THE WHITES ARE

ENEMIES OF HEAVEN

THE WHITES ARE

ENEMIES OF HEAVEN

Climate Caucasianism and
Asian Ecological Protection

MARK W. DRISCOLL

Duke University Press *Durham and London* 2020

Designed by Courtney Leigh Baker
Typeset in Garamond Premier Pro by Westchester Publishing Services

Library of Congress Cataloging-in-Publication Data
Names: Driscoll, Mark (Mark W.), author.
Title: The whites are enemies of heaven : climate Caucasianism and Asian ecological
protection / Mark W. Driscoll.
Description: Durham : Duke University Press, 2020. | Includes bibliographical
references and index.
Identifiers: LCCN 2020018211 (print)
LCCN 2020018212 (ebook)
ISBN 9781478010166 (hardcover)
ISBN 9781478011217 (paperback)
ISBN 9781478012740 (ebook)
Subjects: LCSH: Imperialism—Environmental aspects—China. | Imperialism—
Economic aspects—China. | Imperialism—Environmental aspects—Japan. |
Imperialism—Economic aspects—Japan. | Imperialism—Sociological aspects. | China
—History—19th century. | Japan—History—19th century.
Classification: LCC GF13.3.C6 D757 2020 (print) | LCC GF13.3.C6 (ebook) | DDC
304.2/8095109034—dc23
LC record available at https://lccn.loc.gov/2020018211
LC ebook record available at https://lccn.loc.gov/2020018212

COVER ART: Ippōsai Yoshifuji, *Yokohama Sumo Wrestler Defeating a Foreigner*, 1861.
Woodblock print. Courtesy of The Metropolitan Museum of Art, New York.

In memory:

Eugene W. Driscoll III, Srinivas Aravamudan,
David Bell, and Randy Martin

Contents

Preface and Acknowledgments

This book begins around 1800 when China had the world's largest economy and Japan was so prosperous it doubled its population in two hundred years without a drop in median income. The huge East Asian economic sphere was also what we would today call sustainable: responsible for less than 1 percent of global carbon emissions. The next hundred years saw a massive transformation in world-ecology as Japan and China were turned into peripheries of US and British capitalism under an emerging formation of white supremacy and the systemic plundering of the earth I call Climate Caucasianism. Focusing on the drug, human, and weapons trafficking that gave birth to the carbon-intensive capitalism of the US and UK (responsible in the mid-nineteenth century for between 70 and 80 percent of emissions) and were the driving forces behind this shift affords a new reading of our current moment of the Anthropocene. While I wholeheartedly agree with Jason Moore who suggests replacing the unmarked humanity (*anthropos*) of the term Anthropocene with Capitalocene, white supremacy features extra-economic drives that exceed a logic of capitalism. In other words, climate breakdown is both capitalogenic and raciogenic.

The perceptive Commissioner Lin Zexu, the Qing official who tried to stop British opium trafficking to China, intuited how Euro-whites were attempting to overthrow moral economies, ecologies and cosmologies. In 1839 he identified the problem: "Whites are Enemies of Heaven." With this cue I name this racecological formation Climate Caucasianism and CO_2lonialism to help focus on a capitalist logic centered on extraction (of nonwhite humans and most women, nonliving fossils, living, extrahuman nature, rent, data; etc) and an epistemic logic of what I call "extra-action"—the domination of "inferior" humans and nonliving extractables from outside and above. I show the rapacious "superpredation" necessary to consolidate this planet-endangering project and, following Arturo Escobar, its audacious deforming of language to call it freedom and development.

The events that consolidated Climate Caucasianism were the First (1839–42) and Second (1856–60) Opium Wars with China and the US gunboat invasion of Tokugawa Japan in 1853–54. As the wars with Qing China were launched to remove the obstacles to white UK narcotraffickers, they are more correctly called Wars *for* Drugs. Similarly, while still referred to as the benign "opening of Japan," the US operation against the Tokugawa *bakufu* quickly unleashed white arms traffickers and contraband gold dealers to plunder Japan of much of its wealth. What Marx called the "ruthless terrorism" of white US and UK capitalists shocked Asian elites into restructuring their economies at the end of the nineteenth century, following the Anglo-American templates of extraction and extra-action, effectively globalizing Climate Caucasianism. Japan underwent this transformation before China and, as I showed in my last book, managed to leverage its own capitalist extraction into imperialist extra-action, becoming a colonial power in East Asia by 1905.

Yet this book also tells a powerful counternarrative: the stories of people in Asia who resisted capitalist and white racial terrorism from within very different ecological and ontological worlds than those being imposed from the West. Borrowing a term from Indigenous protests against capitalist extraction, I call these actors "eco-ontological protectors." They battled against Western power not extra-actively, but immanent with nature and extrahuman entities in a mode the philosopher Karen Barad calls "intra-active." While often ruthlessly exterminated, they created an Asian undercommons that stretched across South and East Asia and enabled world historical events like the samurai rebellions in Japan and the Boxer Uprising in China. I will argue that they were also vital to the overthrow of millennia-old dynastic rule in China and offer compelling stories for earthly survival today.

This material is based on a decade of archival work in Chengdu, Sichuan, Fukuoka, Kyushu, Tokyo, Washington, DC, and Princeton University with Japanese- and Chinese-language sources. Sincere thanks to the countless librarians who assisted me at the above archives. Closer to home, the Chinese librarian at UNC, Chapel Hill, Hsi-chu Bolick, was immensely helpful in locating obscure Qing dynasty material for me. The Japanese librarian at Duke, Chris Troost, successfully dug up equally obscure Japanese-language sources.

This book first took shape during a one-year residence at Princeton's Institute for Advanced Studies in 2012–13, where I was warmly hosted by Nicola Di Cosmo. Conversations there with David Eng, Hyun-Ok Park, and Moon-Kie

Jung helped sketch the early contours of this study. The project moved forward over a total of two years spent reading, translating, and researching in Chongqing, Sichuan. Professor Diego Gullota generously put me up in his small apartment in Shapingba for several months in 2013, which was the first of several long stays in the city.

I want to thank my UNC, Chapel Hill, students for their critical engagement with most of this material, especially those in ASIA 244, JAPN 375, GLBL 383, and GLBL 413. I also received invaluable feedback from invited presentations over the last decade. While I don't have the space to mention every institution, lectures and conversations at Pratt Institute hosted by Jon Beller; at Duke University hosted by Michaeline Crichlow; at the University of Toronto hosted by my brother Ken Kawashima; at UCLA hosted by Bill Marotti and Kats Hirano; at the University of North Georgia hosted by Sungshin Kim; and at the University of Chicago hosted by the PhD students in East Asian studies were particularly fruitful. Professor Wang Di made it possible for me to share my ideas on opium production and consumption in the late Qing period with faculty and graduate studies of the History Department at Sichuan University in Chengdu, after which I was granted access to the Sichuan Provincial Archives.

Several people commented on the manuscript, and I want to single out Harry Harootunian (who else?) and Michael Eng, who provided particularly insightful suggestions. Two anonymous reviewers offered crucial suggestions and correctives. My editor Ken Wissoker was both encouraging and patient with the project from the time I proposed it five years ago.

This project is unimaginable without the inspiration, teaching, and love of three special people. Over the last fifteen years Wahneema Lubiano has patiently mentored me in Black studies, providing in-depth critiques and overviews of the most important global thinkers of the twentieth and twenty-first centuries. Everything that appears in this book related to race is directly or indirectly inspired by her. Arturo Escobar is my guru in decolonial theory and politics. Whether involved in protest plans against the lack of diversity at Weaver St. Market, participating in his countless colloquia and seminars over the last twelve years, or breaking bread together in Carrboro and Chapel Hill, my life and thinking have evolved considerably through his friendship and writing. Finally, my life and love, Diane Nelson, read and commented on every sentence in this book and was the main interlocutor for each thought in it. Even more than my last book, this one is *from* her.

The book is dedicated to the memory of my younger brother, Eugene William Driscoll III, and to three friends who also passed prematurely during its production: Srinivas Aravamudan, David Bell, and Randy Martin.

The Speed Race(r) and the Stopped Incarce-Races

The devil never made a wiser move than when he introduced opium smoking among the Chinese. It just suits the natural disposition of the people, as alcohol suits the active, impetuous disposition of the West.—Reverend R. H. Graves, *Forty Years in China*, 1895

The Japanese see that their system of locking themselves in . . . has taught them nothing and only stopped their growth. Like a school plot, it has collapsed instantly with the appearance of the teacher.—Ivan Goncharov, *The Frigate* Pallada, 1858 (in Lensen 1959)

Move fast and break things.—Facebook's corporate motto, 2010–14

Wars for Drugs

In February 1839 the Qing Commissioner Lin Zexu wrote to Britain's Queen Victoria in one of the most famous appeals in the history of international relations.[1] He reminded her that her "honorable country" had benefited from trade with China for two hundred years but that "there are now as many evil foreign traders as good ones. The former are opium dealers who are only concerned with profit and couldn't care less about the harm their products do! These drug traffickers are both enemies of Heaven's way [天道] and universally despised by humans with a heart" (Gong 2010, 694). Appointed by the Qing Emperor Daoguang to halt the illegal flood of Anglo-Indian opium—the nineteenth century's crack cocaine[2]—Lin went on: "Your country is sixty or seventy thousand li away. Nevertheless, your ships frantically rush here to do business and reap huge profits. . . . But how do your people justify selling drugs that injure Chinese people? Even though these dealers may not intend to do us harm [未必有心为害], insatiable greed makes them pursue profit to such an extreme that they are blind to the disastrous effects of drug trafficking. We ask: where is the conscience in all of this?" (695).[3]

Nothing in their experience had prepared Lin and his associates for a market system so indifferent to its deleterious effects. One of the reasons for their naïveté was that Qing dynasty (1644–1911) officials lacked information about a crucial precedent for British narcotrafficking—the systematic human trafficking of enslaved Africans by white Euro-Americans across the Atlantic.[4] However, the main reason for their dismay at the amorality of capitalist profiteering was that many Qing officials still configured trade in moral terms as an act of reciprocity, and in basic market terms as the purchase of a commodity by a merchant who then resells it for a modest gain. A standard way to vouch for products was for merchants themselves to be owners and acknowledged users of their product. One of the things that irked Chinese elites like Lin was that the British opium dealers weren't smokers—Lin scolded Victoria, "you do not take it yourself"—and, as far as they knew, opium was illegal in England.

Lin Zexu and his associates consulted both Christian doctrine and the main textbook of European international law at this time, Vattel's *Le Droit des gens*.[5] Their appeal to Queen Victoria combines these frameworks with Chinese philosophy to undergird a universal moral code the white narcotraffickers were violating. I will flesh out this code in several East Asian philosophico-spiritual discourses in this book. Suffice it to say here that the Chinese officials assumed that humans are morally bound to a Heavenly realm populated by deities. (In fact, when Lin dumped twenty thousand crates of contraband British opium into river trenches in Guangzhou starting on April 11, 1839, he prayed for forgiveness from the river divinities.) It is the responsibility of humans to steward a just, harmonious relationship between the spheres of Heaven and Earth. As deployed in the canonical texts *Analects* and *Mencius*, Heaven requires humans to be accountable to its "way [天道]" and its fateful "mandate [天命]." In this neo-Confucian cosmology, humans are located between ethereal entities and earthly nature in a system held together by rational principle or 理 (*li*). Through no fault of their own, Lin and his associates were unable to fathom an emerging global capitalism where, as Slavoj Žižek quips, erstwhile human Subjects are emptied out by capitalism as $ubject (1993, 27–28).[6] There was no precedent available in Chinese thought that could legitimate the usurious, predatory behavior of the British $ubjects Lin denounces. Equally unthinkable

was waging a war with new carbon-spewing gunboats in defense of these predators, as Great Britain was just about to do.

Climate Caucasianism

Britain launched the First Opium War (1839–42) in response to Lin's actions.
This book construes it as the First War for Drugs[7] and argues that it was a
crucial event in the shift from the Holocene to the Anthropocene. The new
geological era of the Anthropocene has been conceived recently by earth scientists to signal the end of the stability of the Holocene Optimum of the previous
twelve thousand years and marks the beginning of climate breakdown, a collapse of biodiversity, and major disruptions to biogeochemical cycles of water,
nitrogen, phosphate, and carbon. However, I refuse the generic "humanity" in
the Anthropocene, as this was the age when white racial capitalists assumed
global control over nonliving minerals like fossil fuels, nonwhite humans, and
extrahuman nature. Through this control, white men transcended their role in
the Holocene as one biological actor among others and became the dominating geological force of what I will call "Climate Caucasianism."[8]

There should be no doubt that European capitalism altered the global climate. The first clear evidence of this is what Lewis and Maslin (2018) call the
"Orbis Spike." They demonstrate that the significant global temperature drop
between 1550 and 1700 was caused by the Spanish and Portuguese genocide
of 90 percent of the Indigenous peoples of the Americas. This wiped out
most agriculture and infrastructure and allowed an extensive forest regen-
eration, which sequestered so much carbon that atmospheric CO_2 levels fell
by 6 parts per million between 1520 and 1610. Colder and wetter weather
in Europe reduced agricultural yields and put downward pressure on profits
pushing capital to intensify its push into the warmer tropical areas in the
Americas, this time forcing African slaves to clear forests and work plantations from Brazil to Maryland (Moore 2020). By 1875, atmospheric CO_2 levels
had risen by 4 parts per million from 1650 levels. Relentless global warming had begun.

While Climate Caucasianism built on the conquest of the Americas and the
subsequent trafficking of nearly 13 million African slaves across the Atlantic,
it ultimately achieved planetary preeminence by military subjugation of the
prosperous polities of China and Japan in the Asia-Pacific. It is impossible to
understate the impact of this forceful decentering of the Sinocentric trading
area (including Japan) on world-ecology. Just before the First War for Drugs,
the UK was responsible for over 80 percent of global CO_2 emissions (Malm

2015). China, on the other hand, was responsible for less than 1 percent, even though it had the world's largest economy (Maddison 2007).

More specifically, Climate Caucasianism's power was consolidated through an intricate circuit of high-tech, weaponized clipper ships that trafficked opium from British India to China; Indian and Chinese "coolie" captives trafficked to British colonial territories in Asia and Africa and across the Pacific to supplement and replace Afro-descendant slaves in the Americas;[9] contraband weapons trafficked to East Asia by white arms dealers; and investor capital. Readers are seeing a veritable traffic jam here, and I ask you to patiently idle in it for a while. I will insist in this book that drugs, arms, and human trafficking were not anomalies in the reach of Anglo-American power to the Asia-Pacific, but rather representative instances of what Marx called capitalism's "ruthless terrorism" required to establish the conditions for what we call today rapid economic growth (1977a, 895). Although scholars have drawn attention to the ways opium trafficking to China paid for Britain's empire in the nineteenth century (Trocki 1999), in this book I go beyond this to insist that the clipper-coolie captive-contraband-capital (or 4C) circuit opened new frontiers to plunder nature; extracted large numbers of cheap Asian service and sex workers; and enclosed areas in China and Japan for the newest forms of what I will call CO_2lonialism, increasing carbon emissions and intervening in the global climate once again. The 4C circuit itself was activated by a structural inequality based in three asymmetries: those of (1) warfare; (2) lawfare, where law, including European "rationality" and representation, is war by other means; and (3) rawfare, in which nonliving minerals, most women, nonwhite humans, and extrahuman nature are all alienated and reduced to "raw" materials. Although the three "fares" of war, law, and raw all have distinct histories, the focus in this book will be on the ways that the nineteenth-century sciences of philosophy, raciology (scientific racism), geology, and meteorology rationalized them. But let's get back to the white guy narcotraffickers that Commissioner Lin denounced as enemies of Heaven. As I will show, as the vanguard force for Climate Caucasianism in the Asia-Pacific, they were hardly friends of the earth either.

The spike in contraband drugs sold to Chinese by white narcos (four thousand 140-pound chests of opium annually in the 1780s ballooned to over forty thousand in 1839) and the subsequent forced migration of many victims of these black markets invites a comparison with the US crack cocaine epidemic of the 1980s and 1990s. First there was the shift in forms of ingestion—in China from swallowing opium and in the US from snorting cocaine to smoking in both places. Second, when trafficked weapons and drugs rushed into an area, money and captive bodies rushed out. As Chinese opium consumption expanded exponentially in the early decades of the nineteenth century, peasant families were forced to sell off their possessions and even their kids to human traffickers, falling prey to the "symbiotic horizontal integration" of opium and forced migration (Marez 2004, 49). As it had earlier with profitable investments in the African slave trade, Euro-American investor capital swarmed into this labor market when the intoxicating news began to circulate of the 200–400 percent profit made when Chinese from Guangdong province were sold in the Americas as plantation workers (Yun and Laremont 2001, 107). Similarly, in the US case, sentencing disparities force Black and Brown people from their communities into jails and prison labor, feeding the prison-industrial complex. While locked away, their homes can be repossessed by white bankers, and their assets "forfeited" to police.

The First War for Drugs brought widespread destruction and death to coastal southern China, thwarting Commissioner Lin's attempt to protect China from the scourge of white narcos. It opened the door for Anglo-American drug cartels, partnering with British and Spanish human traffickers, to press-gang over a million Chinese across what Christopher, Pybus, and Rediker (2007) call the newest Middle Passage of the Pacific. Eyewitness accounts reported that some Chinese captives were auctioned off exactly as African slaves had been decades before (Swinton and Swinton 1859, 15). Evidently, Anglophone capitalists understood the close connection of contraband opium to Chinese captive labor, cynically linking them as "poison and pigs" (Lowe 2015, 110)—their cash cows.

The profits from opium "poison" extracted by white drug cartels such as Jardine, Matheson & Co. and Russell & Co. (headed by Warren Delano, grandfather of US President Franklin Delano Roosevelt) were recycled into expropriating natural resource frontiers in the Americas and into supplying the "pig" (or "coolie") laborers who worked and died on plantations and built coal-powered railroads cheaply that enclosed this now privatized nature. What is rarely mentioned in the scholarship is that the clipper-coolie captive-contraband-capital circuit also kickstarted the first appearance of the military-industrial complex (McNeill 1982). The trickle of arms sales in the 1830s and 1840s to Asia turned into a tsunami in the 1860s as British and US traffickers, covertly supported by their nations' respective diplomats, rushed to Japan to sell expensive weaponry to the clan domains battling each other and the Tokugawa rulers, as I will show in chapter 1. In 1842 Hong Kong became the central weapons entrepôt in the Asia-Pacific (Blue 2000). After the Second War for Drugs (1856–60) against Qing China, sales restrictions were lifted, allowing arms traffickers to profit from the spike in weapons purchases by both the Qing government for its self-strengthening impetus of the 1870s and by its mushrooming opposition. These weapons sales and subsequent wars were climate-intervening as they unleashed greenhouse gas emissions and poisoned environments.

The events set off by the 4C circuit are still applauded by mainstream scholars as the "development" of East Asia. Conversely, my eco-Marxist perspective draws attention to the ways Climate Caucasianism, as the cumulative effect of the 4C circuit, devastated mineral, human, and extrahuman natures everywhere it turned. While Climate Caucasianism is not the same thing as white (people's) weather, nevertheless Climate Caucasianism deepened when white capitalists profited from extreme weather events, as I will show.

Clipper Ships and Capitalist Extra-Action

Lin Zexu's indignant letter to Queen Victoria calling out whites as enemies of Heaven intuited the larger structure I am insisting on here: the centrality of drug trafficking to the new capitalist and climate regime. While China enjoyed a GDP larger than the combined total of Western Europe and its colonies at this time, many Chinese trading practices were similar to British ones (Pomeranz 2000). However, the new regime of a globally extractive capitalism inaugurated formations that were incomprehensible to Qing officials like Lin. First, there was nothing in China comparable to the "coolie" captive trade across the Pacific. Second, the logistical complexity of Anglo-American narcotrafficking to China was unprecedented. For example, profit could be accrued at several points in the opium commodity chain: from weapons and ships, from contracts and insurance, from financing and credit, and from buying and selling the laborers needed to move the narcotics long distances. While the English "country trader" who purchased British East India Company (EIC) opium in Kolkata, India, and then acquired the necessary crew and infrastructure to get the narcotics to China took the most surplus, many others profited. More importantly, Euro-American capitalism pioneered a process whereby surplus profits were ineluctably invested back into the system in search of even more surplus, kickstarting a process of endless accumulation. Unfortunately, most of the profit opportunities were in climate-interfering industries that emitted high levels of greenhouse gases (Bonneuil and Fressoz 2017, 118).

In the late 1700s some Europeans viewed opium trafficking from British India to China as crucial to even out centuries-old trade deficits caused by strong Western demand for Chinese tea and porcelain, and the lack of Asian interest in European products. While it was already reaping large payouts, systematic narco-capitalism appeared when Warren Hastings was named governor general of India in 1773 and assumed control of the East India Company's new opium monopoly the next year. Attempting to integrate disparate aspects of the monopoly, Hastings began transforming rivers and building roads to ensure the quick movement of opium to—as we can see in the images—the surprisingly modern EIC drug labs and industrial processing facilities, and then finished opium cakes to the export platform in Kolkata.

Vipul Singh shows that this is when the EIC began to see the sacred Ganges and other Indian rivers solely as "resources for accumulating capital" (2018). It's important to highlight these riparian (river and land) zones as also victims of Climate Caucasianism. As I explore in chapters 2 and 6, they feature a diverse habitat and interactions among different kinds of entities not found in other biomes, what Donna Haraway calls a "multi-species democracy" (2007, 262–63). In such zones, dynastic rulers such as China's Qing and Japan's Meiji (1868–1912), as well as CO2lonial regimes like the East India Company tried to practice what I will call "extra-action"—utterly different from more local experiences of interaction or from what Karen Barad calls relational "intra-acting" (2007, 178). Extra-action seeks to dominate from outside and above and features a mode of perception based on separation and superiority, facilitating the making of violent abstractions like those Sylvia Wynter identifies as the "reduction of Man to Labour and of Nature to Land" (1971, 99), the intervening in climates, and the hoarding of biomass. In British India the extra-acting and extracting East India Company transformed riparian zones to facilitate drug trafficking.

Of course, riparian worlds were not the only entities extra-acted upon. Hastings set up a contract system with purchasing agents responsible for delivering a fixed amount of opium to the East India Company for an agreed-upon price. The EIC wanted to procure the drug as cheaply as possible, and the money paid out rarely covered the costs of opium production (Trocki 1999, 62). On top of this, many EIC agents demanded bribes and stole Company money. When these abuses were publicized in England, the company assumed direct control of opium farmers in 1797 under Lord Cornwallis (Farooqui 2005, 14). From then on, through 100 branch offices of its draconian Opium Agency, the EIC forced landholding *gomostahs* to deliver commissioned amounts of opium to its drug labs and processing centers in Patna and Benares (Bauer 2019). In turn, landlords ordered the primary producers—*ryots* or peasants—to grow poppies. Forced to monocrop opium poppies and jettison sustainable crop rotations, the ryots wound up with depleted soils, microbe invasions, and no subsistence crops (Farooqui 1998). *Papaver somniferum*, the opium poppy, is a particularly hungry plant and exhausts nutrients from the soil in just three

THE EXAMINING HALL,
OPIUM FACTORY AT PATNA, INDIA.

THE MIXING ROOM,
OPIUM FACTORY AT PATNA, INDIA.

FIGURES INTRO.1–INTRO.3. British East India Company's huge drug lab and processing center at Patna in Bihar, India. Courtesy MIT Visualizing Cultures. https://visualizingcultures.mit.edu/.

to four years when it isn't rotated. Aggravating this tendency, the EIC began enclosing tracts of Indian land exclusively for poppy cultivation. Britain's extractive enterprises were, of course, based on a deeply predatory relation to nature within the UK, but in Asia—building on the precedent set by the slave-driven monocropping of tobacco and cotton in the Americas—domestic rules of engagement were altered, intensifying extraction and unleashing Climate Caucasianism (Merchant 2002, 49). In British India, a vicious cycle of maxed-out soils and skimmed-off payments indebted many peasants and some landlords, "freeing" them up for permanent removal from the land and into exploitative waged labor inside India or forced migration abroad—pioneers of the Asian coolie captive trade. Although the practice of waged labor preceded the EIC assuming colonial control over Bengal after the 1757 Battle of Plassey, the different enclosure techniques the EIC deployed multiplied its use. And as Maria Mies (1986) and Silvia Federici (2004, 2012) argue, the spread of waged labor exacerbated unequal gender relations as men monopolized waged jobs while women's concrete labor was increasingly denigrated until it was not even counted as work at all. Conflating women's unremunerated labor with the unpaid costs of despoiling nature, Moore and Patel call this "capitalism's most sinister accounting trick" (2017, 94).

Subsequent to processing and packaging the opium, the EIC auctioned it off to private British drug traffickers at Kolkata. (Until the 1830s, US drug cartels weren't allowed to bid at the EIC auctions and bought their opium in Turkey instead.) After the auctions the EIC regularly pocketed between eight and ten times what it had paid out, an astronomical profit rate. But this was just a hint of the extreme extractions to come.

At Kolkata, India, the clipper ship assumed a central role for white narcos. The antithesis of a "slow boat to China," the clippers were the fastest sailing vessels in the world and were originally built in Baltimore, New England, and Great Britain; some began their careers as slave ships. From the turn of the nineteenth century, some Euro-American clipper ships were made for white narcos much cheaper in Indian ports like Masulipatam and Surat using local teak wood, long valued by Indian Ocean sailors for its durability and resistance to water (Arnold 2000, 101). With the savings from building ships locally in India, drug lords could spend more on weaponry, and the most popular clipper design used to traffic drugs to China until the 1850s was outfitted with twenty cannons. The ships were manned by between 60 and 120 Asian lascar sailors, ten sepoy soldiers, and a core group consisting of a white captain, his two or three European mates, and a British or American officer and drug lord. The only females on board were the slave girls the white narco and captain often took on board as concubines (Jaffer 2015, 64). The standard 25-to-1 ratio of South Asian to Euro-white workers was driven by capital's need to drive down costs and increase profitability through a racist rawfaring (or turning Asian humans into cheap "natural" resources) of nonwhite workers. The discursive lawfare that enabled this rawfaring is explained by Ravi Ahuja: "If an unskilled Asian laborer was not a worker but a 'coolie' and an Indian infantrymen not a soldier but a 'sepoy,' an Indian Ocean sailor was not a seaman but merely a 'lascar'" (2009, 14). "Lascars" normally slept on the decks of the ships exposed to the elements and accounted for less than one-half the food costs of Euro-white sailors (Myers 1994, 12).

In addition to the South Asian sailors and sex slaves, H. M. Elmore, veteran captain of successful opium runs in the 1790s, described the hardware required for a successful trip to China from Kolkata: "The ship, in addition to the necessary ammunition for her [twenty] guns, muskets, and pistols, should have a box containing fifty hand grenadoes in each top; together with an arm chest containing muskets and ball cartridge . . . the commander ought to be well supplied with boats. The long-boat should carry two (at least) or four chambered swivels, of three pound caliber; the second boat two; and third boat one; with grape canister and langrage shot sufficient for them" (in Parkinson 1966, 348).

With this amount of weaponry it is no surprise that historian C. N. Parkinson uncovers in captains' memoirs of opium trafficking "nothing but tales of smuggling at the pistol point" (1966, 349). Indeed, exasperated commander-in-chief Rainier of the Royal Navy's East Indies station from 1794 to 1805 described the British narcos' activities as "mere buccaneering" or piracy (346). But this is actually unfair to pirates, disregarding the intricate cooperation and collaboration piracy was based on at this time, as I explore in chapter 4. Instead, individualistic Euro-whites who trafficked contraband drugs and weapons to China exhibited a paranoid fear of everyone involved in the business, combined with a homicidal amorality. Parkinson puts it this way: "the trader was at once bold and guarded . . . eternally watching for symptoms of treachery, both in his crew and among his customers. He was always ready to shoot" (348). While Farsis and Indians also trafficked opium to China, white British and North American narcos came to dominate the lucrative trade, but not because of their superior business acumen or inherent knack for risk management. Rather, as Parkinson argues, they were able to succeed because of race privilege—"they were white men and therefore able to inspire confidence in other white men" (320)[10]—and because they were more cold-bloodedly violent than their nonwhite competitors. Euro-American and South Asian investors were confident that white narcos would stop at nothing to get their contraband drugs to the vaunted China market.

Corroborating further their reputation as "enemies of Heaven," these drug cartels occasionally conducted armed raids on Dutch East India spice plantations in Java. Twenty cannons became standard equipment for the Anglo cartels at the turn of the nineteenth century because the Dutch gunboats guarding their colonial possessions were equipped with only eighteen, so the US/ UK dealers were bound to be victorious in any "White-on-White" firefight (Parkinson 1966). But it wasn't just the numerical advantage that underwrote their monopoly of force. White narcos were the first to feature the carronade, a light but devastatingly powerful short-barreled cannon. Developed by the Scottish Carron Company in 1778, carronades became their weapon of choice because their weight didn't hamper the clipper's speed (Roger 2004). Especially after the Qing Emperor Jiaqing reinforced the 1729 ban on opium trafficking to China in 1799, Anglo-American drug cartels needed both speed and an asymmetry in force projection to outgun and outrun Chinese, Vietnamese, and Malay pirate groups. These carronade-equipped clipper ships were so effective that the Royal Navy leased several from Jardine, Matheson & Co. in 1840 for the First War for Drugs, supplementing steamships (Hayes 2019). After this war against Qing China, coal-powered vessels gradually replaced the wind power of the clippers throughout the Asia-Pacific—a significant climate-intervening event. To facilitate this, by the late 1840s the Royal Navy was working with the British Geological Survey to map the planet's coal resources for UK supply lines, identifying assets in Bengal, Australia, Java, Malaysia, New Guinea, Aden, Japan, and Syria (Bonneuil and Fressoz 2017, 142). Even more than biopower, Britain's hegemony increasingly relied on what Christian Parenti calls "geopower" (2015, 829).

Opium trafficking was outlawed in many places en route from India to China. Therefore, white narcos had to convince port officials to let them do business at each stop on the way (Parkinson 1966). The rare captain's account of opium trafficking provides hints that Anglo-American narcos offered Asian officials who were unwilling to do business with them a choice that Latin American *narcotraficantes* are better known for: *plata o plomo* (a bribe or a bullet) (Elmore 1802, 50; 125).[11] Bribes were so prevalent that Chinese leaders used the stock phrase "salary from the sea [海俸]" to describe them. One way to convince port authorities of the life-or-death seriousness of these offers was pioneered by the US drug cartel Russell & Co. Russell's clipper ships featured the entrepreneurial innovation of hanging the murdered bodies of those unwilling to cooperate with the white narcos up on their masts, showing to all what happened to human obstacles to Anglo-American capitalist progress (Owen 1934, 203–4). This depravity—a more significant and appropriately named "killer app" (Ferguson 2011, 12) than the clichéd explanations for the rise of the West (the hard-working Protestant ethic, private property, Enlightenment science, etc.)—was attractive to investors and enabled Anglo-American drug traffickers to expand the amount of opium dealt to China, with the corresponding increase in use and abuse (Hanes and Sanello 2002, 34). Similar to the deleterious effects of any drug epidemic, from 1807 the Chinese economy began suffering a reversal of trade surpluses as silver money flowed out of East Asia directly into the pockets of white Anglo narcos and their investors. It's worth repeating that this reversal redistributed wealth from the carbon-neutral Sinocentric trading area to the carbon-intensive capitalism of Climate Caucasianism.

The white narcos and their clipper ships stuffed with opium, cotton goods, and contraband weapons worked their way from Kolkata through Southeast Asia—selling, bribing, and murdering. Before 1800 the final drop-off took place at cartel-owned barges near Guangzhou (Canton) on the south China coast, then at Whampoa until 1821, and finally at Lingding Island and Hong Kong, where the drugs were transferred to receiving barges. These barges—Jardine, Matheson & Co.'s weighed seven hundred tons, a floating opium Walmart—proceeded to hook up with Chinese merchants operating "fast crab" and "scrambling dragon" vessels (Owen 1934, 196). Anywhere from 100 to 500 percent markup was made by white narcos on a successful run, leading veteran dealer Charles Magniac to crow that it was "unequalled in the annals of commerce" (Trocki 1999, 79). Karl Marx exaggerated only slightly when he quipped that these drug traffickers were "cleverer than alchemists" (who had to spend money on metal before turning it into gold) in that superprofitable "primitive accumulation went on without the advance of a shilling" (1977a, 917).

The capitalist alchemy of opium trafficking caused other, equally miraculous transformations. The most important were the extreme corporate makeovers that saw an early nineteenth-century version of low-profile street dealers become CEOs of venerable agency houses like Dent & Co. In David Simons's *The Wire*, the African American drug dealer Stringer Bell makes a similar attempt to launder his ill-gotten gains into real estate and political credibility, but like so many of his real-life Black and Brown brothers and sisters, he ends up murdered. The white narcos I'm studying, however, get to "graduate" from drug dealing. Russell & Co.'s Warren Delano became the grandfather to a US president and publicly *white*washed his criminal business as "honorable and legitimate" (Ujifusa 2018, 46), while James Matheson achieved the ultimate vindication in becoming a baron and member of Parliament. Dent & Co. was the beneficiary of the first corporate makeover, shifting their main business from narcotrafficking into banking and shipping. Jardine, Matheson & Co. followed them by recycling their criminal profits into real estate speculation (BFO 46/87, October 19, 1861), banking, insurance, and coal and copper extraction in Japan and the Asia-Pacific (Hidemura 1977, 56–57). Rather than relegitimize these graduations, we should construe these white men as the original "bad hombres" (as Donald Trump depicted brown Latino drug dealers).

After the British victory over the Qing in the First War for Drugs they extorted a staggering £20 million pound indemnity, a boon that should be understood as yet another extraction elicited by the clipper-coolie captive-contraband-capital circuit. Britain also expropriated the island of Hong Kong to be used for secure trafficking of drugs, arms, and people, and took the first concessions on mainland China with the Fuzhou, Guangzhou, Ningbo, Shanghai, and Xiamen treaty ports. Although there is agreement among scholars writing in English, Chinese, and Japanese to refer to these five treaty ports (and all the others to follow in China, Korea, and Japan) as being "opened,"

I will argue that it is more accurate to depict what happened to them as (en) closure for a new kind of racial capitalist and climate regime.

Marx's Extraction → Extinction Imperative

Together with the conquest of the Americas and the African slave trade, Marx categorized the events surrounding the First and Second Wars for Drugs as paradigmatic cases of the primitive accumulation of capital (1977a, 915). With Rosa Luxemburg's (1871–1919) development of Marx's concept, primitive accumulation is now understood to provide capitalists with opportunities for extreme profiteering and the further plundering of nature. Recent anticapitalist scholarship has reframed primitive accumulation as "accumulation by dispossession" to draw attention to its expropriating destructiveness (Coulthard 2014; Harvey 2005). In this book I will build on recent eco-Marxism that puts in bold the ways primitive accumulation both severs humans from nature and rips them from the land where they could reproduce themselves sustainably and, as we saw above with Indian ryots and Chinese coolie captives, delivers them into unsustainable worlds where they are dependent on the owners of capital for their livelihoods (Burkett 1999; Foster 2000). However, following James O'Connor's (1998) concept of capitalism's second contradiction, I think we can go further in arguing that Marx intuited the unsustainability of capitalism *tout court* as it exhausts and extinguishes human labor and nature.

Marx deployed the concept of primitive accumulation to underline the ways capitalism blithely destroys many forms of life (Saitô 2017, 247–55). More precisely, this happens when humanity's relational "metabolism" (a mid-nineteenth-century synonym for "ecology" before Ernst Haeckel's 1867 neologism replaced it) with nature is ruptured or rifted and then transmogrified into an exploitative system of wage labor and competition between humans, and between humans and nature. In both his early (*German Ideology*) and late (*Capital*, vol. 3) work, Marx diagnosed the ways primitive accumulation alienates humans from what he called our "intimate ties" with nature, bemoaning in the later text the way capitalism produced an "irreparable rift in the interdependent" connection of humans with nature (1981, 949). Capitalism kidnaps humans from their intra-actions within nature, subsequently enabling it to exploit both waged labor and natural entities. To underline this, Marx argued that capitalism exhausts soils "like workers," imposing a "martyrology" on both (1977a, 638). Then it expands its thievery into more abstract modes such as financial rent, patents, and contracts (1981, 641).

Marx helps us understand the centrality of primitive accumulation with his key concept of metabolism, which he used in two ways. First, the original connections humans have to their local environment—what he called "natural metabolism"—are severed (in Saitô 2017, 208). Second, after this irrevocable rift, capitalism installs a "social metabolism" that allows it to further expropriate "martyrs": human workers, agricultural soils, animals, freshwater, air, forests, the sea, mountains, minerals—in other words, most living and nonliving entities on the planet. In the case of the Wars for Drugs in China, Marx saw how British capitalism "every hour is bringing new victims to a Moloch which knows no satiety" (1968, 53). His attention to how capital demands live sacrifices reveals a crucial practice of Climate Caucasianism, where capitalist extraction leads to exhaustion and extinction, what I'll call the extraction → extinction imperative. While extraction → extinction appeared first for Marx in the genocide of Indigenous peoples enabling the European theft of American gold and silver, he also lamented the necropolitical "turning of Africa into a warren for the commercial hunting of blackskins" in the slave trade. Further, he denounced the "destruction of the human race" following the flooding of China with Anglo-Indian opium, leading to a death rate of 15 percent for trafficked Chinese captives crossing the Pacific and a mere 50 percent survival rate for the period of indenture of Asian forced migrants in the Americas (1977a, 915, 587). With a surprisingly wide extrahuman optic, Marx in volume 3 of *Capital* underlines the way capitalism exploits workers and the natural environment in the same way—"ruining and laying waste" both to workers in factories and to soils in large-scale capitalist agriculture (1981, 949–50). Marx denounces capitalism's cold disregard for pushing living things to "the point of no return," or beyond the threshold of existence into extinct martyrdom (1977a, 342).

I need to clarify that nonrelational, extra-active postures and extractive operations preceded the arrival of Euro-American capitalists to East Asia. These featured mineral extraction and river management in Japan and salt, coal, and copper mining in China, where dynasties assumed the position of Heaven and possessor of its mandate (天命). The canonical works on anthropogenic climate change in China, Elvin's 2006 *Retreat of the Elephants*, and in Japan, Walker's 2005 *The Lost Wolves of Japan*, make this argument convincingly.[12] Nevertheless, the toxic combination of Euro-whites claiming to be uniquely self-determining and extra-actively separate and superior to nonwhite humans and extrahuman nature, with a $ubjectivity whose sole concern is profit, was a novel entity in Asia. To be sure, Asian hydraulic dynasties influenced their local environments. At an entirely different scale, however, Climate Caucasianism should be seen as a global power wielding unprecedented force to both directly intervene in, and less directly, interfere with the planet's biosphere, hydrosphere, and atmosphere. Following from Climate Caucasianism's planetary reach, one of the main arguments of this book is that subsequent to the First War for Drugs (1839–42), Chinese and Japanese elites were compelled to intensify their own endogenous practices of extraction and mimic Euro-white templates in, for example, capital-intensive coal mining that will be discussed in chapter 1 and the conclusion. With an eye toward understanding the origins of today's extractive capitalism in the form of mountain-top removal for coal, hydraulic fracturing for gas, and deep-water drilling for oil, I will show how the agents of Climate Caucasianism in Asia in the nineteenth century can be characterized as extractiv-eyes/Is.[13] That is to say that white extractiv-eyes/Is were fixated on what they could expropriate from a specific environment, with no consideration of giving back or replenishing. W. E. B. Du Bois called this "the divine right of white people to steal" (1920, 48).

Let's look at the case of Chinese tea to elucidate some of the ways British capitalists activated the extraction → extinction imperative through warfare, lawfare, and rawfare. You'll recall that the original raison d'être for the clipper-coolie-contraband-capital circuit was to eliminate the large trade deficit of tea imports from Qing China with contraband opium sales. This was so successful that it morphed into a plan to replace Chinese tea altogether. First, during Britain's colonial war against Burma in Assam (1824–26), British East India Company officer Robert Bruce stumbled across tea plants growing there (Antrobus 1957, 17–18). Once Assam was removed from Burmese control, in 1834 the British governor general of India, William Bentinck (1774–1839), via a Parliamentary minute, called for tea plantations to be established. Bentinck trumpeted the urgency for "Our Empire to annihilate . . . the Chinese monopoly" over tea by growing it in Britain's India colony (in Liu 2010, 77–8). This was the lawfare that began the installation of brutal plantation capitalism, reducing the rich ecology of Assam to "worthless" rawfare. To push this forward, in March 1838 the British administrator, Captain Jenkins, working closely with Bentinck's appointed Tea Commission, convinced the colonial government in Bengal to pass the Waste Land Settlement Rules for Assam. This forced locals off their commons and enclosed huge tracts to be handed over to white settlers for free, with zero taxes for fifteen to twenty years. "Waste Land" signified any land lacking in cash crop agriculture (Chakraborty 2012, 9–10). When the Kachari people native to Assam refused to work for British capitalists for the exploitative wages of 1–2 rupees a day—evicting their clanfolk from the area, assarting trees and deforesting—the British colonizers attempted to cut off the supplies of opium that many Kacharis smoked regularly (Varma 2017, 38) Failing at this, the British considered small warfare in the form of mass shootings—similar to the extermination of local labor that Donna Haraway (2016, 557) argues was standard for white planation capitalism—before deciding to assassinate several of the Kachari leaders (Imada 2000, 131). Ultimately, Kacharis were lawfared as worse than natural "waste"—constitutionally "wasted" on opium and non-civilizable. But the problem of cheap labor remained unsolved.

A new round of warfare in the form of the First War for Drugs of 1839–42 offered a solution as "coolie" captives began to be rawfared, alienated from inland China and trafficked throughout the British Empire. Furthermore, the enclosure of the five Chinese treaty ports allowed extractiv-eye/I bioprospectors like Robert Fortune to trespass into tea-growing areas in Fujian province and expropriate contraband caches of tea samples and bring them to Kolkata. Almost all of the Chinese plants died before reaching India; even flora were bound by the extraction → extinction imperative (Rose 2011). While the South Asian coolie trade to Jamaica and Barbados had expanded after Great Britain abolished slavery in 1833, the internal trade in Indian coolie captives was still in its infancy (Carter 1995). The Tea Commission, now privatized as the Assam Company, worked to change that (Chakraborty 2012, 12). As informal trafficking of poor laborers into Assam from neighboring Bengal took off in the 1850s, speculative British capital poured into the tea plantations in the early 1860s and, together with a new round of Waste Land grabs, created the "tea mania." White plantation capitalists in Assam urged British rulers in Bengal to make it easier to alienate and extract low-cost workers, and they responded with the lawfare of the Master and Servants Act of 1859, followed by the Bengal Native Labor Act of 1863, which dictated a five-year indenture for all Bengali coolies brought into Assam and imprisonment for those who violated their contracts (Stanziani 2018, 109). Of course, many plantation owners refused to honor their part of the bargain by violating the terms of the 1863 Act which called for a minimum wage and food rations. When the luckiest of the coolies sponsored by the Bengali Labor Act finally arrived to Assam plantations on coal-powered steamships (the death rate for the month-long trip on the Brahmaputra river was between 20 percent and 50 percent [Varma 2017, 47])—they realized that the labor brokers who had recruited them in Bengal had lied about the wages and labor conditions; they immediately began resisting (Lees 1867, 207–8). As soon as the Bengalis insisted on their humanity and refused their devaluation to rawfare with work stoppages and desertions, lawfare kicked in again, this time in the form of the Assam Contract Act of 1865 allowing plantation managers to arrest deserters personally and take the law into their own hands, similar to slave patrols in the US South (Varma 2017, 49). In practice, this meant the colonial government turned a blind eye to floggings of workers when plantation owners realized that jailing their workers for contract violations was counterproductive. Like the racially terroristic whippings that white plantation owners used to raise slave labor productivity in the US South (Baptist 2014), Nitin Varma details the systematic nature of torture of re-rawfared coolies by white capitalists in Assam. Each round of torture was overseen by the plantation doctor to ensure that overzealous plantation managers didn't kill the Bengali workers (2017, 57–63). Nevertheless, regular abuse added to the extraction → extinction toll. When combined with inadequate food supplies and the arduous labor of clearcutting jungles, along with the effects of foreign microbes, only 60 percent of the Bengali coolie captives survived their five-year indenture.

The Assam plantations were similar to the environmentally destructive plantations relying on slave labor in the US South that Markewitz and Richter (2007) have studied—depleting soil nutrients, shrinking biodiversity, and raising mortality rates for humans and fauna. By the 1880s coal-powered drying and rolling machines for tea leaves were common in Assam (Varma 2017, 80). In other words, Climate Caucasianism's extraction → extinction imperative performed its role very well in Assam. So well that, as Sarah Rose (2011) ironizes, by 1900 "all the tea in China" was replaced by all the tea in British India.

The Two Ecologies

Moore and Patel underline that capitalism isn't merely one part of an ecology, "but *is* an ecology" (2017, 38). We saw above how destructive that ecology is when it fixes itself in space. However, this book will also highlight different assemblages of human and extrahuman nature I will refer to as "eco-ontologies." By eco-ontology I mean ecology as "house" or "home," together with ontology as "Being" or "beings." Eco-ontology is therefore a nonanthropocentric commune of coexisting beings. Far from being particularistic deviations from a universal form, the East Asian eco-ontologies I address in this book were structurally similar to most examples elsewhere, especially Indigenous ones. For this reason I will make the case that white capitalism—based on a possessive individualism we could name "ego-ontology"—was the deviant particularism, albeit one driven by ruthless terrorism to plunder and rape its way to claims of universality. Moreover, I will try to expose and then displace Climate Caucasianism's false universality in favor of what Latin American decolonial thinkers call pluriversality (Blaser and de la Cadena 2018; Escobar 2018, 2020). Pluriverses are embedded in distinct eco-ontologies and, while obviously shot through with power hierarchies, are not invested in CO2lonialism and conquest. Rather, the pluriverses discussed in this book will be shown to be defending these very eco-ontologies threatened by Euro-white and Chinese and Japanese capitalists. In this sense, they are similar to contemporary Indigenous struggles to protect local land and water and preserve nonanthropocentric forms of relationality. Because the condition of this human "subject" is intra-actively enmeshed with and dependent on other forms of life, it is more correct to depict it with the and/& character as "&bject."

Race as Yellow

In the examples above of primitive accumulation Marx intuited how global capitalism works through white racial domination. What Cedric Robinson synthesized as "racial capitalism" (2000) shows that capital's ruthless terrorism normally requires racial terrorism. Therefore, after the first homologue with the crack cocaine panic in the shift to smoking, and the second—asset forfeiture, dispossession, and the rendering of rawfared bodies of color into prisons and exploitative labor—we arrive at one final element delivered by Euro-American capitalism in the early nineteenth century with narcotrafficking: race.[14] Smoking opium was thought by white people to bring out a latent jaundiced color in Chinese skin, initiating a racial classification of "yellowness" (Keevak 2011). From the "sickly yellow" of their epidermal hue, an entire algorithm of East Asians was calculated that posited them as decayed (and decadent), mellowly unmotivated, and stubbornly holding on to ingrained "habit"—traits directly attributed to regular opium smoking. But don't go blaming Anglo-American narcos for this. As the US missionary Graves claimed in the epigraph, most Caucasians rationalized that the sedative effect of opium suited perfectly the "natural" inertia and slow-motion disposition of Chinese people, as alcohol was the appropriate intoxicant for "active and impetuous" white men. In fact, a handful of Europeans were willing to smoke opium with their Chinese acquaintances but grew frustrated by how long it took to prepare and thought the whole process of getting high was agonizingly time-consuming (BPP 1894, 109–10). White men's tight pants also didn't make it easy to lie down and enjoy a pipe, unlike the "dresses" that some Westerners described gender-troubled Chinese men as preferring. More importantly, the lethargic conditions of supine, stupefied, and slow (opium "stupefaction" was normally brought about by smoking while lying down on couches, beds, or floors) were unacceptable for upright, on-the-go white men in Asia intent on—as Facebook brags—"moving fast and breaking things." It was no coincidence that the whiskey and beer preferred by Euro-American

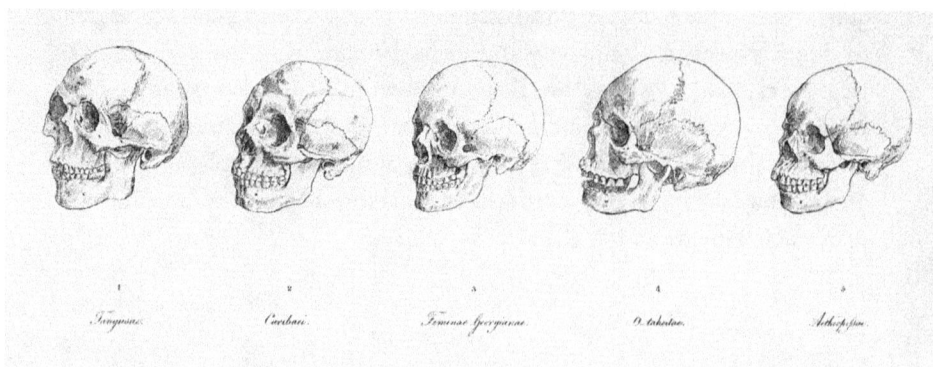

FIGURE INTRO.4. J. F. Blumenbach's five races. What Blumenbach called the "beautifully" contoured Caucasian skull is in the middle, flanked by the Black (Ethiopian) on the far right and the oversized yellow (Tungusae) on the far left (Blumenbach 1795).

men were consumed in an elevated position on bar stools, or better, from hip flasks while striding (or stumbling) forward.

While the "fix" that Chinese opium smokers derived from the drug served to "fix" or repair the British empire's balance of trade, it also performed a third service to "fix" or hold in place globally Euro-American racial science, what Paul Gilroy calls "raciology" (2000). By the 1850s the crayon color "yellow" had become the standard reference to the German anatomist J. F. Blumenbach's influential 1794 racial classification of East Asians as "Mongolian." As we can see in the illustration from his *Natural Varieties of Mankind*, he ranked the Mongolian with the Ethiopian below the superior white. The Mongolian phenotype included jaundiced, yellow skin, sinodonty (crooked "Chinese teeth"), and neoteny, or "youth (*neos*) extended (*teinein*)"—that is, childlike features (Kowner and Demel 2015, 55–76).

Therefore, Euro-American raciology insisted Mongoloid adults resembled sick, bucktoothed, and bedridden white children.[15] In 1843 the US narco Warren Delano casually drew on the racism of neoteny, denigrating his adult Chinese servants in Guangzhou as "talking and thinking like foolish little children" (Ujifusa 2018, 61). Less casually, the French anatomist E. R. A. Serres (1786–1868) provided the scientific foundation for neoteny in the 1820s and '30s with his theory of recapitulation, holding that superior racial groups repeat and surpass inferior raced adults in their growth process (Kowner and Demel 2014, 87–125). In the late 1850s and early 1860s the English physician John Langdon Down (1828–96) applied recapitulation to his research on developmental disorders in children, arguing that arrested development in Caucasian kids demoted them to yellow Mongolians. His 1866 paper etiologized whites with mild cognitive impairment as "Mongoloid idiots" who took on a racial phenotype more characteristic of "orientals" (Down 1866).[16] After his death this condition was reframed as "Down syndrome," although the original racist name would survive colloquially well into the late twentieth century (Keevak 2011, 6). Here too, the association of "idiocy" with yellow Mongoloids was taken from British depictions of Chinese opium smokers in the 1830s. Royal Army doctor Lord Jocelyn famously described the "idiot smile and death-like stupor" of Chinese lying around supine in opium rooms in Singapore (1841, 38).[17] Similarly, an anonymous British army officer based his best seller, *The Last Year in China to the Peace of Nanking*, on his experiences in the First War for Drugs, writing: "The effect of excess in opium is more like idiocy, than ordinary intoxication. It steals away the brain, like drink, but does not substitute fire, as the latter appears to do" (1843, 29). For our purposes, this depiction of layabout, confused, and stoned Chinese became so prevalent among Euro-whites that I will use the single phrase supinestupefiedyellow to code it. The denigration of opium prostration had an analogue in what Euro-whites saw as the ubiquitous East Asian practice of the "kowtow" (Chinese, 叩头). Westerners construed the bowing protocol as evidence of the benumbed slavishness that Chinese and Japanese exhibited toward their emperors and leaders (Hevia 2003). I will show that when erstwhile supinestupefiedyellows refused racialized deference—the examples put forward here are the Gelaohui brotherhood in southwestern and central China, the Boxers in Shandong province, and the rogue samurai in Japan—what Carol Anderson calls murderous "white rage" often ensued (2017).

. . . and in Japan

The racial prototype for neoteny also informed the profiling of "Mongoloid" Japanese. In the epigraph the writer Goncharov documented Russia's 1855 Japan Expedition by depicting Japanese adults as mischievous schoolkids who have "stopped their growth" (in Lensen 1959, 343). Although Euro-Americans smuggled opium into Japan as well, their apparent subservience to white men led Westerners to depict Japanese as less idiotic and less rooted in habit than opium-addled Chinese. British officials in the late 1850s and early 1860s like Ernest Satow and Lord Elgin delighted in noting Japanese people's deference to Euro-whites; they were, as Elgin wrote, "gentle and submissive" (BPP 1859, 371).

They would soon realize that this was a partial story at best. What was more representative of Japanese elites' opinion of Westerners appeared in a text that circulated in official circles fourteen years before Lin Zexu's 1839 letter (but not published until 1858)—Aizawa Seishisai's *New Proposals* (新論). It was first written as an explanation for Japan's Tokugawa rulers' Expulsion Edict of 1825, which overturned a decades-long policy of allowing Euro-American whaling ships into Japanese ports to buy coal and provisions. Japan's Tokugawa *bakufu* government (1603–1868) had become increasingly alarmed both by white sailors' violent behavior and rumors of missionary attempts to propagate Christianity. With the new edict, coastal Japanese domains were compelled to fire on unannounced European ships. The Expulsion Edict stated: "When the English and Russians come ashore, they are more and more disrespectful of our laws. Moreover, they seem to be spreading their wicked religion among our people.... Please note that Chinese, Koreans, and Ryukyuans can be differentiated from [Westerners] by physiognomy and ship design, but this is not the case with Holland. Even so, don't worry about firing on the Dutch by mistake" (Wakabayashi 1986, 60; translation modified).

Beginning around 1640, Tokugawa Japan conducted regulated trade with China and Holland through the western port of Nagasaki. The Dutch were the sole European power to be granted trading rights by the Tokugawa rulers because: first, they weren't proselytizing Christianity; second, unlike Portuguese and Spanish, they weren't publicly involved in trafficking Japanese slaves;[18] and later, they weren't known as narcotraffickers. The precocious deployment of a European-style concept of racial phenotype, or visible biological distinction, in both the 1825 Expulsion Edict and *New Proposals* text signals absorption of Dutch medical and scientific knowledge laid over the proto-caste structure of Japanese society. Early modern Japan was ruled through a caste/status system, with educated samurai at the top and outcaste *hinin* at the bottom, which, as Maria Elena Martinez argues (2008), assumed forms of innate difference—a crucial precedent for modern understandings of race. Perhaps this is why elites in Japan were early adopters of the colored-in, racial phenotypes of white, yellow, black, and red, beating the first major Chinese text on racial classification—Wei Yuan's 1852 edition of *Haiguo tuzhi*—by decades.[19]

Here I want to return to the intellectual endowment that construes the human in much more complex ways than the reduction to rawfared race. While Lin Zexu argued from a standpoint of universality to denounce Euro-whites as enemies of Heaven, the Japanese scholar Aizawa identified a particular East Asian ecology nested in a specific ontology where certain beings are co-present. The "spiritualized nature [神道]"[20] Aizawa claimed was omnipresent in East Asia decenters living humans as only one part of an eco-ontology consisting of metaphysical entities together with varieties of extrahuman life.

The reciprocal intra-action of these different entities is underwritten by divine reason li (理) and channeled into organic forms by primordial matter or *qi* (気).[21] The li–qi couple links the realm of human beings with earth and supernatural Heaven, and disruptions to the circulation of li–qi will impact all three. Unlike the masculine subject-centeredness of Cartesianism and its ontology of binary opposition (mind/body, spirit/matter, culture/nature, male/female), the task of the human being here is to intra-actively maintain a harmony of li–qi (Aizawa 1931, 67–70). Aizawa insists that Europeans are ignorant about humanity's "proper place" in the relational ontologies of East Asia. Therefore, rather than accept the hierarchy of European raciology, *New Proposals* argues that because of white people's myopic "pursuit of profit," their "destruction of local practices of spirituality," and their "decimation [荒] of local ecologies," they barely qualify as human at all (37, 14). Sounding here like an anticapitalist land and water protector, Aizawa uncovers a hidden truth of Euro-American trade as that which "doubly profits [一挙而両利]" by selling far above the cost of production as it facilitates dispossessive occupation of foreign territories (36). For Aizawa this double profiting results in multiple losses for the Asian country when Westerners, driven by the extraction → extinction imperative, wipe out the natural resources in their own countries and, subsequently, come to Asia to "extract lead, copper, iron, sulfur, and other precious minerals from their overseas possessions" (52). This urtext of Japanese decolonial thinking offers other striking insights into Climate Caucasianism. This is why I render its anti-Western cry 尊王攘夷, normally translated as "Revere the Emperor, Expel the Barbarians!" as "Revere the Emperor, Fight the Whites!" following Aizawa's understanding of phenotype as described above.[22] *New Proposals* instigated dramatic changes in Japan's politics of the 1860s, as I show in chapters 1 and 3.

As we've seen, both Lin Zexu in Qing China and Aizawa Seishisai in Tokugawa Japan strongly rejected the determinations from Euro-American raciology that they were inferior, backward people. Rather, they denounced Westerners as vile predators who transgress all known norms of conduct from a position of extra-active superiority. Their ultimate violation was to initiate the First War for Drugs, a major asymmetric war against China, as justification for the lowest form of predation. Ranajit Guha calls this kind of antithetical refusal of Western discourse in Asia a "negative and inversive procedure" (1983, 9). In other words, in China and Japan, all that was proclaimed as upright and universal by the US and UK was largely negated as degenerate and particular to Caucasians, Christianity, and capitalism. There was, however, one additional aspect of Euro-American deportment to be inverted.

Qing officials and Japanese policy intellectuals also singled out Euro-whites' excessive speed as an offense to Heaven. Caucasian hypermobility was seen as the key to conquering distant lands and reducing humans and nonhuman animals and nature to extractable rawfare. Especially for the Japanese Mito scholars like Aizawa, growing familiar with the new language of raciology, the people who phenotypically look and act the same—Dutch, British, Russians—travel restlessly all over the world in expensive ships armed to the teeth. With a powerful rapidity previously reserved for supernatural beings and extrahuman entities like typhoons, Euro-whites had transgressed the proper order of Heaven, humans, and the earth. The Qing officials joined Aizawa and the Expulsion Edict in decrying the cumulative effects of Euro-American predation in East Asia as local ecologies and economies were disrupted and millennia-old moral systems were stomped on by Christian missionaries. The ecology or "home" they shared with various beings was morphing into something unrecognizable. Just who were these impetuous predators, trying to exploit East Asia from all the way across the globe?

In these horrified attempts to categorize and contain this entity, East Asians were sketching a critical profile of racial whiteness. Beginning with the warfare characteristic of capital's primitive accumulation—which allowed a subsequent plunder and appropriation of rawfare—followed by the attempt to destroy polytheistic Asian beliefs and replace them with Christian lawfare, the most shocking trait of Euro-whites was their deranged transgression of the normative limits on human movement. Not yet understanding the need for capital's quick turnover time, in the first decades of the nineteenth century Japanese and Chinese officials critically highlighted this hyperactive, stressed-out mobility. From the East Asian perspective, Caucasians were the dangerously velocious Speed Race(r), and, by usurping the capacity for rapid movement previously belonging only to divinities and the winds, they were violating the laws of spiritual nature. For many Japanese and Chinese, the joyride undertaken by Euro-whites was destined for a serious crash, or at least a bad fender bender—the Occi*denting* of East Asia.

As expressed in Aizawa's text, in early modern Chinese and Japanese thought humans are embedded eco-ontologically in an overarching cosmological order. Beginning in the nineteenth century, Europeans became manifestly disdainful of this refusal of anthropocentrism in Asia. The German philosopher G. W. F. Hegel (1770–1831) was the most famously dismissive. For Hegel, firm connections to local ecologies and cosmologies doomed East Asians philosophically, politically, and racially. While lauding Europeans' aptitude for abstract thought, Hegel condemns Asians, asserting: "In the Orient neither consciousness nor morality exist, only natural order." The geopolitical effects of Asians' inability to think abstractly meant that "Asian states belong to mere space" while, contrastingly, Euro-America exists in "the Form of time" (Hegel 1956, 105–6; citations to follow). China's severe philosophico-political disability elicits the philosopher's trash-talking verdict that the erstwhile Middle Kingdom is "outside of the history of the world" (117). This is similar to Hegel's white supremacist denunciation of the "Negro" as exemplifying "natural man in his completely wild and untamed state" (99, 93). Hegel concludes his gloss by praising Euro-whites as the race built for speed, while East Asians are maligned as passive, fossilized in the earth, and immobile. Oblivious to the supernatural overcoming of place by the Speed Race(r)—jacked up on sweetened tea and coffee and made impetuous by whiskey and beer—supinestupefiedyellows and stuck-in-the-mud Blacks are too spaced out to be going anywhere at all. They are clearly at the bottom of what Mel Chen calls the "animacy hierarchy" (2012, 13). Therefore, opposed by Hegel to the accelerating Speed Race(r), Asians and Africans are rawfared together with inert nature as outmoded fossils, what I'll be calling the Stopped Incarce-Races (think stop and frisk, stopped or "arrested" development, racist traffic stops, etc.). We will see later that some Euro-whites promoted East Asians to the rank of the Slow Races, or those nonwhite others who proved to be more than inert fossils by their deference to pale males. Many were extracted and made to work like the fossil fuels oil and coal. I will show in this book that the hypermobile animacy of the white Speed Race(r) depended on the Incarce-Raced captivity, fossilization, and inanimacy of all other living beings.

#WorldSpiritSoWhite

I'm turning to European philosophy here to help tell a story of whites as enemies of Heaven because all too often the narratives about their pedal-to-the-metal, carbon-intensive incursions into China and Japan are written as normative ones of the extension of political liberties, private property regimes, and techno-science into "traditional" East Asia. Similar to the narrative about capitalist globalization today, we are still expected to applaud its universal rationality and not criticize it as hastening the planetary Sixth Extinction. Again, contemporary Indigenous movements like Idle No More and women-led peasant movements like Via Campesina struggling against resource extraction and for a more interdependent, nonanthropocentric world are particularizing Climate

Caucasianism's extra-actions and extractions as the truly deviant phenomenon (Desmarais 2007; Four Arrows 2016; Simpson 2017). In a similar vein, this book will show the ways East Asian resistance to Euro-white asymmetric warfare, lawfare, and extractable rawfare (both nonliving things and the non-white humans Mbembe calls "bodies of extraction" [2017, 18]) was nourished by their relational eco-ontologies. To illustrate this, I will draw on recent post- and anti-anthropocentric approaches of actor network theory (ANT), decolonial and Indigenous relationality (de la Cadena, Escobar, Rose, TallBear), and object-oriented ontology (OOO).[23]

After the postcolonial work of Edward Said (1978, 1993), Gayatri Spivak (1999), and Teemu Ruskola (2013), it's fairly straightforward to expose the biases in Hegel's philosophy of history, which is also a geology of history based on his conflation of Africans and Asians with nonliving fossils. However, this is only one part of a still underexplored system of European supremacy in post-Enlightenment philosophy, an instance of what Du Bois called a "white blindspot" (1935, 577).[24] Because Denise Ferreira da Silva's *Toward a Global Idea of Race* (2007) detects this blind spot better than anything I know, it will be introduced here. More importantly, Ferreira da Silva's genealogy of modern race provides a theoretical lens through which we can clarify what I'm calling extra-action. It can also elucidate how Kantian and Hegelian thought functioned as a philosophical platform for Climate Caucasianism.

Toward a Global Idea of Race makes three main points. First, against the easy dismissal of the "pseudo-science" of nineteenth-century raciology still common in our age of genomics, Ferreira da Silva argues that the two bodies of knowledge that consolidated white supremacy—historical science and evolutionary science—have yet to be overturned. Hegel's oeuvre was one front in the battle that philosophy waged against Newtonian science to prove that Euro-whites were uniquely self-determining entities free from the constraints of relational other-determination that burdened non-European and extrahuman life. In her analysis, the science of evolution effectively ended the tense standoff between philosophy and the life sciences. Ferreira da Silva insists that Darwin built on Hegel's work in securing European self-determination, reminding us that, as he put it in *The Descent of Man*, only white people are able to "defie the regulative and productive force of nature" (2007, 111).

The marriage of Hegelian historicism and evolutionary science helped whip up a Euro-American hurricane, fed by the winds of racial capitalism. But this could only be achieved philosophically after Hegel reclaimed Euro-white self-determination by upgrading the dry formalism of Immanuel Kant's transcendental philosophy with the power to appropriate and/or extinguish all exteriority. This is the second of Ferreira da Silva's main points.

As is well known, while he was contributing to European raciology with his 1798 *Anthropology from a Pragmatic Point of View*, Kant installed the human capacity for reason inside the transcendental I or ego. Arguing that the external, empirical outside ruled by nature is chaotic and in flux, Kant insisted that humans require an internal a priori (before experience) system to intellectually organize external nature. Accessing the transcendental app and submerging reason within it guarantees that the a priori categories (quantity, quality) and forms of intuition (time and space)[25] that constitute reason map onto and correlate with empirical exteriority—a reduction of what counts as reality as only that which appears to human consciousness. Quentin Meillassoux calls this the "Kantian catastrophe" (2010, 124). The transcendental-empirical (or inside/outside and ahead/behind) split is featured in Kant's famous *Critique of Pure Reason* (1781), but he also treats the issue in a more straightforward way in his next work, the *Groundwork of the Metaphysics of Morals* (1785). "Metaphysics of morals" means that rational laws governing what is disinterested must originate not from local culture and custom—this would make morality merely particular to one place—but from pure concepts of the mind and therefore universally applicable. The test of who acts morally is actually a test for who is unhinged from physical desires and extra-actively distanced from natural environments, and therefore possesses the capacity for "pure" unbiased reason. Those Europeans who are successful in this white flight from nature and local custom use their free will to produce laws and codes of conduct that they imagine would be shared by other rational beings similarly freed from local and empirical constraints. Ferreira da Silva builds on previous scholarship (Mills 1997) that criticizes Kantian reason as established by and for Euro-white men. However, her main concern is to show how Kant's transcendental I restores an isolated interiority and auto-determination for these European men after the challenges posed by Newtonian science (2007, 57–68).

Ferreira da Silva reminds us that Hegel critiqued Kant's transcendental I as too distant from and transcendently cut off from the down-to-earth empirical. Trying to answer the question that she insists hasn't been confronted by critical race theory—"How did whiteness come to signify the transparent I and blackness to signify otherwise?" (8)—she demonstrates the ways in which Hegel enhances Kant's transcendental I with the fast-forwarding powers of progressive temporality and spatial conquest. Kant's clear separation of the interiorized transcendental human from exteriorized empirical nature was incapable of insulating Euro-whites from "becoming a thing of outer determination—affectability"

(70). The problem for Kant lies in the fact that transcendental law and rationality are inevitably applied to empirical things in the world, and this exposes their formal purity to a threatening enmeshing in nature. Hegel's solution is to unleash the transcendental and allow it to get down and dirty by aggressively engaging with external things, upgrading itself in the process. This is to say that Ferreira da Silva sees Hegel going beyond Kant's formalistic by "weaponizing" the transcendental I with the power to either "engulf" (partial violation) or "murder" (total annihilation) what is exterior (28–29). Indeed, in Hegel's 1817 *Philosophy of Nature* he urges humans to "do violence" to nature (in Stone 2005, xiii). With the transcendental armed and dangerous in this way, the transparency and self-determination of Euro-whites is, once again, secured. More importantly, it privileges extraction as the vehicle to deepen self-determination.

She summarizes the important shift from Kant to Hegel this way: "Hegel reconstituted the Kantian formal ('pure reason') universal, the transcendental, as a historical (desiring or living) thing, namely, productive (interior-temporal) force, 'Spirit,' the transcendental 'I.' By resolving Reason into Freedom, Nature into History, Space into Time, things of the world into the (thinking, knowing, acting desiring, or living) subject, Hegel rewrote the Kantian play of reason as transcendental poesis" (71–72).

This is a mouthful, for sure. But to conclude this brief synopsis of Ferreira da Silva, her third point sees Hegel taking the main Kantian postulates (Reason, Nature, Space) and turning them into full-throttle dynamos (Freedom, History, Time). While the transcendental app in Kant was deployed to extra-actively map outside things by the internally contained subject, Hegel's transcendental I (aka World Spirit) aggressively makes/produces external things through appropriative extraction, with "make" or "produce" the standard English translation for the Greek word *poesis*. In other words, the Kantian correlation between internal reason and external objects becomes for Hegel coercive appropriation by Euro-whites in the best case, and genocidal murder in the worst. Calvin L. Warren calls this the "metaphysical holocaust" perpetrated by European thinkers (2018, 13). In the *Phenomenology of Spirit* Hegel wrote that this transcendental self "seeks its 'other,' knowing that therein it possesses nothing else but itself, . . . and it strides forward in this belief to a general appropriation of its own assured possessions, and plants the symbol of its sovereignty on every height and on every depth" (1977, 146). Hegel is confident that the trajectory of the (white) World Spirit is indexed precisely to historical progress; for the first time the "strides forward" of Europeans colonize every part of the earth.[26] I see the intellectual antecedents of Climate Caucasianism beginning with Descartes, but Hegel endows European men with the confident possession of a world that they construe as "liberated" from the wretched (of the) earth—albeit an earth that the white world needs to feed off and prey on.[27]

My own understanding of the intellectual history of race and evolutionary science urges an amendment to Ferreira da Silva's analysis of a fully contained, self-determining Euro-white masculinity. I see a continuity between Hegel's forceful management of a transcendental/empirical (or inside/outside and ahead/behind) dialectic and adaptation as it was construed by Lamarckian evolutionists. After all, J. B. Lamarck's (1744–1829) insistence that the struggle for survival impelled self-improvement that could be inherited was the basis for Social Darwinism. Remember Lamarck's thesis of the giraffe gradually passing down to its genetic successors the long neck it had acquired by stretching to reach the leaves of tall trees. In *Physics and Politics* the white supremacist Lamarckian Walter Bagehot (1826–77) deploys this concept to argue that cultural techniques like military prowess could be passed on biologically by superior individuals, enabling them to control their environment and dominate inferior people.

This substitution of Lamarck for Darwin (who agreed with much of Lamarck) allows us to extend Ferreira da Silva's analysis into the most serious threat posed to nineteenth-century white supremacy: the science of thermodynamics. While the first law of thermodynamics stated that energy was constant and available, the second law's emphasis on entropy and burnout revealed limits to both Caucasian evolution and capital accumulation. Where would the ever-expanding energy needed to power the Speed Race(r) come from when the new concept of entropy promised irreversible deterioration and waste for all systems?

As Cara Daggett (2019) argues, scientists of energy like Lord Kelvin came to the realization in the 1850s that the second law of thermodynamics didn't necessarily mean that energy was irrevocably lost and capital accumulation accordingly halted; in fact, the first law contravened this. Rather, energy came to be understood as more widely dispersed in the environment than was first thought. In order to avoid waste, more capital would need to be directed to capture diffuse energy and put it to work for Caucasians. This meant that the extraction → extinction imperative would have to be made fully operational, digging deeper into the earth and reaching higher into the atmosphere. In volume three of *Capital* Marx called this the capitalist derangement to "exploit the earth's surface, the bowels of the earth, the air" (1981, 909). To facilitate biospheric and atmospheric exploitations, capitalism would draw on the new sciences of geology and meteorology. While Hegel's World Spirit managed to press-gang entities into working for it, these were limited to humans, flora and fauna. With thermodynamics, carbon, glucose, and oxygen would be enclosed by Climate Caucasianism and inserted as inputs, resulting in more profitable outputs. Therefore, with the demarcations between inside/outside and ahead/behind secured, white Euro-American accumulators versus nonwhite dissipators (like Chinese "wasted" on opium and Japanese exhausted from sexual promiscuity) became the thermodynamic supplement to the binary opposition of the Speed Race(r) and the Stopped Incarce-Races.

Climate Caucasianism's Victorious Arrival

The First War for Drugs (1839–42)—what the *New York Herald* called at the time "not a victory for British imperialism, but a triumph for the Anglo-Saxons"[28]—globalized Climate Caucasianism. When he received no reply in his attempt at interaction with Britain's Queen Victoria, Qing Commissioner Lin Zexu took the unprecedented step of confiscating and destroying 2.6 million pounds of contraband drugs in the Euro-American warehouse area of Guangzhou. This immediately elicited the denunciation that Qing officials had no respect for property and were clueless about modern contracts. As Ruskola argues, from this point forward, Chinese were construed as completely lacking in reasonable jurisprudence, "lawless" (2013, 6).

After months of lobbying effort in the British Parliament, spearheaded by white narco William Jardine himself, Foreign Secretary Palmerston ordered a flotilla of gunboats to punish the Qing. The British refused to commit significant ground forces because they needed them in Afghanistan after militarily occupying Kabul in August 1839. Nevertheless, the British flotilla was beefed up in 1840 by the first all-iron steamship, the *Nemesis*. Under the command of William Hall, the *Nemesis*'s coal power, high-tech guns, impregnable hull, and low draft allowed the British to easily knock out Qing batteries, kill Chinese, and wreak havoc on local environments. With civilian "collateral damage" and significant casualties to the Qing's best soldiers, Chinese officials no longer construed British actions as lacking in divine benevolence (as enemies of Heaven); now they were thoroughly conflated with evil—the *Nemesis* was called the "devil ship [鬼船]" and white people were denigrated as "devils [鬼子]."

Black Ships and Blackface

"White devil" was certainly not the handle that the devout Christian Matthew Perry (1794–1858) identified with, doing what he thought was God's work during the Mexican-American War of 1847–48. Commanding a US squadron that raided and terrorized Mexican ports, Perry personified the Manifest Destiny of the settler colonial United States. After winning California with the thrashing of Mexico, and advocating for free and enslaved Africans to be deported back to Africa, he was dispatched by President Fillmore to lead a gunboat flotilla to acquire coal concessions and landing rights in Japanese ports for US ships engaged in extracting whales, avian nitrate, phosphate, and other rawfared entities in the Pacific. No doubt inspired by the 1848 Treaty of Guadalupe Hidalgo that annexed close to one-third of Mexico, Commodore Perry's mission quickly scaled up to demanding that Japan's Tokugawa leaders accept an Unequal Treaty based on the 1842 accord Britain had wrung from Qing China. What worked for the United States in Mexico—scorched-earth tactics, shelling of civilian areas from the sea—was always an option for dealing with racially rawfared Japanese. Although the Tokugawa rulers had readied thousands of samurai fighters to defend the archipelago, they were overwhelmed by the visitation of the four US war machines on July 8, 1853. Perry's ships were twice as large as any they'd seen before, and the Japanese were at first disconcerted when they couldn't locate sails large enough to move the vessels. They quickly discovered that the smoke enveloping them came from dirty coal. They promptly named them "black ships [黒船]" after the toxic clouds their engines deposited into the East Asian atmosphere.

After Perry presented the US demands, he returned six months later prepared to carry out asymmetric war. Arriving in March 1854 with nine vessels (including three *Nemesis*-like iron gunboats), over a hundred mounted cannons, and a crew of 1,800, Perry threatened to bomb to ashes the huge city of Edo (soon to be renamed Tokyo) and its one million inhabitants if the Tokugawa bakufu refused the transcendentally produced reason of the United States. In effect, Perry threatened the officials with the worst drive-by shooting in history. Moreover, he ordered US squadrons to stay within gunshot range of all meetings with Japanese officials, declaring, "I was determined to prepare against their well-known duplicity." The Tokugawa government never stood a chance against the US assault that was designed, as the American leaders put it, "to command fear" and "astound the Orientals" (McCauley 1942, 24). Throughout the show of force, Perry accessed what Frantz Fanon (1967) called the "historico-racial schema" that profiled Japanese people as "treacherous and deceitful Orientals" (Feifer 2006, 66, 68).[29] Shocked by the display of high-tech killing machines, Japanese leaders were also reportedly awed by the aesthetics of this new raciology—Fanon's "epidermal schema"—on display in the entertainment provided at the signing ceremony on Perry's ship *Powhatan* and depicted by a Japanese illustrator who witnessed it: a blackface minstrel show (Hawkes 1856, 329, 376).[30]

FIGURE INTRO.5. Japanese depiction of US minstrel show. Courtesy MIT Visualizing Cultures. https://visualizingcultures.mit.edu/.

During the long trip from the eastern US across the Atlantic and through the Indian Ocean, Perry often ordered the musicians hired to entertain him with an "Ethiopian concert." This was the colloquial term for blackface minstrelsy, where white men made themselves up as Africans by putting burnt cork on their faces. The motivations behind white minstrels appropriating the music and dance patterns of Blacks at this time were complex, with some scholars of blackface arguing that respect for and envy of Afro-descendants were prominent (Lott 1993). However, this pioneering form of US mass entertainment was conceived entirely by whites to transcendentally produce images of Blacks—highlighting African musical and dance prowess, while depicting Blacks as ignorant, lazy, and grateful for a life of plantation slavery. As such, minstrelsy supports the theory of Climate Caucasianism I'm developing through Ferreira da Silva, where white men alone have the power to appropriate and/or extinguish nonwhite humans and nature. In the 1830s the first minstrel, the white Thomas Rice, sang and danced on the ground with Blacks and subsequently appropriated their best moves, leaving Rice and later other whites alone to represent blackness. I would argue that this dramatizes the synthesis of the on-the-ground empirical with the positioning above and accelerating ahead powers of transcendental production in Hegel's operating system of whiteness. In other words, although the white man Rice was admittedly the loser in impromptu contests with Blacks, white supremacy granted him a platform for extra-acting on and transcendentally producing the "truth" of blackness that was denied to African Americans themselves.

As we can see from the program printed for the event, Commodore Perry's minstrels divided their show for the Japanese officials into two sets, each representing distinct types of Blacks. The first was "Colored Gemmen of the North," about the lascivious dandy Zip Coon, and the second was "Plantation

ΕΤΗΙΟΡΙΑΝ ΘΟΜΟΝΕΣ.

UNITED STATES STEAM FRIGATE POWHATAN,

Hakodadi, Island of Yesso, Empire of Japan. May 29th.

An Ethiopian entertainment will be given by the
JAPANESE OLIO MINSTRELS,
on board this ship, this evening, weather favorable, to which
the OFFICERS invite your attendance.

PROGRAMME.

PART FIRST.
As "Colored 'Gemmen' of the North."
GRAND OVERTURE.
1. VIRGINIA ROSE BUD   .   .   Mr. Dabney.
2. DARKIES SERENADE,   .   .   " DeCosta.
3. LADIES WON'T YOU MARRY?   ·   "   Tripp.
4. SALLY WEAVER,   .   .   .   " Dabney.
5. OH! MR. COON,   Duett, Messrs. Dabney & Reeves.
6. OLD GREY GOOSE,   .   .   .   Mr. Tripp.

PART SECOND.
"As Plantation 'Niggas' of the South."
1. LIFE BY DE GALLEY FIRE, ·   Mr. DeCosta.
2. GET UP IN DE MORNING,   "   Reeves.
3. MASSA'R IN DE COLD! COLD GROUND, "   Pablo.
4. OLD AUNT SALLY,   .   .   " Dabney.
5. SUSEY BROWN,   .   .   .   Full Band.

SOLO ON VIOLIN, by C. McLewee.

The whole to conclude with a burlesque on
Bulwer's celebrated play,

THE LADY OF LYONS,

introducing a new and much admired pas de deux, with
the following cast of characters:—
CLAUDE MELLNOTTE, alias SAM JOHNSING, Mr. Dabney.
PAULINE, alias POLLY ANN,   .   .   Miss Tripp.
GINGER, ...   Mr. McLewee.
MINSTRELS, &c.,   .   ·   .   .   By the whole band.

Manager, Mr. W. J. Dabney.
Musical Director, Mr. C. McLewee.
Performance to commence at 7 o'clock, precisely.

Japan Expedition Press.

FIGURE INTRO.6. Program for US minstrel show. Courtesy MIT
Visualizing Cultures.https://visualizingcultures.mit.edu/.

Niggas of the South," which showcased happy, infantilized slaves grateful for all their benevolent white masters had given them (Yellin 1996). Featured songs included "Darkies Serenade," which highlighted the inferior intelligence raciology insisted was characteristic of all Blacks. The main events for the celebration concluding the signing of the Treaty of Peace and Friendship featured, on the Japanese side, a Kabuki play and, for the US, military band music and the minstrel show.

Surprisingly, the program referred to the blackface performers as "Japanese Olio Minstrels" (Perry 1854).[31] Why would the North Americans refer to the blackface performance as conducted by Japanese?

As there was no translation of the program into Japanese, the reference to the white sailors doing blackface as "Japanese minstrels" was meant for the English speakers alone. Although I am unaware of any commentary on this in the voluminous literature on the Perry mission, I find it useful to construe this peculiar framing through the terms laid out above from Ferreira da Silva. Whatever else the motivations for blackface minstrelsy—money, racist humiliation, love, jealousy—it was obviously another instance of Euro-white engulfment of people of color that Ferreira da Silva uncovers in Hegel. The inside joke of the blackface performers referring to themselves as "Japanese" should be seen as a racial threat: just as they transcendentally rawfared Africans, Climate Caucasianists were coming to terrorize Japanese people and nature next.

Asymmetric Lawfare

Coming on the heels of the US invasion of Japan, the Second War for Drugs (1856–60) in China legalized the trade in opium and coolie captives and forcefully enclosed the major Chinese city of Hankou (some five hundred miles inland from Shanghai) as a treaty port. In violation of recognized standards of conduct in war, the British commander, Lord Elgin, ordered the destruction and looting of the vast complex of Qing palaces, gardens, and libraries known as the Summer Place as retribution for the torture and death of several Westerners captured by Qing soldiers (Hevia 2003). After the conclusion of military operations, the British and French decided it was time to force the Qing into accepting the "universal" laws transcendentally produced by and for the white Speed Race(r). So British officials established an agency to tutor Chinese in the new game of capitalist lawfare—the Imperial Maritime Customs (IMC), tasked with stabilizing Chinese foreign and domestic customs revenue. After a shaky first few years, the leadership of the IMC was given to Robert Hart (1835–1911) as inspector general in 1863. He spoke fluent Chinese and has been revered by important Euro-American Sinologists as someone who brought the modern world to backward China (Bruner and Fairbank 1986).

While Hart ran the IMC for over four decades, it morphed, after the chaos of the Taiping Rebellion (1850–64), into the principal purveyor of extra-action and extraction in China. It pioneered meteorology in China as a way to manage weather and mitigate the negative effects extreme events had on capital accumulation (Bickers 2012). In so doing, the IMC transformed the eco-ontological intra-actions humans had had with the weather (and the cosmos) in China for thousands of years into an extra-active relation of exteriority. Telegraph wires the IMC installed in the 1890s made possible the first weather map in China.[32]

Building on the barometers and thermometers Europeans had brought to China, the weather map allowed IMC engineers to depict exteriorized weather on a large scale, seeing how a collection of local air moistures, wind speeds, and atmospheric pressures could build up to reveal patterns that could be reliably identified. Until this time weather in China was a local phenomenon that was inextricable from morality and cosmology. The Climate Caucasianism of the IMC turned weather into a discrete entity disembedded from human and extrahuman forces.[33] While it isolated weather so as to manage it better, the IMC's Marine Department similarly transformed rivers and ports into spaces supposedly immune to the constraints of diurnal and seasonal changes; putting in lighthouses and signal systems and undertaking major hydraulic transformations (Bickers 2012).

Robert Hart's IMC also aggressively applied the European science of statistics to mathematically determine the value of human and extrahuman nature (Chen 2002). This included putting a price tag on human life itself, disconnected from its mesh of relations—and the new nineteenth-century science of raciology dictated that Chinese life was cheaper than Euro-American life. For example, Hart routinely devalued Chinese people during the negotiations over the large indemnities paid to Euro-American countries by the Qing government. The inspector general of the IMC wasn't shy about raciologically rawfaring Chinese in his personal life either. Hart rationalized one of his discount purchases of teenage sex servants in October 1854 this way: "some of the China women are very good-looking: you can make one your absolute possession for 50 to 100 dollars and support her at a cost of only 2 or 3 dollars per month" (Heaver 2013). What's important to flag here is not only the dehumanizing creepiness of this extractiv-eye/I but the lawfare that leads Hart to reduce them to a low dollar value. While sex work had been a feature of urban East Asian societies for over a thousand years, white capitalism will systematically extract these girls from their immeasurable eco-ontological relations and rawfare them as measurements—50 dollars down and only two or three bucks a month to allow Hart to always, as he put it, "have a girl in the room with me, to fondle when I please" (Coble 1991, 179).

Perhaps the most significant instance of his overvaluation of white life came with the Margary Affair. Augustus Margary was a British consular official carrying out geological surveys and exploring an overland route for trade in opium and cotton from India through Burma (Chen 2010, 142). He was killed in February 1875 in Yunnan province by unknown actors, and his death was exploited for a full-on expansion of Climate Caucasianism. While some Europeans claimed the murder was a casus belli, more savvy imperialists like UK minister Thomas Wade wanted to leverage it both for a large indemnity payment and to push for new privileges for white extractive capitalists in China. Robert Hart wrote the proposal submitted to the Qing government's Zongli Yamen (Foreign Ministry) on January 23, 1876, laying out precisely what he and Wade thought these new privileges should be, indexed to the inflated value of the life of Margary. The proposal first outlines basic disagreements between Westerners and Chinese: Euro-whites want their imported goods to be taxed only once at the low rate of 5 percent, while Qing officials want to maintain the additional *likin*, the tax on interprovincial trade. So right away in the introduction, Hart's extractiv-eye/I puts forward the British negotiating position:

> If it is asked what more the foreigner wants in China . . . the reply is, that on the foreign side the end now sought for is freedom for every kind of trading or industrial operation. . . . [This] means that the foreigner wants unrestricted access to whatever place interest suggests; development of local natural resources; etc. On the Chinese side, the object hitherto and still kept in view has been, and is, self-preservation; change is not welcome . . . change is rarely accepted on foreign suggestion except when imposed by force. (BPP 1971, 739)

While Robert Hart reminds the Qing officials of their recent defeats in the First (1839–42) and Second (1856–60) War for Drugs, he asserts the right of Climate Caucasianists to do anything they want with rawfared nature. He also states limpidly that if Qing officials attempt to obstruct Euro-white extraction ("unrestricted access") the British government will not hesitate to kill Chinese. This was the typical negotiating position of Euro-whites outside the North Atlantic at this time.

Next, Hart elaborates on China's endemic conservatism in a section called "Administration," rolling out Orientalist stereotypes of the sort we witnessed in Hegel's writing above: "Chinese are a very conceited people," and Chinese are delusional and paranoid: "[Chinese] have been suspicious of the foreigners' intentions, and still think every word must have some ulterior object, and every suggestion some sinister motive. . . . But, obstacles though they long have been and now are, they are nevertheless forces which must decrease. . . . But alongside of these Chinese forces exists another set of forces" (750).

This "other set of forces" is nothing but the march of Hegel's World Spirit, moving in lockstep with white capitalism's haste to extract. Hart himself provided specifics about these forces in his introduction when he insisted that on-the-ground reality in China in 1876 must not reflect the status quo ante, dictated by what he calls "defensive extraterritoriality," or mere immunity from Chinese law. Although this might have been appropriate European policy for the 1840s and '50s, Hart insists that the transformed political situation of the 1870s calls for much more. Therefore, Qing officials must install the political protections for a new "aggressive" or offensive extraterritoriality for Euro-whites (740). What Hart here calls defensive extraterritoriality was the set of privileges granted to Euro-Americans after the First War for Drugs and in Japan after the 1858 treaties with the US and the UK. Ruskola writes that even in this limited form, when Euro-Americans entered China, "their law traveled with them" (2013, 111). But offensive extraterritoriality goes well beyond this. In this new upgrade, Euro-whites must be provided with complete protection from local Qing officials as they exercise, anywhere in China they want, their "freedom for every kind of trading or industrial operation," underwritten by "unrestricted access . . . to work mines, or introduce railways with carte blanche" (BPP 1971, 749). In other words, this new extraterritoriality unleashed Euro-whites to extract human, extrahuman, and mineral rawfare completely above and beyond Chinese laws. In the face of saber rattling, the Qing ratified Hart and Wade's demands for offensive extraterritoriality in the Chefoo Convention of August 1876, concluding the Margary Affair. It transformed the Qing government's primary responsibility from providing for their own subject people to shielding and protecting Euro-white men as they transmogrified China into a shopping mall, open-pit mine, brothel, and outhouse.

White Superpredation

One could argue that offensive extraterritoriality was already understood to be the law of the land in China after the Unequal Treaties of 1858 and 1860 concluded the Second War for Drugs (1856–60). These agreements removed the remaining obstacles to the clipper-coolie captive-contraband-capital circuit by decriminalizing narco and other kinds of trafficking, while it pried loose China's interior to Christian missionary occupation. One underacknowledged effect of this was an intensified sense of impunity on the ground that allowed white supremacist violence against Chinese to become routine and, as I will show, enjoyable. This phenomenon emerged initially at the end of the First War for Drugs with widespread beatings of Chinese men, rapes of women, and looting carried out by Euro-white and colonized Indian forces (Fay 1975, 224–25, 315, 318).

The prevalence of White-on-Chinese violence got so out of hand that British officials in the treaty ports who had otherwise been full-throated supporters of Anglo-American imperialism were aghast. The British consul at Guangzhou in 1857–58, Rutherford Alcock (1809–97), was irate over the predominance of what he called "offscum" among Euro-whites in China. He argued that extra-territoriality "brought with it an evil progeny . . . license and violence wherever the offscum found access and peaceable people to plunder" (BPP 1859, 56). An example of the offscum modus operandi in Guangzhou in 1857 featured "three or four ruffians of a Western race, armed with revolvers and bowie knives, [who] put a whole district under a levy of blackmail by the terror they inspired"—acts of white terrorism that Alcock first observed in Shanghai in 1852 carried out by heavily armed men from Sydney and San Francisco (1863, vol. 2, 366). For him the treaty port enclosures opened a window into the ubiquity of Euro-American criminality and made him fearful that it was jeopardizing the British imposition of free trade and other lawfare in East Asia. For example, the belligerent UK diplomat in China C. G. Alabaster (1838–98)—reportedly nicknamed "the Buster" for his predilection for punching people in the face—reminisced fondly about the "fun" British sailors experienced while on leave in the treaty ports in the 1860s, when they immediately got drunk and roamed the streets looking for Chinese to assault (Coates 1988, 48). While I will demonstrate in this study that, although punching and whipping were the preferred ways to elicit this fun (in East Asia the whip became established globally as the essential accessory for alabaster-white supremacists), Euro-American men also used knives to stab and cut off the fingers and ears of innocent Chinese. Firearms came out when Chinese offered the slightest resistance to white terror—"resistance" often being construed as nothing more than refusing to avert one's gaze from a white guy—close to what whites called "reckless eyeballing" as a justification for lynching Blacks in the US South (Goldsby 2006, 249). Tragically, these nights of Westerners "wilding" in China and Japan often culminated in brothels, where they had their way with young East Asian women and girls until they passed out. Like Hart, the more middle- and upper-class white men bought concubines so they could act as if they were above such lowlife activities (Coates 1988; Hoare 1994).

Even Lord Elgin, the man who ultimately ordered the sacking and looting of the Qing Summer Palace in 1860 and recommended that British men needed to "bully and then stand firm" in China, was himself scandalized during visits to treaty ports in 1858. There he couldn't but notice the "foreign adventurers . . . who take advantage of the laxity of the Consular systems, and the immunities attached to extraterritoriality, to commit outrages on the natives" (BPP 1859, 260). Terrorizing Chinese in this way, Elgin fumed, saw "the worst class of foreigners profit at the cost of the more respectable" (346). However, Elgin found it difficult to identify such "more respectable" Euro-American businessman working in the Ningbo and Fuzhou treaty ports (255). No doubt this was because the most respected were the drug cartels Jardine, Matheson & Co. and Dent & Co. Clearly, respectability was in short supply in 1858.

Chinese Are Entirely at Their Disposal

Nowhere was this more the case than in Shanghai, ground zero for white racial capitalism in Asia. Euro-American missionaries and travelers to the city corroborated Alcock's depictions of "license and violence" and Elgin's "outrages on the native." Some white men appeared to do nothing but go to the brothels and bars, and when they ran out of money they found mercenary work or, alternatively, extracted food and sex at gunpoint from local Chinese (M'Ghee 1862). The British consul at Ningbo, D. B. Robertson, tried to prevent all Anglo-American sailors and merchant marines from disembarking at this treaty port in 1858, as they "consider the persons and property of Chinese to be entirely at their disposal" (Coates 1988, 48). What facilitated robberies and rapes is that white men often carried firearms. In fact, many Westerners residing long-term in China possessed a private arsenal both to hunt game and to terrify Chinese (Wood 1998, 120).

Higher up the social ladder from the so-called "worst class" of whites, middle-class businessmen thought nothing of assaulting Chinese in the streets. The veteran Scottish merchant in Shanghai, John Scarth, bragged that "if there is a coolie doing something vexatious, and an angry foreigner gives him a good punch in the ribs, the Chinamen will drop down and have his cry" (1860, 149). Many white capitalists refused on principle to learn Chinese and some also disliked hearing it spoken, calling it aggravating "clatter and chatter" (Marez 2004, 115). On July 4, 1846, in Guangzhou, the British merchant Charles Compton yelled at a perplexed Chinese street fruit seller in English, telling him to stop hawking his wares across the street from his corporate office. When the peddler didn't understand and continued working, Compton flew into a white rage, punching the man and kicking his fruit stand over into the street. When Cantonese locals started gathering in protest, an armed white mob led by Compton responded by shooting at the indignant Chinese, killing three and seriously wounding six. Compton did not serve any prison time (Morse 1910, vol. 1, 381–84).

Frederick Bruce, Lord Elgin's brother and the British envoy to Qing China from 1859 to 1863, was called on to support British consuls fining and jailing white men for murders and assaults of Chinese, a system that Rutherford Alcock first tried to formalize in Shanghai in 1847 when he became disgusted by the widespread brutalization of Chinese servants (BFO 228/76, Shanghai 32, 1847). Bruce was similarly shocked at the ubiquity of white criminality in China's treaty ports, writing to his sister in April 1858 describing Euro-American mercenaries and traffickers as "the scum of the earth . . . attracted to a country where they can commit excesses without restraint" (in Gerson 1972, 211). While he held out hope that the "more respectable" capitalists would carry themselves differently, these were soon dashed. Commenting on a White-on-Chinese assault case in Shanghai in 1862 involving the "brutal and unprovoked attack upon an unoffending coolie in his employ," Bruce conceded that this seemingly respectable British trader represented "a type too often found among our middle class in China, with the brutal courage of a prizefighter, unchecked by a single chivalrous instinct. . . . They acquire a taste for inflicting suffering and practicing it upon people who don't resist" (in Checkland 1989, 17–18). What particularly bothered Bruce (and other honest diplomats) is that there didn't seem to be any discernible point to the brutality. The white men who assaulted and stole from Chinese were already living well, and, different from the white plantation masters who systematically tortured Bengali peasants in Assam, India and African slaves in the US South, the capitalists who whipped and kicked their Chinese servants generally weren't successful in making them more productive. Perpetrators of white racial terror simply claimed that they were relieving boredom or "having fun." To understand this we will have to go beyond an economic logic focusing on the exploitation of humans and nature for profit to a psychic one that construes white supremacy as compensating itself "psychologically," as W. E. B. Du Bois famously theorized (1935, 700–01) and chasing what followers of the psychoanalyst Jacques Lacan call "obscene enjoyment" (Žižek 1989, 1993).

Because of drunk and marauding lower- and middle-class white men, Shanghai's International Settlement was already off limits to Asians and all women after dark by 1855—the first sundown town[34] in Asia (BFO 228/196, Shanghai 53, 1855). Japanese visitors to Shanghai, after Japan's own coerced entry into global trade in July 1859, experienced this firsthand and registered shock at how Chinese were treated. After several days in the city in 1862, the Japanese samurai Takasugi Shinsaku—protected by his two swords—realized that Shanghainese "scurry away in fear" from white men on public streets to avoid being arbitrarily assaulted or shot (1916, 79–80). Frustrated British consuls in Shanghai and Guangzhou were finally forced to increase the fines in an attempt to curb the assaults (Miyazawa 1997, 44–45). Unlike the diplomats, however, most rich capitalists on the Shanghai International Council seemed less worried about pugilistic traders abusing Chinese in the privacy of their residences or offices than the optic of Euro-white mercenaries and sailors loot-ing and murdering in public. Some of the businessmen on the council who hired these same men as police and security no doubt realized that it was, as we say today, a "cost-effective" savings for them when food, sex, and lodging could just be taken for free by white mercenaries at gunpoint, meaning that wages ordinarily used for these needs could be reduced accordingly. However, the majority of the Shanghai Council understood they had to do something after a series of homicidal rampages in the Hongkou neighborhood of the Interna-tional Settlement in 1862–63. So, they took the unprecedented step of ordering one of the mercenary perpetrators, the American John Buckley (who had pre-viously worked as a policeman for the same council), hanged for the senseless murder of a Chinese man (46; Bickers 2011, 180).

This toxic mix of extraterritorial lawlessness and Euro-white predation was exported to Japan when treaty ports were enclosed by the Euro-American pow-ers in July 1859. Nagasaki and Yokohama were immediately occupied by both drug cartels and arms traffickers like Jardine, Matheson & Co. as well as the more numerous middle-class capitalists whose curriculum vitae featured what J. E. Hoare calls "years of opium smuggling and ruffianism" in China (1994, 6). Rutherford Alcock was promoted and sent to Tokugawa Japan in late June 1859 as the first British minister and witnessed an uncannily familiar license and violence there. As I will show in chapter 1, once in Japan Alcock became much less concerned with white working-class offscum than with what he called the more pernicious kind—the obnoxious white traders and corporate capitalists like Dent & Co.

Then there was what we might call the "onscum"—the diplomats them-selves, the ones the Chinese and Japanese officials who had to deal with them called truculent "fist-pounding foreigners" (Wilgus 1987, 91). In addition to the aptly named "Buster" Alabaster, there was the combative Harry Parkes, the second British minister to Japan, who will feature in chapter 1. In fact, in China Frederick Bruce didn't confine his outrage to middle-class racial terrorists but asked for advice from the Foreign Office in London about how to stop "persis-tent acts of violence by consuls" like Alabaster and Horatio Nelson Lay (Coates 1988, 152).

Although Robert Hart and Thomas Wade succeeded in leveraging the death of Augustus Margary into an expanded set of privileges summed up as offensive extraterritoriality, damages were rarely paid by the Euro-American powers to Chinese unlucky enough to be on the receiving end of a lethal blow.[35] Only mass protest by Chinese was able to elicit investigations by Euro-American consuls.[36] Furthermore, as all non-aristocrat Chinese women and girls were assumed to be dehumanized rawfare by white men, rape being a crime was inconceivable. This absolute opposition between the value of rawfared Chinese and lawfared whites was succinctly explained in the mid-1860s by the British consul at the central Chinese treaty port of Hankou, Walter Medhurst: "The foreigner . . . is regarded, and with reason, as the depository and source of all wealth, influence, and power. Foreigners own the most magnificent houses and conduct the most wealthy banks and firms; foreigners own and command the finest ships and steamers. . . . In fact, foreigners are everything" (in Bickers 2011, 184).

Notwithstanding what Du Bois called the "Heavan-defying audacity" (1920, 43) of these kinds of declarations of Caucasian supremacy—what the comedians Desus Nice and Kid Mero conflate as "Caucasity"—there was an improbable consensus among Chinese officials like Lin Zexu and Anglophone diplomats like Rutherford Alcock in calling the behavior of Euro-whites in East Asia "predation." This book shows how this predation flourished in East Asia by activating asymmetries in warfare, lawfare, and the extraction of rawfare. It's worth underlining the fact that in the seventeenth and eighteenth centuries, Chinese and Japanese repeatedly said that they didn't need anything from Europe. But on the contrary, Euro-whites didn't hide the fact that they needed tea, silk, and "china" from East Asians, and the only way to guarantee continued access was through escalating violence. Here, as Frederick Bruce and Alcock recognized, white male predation in the East Asian treaty ports was a form of merciless conduct that acknowledged no higher juridical or moral law. Echoing the terms of tough-on-crime leaders in the 1990s like Bill and Hillary Clinton defaming African American teenagers, Euro-whites in China and Japan exhibited "no conscience, no empathy." However, to displace the Clintons' racist profiling of Black youth as "superpredators," when we consider the problem of Euro-white predation from the fuller analysis developed through Ferreira da Silva, it's clear the denunciations of Qing officials and British diplomats didn't go far enough. That's because they couldn't grasp the ways in which the joining of the empirical, on-the-ground conflict with up-in-the-clouds transcendental extra-action allowed white predation to be uploaded and recoded into rational truth. In the era of liberalized trade and the Climate Caucasianist despoiling of nature in East Asia, these truths would include the Social Darwinian "struggle for existence," the capitalist ideology of "free market competition" and nature as a "resource," and the Smithian "invisible hand" justifying extractive greed. Reframed in this way, one could argue that when extra-active transcendental reason was downloaded into the on-the-ground empirical, the predatory actions of Euro-whites weren't at all lacking in rationality but became grounded on principles authorized by a constantly transforming transcendental production. In other words, the expropriation of the rawfared "outside" by the "inside" and the "behind" by the "ahead" rationalized multiple forms of Euro-American brutality, and then allowed those "truths" (race war; the putative public good of vile, private greed; extraction as civilizing development; etc.) to then guide and direct further actions on the ground. Therefore, together with a basic predation determined solely by plunder and pleasure, we should construe Euro-white actions as more complex, transcendentally extra-active endeavors involving classifying, calculating, and coding—in other words, "Superpredation." Supported by the nineteenth-century sciences of philosophy, raciology, geology, and meteorology, Superpredation defined the attitude toward nonwhite humans and nature in the era of Climate Caucasianism.

Chapter Outline

Chapter 1, "J-hād against 'Gorge-Us' White Men," and chapter 2, "Ecclesiastical Superpredators," are introductory chapters on Japan (1854–81) and China (1839–91), detailing the ways in which locals defended their eco-ontologies against the onslaught of white racial capitalism. These chapters use decolonial, relational theory and eco-Marxism to reject the standard descriptions of this period ("opening" of treaty ports; capitalist "development") for a framework that emphasizes dissymmetries in warfare, lawfare, and the extraction of cheapened rawfare. These chapters also reveal the climate-intervening and climate-interfering aspects of white capitalism.

The next four chapters are based on a decade of archival research in both China and Japan on two insurgent groups I call "eco-ontological protectors." In chapters 4 and 6 on China, I focus on the outlaw brotherhood the Gelaohui (GLH). GLH membership exploded in central and southwestern China after the Taiping Rebellion (1850–64) was crushed and after major peasant uprisings in Yunnan and Sichuan resulted in small farmers adding opium poppies to their crop rotation. Growing poppies both for their own use and to sell to local Gelaohui dealers led to a substitution of Anglo-Indian opium for Sichuanese product. As more and more peasants took to growing poppies as their winter crop, opium smoking spread from being an expensive habit for Qing officials and rich gentry to an affordable form of recreation and relaxation available to all. But this sudden increase in opium smoking didn't lead to spikes in addiction and delinquency as white Protestant missionaries warned in their War on Drugs launched in China in the 1870s. Rather, it resulted in sustainable economic growth in Sichuan, where sales of the organic product spurred an increase in market towns and new opium establishments and restaurants where peasants could both deepen existing friendships and make new ones. These regular encounters in opium rooms supplemented the traditional function of the Sichuanese teahouse in spreading news and gossip. As Euro-white missionaries flooded into central and southwestern China after the Second War for Drugs, they denounced opium smoking and the "devilish" places where people gathered to smoke it. When news of Euro-whites' attack on the local product that was penetrating deeply into the lives, lungs, and even spiritual practices of Sichuanese peasants reached opium rooms and teahouses, this intensified the opposition to Euro-American Christianity. Sichuan witnessed the greatest number of attacks against Euro-American Christians (教案, *jiao'an*) until the more famous Boxer Rebellion of 1898–1900. Finally, when the Qing government itself launched a draconian opium suppression campaign in 1906, it was opposed by a wide swath of political actors in Sichuan. No one group was more militant in its opposition than the outlaw brotherhood the Gelaohui. In a new analysis of the causes of the overthrow of dynastic rule in China, I will argue that the anti-Qing uprising in Sichuan—usually considered the second most important site of confrontation after Wuchang, Hubei—resulted from this widespread opposition to opium suppression as much as the frequently noted Sichuanese anger at being denied the right to build a railroad linking Sichuan's capital of Chengdu to Yichang, Hubei.

In chapters 3 and 5 I focus on the important southwestern Japan group Genyôsha, from Fukuoka, Kyushu. Inheriting a tradition of anti-Westernism from rogue samurai known as principled protectors (志士, *shishi*), Genyôsha was a major force in the sociopolitical movement known as the Autonomy and People's Rights (APR) movement. Although the APR has been well documented in English and Japanese, there are significant gaps that I have tried to fill. The first is what is known as the Osaka Incident of 1885, where Genyôsha allied with several other armed APR groups in an attempted simultaneous uprising inside Japan—and in Korea and China—to overthrow the Meiji oligarchs. The second gap in APR scholarship is the attempts by local groups to delink from both the centralized capitalism of Tokyo and the carbon-spewing economic system subtending Climate Caucasianism. Genyôsha was one of the groups involved in an attempt in Fukuoka, Kyushu, to do this in 1880–81.

In these two chapters on Genyôsha I return to one of the central themes in this book to analyze the contentious issue of coal extraction in western Japan. As coal mining was being monopolized by large capitalist companies like Mitsui and Mitsubishi with connections to the Meiji oligarchs, many APR groups opposed it, and Genyôsha was no different. However, when the Tokyo leaders imposed a crushing austerity program in 1882, the APR opposition saw its resources vanish. Inside Genyôsha, a fierce debate took place from 1884 to 1886 about moving into coal mining. While nearly all members opposed it, a new pragmatic and proextractivist faction emerged, led by Tôyama Mitsuru, who managed to convince a few of the members to join him in the outright buying of coal resources and investing in other mining ventures. This infuriated Genyôsha's President Hakoda Rokusuke and internal fistfighting and name-calling continued for three years until Hakoda's suicide in 1888.

In the conclusion, called "'Undermining' China and Beyond Climate Caucasianism" I bring the main theme of resistance in East Asia to the extra-action and capitalist extraction of the "enemies of Heaven" to a close with a discussion of two of the most important thinkers of turn-of-the-century East Asia, Zhang Taiyan and Tanaka Shôzo. Zhang was a fierce critic of Euro-American imperialism, but he separated himself from other critics by attacking both the philosophical premises of Western power and its on-the-ground practices. He was also a supporter of the subaltern Boxer and Gelaohui insurgencies. Tanaka was the first environmental activist in Japan, and he was supported financially by Genyôsha.

I

J-hād against "Gorge-Us" White Men

As was appropriate for a man who did "everything at full speed," Parkes walked "at four miles an hour" and on horseback "galloped all the way."—S. Lane-Poole, *Sir Harry Parkes in China*, 1901

As a miraculous act, colonialism frees the conquerors' desires from the prison of law, reason, doubt, time, measure.—Achille Mbembe, *On the Postcolony*, 2001

Gorge-Us

Inserted into the same phenotypical category as Chinese people, Japanese were profiled by Euro-American raciology as "Mongoloid," which highlighted their incomplete sexual dimorphism (little distinction between biological males and females) and neoteny, or the abnormal presence of infantile and juvenile physical traits in adults. Therefore, beginning in the 1850s and continuing directly through the nuclear bombing and occupation of Japan (1945–52), from the British diplomat (Ernest) Satow to (Dr.) Seuss, Japanese adults were said to be childish and easy to control. Taking advantage of the cessation of fighting in the Second War for Drugs (1856–60) in China, Lord Elgin headed up the British diplomatic trip to Japan in August of 1858 to finalize the UK's Unequal Treaty with the Tokugawa bakufu government (BPP 1859, 58). Accompanying Elgin were two members of the British Geological Survey who would conduct investigations for copper and coal extraction. While riding on the gunboat *Furious*, Elgin reported to Foreign Minister Malmesbury in London confirming the Mongoloid racial profile, writing that with the exception of the obstreperous samurai, Japanese are childlike and "gentle," with a "great desire to learn from and even to cultivate closer relations to foreigners" (BPP 1859, 370). Elgin's personal secretary in China and Japan, Laurence Oliphant (1829–88), expanded on Elgin's narcissism in his popular travelogue, *Narrative of the Earl of Elgin's Mission to China and Japan in the Years 1857, '58, '59.*

Oliphant drew a strong contrast between Japan on the one hand, and China and India on the other, where he and Elgin briefly witnessed the 1857 Indian Mutiny against British rule. Seconding Elgin's observations, Oliphant projected that because of their innate "docility," the pliable Japanese "are in a condition to profit by the flood of light that is about to be poured in upon them" (1860, 441; citations to follow). The British diplomats and officers sailed to Nagasaki from Shanghai, and the western Japanese port city immediately impressed with its picturesque harbor featuring quaint temples and teahouses sprinkled on surrounding mountains. The first section of the *Narrative* is aptly called a "Surfeit of Sensations" and details the seductive effect Nagasaki had on Elgin's group. This seduction emerged fully formed when Oliphant shifted abruptly from describing their first perceptions of Japan to an anecdote from eighteenth-century Nagasaki when the Dutch were the only Europeans allowed to trade with Japan. Called "Smuggling Skipper," the snippet depicted the ease with which a Dutch captain smuggled contraband goods into urban Nagasaki from their separate settlement in Dejima. Oliphant bemoans the fact that Euro-white "commercial dishonesty" in Nagasaki has continued right up until 1858 (now personified by the ubiquitous "British smuggler") and that the blithe European disregard for Japanese law "worked to the prejudice of the foreigner in the mind of the Japanese" (308). But the Lilliputian Japanese are so clueless about how to deal with smuggling that the only punishment for Dutch violators of Japanese law was house confinement together with one of the "sundry pretty-looking female Japanese" sex workers assigned to the criminal traders by the Nagasaki officials (308). Right away, Oliphant establishes what Edward Said famously called "the association between the Orient and the freedom of licentious sex" (1979, 190).

Considering this improbable deterrence, Oliphant isn't at all surprised to discover in Nagasaki "bazars crowded with British purchasers"—most of them criminal smugglers (331).[1] In fact, soon after their arrival on August 3 there would be even fewer constraints to trafficking contraband goods than in the eighteenth century, as most of the remaining obstacles to trade were lifted with the granting of extraterritorial immunity to British citizens in the Anglo-Japanese Treaty of Amity and Commerce of August 26, 1858. As I will show in this chapter, extraterritorial privileges for Euro-whites would not bode well for the Amity half of the treaty, but it would certainly lubricate the wheels of contraband Commerce; the clipper-coolie captive-contraband-capital circuit directly impacted Japan from this point on. And while Oliphant is concerned with guiding the reader's attention away from British capitalists' flagrant disregard for Japanese law, his text quickly returns to what for his extractiv-eye/I is the most interesting item of commerce—Japanese women and girls. He informs his readers that for only a few pennies white men of all classes can purchase for recreational sex many of the female "sprites and nymphs" populating Nagasaki from the time they turn fourteen (305).

Soon to be followed by R-rated best sellers like Pierre Loti's 1887 *Madame Chrysanthème* (which I will discuss later), Oliphant's book was the first popular adult-themed introduction to Japan. With its insistence that white male extraction was inherently civilizing and an indisputably positive force for Asia, it made a subtle, but not insignificant contribution to Climate Caucasianism. The travelogue begins with Oliphant's obsession with young sex workers, a phenomenon "so singular to Japan and so prominent" (608). What is even more alluring for white men than the easy expropriation of rawfared Japanese females is the sense that, different from other global spaces, the "social evil" of prostitution isn't opposed in any way to Japanese religious sensibility. In fact, it is an essential aspect of it: "In Japan, religion is not used . . . to conceal immorality, but rather to give it support" (335). Underlining the Japanese "active commitment to sensual pleasure," and forgetting that Euro-American raciology had always depicted nonwhite people as morally degenerate and lascivious, Oliphant finds "very little difference here between temples, teahouses," and brothels (441, 335). Incontrovertible evidence of this conflation emerged later during a sightseeing excursion in the political capital of Edo's (soon to be renamed Tokyo) Asakusa Kannon area, one of "two distinct quarters of this vast city set apart for purposes of debauchery" (638). After concluding that in Japan "Vice itself is systematized," Oliphant and Elgin are informed by their guide that they are behind schedule and won't have time to visit the famous Yoshiwara brothel district adjacent to Asakusa. Oliphant promises to return later for what he calls "nayboen."

Nayboen is a phrase that Oliphant data-mined from the authoritative Western book on Japan at the time, *Manners and Customs of the Japanese in the Nineteenth Century* (von Siebold 1981). Compiled from the notebooks of the Dutch physician at Dejima in Nagasaki, Phillip von Siebold, nayboen appears in the 1841 text simply as "many Japanese of higher order die nayboen," meaning that the family doesn't report the father's death until an heir is identified (192). Oliphant transmutes this rare aristocratic code into the prototype for what would emerge as a key ethnoracial characteristic of Japanese people: the duplicitous shifting back and forth between *tatemae* (social façade or "face") and *honne* (real feelings): "In a country governed by etiquette, and in which every individual is a slave to conventional rules, it is necessary to have a loophole which enables them to sink to the level of ordinary mortals; in other words, to indulge their natural appetites for pleasure or vice. This is the convenient system of 'nayboen'" (Oliphant 1860, 393).

Leaving open for now the extent to which nayboen indexes anything at all in Japanese behavior, the work it does here is to both solidify Frantz Fanon's racial database (the combination of the "historical-racial" and "epidermal" schemas) and justify predatory "appetites for pleasure or vice" in Euro-white men. They too are thankful for loopholes where they can take off the mask of decorum (tatemae) and indulge themselves to the core of their true being (honne) (330). Evidently, innate desires for pleasure or vice have plenty of available outlets in Japan—most prominently with sex workers but, as I will detail here, in ubiquitous Euro-white practices like smuggling, assault, monetary fraud, grave robbing,[2] extortion, and deforestation.

As we saw in the introduction with Robert Hart in China, Oliphant connects the act of expropriating life and labor from East Asian teenagers to extracting resources from Japan's plentiful mountains and rivers—all of these are rawfared by the extractiv-eyes/Is of Climate Caucasianists. And buying Japanese sex workers exemplified Marx's extraction → extinction imperative discussed in the introduction. A British embassy investigation of brothels in Yokohama conducted by Dr. Willis determined that one-third of the Japanese women and girls selling their bodies to Euro-Americans died from syphilis before they finished their terms of indenture at age twenty-two or twenty-five (BFO 46/97, September 22, 1868). Exactly as Aizawa Seishisai had warned about Euro-whites in his 1825 *New Proposals*, the greed for extracting humans is equaled by their desire for minerals (copper, gold) and coal, evident here in the policy recommendations Oliphant puts forward (468). Although he tries to camouflage this greed by asserting a "universality" of free trade, Oliphant underlines the huge market potential of Japan's coal and copper. And, as Robert Hart will insist on in his promoting of "offensive extraterritoriality" in 1876, Oliphant states in 1860 that there is no alternative for Japanese but to accept these Euro-white freedoms to extract unlimited rawfare as a universal "law of civilized nations." As it stands in 1860: "A Japanese has no more idea of individual freedom than a child of three years old, and is about as learned in matters of trade. He has always been in the nursery. . . . When the Englishman comes into business contact with a slave instead of a free man, it requires no prophet to foretell the results" (468–69).

The only problem with dealing with Japanese as the racially othered "slaves" that they obviously are is the inappropriateness of chattel slavery for the new liberal era of individualism and free trade that Elgin and Oliphant claim to be bringing to Japan. From this point forward, Japanese have to be impelled to act through their own volition—as Michel Foucault claimed about the ideology of liberal biopolitics (2008). The problem from the perspective of Anglo-American CO2lonialism is that any liberatory freedom for the nonwhite slaves must not prevent white racial superiors from extraacting on and extracting Japanese rawfare. The trick will be to construct a system that naturalizes and biologizes the power hierarchy characteristic of white masters and nonwhite slaves, yet also solicits some degree of voluntary consent from East Asians and thereby sustains the ideological fiction of freedom—Japanese volition must enable white male violation.[3] The lawfare of nineteenth-century raciology will be the mechanism that accomplishes this and will alert Euro-Americans to how and what Japanese desire. As Achille Mbembe argues, race here is "at once an ideology and a technology of governance" (2017, 35).

As we saw in figure INTRO.4 in the introduction, where the "typical" Mongoloid head was larger than the "typical" Caucasian head, but Mongoloid legs and arms were considerably shorter than standard Caucasian appendages, this neoteny phenotype emerged in the 1850s to produce for Euro-whites the East Asian adult child. While neoteny's primary function was to construct the binary opposition between the Speed Race(r) and the Stopped Incarce-Races, in Japan it offered the added benefit of construing for Oliphant and his fraternity of readers Japanese women and girls as "freely" desiring white men. As can be seen in neotenized depictions of some of the first Western photographs of Japanese females, the oversized head in relation to the "abnormally" short arms (visually shortened by long kimono sleeves) and legs (that can't reach the ground from the bench) creates the effect of a young female soliciting parental attention as a much younger child would.

Neotenizing Japanese females in this way posited them as adolescents obsessed with getting on and down with paternal white men—a new iteration of the supinestupefiedyellow.[4] For Caucasians this racialized "fact" facilitated Euro-white penetration into East Asia. More importantly, it consolidated the "white guy in Japan" genre as the ideal vehicle for extraction in the age of Climate Caucasianism. Borrowing Mary Pratt's insight, Oliphant's text can be understood as an "anti-conquest narrative," whereby Euro-Americans "seek to secure their innocence in the same moment as they assert European hegemony" (1992, 7).

JAPANESE WOMEN, SIMODA.

FIGURE 1.1. Japanese women in Yokohama in the 1850s. Courtesy MIT Visualizing Cultures. https://visualizingcultures.mit.edu/.

FIGURE I.2. Laurence Oliphant in the mid-1860s.

Just a few years after the publication of the *Narrative*, Japanese-speaking white men proposed a meme to normalize racial extraction once and for all. Beginning in 1865, British officials Ernest Satow (1843–1929) and Algernon Mitford (1837–1916) translated the standard Japanese expression of *gochisô* (ごちそう), which is a form of gratitude meaning "thank you for the feast," into English as "gorge-us." Concocted first by Satow to describe a sex party arranged by a Satsuma-domain patron of British contraband arms traffickers, the men referred to in Japanese as *onna gochisô* (女ごちそう), this phrase can be rendered into English as "orgy" or "debauche" (Ruxton 1998, 58). However, Satow's symptomatic translation of gochisô as "gorge-us" was designed to highlight the desirability (cum gorgeous) of white men as it also celebrated predatory extracting, or "gorging." For gorge-us white men in Japan, "us-gorging" on teenage girls and Japanese coal, copper, and gold was construed as a God-given right.

Fleshly Extractions

Right after the successful conclusion of Britain's Unequal Treaty with Japan on August 26, Oliphant wrote to his mother in London that he would "willingly go to Japan" for a diplomatic post, adding that "I am sure . . . you and papa would like it" (1887, 233). Oliphant could barely contain his excitement about returning to Japan, as he was convinced that the cutely neotenized Japanese would welcome white men to Japan even more enthusiastically in the future. Although Lord Elgin was surprised at how Japanese "have a great desire . . . to cultivate closer relations to foreigners," Oliphant took this one step further. Commenting in a letter to his mother about the desperation that he sensed young Japanese women had to be sexually intimate with him, Oliphant's obsession blinded him to his own recent experience with widespread opposition to British CO_2loniality in India and China. And instead of noticing a similar hostility in Japan—taking the form of courageous rogue samurai (浪人) carrying out attacks on Euro-whites—Oliphant fixated on the Japanese women and girls "wild with excitement" at checking out the white guys in the first formal British procession through Edo (1860, 370).[5]

Who could blame Oliphant for finally giving these girls what they innately craved? This is apparently what happened during Oliphant's visit to the neighborhood of Shinagawa, which he understood to be the second largest brothel district after Yoshiwara, zoned "solely for purposes of debauchery." Oliphant's most recent biographer claims that the detailed description of Shinagawa in the *Narrative* combined with the depictions of sex workers and female entertainers elsewhere in the book was proof enough that Oliphant was the first Euro-white to pay for sex in the Shinagawa brothels (Casey 2015, 60). Back home in England in 1865, the then thirty-seven-year-old sybarite was bragging to women friends that he was well on the way to realizing his extractiv-eye/I dream of "knowing a thousand women" (92). Therefore, we can be fairly certain that his Shinagawa visit added to his "score." On the other hand, we don't know if coming down at least twice with serious STDs between 1858 and 1864 helped or hindered progress toward his goal.

Oliphant's extra-action generates a sense of being ahead temporally and above and beyond spatially (what Ferreira da Silva [2007, 98] calls "transcendental production), thereby allowing him to represent willing, consensual sex between white men and Japanese girls—what Saidiya Hartman describes as a situation where "domination is disguised as mutual affection" (1997, 89). However, it was impossible for him to find anything consensual in a different kind of interaction taking place between male samurai and the British officials—so much so that we need to supplement Oliphant's romp in the Shinagawa brothels by suggesting that some in the British party knew that this would be an affront to their Japanese hosts. After all, the regular clientele at the Shinagawa brothels were samurai and upscale merchants, while Oliphant was a mere scribe, and a boorishly illiterate (in Chinese and Japanese) one at that.

Here we need to underline the important work raciology does in the new biopolitical age of freedom. Oliphant asserts that the "Oriental" racial characteristic of "face" is found in Japan's honne/tatemae distinction (1860, 333). Now consider the growing frustration that the British party met with in Japan: after their initial warm reception they were ultimately denied audiences with the Tokugawa shogun in Edo and the Japanese emperor in Kyoto. Similar to British imperialists such as Thomas Wade and Robert Hart in China, Oliphant and Elgin scoffed at Japanese officials' haughty pride, which they called "their assumption of superiority" unsuitable for the new age of freedom and equality (466).

This fakeness of samurai superiority—all the officials in the Tokugawa government and in leadership positions in the 260 domains were samurai—called for more forceful Euro-white tactics. Although assigning young Japanese sex workers to Dutch traders inside their private houses in Nagasaki was one thing, for non-aristocratic white guys like Oliphant to be running around upscale brothels that demanded a precise code of deportment was quite another. Because Oliphant was certainly urged by his Japanese guides not to go to the Shinagawa brothels, he may have refused their recommendation in order to produce two salutary effects with one predatory action: ripping off the mask of Japanese countenance while finally having sex with the prostitutes he obsessed about during his entire time in Japan (Casey 2015, 61).

As one part of this samurai face-slap, Elgin insisted that all negotiations take place at the center of Tokugawa power at Edo Castle, not at the remote village of Shimoda, thirty miles from Edo, where negotiations with the United States had taken place and where the British thought the ongoing negotiations with the US consul Townsend Harris had been restricted to. When the Tokugawa representatives continued to insist that Shimoda was the sole appropriate locale, Elgin sent word to authorities in Shimoda that he intended to sail directly up the bay to Edo, where "no Western ship had ever before ventured" (357). So, they picked up the Dutch translator Henry Heusken at the American mission and, turning their backs on the Tokugawa officials, ventured straight up to Edo with confidence that the monopoly of force on display in their flotilla would produce "a most salutary effect upon the Japanese" (356). The hardware of asymmetric war on display here featured the coal-powered *Furious*, weighing 1,300 tons, outfitted with sixteen cannons and manned by a crew of 185; the *Retribution*, weighing 1,600 tons with twenty-eight cannons; and the high-tech HMS *Lee* gunboat. Speed Race(r)s Oliphant and Elgin chortled as they zoomed past the two tiny Japanese ships loaded down with "two-sworded officials tugging hopelessly after us, in the vain attempt to overtake a steamer of

400 horse-power going at full speed" (356). Elgin chest-thumped in his diary that by disregarding Tokugawa protocol and sailing straight up to Edo to perform an "act of vigour . . . we completely foil by our audacity all the poor Japanese officials" (Elgin 1872, 264–65).

Unbeknownst to Elgin, the US beat them to it. After two years of negotiations starting in summer of 1856, the fifty-four-year-old businessman in China and American consul in Japan, Townsend Harris (1804–78), finally succeeded in forcing the Tokugawa to sign a humiliating treaty on July 29, 1858. The cantankerous Harris had continued Matthew Perry's Superpredator negotiating style of threatening drive-by (gunboat) shootings whenever he didn't get what he demanded (Statler 1969, 234–36). Harris thought that constantly browbeating the Tokugawa officials was necessary because, as he wrote in his journal, he knew the "Eastern character" from five years doing business in China—it was unreliable, devious, and foreclosed from the truth. But the Japanese were even more mendacious than their Chinese neighbors: "they are the greatest liars on earth" (237). As was often the case, this imputation of mendacity was a smokescreen for Euro-white license and disavowal of Harris's own behavior. In clear violation of the Perry agreements, Harris attempted twice to sell expensive American weapons to the Tokugawa negotiators under the table (342). Later, he took advantage of the Shimoda governor's inexperience with exchange rates and swindled the Japanese by paying for his annual expenses from 1857 with silver dollars, but lying in his reimbursement claims that he had actually used the same number of gold dollars—silver dollars were one-third the value of gold in Japan's currency exchange at the time (363).

But what qualified Harris himself for the "greatest liar on earth" award was his approach to Japan's culture of non-Christian eroticism. Frequently deriding Japanese people's "lubricity" in his journal, he ridiculed what he called Japanese officials' adolescent obsession with white women's body parts (Leupp 2003, 147). However, Harris accompanied his translator Henry Heusken on his regular voyeuristic sojourns to the local public baths on at least one occasion: Heusken's Peeping Tom angered the local women so much that they altered their regular bathing times to avoid his creepy ogling. When Heusken adjusted in turn, one fed-up woman sent her boyfriend to threaten him (Stadler 1969, 232–33). Finally, at the beginning of June 1857, the Japanese were startled by an extra demand from Harris just when the negotiations seemed to be wrapping up: attractive teenage sex servants provided to both him and Heusken. In fact, Harris threatened to withdraw the entirety of the US agreement if the girls weren't supplied immediately, risking imminent war. So, one week later a reluctant seventeen-year-old named Tōjin Okichi was forced to have sex with the obese and hirsute Harris, but even this wasn't enough as he threw her out three days later after discovering a skin eruption on her back that repulsed him (382–86). Although he had sex with Okichi again, behind the scenes gorge-us Harris demanded "cleaner" girls. It took six months for the Japanese officials to locate young women whose parents would agree to this arrangement, but they eventually did provide him with two new teenagers in the spring and summer of 1858 (Leupp 2003, 149).

After Elgin's initial slap to Japanese face, the British returned to the playbook of insults they deployed against Qing China. Selecting the most efficacious, they initiated a second mode of defacement: prohibiting white men from kow-towing to East Asians; from this point on they would sit in chairs at tables as equals.[6] The truth underscoring this British insistence on equality would later be revealed when the British minister to Japan from 1865 to 1883, Harry Parkes, resorted to making Japanese officials stand at attention during negotiations, while he lounged on a couch. From the comfort of the couch, Parkes would often give the Japanese, in the words of his translator Ernest Satow, "a good rowing" (Daniels 1996, 42). Parkes was also known to leap up off his sofa to scream at and shove Japanese during negotiations. The "wolf-like" Parkes was despised by Japanese officials as exhibiting the "most disgraceful violence and brutality: smashing of glasses at our prime minister's table; physically assault-ing at Hiogo an individual of elevated rank; etc." (in Williams 1959, 220). The act of lounging sultan-like on a divan was the only time Parkes interrupted his frenetic pace in Japan. As we see in the epigraph to this chapter, Parkes exempli-fied the anxious Speed Race(r) by "doing everything at full speed."

While Japanese girls and women were construed as desperately desiring Caucasian men, commoner men were ignored; samurai men were the only ones that mattered for Westerners. Once again, contents from the raciology database would profile samurai as possessing characteristics opposite those of reasonable, self-determining Euro-whites: irrationally violence-prone and slav-ishly subservient to their leaders' orders. While Parkes dehumanized them as possessing "the ferocity of a wild animal as soon as they taste blood" (Daniels 1996, 85), Rutherford Alcock identified their propensity for violence, which made them "quite capable of avenging on the spot any wrong done to them" (1863, vol. 1, 367). Based on this data mining (yet another form of extraction), weren't Anglo-American arms traffickers like Thomas Glover merely respond-ing to the natural desires of samurai men when they illegally sold them 171,934 new rifles, thousands of Armstrong artillery pieces, and hundreds of ships be-tween 1865 and 1868? (Gardiner 2007, 171). In the same way as selling opium to Chinese and offering themselves to Japanese girls and women, white contraband dealers were merely providing Japanese samurai men with what their innate dispositions called for—again, "dispositions" self-servingly generated by the extra-action of transcendental production and transmitted by raciology. And like the Qing Commissioner Lin Zexu, the Tokugawa shogun Iemochi was forced in 1866 to appeal directly to Queen Victoria when all the requests made to the British embassy in Japan to intervene in widespread contraband arms trafficking were ignored (Gardiner 2007, 171).

Laurence Oliphant's ardent wish for a diplomatic posting to Japan came true in 1861 when Lord Russell appointed him first secretary to the British minister Alcock. He returned to Japan at the end of June 1861 and settled in at the new British embassy, housed at a large temple called Tōzenji in a park in Shinagawa—coincidentally, walking distance to the brothel area he visited three years before. Oliphant was no doubt excited to get back to the scene of his pioneering (anti)conquest, but then realized that the picture he had sketched of pliant and doting supinestupefiedyellows was dangerously incomplete. Upon arrival at Edo, he was surprised to find the Tōzenji grounds guarded by some 150 Tokugawa soldiers. In the three-year interim, ports at Nagasaki, Yokohama, Niigata, and Hakodate had been enclosed for Euro-American trade, trafficking, and residence. When the Tokugawa leaders gave in to the threats of asymmetric war and cooperated with the Westerners in building infrastructure in the new treaty ports, this intensified a domestic crisis. While not an Islamic jihād, a Japanese jihād or J-hād against whites and their local collaborators was erupting in the erstwhile fairyland.

Although Oliphant was warned about the dramatically altered situation, his excitement over returning to Edo combined with the beauty and quiet of the new British embassy grounds seemed to have lulled him into a false sense of safety. The convenience of having one or two Japanese sex servants residing at Tōzenji for exclusive use by the five British officials there no doubt contributed to his satiated sense of security.[7] Just a week after his arrival, the famous attack on the British embassy masterminded by the Mito-domain (where Aizawa Seishisai was from) rogue Ariga Haniya took place on the evening of July 4, 1861. Coming face to face with Oliphant, one J-hādi swung his sword overhead to deliver a blow designed to slice Oliphant in half from the shoulder down, but the attacker couldn't see a wooden beam in the dark, which ended up receiving much of the blow. Just at this time, several of the sixteen assassins inadvertently stepped on pins that were being used for Japanese flora and fauna samples stolen for the British Museum in London, screaming out in pain. This alerted the guards outside and the five British inside, and a bloody battle ensued. Minister Alcock managed to quickly patch Oliphant's slight wound and lead him outside, but the woozy Oliphant passed right next to a severed head lying in a pool of blood (BFO 46/87, August 26, 1861). Stunned and on the verge of passing out, he subsequently stepped on a loose eyeball and became nauseous at the squishing sound it made. Oliphant briefly thought he'd stepped on his own eyeball. Did one of his extractiv-eyes/Is itself become extracted during the rogue samurai attack? (Casey 2015, 84–85).

White Scum

Ernest Satow was a nineteen-year-old student at the University of London when he read Oliphant's titillating account of Japan and was determined to do everything in his power to get a position there. So, after passing the first open examination for the British Consular Service in China and Japan in the fall of 1861, he was shipped out to Beijing on November 4, 1861, to start learning Chinese characters. Although he would later be idolized as one of the first scholarly "Japan hands," Satow's life in Beijing was hardly monastic. Later, in addition to checking out the brothels, he admitted to copying what other young Europeans were doing in Beijing: brutalizing Chinese subalterns. One incident saw him assault his own personal servant, who was responsible for getting him washed and dressed every day. For no apparent reason other than the man importuned Satow to allow him to continue on as his servant in Japan, Satow kicked him down two flights of stairs at his residence in the British embassy dormitory (Ruxton 1998, 15).

Satow was transferred to Japan just two weeks after the diplomatic crisis surrounding the Namamugi Incident. Namamugi was the hamlet seven miles from Yokohama where the British trader Samuel Richardson (1824–62) was killed and two other British nationals lightly wounded by samurai attendants escorting the regent and father of the Satsuma-domain daimyo, Shimazu Hisamitsu, from their compound in Edo to Kyoto. There is no consensus on the cause of the fatal attack on Richardson, but the main events can be outlined here. On September 14, 1862, Richardson, who was in Yokohama looking to make some quick money extracting Japanese gold before returning to England, went on a horseback outing to the Kawasaki Daishi temple with two other Yokohama-based capitalists and a woman visitor from Hong Kong, Margaret Watson Borradaile. Ignoring a warning by Tokugawa officials delivered to Yokohama on September 13 that Westerners should avoid the Tōkaidō highway for three days because several daimyo processions were leaving Edo for western Japan by that road, they sent their horses up to Kanagawa village and took a boat to meet them. After riding for an hour along the Tōkaidō, they came upon one of the processions they had been warned about—the powerful Satsuma domain on their way west. It's here where the facts are disputed. Contemporary British accounts of the incident simply reported that Richardson refused to dismount after being repeatedly urged to do so by both his acquaintances and the guards in the Satsuma cortege (BFO 46/39, March 14, 1863). Several Satsuma samurai then attacked the English, which was their right under Japanese customary law. Richardson received a serious wound in his chest and several smaller cuts, but was able to ride a short distance away before falling off his horse fatally wounded. The injuries to the other two British men were less serious, and they managed to ride back safely to Kanagawa. The terrified but unharmed Watson Borradaile was able to ride the seven miles all the way back to Yokohama.

The main Japanese-language account of the incident provides more detail and context. From the beginning of the enclosure of Yokohama on July 1, 1859, horseback riding (and Speed Racing) through the streets of the treaty port was a way for all classes of Euro-American men to perform white supremacy, and Japanese servants—who were not allowed to ride—were often targeted by drunk white men for amusement. One Japanese died and several were wounded as a result of what official British accounts called "furious riding" (BFO 46/97, July 30, 1869; 46/182, September 30, 1869). Richardson joined many of the other Euro-white transplants from Shanghai in taking a liking to the sense of invincibility that they felt on horseback in Japan (Miyazawa 1997, 142–43).[8] This culminated with Richardson brandishing his horsewhip and trotting threateningly back and forth across the Tokaidô road just as the Satsuma procession was about to pass by the four English (147–48).[9] The US embassy's investigation of the incident concluded that Richardson was even more provocative, writing that "the horse of one of the party forced itself between the [daimyo's] norimono and the retainers who marched as a guard beside it," in what doubtless appeared to be a threat against the Satsuma daimyo's life (Black 1880, vol. 1, 134). The American journalist Edward House wrote in 1875 that when a member of the party, William Marshall, grew alarmed at Richardson's deliberate provocation and screamed out, "For God's sake, let us have no row!"[10] Richardson replied, "Let me alone; I have lived in China for fourteen years and know how to manage these people" (134). Moreover, the British, who were planning to picnic at the Daishi temple with champagne (and had already polished off one bottle), used a picnic cloth and a stick to create the impression that they had a long rifle, which they proceeded to aim at the Satsuma group. This was no game, as Euro-Americans routinely terrorized Japanese in Yokohama and Nagasaki at this time by pointing loaded weapons at them (Black 1880, vol. 1, 156–57). The Satsuma samurai were only armed with swords, with three or four hunting rifles packed away in boxes (Miyazawa 1997, 148).

Here we need to append a third mode that Euro-whites practiced in order to rip off the mask of Japanese "face"—physical assault. In tactics derived from Anglo-American plantation slavery and from British India, Anglophone merchants in Japan earned a reputation for racial terror, and Richardson was no different.[11] However, class difference dictated distinct forms of violence. Mercenaries and sailors got drunk and went out wilding, which sometimes culminated in murder, rape, and theft.[12] On the rare occasions when they were brought to a consular court in Yokohama or Nagasaki, they defended themselves by insisting that to get drunk, raise hell, and fornicate was the raison d'être for shore leave in East Asia. Sailors doing anything else would be in dereliction of duty (McMaster 1966, 59). On the other hand, the preferred method of Western diplomats and officers was to kick and/or spit on Chinese and Japanese. As we saw above, Ernest Satow thought nothing of kicking his Chinese servant down flights of stairs, and wrote in his journal that he learned from his time studying in Beijing that assaulting Chinese in this way was normative Euro-white conduct.[13] Finally, although kicking Chinese and Japanese was also practiced by middle-class capitalists, a survey of the incidents[14] supports the observation referenced in the introduction of the British envoy to Qing China, Frederick Bruce. Bruce reflected on the 1862 case in Shanghai of a white British capitalist's "brutal and unprovoked attack upon an unoffending coolie in his employ" and regretted that this shocking lack of conscience and empathy was typical "among our middle class in China" (Checkland 1989, 17–18). In this case and others, Bruce noticed that white merchants preferred to brutalize innocent Chinese with their fists, in the fashion of "prizefighters." According to W. E. Griffis, an American who taught for three years in Tokyo, in the early 1870s British capitalists in Yokohama primarily beat their Japanese servants with their fists, while occasionally mixing in whipping, caning, and kicking. Griffis prefaced his account by clarifying that not every Englishman in Yokohama abused Japanese subordinates, "but a grievously large number . . . are apt to become offensively vaporous in their pretensions. They are the foreigners who believe it their solemn duty . . . to train up their servant 'boys' in the way they should go by systematic whippings, beatings, and applications of the boot. Fearful of spoiling cook, boy, or 'bettô' (groom), they spare neither fist, boot, nor cane" (1877, 342). Some Japanese laborers risked certain death by refusing their dehumanization as rawfare. In 1869 a white British trader named Hoey was killed by two Japanese as retribution for severe assaults inflicted on them (Partner 2018, 58).

The de-facing assault mode par excellence may have only been used on Japanese servants in Nagasaki. There, Anglophone traders would automatically blame their servants for the smallest inventory shortage and proceed to round up several, shackling them and accentuating racial othering by slathering black tar on their faces (Paske-Smith 1930, 254). The Jardine, Matheson & Co. agent in Nagasaki and contraband arms trafficker, Thomas Glover (1838–1911), was known to have taken the law into his own hands by chaining and tarring disobedient servants. Glover doubtless learned from his white capitalist colleagues additional ways to abuse powerless Chinese during his time in Shanghai, and he kept his skills honed after he relocated to Nagasaki in 1860. Although Glover normally assaulted his own servants inside his huge Ipponmatsu mansion, one incident in 1863 caused a minor scandal. On February 21 the Nagasaki governor charged Glover with punching a delivery boy "half to death" at Ipponmatsu. Glover first laughed off this rare Japanese intrusion into Euro-white affairs (extraterritoriality in East Asia made it extremely difficult for Japanese or Chinese to indict Euro-Americans) before agreeing to pay a small settlement to the victim's family (Gardiner 2007, 51). Glover's reputation for personally assaulting his servants and workers was so widespread that the Foreign Ministry in London was forced to warn him that his trading license would be rescinded if he didn't stop the abuse (80). Like Glover, the accounts of Samuel Richardson's Superpredation confirm that it featured fisticuffs, although he was widely rumored to have whipped his Chinese servants as well.[15]

The White-on-Japanese violence was so widespread and public in Yokohama that Euro-American capitalists didn't even bother to refute the criticisms of their brutality, although they did try to shift the blame to mendacious "two-faced" servants who cheated them. After considering the evidence of several assaults in January and February 1866, the pro-British merchant newspaper *Japan Times* unexpectedly took the side of the Japanese servants and advised the Euro-America merchants to drop the default prizefighter responses and be more sympathetic to indigent Japanese workers (*Japan Times*, March 9, 1866).

Samuel Richardson worked in Shanghai from 1853 until 1862, first in the silk trade before getting rich in real estate speculation and rent extraction. After several incidents of unprovoked assault on his own servants, he was finally called to appear at the British consulate in Shanghai on March 31, 1861, and was fined for punching one of his Chinese servants to the brink of death (Miyazawa 1997, 88–89). The British envoy Frederick Bruce monitored the specifics of the Richardson case and struggled to fathom the disconnect between the calm demeanor that Richardson exhibited at the hearing and his serial assaults on defenseless Chinese (Reichert 2013, 67). Bruce could only conclude

FIGURE 1.3. Thomas Glover in the 1880s.

that the fault lay with the ways "the East" so completely corrupted Euro-whites that it quickly stripped them of the Christian moral framework they had been brought up with.[16]

The quaint several-mile stretch of the Tōkaido highway from Kawasaki village to Kanagawa—lined with shops, inns, teahouses, restaurants, and a brothel—was considered by many Westerners to be their prime consumer area in Japan, and they named this their "Avenue." White people regularly ignored recommendations by Tokugawa officials to refrain from horseback riding or partying at restaurants during daimyo processions. Miyazawa Shin'ichi writes that no Japanese could ever tell Euro-Americans what they could or couldn't do on the Avenue, as they considered this their CO2lonial territory (1997, 136–37). Moreover, unlike inside Yokohama, where whites of all classes carried firearms, when they went to this stretch of the Avenue to consume and carouse, many left their pistols and rifles at home.

As Rutherford Alcock was in England on holiday, Colonel Edward Neal was the acting British minister, and while he was under strict orders not to initiate a conflict, he was helpless to prevent a bloodthirsty mob of fifty or so armed sailors and merchants from riding out from Yokohama to hunt down the Satsuma perpetrators of Richardson's killing. Just at this time, the British flagship *Euryalus* sailed into Yokohama harbor, joining two British and three French gunboats. From these six ships, boatloads of armed sailors were ordered by their commanders to land at Kanagawa, Kawasaki, and Shinagawa, terrifying Japanese commoners and merchants. All the while the Satsuma cortege was staying at inns only five miles away.[17]

Evening fell and the white military and merchant leaders gathered to discuss how to proceed against Satsuma. Almost every capitalist in Yokohama was at this raucous meeting, and after several hours a consensus emerged between the soldiers and merchants: a combined force of a thousand armed soldiers backed by six gunboats would pressure Satsuma (with only a handful of firearms among their 150 men) and, if they refused to hand over Richardson's killer, a coordinated attack with ground forces and gunboat projectiles on the coastal Kanagawa village would ensue. The Euro-Americans promised to try to limit the death toll to ten Satsuma samurai. No one present disagreed with what Du Bois called the "Heaven-defying audacity" of this white calculus: ten samurai = one British merchant (1920, 21).

When Neal resorted to threatening the British soldiers and sailors with reprisals, the assault on Kanagawa was called off. However, in violation of all legal precedents, the British demanded a huge £100,000 indemnity from the Tokugawa government (roughly one-third of Japan's annual revenue) plus a £25,000 indemnity from Satsuma, in addition to the immediate trial and execution of Richardson's killers. Back in London, critics pointed out that the entire Japanese government could not be held responsible for the actions of one Satsuma samurai, and furthermore, the punishing indemnities were ten to fifteen times higher than would be the case if England were dealing with a French or Spanish killer (Fox 1969, 117–18).

With Alcock still in London, both the Satsuma domain and the Tokugawa refused to pay the indemnities. In consultation with the Foreign Office, Alcock decided that nothing short of a bombardment from the sea and land invasion of Satsuma's capital of Kagoshima was required to restore British supremacy. Astonishingly, even though only East Asians were raciologically profiled to obsess about the sociopolitical importance of "face," Alcock justified British asymmetric war in these terms. As he put it, English "esteem" was being undermined by the Japanese refusal to pay the indemnities (Alcock 1863, vol. 2, 15). If the UK did not obtain retaliatory justice, Alcock hallucinated, it would be regarded as "dishonored and craven by the Japanese" (17).

Minister Neal and Admiral Kuper began preparations for an attack on Kagoshima. A flotilla of seven ships with 125 cannons, including twenty-four high-tech Armstrong guns, left Yokohama on August 6. Unbeknownst to the British, most of the 180,000 residents of Kagoshima were evacuated in anticipation of a UK assault. After two failed negotiation attempts, on August 14, Kuper seized three Satsuma-owned steamships with a total value of $380,000.

Kagoshima lies right in the middle of a major typhoon alley running from the Philippines to Korea through Kyushu, and lucky for the Satsuma gunners, this was typhoon season. So, the Satsuma soldiers proceeded to fight intra-actively within their environment at hand. They waited patiently until just before a storm developed to launch their attack on the British flotilla that had been parked right in front of them for two days. With surprising accuracy, their eighty-eight guns (bought from British and US arms traffickers) tore into the British fleet, and a single cannonball decapitated two English captains. The British counterattack thirty minutes later was hampered by the intensifying typhoon gales, blowing battle smoke over the Satsuma forts and preventing the British gunners from clearly seeing what they were shooting at. After three hours of fighting, eleven British sailors were dead and fifty wounded. Angry at the surprising accuracy of the Satsuma cannons, as Kuper retreated from Kagoshima harbor and fire from the Satsuma guns waned, he ordered the British gunboat *Havoc* to launch rockets over the Satsuma batteries into the civilian areas of the city—a deliberate war crime as the British didn't know that the city had been evacuated (McMaster 1992, 99). As the flotilla sailed back to Yokohama, Colonel Neal bragged that firing into residential areas of Kagoshima resulted in a million pounds of property destruction (Satow 1921, 92).

Let's do some rough accounting to arrive at the value of Samuel Richardson's life: three Satsuma steamships stolen, looted, and destroyed ($380,000); a significant amount of property damage in the ancient Kagoshima castle town ($4,000,000); five ships in Satsuma's Ryūkyū fleet burned on Kuper's order ($200,000); together with twelve British and five Japanese combat deaths and roughly five hundred Japanese civilian deaths. Not counting the CO2lonial destruction to the environment in the indiscriminate shelling of Kagoshima, the total comes to just over five hundred humans and roughly 5 million dollars, seven to eight times the annual revenue of the Japanese government in 1863 (Totman 1980, 69).

Neal, Kuper, and Rutherford Alcock reasoned that Britain had temporarily regained face, especially after Satsuma finally agreed to pay the £25,000 indemnity and resume diplomatic relations with the UK. But the problem of Euro-America losing face through the bad-boy modus operandi of the capitalist merchants lingered. The first British minister in Japan, Alcock began his diplomatic career in China as consul in the Shanghai and Guangzhou treaty ports. There he grew increasingly disgusted with the behavior of working-class whites, the "desperadoes and lawless persons" he pegged as "offscum." In China, Alcock and Lord Elgin tried (and largely failed) to distinguish these men from "more respectable" white capitalists. When Alcock arrived in Japan for the enclosure to Euro-Americans of Nagasaki and Yokohama on July 1, 1859, he was dismayed to find that almost all of the Euro-American traders in Japan were transplants from Chinese treaty ports, a situation that continued right up until the Meiji transformation in 1868. Frustrated with his inability to separate lower-class offscum from middle-class capitalists in his last years in China, when he reacquainted himself with these same drug cartels and arms traffickers in Japan, he threw up his hands and stopped trying altogether. Although Nagasaki and Yokohama hardly lacked offscum (108 US residents of Yokohama were forcefully deported for "outrages" including rape and murder in a purge in January 1871),[18] the most pressing public relations problem in Japan was the presence of white businessmen like Richardson—who Alcock denounced as "scum," plain and simple (Williams 1959, 214).[19] Like the black teenage "superpredators" that Bill and Hillary Rodham Clinton rawfared in the 1990s as bereft of "all conscience and empathy," white capitalist scum in Japan ignored all morality and routinely resorted to "violence and lawlessness" in their quest for short-term riches (Alcock 1863, vol. 2, 368).

Fiscal Extractions (Taking Gold Candy from Neotenized Babies)

Although Euro-Americans continued to insist that they were bringing the civilizing influences of liberal trade and the rule of law to a stubbornly backward East Asia, more honest British diplomats like Alcock and Bruce saw the situation very differently. After the widespread instances of smuggling—which included trafficking opium into Japan, a flagrant violation of the treaties (Gardiner 2007, 40–42)[20]—the second substantiation of the scummy MO of Caucasian capitalists took place around the issue of currency. With Nagasaki and Yokohama being enclosed for white racial capitalism on July 1, 1859, the Unequal Treaties had to determine the exchange rate for dollars. While the nominal exchange ratio of gold to silver in Japan was five to one, on the global market it was fifteen to one. The Unequal Treaties authorized the exchange of foreign silver for Japanese gold coins on this five-to-one weight-for-weight basis, meaning currency speculators could bring silver coins to Japan and exchange them (after the first three months this practice was outlawed, although the ban was routinely ignored by Euro-Americans) for gold kobans in Japan and reap a 300 percent markup when the gold was extracted and resold in Shanghai, Hong Kong, and San Francisco (Ishii 1976, 92–96). As a result, huge amounts of gold disappeared from Japan (BFO 46/3, November 21, 1859). The journalist John Black wrote that when a US Navy officer heard about the potential for gold profiteering in Yokohama in 1861, he immediately resigned his commission, rented a ship, and started buying as much gold as he could to ship to San Francisco, followed by "nearly every other officer on the ship" (1880, vol. 1, 41). This gold rush angered both anti-Western samurai—the rogue Shimizu Seiichi testified in 1866 that the theft of Japanese gold drove him to kill Euro-whites (Paske-Smith 1930)—and some of the first British soldiers stationed in Japan. One refused to listen to the Western merchants complain of so-called Oriental corruption, instead accusing them of white Superpredation: "Did we teach them truthfulness or honesty when we bought their gold weight-for-weight with silver and drained their treasury under false representations? We call them [Japanese] a semi-barbarous race; but contrast the courteous, dignified bearing, and the invariable equanimity of the lowest official or smallest tradesman, with the insolent arrogance and swagger, the still more insolent familiarity, or the besotted violence, of many a European resident" (De Fonblanque 1863, 70).

Colonel De Fonblanque, who lived off and on in Yokohama for eighteen months, confirmed Alcock's conflation of the working-class sailors with the capitalist merchants. Both classes resorted to "besotted violence" to get what they wanted. Both took advantage of the attractive exchange rate and low labor costs to live in a style impossible in Euro-America. For example, in 1862 about 40 percent of the Euro-white merchants in Yokohama had a live-in sex servant, whom they called a *moosme*. In addition to concubines, all of them had at least one full-time servant and most had a groom for their horse, or *bettô* (Williams 1963, 109).[21] In 1897 there were still on average three Japanese servants for each of the 2,500 permanent Euro-American residents of Yokohama.[22] For the sailors and mercenaries, the cost of living was so low that during leaves they could afford to drink and gamble all day and then buy women and girls on the cheap at night. But as we saw in the introduction, turning Japanese and Chinese into rawfare also meant they could be taken for free. Well-armed Euro-American mercenaries between gigs in Yokohama followed the pattern set by their white brothers in Shanghai and Guangzhou and held neighboring villages hostage, demanding free food, shelter, and sex (Black 1880, vol. 2, 100). One testament to white male depravity is that the area of Yokohama with the densest concentration of bars and brothels was widely known as "Bloodtown." Things got so rowdy there that local Japanese did everything they could to stay away. Although most of the White-on-White and White-on-Japanese violence in Bloodtown was carried out with knives and clubs, most Euro-Americans in Yokohama carried firearms, and they didn't hesitate to use them (Griffis 1877, 373). It was left to the marshals connected to the Euro-American embassies to deal with the most egregious of the ruffians. The US deputy marshal in Yokohama in the late

1860s, William Davis, had been a real prizefighter, and he needed all his boxing skills when trying to chill out wilding Westerners. After failing to apprehend a particularly obnoxious white American, Davis succeeded only by biting off the nose of the man and then handcuffing him (Williams 1963, 119).

Honky Dory CO2loniality

Excepting Davis, Euro-whites avoided biting off noses to spite their face, and the brothels were designed to help with this. Under pressure from US and UK officials, the Tokugawa government built the large Miyozaki commercial sex district, with six brothels to accommodate Euro-Americans and others, when Yokohama became available for Euro-American extraction on July 1, 1859 (Leupp 2003, 152). Miyozaki opened for business on November 10, 1859, and Gankirô was the largest establishment there, with around two hundred indentured sex workers detained in tiny spaces (Bernstein 2009, 211). Exactly opposite to the Euro-fantasy of supinestupefiedyellow girls and women desperate for pale penises, upon learning that their bodies would be sold to Euro-Americans, nearly all Japanese females had to be physically forced to go to the newly opened Miyozaki brothels. For example, brothel owners in nearby Kanagawa were ordered to send a total of forty women and girls to Miyozaki on July 7, 1859, and when the time came to bring them to Yokohama, they cried, screamed, and tried to flee. Each one had to be dragged into small palanquins that were then roped shut to prevent escape en route (Partner 2018, 16). Some committed suicide rather than subject themselves sexually to white men.[23] The suicides continued years after Gankirô opened. Miyozaki sex workers would do anything in their power—feign illness, lie about deaths in the family, and so on—to avoid spending the night at the Yokohama residences of Euro-Americans. One young woman indentured at Gankirô, named Kiyû, ran out of excuses and chose to kill herself rather than be further rawfared by being forced do an overnight with a white man in 1863.[24]

The British consul at Hakodate, Abel Gower, visited Gankirô in 1861 and likened the condition of the two hundred trafficked sex workers there to "horses in stables" and "dogs in kennels" (in Leupp 2003, 152). The US writer and traveler R. H. Dana spent time at Gankirô in 1860 and similarly described the "cages" that held sex workers captive. Dana went further than most Euro-Americans visitors in describing the situation of the Japanese captives as "like slaves" (Lucid 1968, 1018). Many white men extracting women at Gankirô themselves reiterated this language of dehumanization and forced captivity. What is important here is that most of the men who honestly depicted the situation of the trafficked women went ahead and paid for sex with them anyway. How?

The explanation lies in the ways the mechanism of disavowal pushed these clear-sighted observations of dehumanization and extreme inequality to the margins and replaced them with fantasies of consent and reciprocity that we saw with Laurence Oliphant above. The raciological imputation of lasciviousness and moral degeneracy to Japanese people obviously contributed to this disavowal. The objects making up the space of Gankirô (and most other brothels designed for Euro-Americans in Japan) were also important. The centrality of music and dancing inside the brothels was crucial in helping to hide the coerciveness of the sex trafficking of girls and women to white men; it was the Oliphant in the room. Of course, most white men had so thoroughly dehumanized and rawfared nonwhite women that this mechanism of disavowal was pointless; they were mere (lowercase) superpredators possessing "no conscience, no empathy." But for others who didn't consider themselves primarily pleasure-seeking extractors, disavowal was crucial. Dana mentioned the music and dancing at Gankirô in 1864, and the American writer Charles Longfellow depicts it in several brothels in Tokyo in the 1870s (Guth 2004). As we can see from some of the images inside Gankirô from the early 1860s, music played a role in disguising the reality of captivity.

As we will discuss later, men who paid for teenage Japanese sex servants like Pierre Loti wanted them to play music and sing. While music can be inherently sensual, its power in what Saidiya Hartman (1997) calls "scenes of subjection" was arguably to allow some white men to hallucinate that these asymmetrical encounters were merrily consensual. The singing and shamisen-strumming girls were proof that they were sharing in the good time, white guy disavowal held. And even if sex worker captives weren't obviously enjoying themselves, the disavowal initialized by Laurence Oliphant that continues to this day—"They *love* white guys in Japan"—was always available for Euro-American men. They could then proceed guilt-free to the "cannon shot [一炮注意]" ejaculation, as it was symptomatically called in several areas of East Asia at this time (Hershatter 1997, 47). Herein lies the evil genius of extra-active transcendental production for Caucasian Superpredation. In the charnel house brothels in Yokohama and Nagasaki, where young Japanese sex workers had a 65 percent chance of surviving to age twenty-three, what Christina Sharpe (2010) calls "monstrous intimacies" were represented upside-down by many Euro-American men as sites of mutual attraction and consensual sex.

After Gankirô was burned down by samurai rogues in 1866, Jumpirô took its place as the largest brothel catering to Euro-white men. Run by the Miyanoshita

FIGURE 1.4. Japanese sex workers playing shamisen and singing for Euro-American clientele. Courtesy MIT Visualizing Cultures. https://visualizingcultures.mit.edu/.

restaurant family from Kanagawa, Jumpirô became known by its address of Number Nine Takashima-chô. Subsequently made famous by Rudyard Kipling's 1894 poem "MacAndrew's Hymn," the brothel was run by a Miyanoshita daughter known as "Mother Jesus." Beginning in the mid-1860s, when Anglophone sailors were given shore leave at Yokohama, most ordered their rickshaw cab to take them to "Hunky Dory," which was the bastardized name for the main thoroughfare from the Yokohama dock area leading to No. 9 Takashima-chô—Honchô Dôri. Eventually, "Hunky Dory" became the meme depicting imperial surfeit for white men in Japan (Pedlar 1990, 64). Hunky Dory first appeared as the title of a blackface minstrel song composed by Christy's Minstrels in 1861 called "Hunkey Dorey," which featured a blackened-up white man singing about the joyous and carefree—or hunkey dorey—lives of black slaves on plantations in Kentucky in the 1850s.[25] Here again, white men had the power to both raciologically profile black people as lazy and promiscuous (through transcendentally produced lawfare) and then to appropriate these fictive characteristics of Africans when it suited them, which it apparently did every time there was shore leave in Japan.

We can make one final conflation of the behavior of working-class men and capitalist merchants in Japan's treaty ports. While the sailors were only allowed to let the good times roll in the Bloodtowns during shore leave— gambling and drinking during the day; drinking, gangbanging, and visiting Mother Jesus at night—the capitalists were almost always kicking back, feeling honky dory. Although the racist lawfare of (white) accumulators versus (non-white) dissipaters has led many scholars to assume that Western merchants in Japan tirelessly plied their trade as exemplars of the disciplined Protestant ethic, this is but another white lie. Honest visitors and missionaries noticed how indolent the Euro-American merchants were: beginning work at 10:00 a.m., followed by a two-hour champagne lunch—often coming on the heels of an hour of horseback riding—before returning to work briefly to close up the office for the day at 4 p.m. (Williams 1958, 51). This was limited to a five-day week, Monday–Friday. After work the merchants went horseback riding, boating, or played tennis. Following another champagne meal for dinner, they played cards and drank before ending the night by calling for their live-in sex servant or going to Gankirô. There were exceptions to this honky dory schedule, for sure, but even for the workaholics like Thomas Glover in Nagasaki, the most important tasks in every Euro-American company were delegated to Chinese assistants. This was because in the 1860s and 1870s Euro-white merchants in Japan refused on principle to learn any written or spoken Japanese; their communication skills were limited to hand gestures and the treaty port pidgin. Based on a white supremacist disdain of East Asian languages and societies, these capitalists viewed Euro-Americans who were hired as advisers to the Japanese government as contemptible race traitors—white men didn't work with Japanese, they extra-acted over and on them. Climate Caucasianism held that Japanese and Chinese worked for and were worked over by their bio-genetic superiors in the manner of natural resources. This was why, except for concubines and bought sex workers, most whites practiced a racial apartheid completely separate from Japanese. While the prohibition of "dogs and Chinese" entering Shanghai's Huangpu Park is well known, a sign stating "NO NATIVES will be admitted" at the main Yokohama racetrack exemplifies the shared mentality between Shanghai and Yokohama (Williams 1958, 35, 28).

Enclosed for Business

One year after the enclosure of Yokohama and Nagasaki, the Tokugawa bakufu announced that it was setting up a special exchange rate for dollars in an attempt to stop the gold rushing out of Japan, as it was having a strong inflationary effect. Alcock noticed that Euro-white merchants in Yokohama and Nagasaki had basically given up the silk and tea trade in their "delirium" to procure cheap Japanese gold to then resell on the global market (1863, vol. 1, 283).[26] After the first months of this yellow (gold) fever, Euro-American capitalists had picked Japan nearly clean by, as Alcock put it, "shipping off all the gold currency of Japan" (BFO 46/4, November 10, 1859).

With the profits from Japanese gold extraction stuffed in their pockets (some of it subsequently circulated in global financial markets before landing in high-carbon investments), white merchants next turned their extractiv-eyes/Is to the widespread avoidance of the legal tariff. The asymmetric lawfare of the Unequal Treaties established a low tariff of 5 percent on imports and exports, but even this 5 percent was largely symbolic as the most expensive items, like Euro-American weapons and ships, were imported into Japan duty free. The Euro-American powers argued that the increase in trade would help Japanese producers while the tariff duties would fill the coffers of the Tokugawa government and allow them to pay for infrastructure upgrades to facilitate more exchange. The only problem with this was that when the Euro-white merchants didn't cheat the Japanese by refusing to pay any tariff at all, they took advantage of the inexperience of the Japanese customs officials to deliberately undervalue their imports. Amazingly, from 1859 until 1866, the Unequal Treaties granted Westerners the right to assign value to their imports themselves.[27] Owing to the Tokugawa officials' relative cluelessness about global commodity markets, the rare arbitration cases that arose were won handily by Euro-whites.

British officials in Japan admitted publicly that, at a minimum, 50 percent of the tariff went unpaid by their merchants. Later, even pro-British historians conceded that whites ripped off the Japanese government of up to 90 percent of tariff revenues (McMaster 1966, 76–78). The "most respectable" firms like Jardine, Matheson & Co. managed to largely avoid paying tariffs. Looking at their textile shipments brought into Yokohama between August 1861 and April 1863, it's clear they defrauded the Japanese Customs out of 67 percent of the real value of their products (77). Jardine, Matheson & Co. and Dent & Co. became adept at the game of bribery and undervaluing imports they called "Oriental squeeze," having perfected it in bringing contraband drugs and weapons to market in China for decades. Once again, Euro-whites got to write the raciological profile for East Asians—corrupt, duplicitous practitioners of Oriental squeeze—and then violate that profile by usurping supposed East Asian cultural traits (like "squeeze") to enhance Euro-white extraction.

The Eco-Ontology of J-hād

We saw above how the Satsuma domain soldiers dealt with the British gunboat attack. They did this not by mobilizing the Kantian process of correlating internal subjective reason to externalized objects (and then extra-acting on that externality), but through intra-acting with the ecology, or what Arturo Escobar calls "the political activation of relationality" (2018, 95). For the Satsuma fighters, agency generally didn't exist in any single place in the assemblage of typhoon weather system, military technology, human proficiency, and protector deities. However, at times a dominant force could emerge, and the samurai fighters understood this to be a deity of some sort. Drawing on recent scholarship about Japanese animist spirituality, in nineteenth-century Japan the divine was understood to be both present inside things and, less often, outside of them (Clammer and Poirier 2004). Although Japanese popular religion at this time was more animistic than in China, East Asians shared a belief that all life was generated by divinities. But while all action was outsourced to divinities—human acts are, in fact, activations of divine agency—acts were also dedicated to and inspired by dead ancestors. This combination of divine source and ancestral inspiration was often conflated in the Sino-Japanese term "Heaven [天]."

The daring 1861 rogue samurai attack on the British embassy at Tōzenji that nearly cost Laurence Oliphant his life was justified by the assailants in a signed pledge each of them carried to prevent Euro-whites from "polluting [汚] their sacred territory [神州]" (Morikawa 1967, 47–48). Although those J-hādis hoped to receive the "highest praise" for their actions, we shouldn't necessarily construe this in terms of modern secularism, where mirroring is claimed to increase the "social capital" of an individual. As we can see from the testimonies of the most important rogue samurai, much of the approval for the assassins of Euro-whites was sought from metaphysical entities and deceased ancestors. The remainder of the appeal was to like-minded young men who J-hādis hoped would commit similarly heroic acts of ecological protection and ontological preservation.

Arguably the clearest example of this appeared in the rogue samurai assassins who claimed to be exacting revenge for Climate Caucasianism directly through the agency of heaven, what they called "Heaven's vengeance [天誅]." Here, as Kikuchi Akira points out, rogues considered themselves "temporary substitutes" for divine actors (2005, 8–9). A signature Heaven's vengeance activation occurred after the Anglo-Satsuma war in August 1863 and the combined French, British, and US war against the powerful Choshu domain. Subsequent to the defeat of the anti-Western Choshu forces, Euro-Americans hoped that this would mark the end of the J-hādi attacks against white people and the beginning of uninterrupted extraction of rawfare. These hopes were dashed by a series of divinely inspired attacks.

On November 20, 1864, two British officers in the 20th Infantry regiment, stationed in Yokohama permanently to protect Euro-whites following the

Samuel Richardson murder, went on a sightseeing outing to the castle town of Kamakura, about seventeen miles from downtown Yokohama. Haughtily refusing the armed Japanese escorts standard for these excursions, they substituted the security with one Chinese interpreter and their concubines, named Otaka and Osono (Morikawa 1967, 52). When Major George Baldwin and Lieutenant Robert Bird arrived at the famous Daibutsu (Great Buddha) monument, they had already created a stir by promenading with their sex servants, referred to as "foreigners' women [洋妻]." But it was at the Tsurugaoka Hachimangu shrine that things turned ugly. According to the neighborhood guard's testimony, Baldwin and Bird adamantly refused to remove their shoes while inside the main shrine building. They were reportedly drunk and belligerent, and when three guards and a priest tried to remove them from the shrine, the armed Englishmen whipped the Japanese men with their riding crops and kicked them to the ground (53).

About thirty minutes after leaving the Hachimangu shrine, Baldwin and Bird were attacked and killed by the Higo (Kumamoto) domain rogues Shimizu Seiichi and Mamiya Hajime, with Bird's head almost completely severed from his body (BFO 46/98, November 29, 1864). Both murders were accompanied by the channeling shriek "Heaven's vengeance! [天誅]"—the voiceover to about one-third of the assassination attempts from 1860 until 1865. Under interrogation Shimizu insisted that his act of protection was designed to put a stop to the easy extraction of Japanese gold and women and girls by predatory Euro-whites (Leupp 2003, 142). Shimizu had fallen under the sway of the famous Fight the Whites! rogue Kiyokawa Hachirô in late 1861 when Kiyokawa was in southwestern Japan trying to recruit for organized attacks against both Euro-whites and corrupt Tokugawa government officials (Satô 1991, 32–34). Kiyokawa was the mastermind behind the spectacular assassination on January 14, 1861, in Edo of the philanderer and translator for US representative Townsend Harris, Henry Heusken. In addition to his creepy voyeurism that angered women in Shimoda (mentioned above), Heusken was known to go out publicly with his sex servants—a flagrant violation of decorum in Edo at that time (Williams 1959, 81). Moreover, he was often seen galloping his horse Speed Race(r) style through the streets of Edo, deliberately threatening pedestrians.

Kiyokawa (1830–63) was from Shônai han in present-day Yamagata prefecture. Like many rogue samurai, Kiyokawa was himself inspired by the bold assassination of the Tokugawa Chief Minister Ii Naosuke in Edo by Mito-domain rogues at Sakurada Gate on March 24, 1860 (*Yamagata Shimbun*, September 28, 2009). Ii had signed the Unequal Treaty with the United States in

July 1858, was a vocal supporter of exposing Japan to Euro-American trade, and was the architect of the Ansei purge against opponents of the Tokugawa regime's capitulation to the Euro-American powers. Kiyokawa founded a secret society of rogue samurai called the "Tiger's Tail Group," which drew its inspiration from the section of the canonical *I Ching* warning that valorous acts of stepping on the tiger's tail would invite extreme danger for the perpetrators. Tiger's Tail embraced the danger and, while publicly denouncing the corruption and weakness of Tokugawa government, they became the matrix of the decolonial "Revere the Emperor, Fight the Whites!" movement in Edo. By the fall of 1860 they concocted an elaborate plan to kill most of the Euro-whites in eastern Japan by burning down the Yokohama treaty port (the first of many to follow), but they called if off at the last minute (Kiyokawa 1913, 77–78).

Like all the rogue samurai, Kiyokawa was influenced by Aizawa Seishisai's *New Proposals*, and his writings echo that text's denunciations of the selfish consumerism of rich merchants and upper-rank samurai residing in Edo that Kiyokawa witnessed firsthand. However, while Aizawa was careful not to go too far in his critique of the samurai elite, Kiyokawa was one of the first "Revere the Emperor, Fight the Whites!" militant to conflate the depravity of rich Japanese and Euro-white invaders. One of the ways he did this was by foregrounding one of several derogatory Sino-Japanese names for Euro-Americans—"ignorant predator," or 夷狄.[28] In the hands of Kiyokawa, white predators were subhuman both because of their inability to read Chinese characters and because they couldn't grasp the higher ideals of duty (義), rationality (理), and benevolence (仁). Predators ignorant of the reason and righteousness of Heaven are likened by Kiyokawa to greedy pigs and boars, taking what they want at any moment regardless of the effect their self-serving acts have on the environment that sustains them. Even more egregious were the samurai and rich Japanese merchants who willfully rejected Heaven's righteousness and rationality for immoral luxury and wasteful consumption.

In the writings of some rogue samurai, one of the qualities of Euro-whites that justified denigrating them as "ignorant predators" was their assumption that humans are primarily individualistic, or ego-ontological. Euro-whites' lack of benevolence and loyalty followed from this alienated solipsism, as the relative absence of significant others in their environment coupled with their self-understanding as superior beings consolidated an extra-active walled-off superiority. Moreover, both the Japanese upper class and Euro-whites lived relatively isolated existences in urban environments surrounded only by commodities. Contrastingly, Kiyokawa preferred the mountain commons, with its rich habitat diversity of streams, birds, minerals, soils, and extrahuman animals.

Even in the lowlands, his lifeworld remained enchanted—"sentient lands" jampacked with different kinds of entities (Di Giminiani 2018). There is no sense of him being an atomized self; rather, he is an &bject inextricably enmeshed in other entities. Many of these entities were themselves divine. Accordingly, we see references in his writings to the presence of the rain goddess (水神) and the thunder god (鳴る神), a situation typical of the animism of Japanese popular spirituality at this time (Kiyokawa 1913, 72, 126).[29] This awareness of the ubiquity of divinities isn't limited to his frequent visits to shrines; gods and goddesses are ever present, and virtuous humans must be attentive to their moods and temperament—whether divine mood rings show a positive (天の幸) or negative (天の辛) color.

Owing to their preferred locale on mountains or deep in the woods, shinto[30] shrines do provide an ideal place for attunement to divine moods. Unlike praying at Buddhist temples, shinto ritual and prayer were generally not petitionary; no "requests" were made and no wishes proffered.[31] Instead, Kiyokawa makes vows to the gods and goddesses promising deeper intra-action (Kiyokawa 1913, 97; citations to follow). Although the content of the vow is sometimes revealed—normally, to force the ignorant predators out of the realm (天下の為夷狄を払う)—the motivation behind nativist spirituality for Kiyokawa was, as Clammer and Poirier argue, "to affirm and enhance the immanent relation to heavenly deities" (2004, 102). And there is no better way to affirm this relation than, as Kiyokawa vows, to commit to sacrificing one's life for "all the beings in the realm." As Kiyokawa puts it in a poem written during a visit to a shrine in Mito domain:

> For all things in the realm I will bear whatever hardship,
> as there is nothing that can hide from Heaven and Earth . . .
> Resolutely vowing to the gods and goddesses I have no regrets;
> the commitment to death will bring one's eyes to close and
> while everything outside the heart is storming, tears flow involuntarily.
> (97)[32]

The Japanese Eco-Ontology

As Kiyokawa sees it, the crisis in Japan in 1861 and 1862 extends to both the natural environment (然) and human reason (理). While the immediate cause is the arrival of Euro-whites, the tendency for rich Japanese to place themselves and their families above other entities preexisted the US invasion. Although in ordinary times humans are a relatively minor presence among all the beings in the Japanese eco-ontology (神道), the present predicament calls for brave and selfless humans to protect it against both Euro-Americans and unjust Japanese pursuing base pleasures and profit, or 利. Kiyokawa advises that the righteous protector "must understand that the safety of the realm depends on him. Therefore, now is the time to prove his love for words, the wind, flowers, the moon, and the rain" (236). Needless to say, a valorous act such as cutting down a vile predator like Laurence Oliphant is convincing proof of one's love for the multiple beings in the eco-ontology, but Kiyokawa makes it clear that he and his followers are recommending a nonanthropocentric notion of love. Whether it's for supernatural entities like goddesses and gods or natural entities like the wind, flowers, or rain, they are all equally deserving of sacrifice and worship. In the dense web of relations that make up Japan's eco-ontology, each of these entities is immanently intra-acting with others.

The same must be said for human beings as well; human life is similarly indebted to its imbrication with other forms of being. Minus this relational enmeshing, human &bjects would cease to exist. Therefore, principled protectors (志士) of the realm are duty bound to repay the debt to the life-giving eco-ontology when the political situation calls for it. In his writings of 1861 and 1862, Kiyokawa deploys a specific phrase for this—報国之志, which I translate as "repaying the debt that you owe to the realm." He elaborates: "[As] nature [自然] provides the people with food, drink, and everything else they need to live" it's up to ethical men to protect it from destruction (237). The "pollution brought by the ignorant predators [夷狄之汚]" represents an existential threat to Japan's ecology, "poisoning the natural environment that provides the people with food and shelter" (238). The best way to protect the realm from further damage—and to avoid the harsh extraction → extinction imperative undergirding the capitalism of Climate Caucasianism—is by ethical humans deepening their intra-active relation with other entities and "mimicking the resolve of the wind, rain, dragon, and tiger" (240). For when the "human spirit completely loses its connection to nature, there will be deep trouble everywhere" (247). As the "goddesses and spirits" prefer to reveal themselves in outdoor and wild settings, best practices for rogue samurai must include time praying in the mountains and meditating in the forests, far away from the seductions of consumer society in Edo or Osaka, to say nothing of the thoroughly toxic treaty ports of Nagasaki or Yokohama, where all trees have been cut down and marshlands filled in (124–25).

One of the reasons that Euro-whites are disparaged as ignorant is that they don't understand the fundamental relationality that humans as &bjects have with other kinds of being (248). Kiyokawa polemicizes that while most

Japanese adhere to an eco-ontology that stresses the presence of the divine in all things, "the only religion the Western predators understand is money, and they accumulate it through evil practices [奸計] and devilish cunning [邪智]" (249). He concludes that in addition to the monomaniacal pursuit of money, because they have "trampled all over the natural environment of the realm [天下之然] ... whites are enemies [夷之仇] of our Heavenly land" (248). Unlike the beings residing in the Japanese eco-ontology that have respect for the divine in all things, the ignorant barbarians "recognize no limits to their vile insatiability; nothing is safe here until they have been driven from the realm" (248).

Kiyokawa's animist sensibility makes him particularly sensitive to transformations in the natural environment. Therefore, the climate-interfering presence of Euro-American steamships and high-tech weapons poses a significant "harm to the environment [傷之然]" (249). "Polluting Westerners [夷狄之患]" are actually bringing about "changes to the climate [変之然]" (271). In his final work, *Senchû Kiji*, he notices how unusually hot and dry the weather is in the fall of 1862 and connects the strange weather to the political and moral crises in the realm (247). Kiyokawa most certainly picked up this connection linking political and ethical crises and natural disasters from the Japanese Mito school writers like Aizawa of the 1820s and '30s. As Tadano Masahirô writes, for Mito thinkers it was no coincidence that the remarkable series of strong earthquakes that struck Japan in 1854 and 1855 (the Ansei-Tôkai and Ansei-Nankai quakes in 1854 and the massive Edo quake in 1855) happened during the years that the Tokugawa bakufu capitulated to the threats of asymmetric warfare made by the United States (2014, 65–67). Mark Elvin calls a similar conflation in China of political virtue with climate events a "moral meteorology" (1998, 2).

Although Kiyokawa didn't write explicitly about the earthquakes, early modern Japanese myth held that earthquakes were caused by the demon catfish Namazu (technically a *youkai* monster) who resided under the Japanese islands. When the god Kashima, responsible for containing Namazu, gets distracted or tired, Namazu can take the opportunity to wag his huge tail and bring about devastating cracks in the earth. It was widely believed in the mid-nineteenth century that Kashima deliberately allowed Namazu free rein and, with other deities, was intent on punishing Japan for widespread greed and the neglect of righteousness and benevolence (Bressan 2012). As a practitioner of (lowercase) shinto, Kiyokawa's texts are similarly filled with demons (鬼神), proof that there is too much pollution in the realm. It is evident to him that reading these signs of ecological harm isn't indicative of any special talent or intellectual acumen—anyone who commits to living intra-actively and relationally in the Japanese eco-ontology is capable of this. Unlike the more famous rogue samurai thinkers (Yoshida Shôin, Kusaka Genzui), Kiyokawa exhibits an intellectual humility. He doesn't understand the task of the principled protectors (志士) to be offering new ideas and innovative policies. His commitments are to renovation, not vanguardist innovation; restoration, not revolution.

The crucial nativist code "pollution [汚, *kegare*]" is normally understood to demarcate a firm inside/outside binary in Japanese spirituality and is considered the main code for its deep-rooted xenophobia. There should be no doubt that in Kiyokawa's texts there is an "us" that is under threat by a predatory "them" that brings contamination through moral and ecological crises. However, it's also clear that rich Japanese merchants and Tokugawa government officials are carriers of this toxicity as much as the Euro-white predators. Consequently, Kiyokawa and other rogue samurai want them banished from the realm as well.

What I want to underline in closing this analysis of Kiyokawa is that pollution is mythic, ecological, and political for many rogue activists of the 1850s and '60s.[33] Both Euro-American people and their coal-powered machines are dangerously contaminating agents for the Japanese eco-ontology, or "shinto." It should go without saying that the animism in Kiyokawa prevents an association of pollution with greenhouse gases and disruption in the hydrological cycle. Nevertheless, while metaphysical entities (deities and dead ancestors) suffer from Euro-white toxicity, geophysical entities experience the effects as well. Therefore, nativists like Kiyokawa insist that multiple forms of metaphysical and physical life deserve to be protected from threatening pollution. Underneath, but immanent to the gods and goddesses, all things are part of the ecology of Japan, ecology here being construed as "home." The ethno-racial aspect of who belongs in the home and who does not is secondary to who understands the ethical and ecological criteria of the realm. Who is honest enough to acknowledge their fundamental reliance on the eco-ontological whole? And who is willing to sacrifice their inconsequential human life to protect the eco-ontology?

Yokohama Is Burning

After Kiyokawa's death in 1863, other rogue samurai pushed ahead with decolonial attacks on Euro-whites and Tokugawa officials. These peaked with the killing of four French sailors in Yokohama in September 1866. According to Morikawa Tetsurô, a group of eight Frenchmen were barhopping in Bloodtown and ended up in a brothel. After the sailors had roughed up four of the women they had paid for, the sex workers decided they'd had enough and tried to flee. Two French sailors caught them outside, and together the now ten French slapped the women around and trashed the waiting room (Morikawa 1967, 67–68). The situation was so chaotic that the brothel owner took the unusual step of summoning the magistrate. But by the time he arrived the French were out in the street, fighting with random people. At this point several local "toughs [力士]" and two rogue samurai took control of the situation, killing four of the drunken French before managing to escape.

The ensuing hearing was a public relations nightmare for Euro-whites as Yokohama residents testified about the routine violence visited upon them by Westerners. For the first time, several sex servants of French nationals testified publicly about the regular abuse they had to endure, echoing sentiments expressed indirectly by indentured sex workers at Gankirô who killed themselves rather than subjecting themselves to a night of violence at the hands of Euro-American men. The French minister's own sex servant, Otomi, detailed his harsh treatment of her (Morikawa 1967, 69). None of this deterred the French from pursing a punishing indemnity and insisting that the Tokugawa government round up and imprison all rogue samurai in the area. Japanese businesses catering to the Westerners—including sex workers—responded with the first general strike in modern Japanese history, lasting six weeks. The terrible fire that broke out in the Miyozaki licensed sex district on November 26, 1866, was one part of this larger uprising in Yokohama (Ishii 1976, 138–39). Most likely the work of eco-ontology–protecting samurai, the fire was designed to kill Euro-Americans frequenting the brothels. Tragically, it ended up killing thirty-five young sex workers. However, the terrible fire ended up corroborating the denunciations of whites as "enemies of Heaven" when British sailors, called in to put out the fire, instead looted all the valuables from the houses they were supposed to be saving (Black 1880, vol. 2, 17–24).

"We Need a Bloodbath"

The standard scholarly interpretation of Anglo-American policy decisions of the mid-1860s in Japan is that the UK/US diplomats slowly realized that the anti-Tokugawa forces in the southwestern domains of Choshu and Satsuma were gaining strength, and that the Anglo-American powers increasingly supported them despite official positions of neutrality. British officials like Harry Parkes and contraband arms dealers like Thomas Glover are often singled out as having been the most public about their prescient endorsement of Satsuma and Choshu as capable of securing the requisite peace and security for unhindered extraction. At the end of his life Glover went so far as to take full credit for the defeat of the Tokugawa and the Meiji Restoration, bragging, "I believe that I was the greatest rebel of them all against Tokugawa" (Gardiner 2007, 72). "Gorge-us" Ernest Satow similarly felt that an essay he published in Japanese in 1866 advocating a political transformation toward a British-style constitutional monarchy was crucial for Japanese to finally realize that the "Satow plan" was the best way forward for the country (Ruxton 1998).

Ignoring this standard white guy narcissism for a moment and looking deeper into the diplomatic archive, it becomes clear how erroneous this is. Harry Parkes was one of the two or three most powerful British officials in East Asia in the 1860s, '70s, and '80s. As we saw above, by Japanese accounts he was irascible, arrogant, and, on occasion, physically violent in his diplomatic dealings—he was the quintessential Superpredator diplomat in East Asia. The ongoing attacks on Euro-whites in 1865 and 1866 infuriated Parkes so much that he considered a significant part of the samurai impossible to appropriate and manage. Rewinding to Ferreira da Silva's theory from the introduction, she argues that whites deal with people of color in one of two ways—appropriation or obliteration. It became obvious to Parkes that at the very least the incorrigible "Fight the Whites!" faction of the samurai needed to be extinguished for anything good to come out of an Anglophone CO_2lonial project in Japan. What would be an appropriate Superpredator solution?

We have only a few recorded hints that Parkes (and other Euro-Americans) wanted to incite a kind of gang warfare between different factions of samurai, knowing that Japan would be easier for white capital to extract rawfare from if many of the anti-Westerners were permanently disposed of. I hope it's at least plausible that this is what Parkes meant during the Boshin War to overthrow the Tokugawa when he wrote to London in early 1868 that it might be in the best interests of both England and Japan to have a "blood bath" before a settlement was reached (BFO 46/97, October 7, 1868; cited in Daniels 1996, 89). Parkes's biographer Gordon Daniels analyzes his letters and communiqués from amid the chaos of the start of the Boshin War in January 1868 (when deCO$_2$lonial attacks against white people occurred) and writes that Parkes "turned to the view that war . . . might be a purifying force which would place Japan on the path to progress" (1996, 74). When this didn't happen and Westerners learned of the disappointingly low death toll of approximately nine thousand, Parkes regretted that the civil war was "too short and that a longer conflict would have destroyed the forces of reaction" (108).

Of course, extermination of anti-Western samurai was only desirable if it didn't interrupt British profiteering, as Parkes hinted at in his necropolitical musings. If Thomas Glover hadn't turned himself into a borderline persona non grata by ignoring warnings from UK officials to stop trafficking contraband armaments, he could have reassured Parkes that a samurai blood-bath would be, in and of itself, a major boost to British arms sales. In fact, there's evidence that Glover seconded Parkes in hoping for just that as, in a calculated risk, he bet on a protracted civil war in Japan with large purchases by his trading company in Nagasaki of Enfield rifles and Armstrong cannons (McKay 1993, 85). When Glover returned to Japan on January 27, 1868, after a short trip home to Scotland to deliver steamship orders, he knew his business was in trouble when he heard that the worst of the fighting concluded quickly (Gardiner 2007, 86). The price of the thousands of weapons lying unsold in his Nagasaki warehouse was plummeting by the hour, as it became clear that there would be no samurai slaughter. In Glover & Co.'s account books for the summer of 1870, there are references to "stocks" of rifles still unsold (Checkland and Checkland 1984, 153). His serious financial problems began when the bloodbath he speculated on didn't happen.[34] Alas, what Rutherford Alcock called "merchant scum" would seek out other ways to make a killing.

For Glover that way was the principal extractive operation of Climate Caucasianism—industrial coal mining. If Glover couldn't profit from the death of Japanese in the civil war, he was determined to profit from other kinds of death. As a last-ditch attempt to recover his business from losses incurred from bad bets on mass killing, he managed to get financing and turned his extractive-eye/I toward opening the first mechanized mining operation in Japan at Takashima, an island ten miles from Nagasaki harbor. The 1869 joint venture between the Hizen domain and Glover's company unleashed climate-intervening violence previously unseen in East Asia: two-hundred-foot pits where steam-driven winches lifted coal to the surface, coal-powered pumps were used for draining, and its own railway system hauled coal from the mouth of pits to the piers (McMaster 1963). Glover's megalomania led him to overestimate the amount of coal he could rip from the earth daily. While his inflated estimates gained him short-term financing for the Takashima project from European investors (who benefited from the profits generated from the clipper-coolie captive-contraband-capital circuit), it also impelled him to work his managers and miners into the ground by extending working hours when the mines didn't reach the projected 350–400 tons of coal per day—a classic example of what Marx called the extraction of "absolute surplus value" (1977a, 646). In fact, in 1863 Marx focused on capitalist mining as the site where "the increase of labor's productive force serves only as compensation of decreasing natural conditions of productivity, as seen in certain cases of agriculture, extractive industry, etc." (in Saitô 2017, 134).

After two miners died and labor conditions didn't improve at Glover's Takashima operation, three major uprisings by workers took place in the first full year of operation in 1870 (Hidemura 1977, 54). As we can see in figure 1.3, the prematurely balding and graying Glover was being hounded by his creditors, so he stopped commuting from his Ipponmatsu mansion on Nagasaki Bay and built a small shack right at the main Takashima mine in 1871, where he would live for a week straight amid the coal ash and the machine shrieks (Gardiner 2007, 93). His only respite from this nightmarish activity was one day a week back at his mansion with his new seventeen-year-old sex servant Tsuru (McKay 1993, 86). There the pioneering Climate Caucasianist in Japan would drink and fornicate until he passed out, doing this for thirty-six hours before returning to his toxic shack at Takashima—shuttling back and forth from one site of extraction to another.

2

Ecclesiastical Superpredators

You know the Ten Commandments of the Catholics? Well, those people break every one of them. Take for instance Number Five, which calls for respect for one's parents. But the Catholics order their converts to reject their parents. Number Six says one can't kill another human, while Number Seven says you can't lust after your neighbor's wife; Number Eight forbids stealing. These are all opposite to how French Catholics in China behave. Have the Catholic missionaries even read the Ten Commandments?—Qing High Commissioner for Border Affairs Chong Shi in the 1860s (in Qin 2006)

Colonies, we call them . . . ; they are those outlands where like a swarm of hungry locusts white masters may settle to be served as kings, wield the lash of slave-drivers, rape girls and wives, grow as rich as Croesus and send homeward a golden stream.—W. E. B. Du Bois, *Darkwater: Voices from within the Veil*, 1920

White Lies

The treaties and tariff agreements concluding the Second War for Drugs in China (1856–60) lifted nearly all the restrictions on Euro-American drugs and human trafficking. The new agreements also allowed European Catholic missionaries to move wherever they wanted to proselytize, buy and sell real estate, run climate-interfering extractive enterprises, and establish what Ernest Young calls "ecclesiastical colonies" (2013). Finally, an important new Yangzi River treaty port was enclosed at Hankou in central China—where the British consul Medhurst would declare after the first few years of settlement that white people "are everything"—with more to follow in the upper Yangzi. The rawfaring and cheapening of Japanese human and extrahuman life we discussed in the previous chapter was set to intensify in China, as the clipper-coolie captive-contraband-capital circuit went into full throttle.

However, unlike the 1830s when Lin Zexu and other Qing officials were caught off guard by the complexity and brutality of what Marx called white racial capitalism's "ruthless terrorism," Chinese on the ground had now had thirty years to either personally witness or hear first-hand accounts of Euro-white behavior in China. Therefore, when the British began exploring and then CO_2lonizing the important southwestern province of Sichuan in the 1870s, they became concerned that in towns and cities Sichuanese hung out and talked somewhat more than people did on the east coast. This primarily took the form of the ubiquitous informal "bullshitting [白龙门谈]" sessions or happened in the more time-honored Sichuanese setting of the teahouse, or the latest version of that in the opium room. As the British feared, the content of these hangout chats often featured them and other Euro-whites (Li 2004, 485–86).

Local Chinese officials realized even before the white settlers that this casual banter excited decidedly noncasual insurrections against Euro-American Christians like the one that took place in Chongqing, Sichuan, in July 1886 (QMJA 2:449–52, 458–61). This was the period when Chongqing, already the commercial matrix of southwestern China, was bracing to be the first Chinese treaty port west of Hubei province to be enclosed by the Euro-American powers in January 1891, which forced the Qing government attendant for eastern Sichuan to put up official announcements threatening immediate arrest of anyone caught spreading "wild rumors" about Euro-whites (BFO 228/886, November 10 and 13, 1890).[1] Although scores of poor people—out-of-work actors performing in the streets; boat pullers left stranded in Chongqing after hauling boats up the Yangzi from Hankou and Yichang, but out of luck when only one-third of this labor force was needed to guide the boats back down the Yangzi to the east; and so on—were rounded up, beaten, and thrown in jail for doing just that over the course of the next decade, this didn't stop the circulation of these rumors.

One tale from the early 1890s would not be considered rational by the lawfare of Western representation. That's because this story and others like it emerged from an eco-ontology where myth was central, in particular myths warning about the threats posed by greed and extraction—a far cry from European capitalist lawfare that dictated that private avarice benefitted the greater good and extraction was essential for modern progress. It went like this: In downtown Chongqing there is a small street called Golden Duck (金鸭) Lane. Reflecting Chongqing's centrality in China's trade network, the city was said to feature several places rumored to contain hidden treasures; one of these cryptic treasures was a gold duck located at a small lane off the main thoroughfare, Shanxi Street. Apparently, part of the time it hid inside a wall and part of the time hid itself away under the earth. Although none of the locals could ever recall seeing the duck, anyone passing through the lane who clapped their hands insisted they heard the gold duck respond with a loud quack. Children were especially fond of this multispecies (bird and human) call and response. However, when Euro-whites got wind of the story, one guy in particular was able to ascertain the duck's location. After bribing local Qing officials, the yellow (gold) fever–stricken Westerner was able to get his hands on the treasure and make off with it. Subsequent to the theft of the golden duck, no matter how committed locals were to invoking the duck by handclapping, no duck quacks were ever heard again in and around Shanxi Street (Jin and Zhong 1992, 36–37).

Structurally similar to several Sichuanese tales from the 1890s featuring the predatory extractions of gold, silver, and jade by Euro-Americans mentioned in Li Jieren's 1930s historical novels about Sichuan's capital city Chengdu, here what was a multispecies intra-action for Sichuanese and the goose-like duck was merely $ubject for the Euro-white gander (Li 2012a, 36–37). However one wants to construe it, this content was mild compared to more adult-entertainment myths.[2] More explicit Chinese narratives often featured sadistic acts such as Euro-whites slicing off the genitals and limbs of Sichuanese children, actions that would usually be followed by cooking them up and eating them. Stories about Euro-American missionaries cutting out the eyes of Chinese converts to Christianity were also popular.[3] One incendiary Chinese placard put up in public squares in the Hankou, Yichang, and Chongqing treaty ports in 1891 was titled "A Man Should Not Become a Devil," and singled out Catholicism. "The Roman Catholic is a devilish religion. It comes secretly, deluding good men and changing them into devils, and drugging and polluting women and girls. Its living victims are mutilated, and when they die their eyeballs are gouged out. Men and women are drugged and deprived of their reason" (BFO 2012b, 76).

The explorer Isabella Bird wrote that the Chinese she met in rural Sichuan in 1899 would often transmit these mythic beliefs to her in a relaxed, "good-natured" way. She recalled one rumor popular in Sichuan at the end of the nineteenth century in which locals thought that Protestant missionaries bought houses for two reasons only. The first allowed them to secretly dig holes all the way to England "so that foreign soldiers would come by it and take their lands," while the second was the extractivist myth that white people needed the houses to store the gold "which they dug out of the mountains by night" (Bishop 1972, 122, 329). "White lies!" cried Euro-American officials in Sichuan and pressured the local Qing officials to do whatever they could to silence them. Despite threats and punishments, these kinds of myths persisted right up to the 1911 overthrow of Chinese dynastic rule and insurgent uprising against Climate Caucasianism. The British consul in Chongqing could only wring his hands and complain, "It seems incredible to report that a majority of Chinese are from time to time induced to believe the lying stories foreigners consume human flesh [and are] considered to be endowed with devilish powers" (BFO 228/1403, August 19, 1901).

The Euro-American regime of treaty port enclosure was advertised as bringing multiple forms of freedom (trade, expression, association) to "closed-off" Japan and China, places populated by Stopped Incarce-Races stagnating either because of biological anatomy or owing to the absence of political and economic freedom in their feudal countries. Despite these public policies, British officials in the treaty ports and in Beijing regularly tried to block freedom of expression and censor any Chinese from referring to Euro-whites as "devils" or "barbarians." Similarly, the newest British consulates in the treaty ports up the Yangzi in Yichang, Hubei (1876), and Chongqing (1891) conducted suppression campaigns against what they thought to be the childishly irresponsible ways local Chinese in the interior used language, especially when it reflected Euro-whites in an unflattering way (SJYD, 486). For Western officials the proper use of words and images was restricted to functioning as correlates for external, empirical things, as Kantian philosophy espoused. Or rather, as Robert Hart's use of statistics in the Imperial Maritime Customs would have it, as a science where numbers modestly stand in for actual things—say, a crate of opium, the labor of a sex servant, or the future profit from a copper mine. But the deployment of (Chinese) language in the placards and in the everyday Sichuanese disdain for Euro-Americans as "white foreign devils [白外鬼子]," predatory "pigs [猪]," or "enemies of Heaven [天为仇]" was condemned by the British as criminally nonreferential—fake news created by Chinese heathens. A different kind of white lie needed to contend that there was absolutely no truth content to Chinese myths.

Euro-white settlers in Sichuan thought that at least some of the Chinese could be coerced into using language in an objective European way, and surprisingly despotic, nonmodern methods like ordering one hundred lashes of the whip, or a month in the dreaded *cangue*, were advocated by British officials in Sichuan as, in Enrique Dussel's construal, the "violent pedagogic actions" designed to correct them (1995, 66). Some of the Protestant missionaries flooding into Sichuan after Chongqing was enclosed hoped that using language in a nonreferential way didn't necessarily have to result in corporal punishment.

The pedagogy they preferred was to put up their own placards right next to the Chinese placards denouncing Westerners, intentionally mocking local Daoist and Buddhist practices (BFO 228/1115, September 26, 1893).

On the afternoon of June 25, 1893, a relatively rare fire broke out in wet and rainy Chongqing, ending two days later with over four hundred houses burned down, ten people dead, and the magistrate's *yamen* office up in smoke. With the cleanup still going on and the city's charities desperate for donations to help those made homeless, British missionaries from China Inland, flaunting a superpredator-like absence of "conscience and empathy," decided that they would taunt and troll what they called Sichuan's "heathen beliefs." As the annual procession for the Daoist fire deity Zhurong had coincidentally taken place two weeks before the outbreak of the fire, the missionaries put up several placards in Chinese around the city, including in the neighborhoods that suffered the worst damage. With a tone-deaf insensitivity to the loss of life and shelter, the Westerners' text mocked Chongqing residents' worship of Zhurong; propitiary devotions to this fire deity were evidently pointless. Moreover, the practice of idolatry demonstrated how "childish" the locals were, confusing signs and symbols with real things—"It's just a small piece of wood, not a God!" the placard ridiculed, concluding that Jesus was the only god who could truly protect them (BFO 228/1115, July 31, 1893). Even to the point of self-parody, these missionaries demonstrated a cruel commitment to enforcing their own method of representation. Infuriatingly for the locals (the Unequal Treaties prohibited all Chinese from interfering with Christian preaching and proselytizing), the placards remained up in the city until mid-August, when after several angry letters to the British consul E. H. Fraser, he convinced the head of China Inland to have them removed. Fraser wrote to the British legation in Beijing explaining: "The zeal of the missionaries often outrun their discretion. . . . It is inevitable that some should feel impelled to attack the religious practices of the natives with unsparing criticism" (BFO 228/1115 November 8, 1893).

Whenever the missionaries' right to "unsparing criticism" of Chinese religious practice was questioned by the diplomats or when Sichuanese locals took things into their own hands, the "white fragility" (DiAngelo 2018) of Euro-American missionaries led to self-righteous "indignation meetings," and Chongqing saw several of these (BFO 228/1115 November 8, 1893). The largest took place in Shanghai in the summer of 1893 when some Protestant leaders called for missionaries in the interior to be heavily armed. Pistols and rifles were evidently losing their power to adequately persuade and police Chinese, but if columns of missionaries were trained to wield repeating weapons like

Gatling guns, as some recommended, this would surely get the heathens to be more deferential toward God's representatives on earth (Wehrle 1966, 74).

For impatient white missionaries, a more forceful form of persuasion was felt to be particularly urgent in Sichuan, a place that was seen by them as wild, backward, and long isolated from the east coast and Beijing by mountains and the treacherous gorges (especially the famous three) and rapids that made river travel up the Yangzi from the east so risky. Depending on the season, water flow rate in the upper Yangzi could abruptly change in ten miles from 200 cubic feet per second to 25,000.[4] Cut off from the maritime cosmopolitanism of the treaty ports in the east, and surrounded by similarly xenophobic Tibetans to the west, Muslims to the north in Gansu and Xinjiang provinces, and minority populations (referred to not as heathen like Han Chinese, but "savages") to the south in Yunnan province, Sichuanese were, in the words of a British missionary in 1886, the most "irrationally suspicious of foreigners" in the whole of China (BFO 228/829, August 19, 1886).

But was Sichuan really that cut off and isolated? Only if you were looking at the province from the vantage point of the stolen territories of Hong Kong and the east coast treaty ports. But as the omnipresent Sichuanese Gelaohui (GLH) would counter in proclamations against Westerners that will be a focus of this chapter, Sichuan featured what decolonial theorists call a "pluriverse" of ethno-epistemologies: Tibetans, Chinese Muslims, Central Asians, South Asians, Manchurians, and Burmese traders all lived in or frequently passed through Sichuan (Escobar 2020). Referred to publicly as "Guys in Gowns [袍哥]" in Sichuan, the GLH went so far as to proclaim that Sichuanese had flexibly adopted some of these people's spiritual beliefs and aspects of their cultural practices, and rarely had there been any conflict. They drew a stark contrast, however, between these Asian groups and those who they sometimes colorized as white people (白外人).[5] Invariably, whites weren't willing to intra-act with people different from themselves; they only wanted to extract nonreciprocally and dominate extra-actively.

Take Me to the (Yangzi) River

Dreams of dominating the Great Game of empire were what the British had in mind after the 1876 Treaty of Yantai (Chefoo) legalized offensive extraterritoriality and enclosed Yichang in Hubei, with the promise of a bigger prize, Chongqing, to follow quickly. For as the 1876 treaty set apart de jure new treaty ports, it also opened de facto the great Yangzi River running from east to west directly through the heart of China. For many Euro-whites, the upper Yangzi was the royal road to the riches of inner Asia, connecting Nanjing and Shanghai on the east coast through the commercial centers of Hankou, Yichang, and Chongqing, and then on to the trading hubs and oases of the southern (starting 165 miles west of Chongqing in Chengdu, Sichuan) and northern (from Xian through Xinjiang to Kashgar at the border of the Ottoman Empire) Silk Roads in western China and Central Asia. But the Yangzi was also instrumentalized as a highway to carry the matériel and float the coal-powered gunboats needed to win the Great Game against Russia in Tibet and Central Asia. French Missions Étrangères de Paris (MEP) priests in Sichuan urged an even Greater Game than the mere domination of Tibet and Central Asia, with a Bishop Delacroix writing to the French delegation in Beijing from Chengdu in the mid-1890s that "You can draw a territorial line running from Tokyo Bay all the way to the upper Yangzi. If we don't make this ours, then somebody else certainly will" (SJYD, 597). The British, salivating like urban drug dealers when college students gentrify a poor neighborhood and multiply their customer base overnight, felt confident that their previous successes in trafficking "poison" (opium) and "pigs" (captive coolie laborers) would easily be repeated in this newly appropriated territory. The second British consul in Chongqing, E. H. Parker, set a superpredator precedent in the 1880s by regularly assuming the "up with my fist" prizefighter position and knocking harmless Chinese through walls for very little reason and "punching the people's heads" who were teasing him on the streets (Parker 1909, 91, 104). Consequently, as we saw Ferreira da Silva argue in the introduction, all that nonwhite and extrahuman rawfare can ostensibly do is await the fate handed down by the accelerated Speed Race(r): extractive appropriation or obliterating extinction. But neither was to happen without a fight, and the tools of battle would be the stories we introduced above, human &bjects, and extrahuman entities. That's right: we'll see the Yangzi and its riparian zones join the anti-Western insurgency as what Donna Haraway calls a "witty agent and actor" (1991, 201).

As we saw with the Ganges and other rivers in India, for Climate Caucasianists the Yangzi River was primarily a means to the end of rawfaring and extracting resources and winning the Great Game in Central Asia, what Dilip da Cunha calls "river colonialism" (2019, 273). However, in the eco-ontologies of southwestern China rivers were an aquatic commons central to people's physical and spiritual well-being. Sichuanese bathed in them, washed clothes in them, played in them, fished them, and navigated boats on them. They also prayed to them, wrote poems about and to them, and offered sacrifices to them. (Like all entities, and in the idiom of object-oriented ontology, these myriad uses didn't exhaust the potential of the river.) Yangzi boat trackers and sailors working the Yichang, Hubei, to Chongqing, Sichuan route in the 1880s and '90s were expected to make offerings at all the temples in Yichang before launching, in addition to sacrificing a chicken to the river deities and spreading its blood over the bow and stern of their boat (Bishop 1972, 117). They also scrawled prayers and incantations on small sheets of paper and "pasted them on oars, sweeps, mast and runner, and hung them over the boats' sterns" (162). These included a few longer prayer streamers (风马旗) that served double duty in both appealing to the river deities and helping ascertain the wind direction. Along the way, boatmen sang songs to ward off evil spirits, as the more than one thousand rapids endangering boats on the three-hundred-mile trip were said to be populated by ethereal malefactors. Boats would also stop and make offerings at gorges where locals had carved, painted, and gilded images of the Three Water Guardians deep into the rocks (Bishop 1972, 171). Moreover, Chinese sailors were expected to propitiate monkeys along the route, and the failure of Euro-whites to do so led some monkeys to push rocks over cliffs and hurl stones at the first coal-powered steamships traveling up the Yangzi from Yichang (Matthews 1999, 139). Finally, boatmen were expected to sacrifice yet another chicken to the river deities upon the successful completion of a trip to Chongqing and leave offerings at the large statue of Buddha at the Chaotianmen wharf there (Jin and Zhong 1992, 61–62). Failure to properly perform these rituals was believed to be the number one cause of calamities on the Yangzi. Like riparian zones elsewhere, the upper Yangzi elicited a rich intra-activity between different deities, humans, monkeys, birds, and fish; the water itself; the lush vegetation and fertile crops including poppies; and ghosts and demons of different sorts.

Fundamentally opposed to the intra-actions taking place in the upper Yangzi biome, Euro-whites wanted to extra-actively command the river for capital accumulation. The English businessman Archibald Little tried for over ten years to get a coal-powered steamship through the gorges and rapids of the upper Yangzi to Chongqing, failing miserably until finally succeeding in February 1898.

Following right behind Little two years later was a British gunboat, soon to be joined by two French warships and additional British ones regularly patrolling the upper Yangzi until 1912 (Chen 2010, 156–57). Little saw the whole Yangzi from the east coast to the Tibetan plateau through his extractiv-eye/I as representing "a magnificent prospect for British enterprise." The technological and military domination of the environment of the upper Yangzi would multiply "by ten" the profit generated by low- and no-tech Chinese boats. And because of this potential for profit taking, an accelerated Speed Race(r) approach was the only realistic one: "we must lose no more time in securing the

FIGURE 2.1. Archibald Little dining with gentry in Chongqing in the late 1890s (Little 1902).

region allotted as our sphere by effective occupation" (Little 1898, xxi–xxii). Although his book about journeying up the Yangzi from Yichang to Chongqing is filled with detail about the sublimity of the gorges, his observations consistently return to the Climate Caucasianist compulsion to extract coal—Sichuan's deposits were thought to be the "most extensive in the world"—and other speculations on how Western entrepreneurs could gorge themselves on precious metals available only here (192). Little suggested that the sole obstacle to the march of capitalism was that Chinese people—themselves raciologized as "wasted" on opium—would inevitably waste and despoil the beautiful things that Westerners built in China, including industrial coal mines and urban infrastructure like the International Settlement in Shanghai (132). Therefore, it was imperative that white people find a way to keep Chinese from ruining the "progress" that they had worked so hard to achieve. Keeping one step ahead of Chinese scientifically and economically was Little's preferred method. He also saw advantages in a system of racial segregation in which only Chinese servants were to be allowed in Euro-white treaty port enclaves, but then forced to return home at night.

Therefore, the extractive operations that Little planned for the upper Yangzi region were inconceivable without the pioneering visitation of Euro-American coal-powered gunboats and steamships to Sichuan. Ensuring their speedy passage required waging small warfare on the environment of the upper Yangzi, featuring what Little called "a few tons of dynamite judiciously expended" (1910, 149). Although Chinese engineers had used natural gas for hydraulic operations since the Ming dynasty, the use of dynamite and naval mines in river and stream design was introduced by British engineers working in the Lighthouse Department of Robert Hart's Imperial Maritime Customs in the 1870s, becoming routine by the 1880s. The British engineers found the standard Chinese method for rock removal—wood or coal was placed against the rock and burned off, which allowed the brittle rock to be removed with axes—tedious and ineffective. Chinese engineers followed suit and started using dynamite to construct tracking paths and bridges in the late 1880s in the middle Yangzi (Changjiang Liuyu Guihua 1979, 169–71). An extensive operation to build nineteen miles of tracking path at the Wushan Gorge in 1889 was the first time Chinese engineers used dynamite in the upper Yangzi (Kim 2009, 676). However, Qing officials in Sichuan and Hubei depended on British engineers for hydraulic operations involving extensive dynamiting and Jacobi mines until the 1911 Revolution (Little 1910, 136–37).

The British expected newly available southwestern China to be filled with nothing but rawfared humans and resourced nature. Here, the connection so crucial for Climate Caucasianism between the denigration of nonwhite humans and a similar treatment of the natural world was first pointed out by Marx in the 1840s. As he wrote in in the *German Ideology*: "the identity of man and nature also appears in such a way that the restricted attitude of men to nature determines their restricted relation to one another, and their restricted attitude to one another determines men's restricted relation to nature" (Marx and Engels 1975, vol. 5, 44). In a similar critical manner, Saidiya Hartman reminds us that the West African British CO_2lony the Gold Coast (now Ghana) was called simply "the Mine," as Euro-whites extracted both slaves and gold from it (2007, 51). Nevertheless, in the case of Sichuan and southwestern China, the appropriation or obliteration of everything external to the extractiv-eye/I wasn't going to be the exclusive privilege of Great Britain. When Augustus Margary was investigating Sichuan, Guizhou, and Yunnan with a British consular team in late 1874, he was disconcerted by the extent of French Catholic incursion in the region, with some of it happening during the 1840s and '50s in flagrant violation of treaty agreements. These gains were bragged about during Margary's meeting with the powerful MEP Bishop Eugène Desflèches in Chongqing in December 1874 (BPP 1971, 695). Desflèches also supplied Margary with crucial intelligence and a recommendation to enhance his armed security; for over a decade Desflèches was protected by his own well-armed militia made up of Catholic converts. Although Desflèches said nothing about this, some Euro-white priests themselves brandished rifles and pistols when they went out in public (Coates 1988, 178; Bulfoni and Pozzi 2003, 59). The fact that some MEP priests would have access to armed security shouldn't be surprising given that many Chinese converts in central and western China were ex-convicts and crooks who decided to enter the Church primarily because of the immunity it provided their criminal activities—what was called a "protective talisman" (護符).[6] It was almost universally acknowledged in central and southwestern China that, as the Japanese consulate researcher Yamaguchi Nobu noted in 1910, the overwhelming majority of Catholic "converts don't believe in any of the teachings of Christianity"; they converted simply because "they wanted to be protected." Because of the power of extraterritoriality, white "Catholic missionaries have taken the place of the law in many parts of China" (JFMA, "Chinese Secret Societies," 1078).

In addition to the valuable protection the MEP Catholics offered against Qing authorities, the more astute of the criminal converts may have admired the ways the MEP itself acted like a powerful criminal organization in routinely violating the treaty agreements and flouting Chinese law; its infrastructural presence in central and western China before the 1860 Beijing Convention was completely illegal. While many Euro-Americans were outraged over the 1856 killing of the French priest Auguste Chapdelaine in Guangxi province, others wondered why there weren't more attacks against insolent white Catholics. Rutherford Alcock once again refused the CO2lonizers' discourse vis-à-vis the killing of Chapdelaine when he wrote in 1858 that, "with such legitimate grounds of [Chinese] alarm and hostility, it must be a matter of surprise that a single missionary of the many hundreds in the interior has been left alive— not that one should have been sacrificed" (BPP 1859, 57). As Alcock intuited, French Catholics were on their way to becoming the pioneering white Superpredators outside the treaty ports.

What the Catholic inroads into central and southwestern China meant for those being turned into rawfare is crucial in order to understand the general hostility the British team met with, culminating in the murder of Margary in Yunnan province. In addition to Sichuanese indignation over MEP Catholic arrogance, trade and the movement of people up and down the Yangzi from Nanjing all the way to central Asia linked Sichuan in a network that disseminated information about of Euro-whites in their nearby colonies (Vietnam, Burma, Hong Kong, Singapore) and treaty ports. Although the British had profit and pleasure clouding their extractiv-eyes/Is, local Sichuanese were clear-sighted about what was to follow from the enclosure of Chongqing as a treaty port. From the standpoint of Sichuanese locals—as well as accounts from Japanese anti-Western activists supporting anti-Western struggles in the region in the 1880s and '90s (OSS 1944)—Europeans were construed as a toxic visitation. The historian of the anti-Christian movement in Sichuan, Hu Qiwei, proffers that the combination of extraterritorial immunity for whites, French Catholic arms and human trafficking, and militarized capitalism elicited a rejection of "all aspects" of the Western presence (1986, 106).

Catholic CO2loniality

Long-term residence of French priests in Sichuan took off in 1840 when Eugène Desflèches joined three other MEP missionaries in Longshui (in Chongqing prefecture) to supervise the first Catholic infrastructure project in China since Christianity was outlawed in 1724. Many changes in the world were impacting the Catholic Church in Europe, and these transformations fed forward into its activities in China. The most important was the spasm of imperial nationalism, which emerged in a particularly virulent form in France during the Napoleonic Wars (1803–1815). With some French Catholics increasingly frustrated by the power of the Vatican in Rome, they established autonomous organizations. These were given full-throated support during the reign of Emperor Napoleon III (1852–70).

One of the most important of these was the Missions Étrangères de Paris (MEP), which had a seminary in Paris and began sending priests out of France in large numbers in the 1830s. Supported financially by the Society for the Propagation of the Faith and the Holy Childhood Association, most of the Catholic missionaries in China in the nineteenth century came from MEP (Lesourd 1947). After the failed revolution in France of 1848, the MEP developed a close relationship with the French Foreign Ministry, and through this relationship the French Religious Protectorate in China was born.

Unlike the US and the UK, France had almost no merchant presence in East Asia at the time of the 1842 Treaty of Nanking.[7] Therefore, in the great power competition in East and Central Asia, the French state was forced to rely on the Catholics missionaries as their ears and eyes on the ground. This would prove to be decisive for both the MEP and France. Although France was neutral in the First War for Drugs (1839–42), it took advantage of the Qing court wanting to play the Euro-American powers off against each other. After the French plenipotentiary Théodore de Lagrené signed the first Sino-French treaty in 1844, which gave France all the privileges granted to England in the Treaty of Nanking, Lagrené wanted more (Wei 1991, vol. 1, 269–81). Backed by a six-ship naval escort (plus two gunboats) the French side whispered to the Qing negotiator Qiying that they could play a role in hindering further British advances in China and, regardless of whether the Qing agreed to play ball in any covert Sino-French diplomacy, Lagrené let Qiying know that France was perfectly willing to initialize asymmetric warfare—à l'anglaise. Pressured by the thirty or so MEP missionaries already in China, Lagrené convinced Qiying to propose to the Qing Emperor Daoguan that Catholicism be decriminalized in China. Surprisingly, a December 1844 imperial edict did just that, provided that Catholicism was not used again, as it had reportedly been during the seventeenth and eighteenth centuries in China, "as a cover for evildoing [借教为恶]" and so long as Catholic priests did not "seduce and defile women [诱污妇女]" (Wei 1991, vol. 2, 424–25).[8] Although practicing Catholicism was no longer a crime for Chinese, this Qing edict reiterated that Euro-American missionaries were absolutely forbidden from traveling beyond the five treaty ports. Well outside Qing intelligence networks was the fact that French priests like Desflèches were already using extra-active lawfare to justify their outlaw incursions into China's interior.

Even after Lagrené succeeded in getting Emperor Daoguan to issue the 1844 edict, the MEP would soon score another victory thanks to their missionaries haranguing French diplomats. The payoff was a second Qing edict of 1846 that promised to punish Chinese officials who persecuted Christians based solely on their religion (Wei 1991, vol. 2, 552–55). Forebodingly, it also provided that European churches proven to have been built during the reign of the Qing Emperor Kangxi (1661–1722) be returned to local Catholics, with the exception of churches that had been turned into temples or official government buildings by locals. This last clause should have greatly reduced the opportunities for Catholic repossession, as it was highly unlikely that large stone buildings would have been left unused in poorer areas in the Chinese interior.[9] In addition, the 1846 Qing edict restated the firm ban on Euro-white missionaries traveling outside the five treaty ports. Readers should understand that until 1860 all Chinese officials were required to arrest any Euro-American missionary found outside the treaty ports. Accordingly, the best way for Catholic priests like Desflèches to survive and thrive was to have armed protection; the three who didn't before

1860 ended up dead.[10] While the two new edicts generated novel protection for Euro-Catholic missionaries, they also provided enough ambiguity to push for even much, as the new privileges were understood by most Qing officials in the interior simply as the "legal protection for Catholicism [保教权]." But did these legal protections provide complete immunity from Qing law for Euro-white and Chinese Catholics alike?

As the Boxer Rebellion in eastern Shandong province has attracted much of the scholarship on the issue, it's not often recognized that Sichuan had more battles against Christians than any other Chinese province from 1860 until the rebellion of 1898–1900.[11] While there is no scholarly consensus on the reasons for this,[12] my argument here will illustrate the ways in which the mutual-aid outlaw brotherhood Gelaohui (GLH) led a campaign of eco-ontological protection against Euro-whites in Sichuan. I want to contextualize this campaign first by introducing an incident of white racial terror and then build on that to flesh out my argument in this chapter.

In western Sichuan's Yanjing county there was a resident MEP priest in the early 1900s named E. T. Vignal. Vignal had been involved in armed skirmishes against Tibetan and Sichuanese locals just across the western border of Sichuan in Tibetan Batang. For over three decades the MEP had been trying to maintain a Catholic mission compound and adjacent army base since originally making an incursion into Batang in 1863 with seven armed priests supported by their own militia of Chinese Catholics (Launay 2008, 155). In 1905 Vignal was lightly wounded in one of the uprisings against the French at their mission in Batang and was convinced that he suffered his injury during a night raid carried out by Tibetan monks. Over a year later, Vignal was traveling in nearby Deyin county, Sichuan, when he spotted the bald head of someone he thought was a Tibetan monk in a town called Nagu. The man was named Ci and, when threatened in front of his house by Vignal, he insisted he had no connection whatsoever to institutional Tibetan Buddhism. But Vignal had been plotting for a year to exact revenge against the first Tibetan monk he met up with and was convinced that fate had brought him face to face with Ci. Screaming wildly to a few bystanders that Ci had been involved in attacks on Catholics, he proceeded to cut the Tibetan's head completely off with a swift scimitar blow and then, as the Sichuan governor general's investigative memorial to the Zongli Yamen in Beijing alleged, "tore the man's heart out of his chest [挖心]" with a knife. But Vignal wasn't done. Ci's wife came screaming out of the house, and Vignal tried to separate her head from her body as well, which resulted in a serious head injury and one of the woman's ears hacked off. Leaving her bleeding on the ground, he reportedly ransacked their house and made off with a horse, a cow, and some of Ci's clothing—stolen goods that, as the official report concluded from testimonies of local Chinese Catholics, weren't donated to the local Catholic mission, but "put into his own pocket." The memorial concluded that that although Ci was ethnic Tibetan, he was definitely not a monk (Qin 2006, 228–29).

The Vignal case is one of only a handful in which Euro-white priests premeditatedly murdered Asians. But it's a good place to begin to unpack the condemnation of Catholics made by the Qing high commissioner for border security, Chong Shi, in the epigraph to this chapter. Chong was in a good position to make a well-documented assessment, as he was the Qing official responsible for handling all problems with Catholics in Sichuan and Yunnan. MEP priests thought extremely highly of Chong, and successfully pushed to raise his authority over that of the Qing governor general of Sichuan. Nevertheless, Chong didn't reciprocate in his opinion of the MEP missionaries, observing in the epigraph that there was an unbridgeable chasm separating Catholic religious doctrine from the actual deportment of white priests in China. At the very least, Chong's observation of the endemic hypocrisy in the Church supports our argument put forward in the introduction and advanced in chapter 1: the power to both transcendentally produce the law (in this case, establish the Ten Commandments as the basis for Catholic morality) and then proceed to contravene or ignore that same law qualifies some Catholics in China for consideration not as mere (lowercase) superpredators, but as ecclesiastical Superpredators.

To understand this conjuncture, we need to rewind to the introduction and Robert Hart's distinction between defensive and offensive extraterritoriality for Euro-Americans in China. While these defined the parameters for juridical immunity for secular white people, Christian missionaries actually enjoyed a wider spectrum of immunity. Although the precise terms of the "guaranteed protections for Christianity" won by force of arms would be fought over until the end of the Qing dynasty in December 1911, it was mobilized by MEP Catholics to access the entire playbook of Superpredation: extortion, homocide, human trafficking, sexual assault, and theft ranging from the petty burglary of the sort Father Vignal allegedly committed in 1906, to the dispossession of the large temple Chongyin at Qixinggang in Chongqing in 1862 by the bishop of eastern Sichuan, Eugène Desflèches. By the summer of 1863 Desflèches had already finished the foundation, underground vault, and brick walls for a large Catholic church, obliterating Chongyin.

While the protection provided to Euro-white Catholics turned out to be basically unconditional, that was never the understanding for Chinese Catholics.

Nevertheless, the MEP would do everything in its power to shield Chinese converts from Qing law. After all, their raison d'être was to convert nonwhite heathens to Catholicism, and both local Catholic missions and the regional bishops were under pressure to demonstrate steady growth in converts. One of the proven ways to do this was to offer protection for petty thieves and criminals, who constituted one of the two main streams of converts. This was so widely known that a popular phrase was already circulating in Sichuan by the mid-1870s—"thieves don't have to be afraid of the police, all they have to do is get a priest to take care of everything [拉抢不怕官快把司铎搬]" (Qin 2006, 229). And on the rare occasion that a determined magistrate still pursued thieves after they converted to Catholicism, once in court another Sichuanese saying held: "become a Christian sheep, and the judge will even do obeisance to your shit" (Han 1965, 65)

The second stream of Catholic converts consisted of poor peasants, who often converted with their families in the face of starvation. In central and southwestern China these converts were referred to derogatorily as "sponging off the Church [吃教]." As I will demonstrate below, the extractive practice of indemnification that came to define MEP Catholics in southwestern and central China would contribute directly to the increase in impoverished converts. For there was a circular causality here that saw Catholics impoverishing local governments with punishing indemnities, which left no money for relief after famines or floods; this resulted in the desperately poor having no viable option other than converting to Catholicism. Qing government relief was also impacted by heavy indemnities paid out to Euro-American countries and their missionaries, infamously in the drought-caused famine in north China of 1876–79. While Qing borrowing for its wars against Muslims in Gansu and Xinjiang was also a factor (as was endemic corruption), nonstop indemnity payments impacted emergency rice and wheat stores, contributing to the millions of deaths from drought and famine in the late 1870s. While we can't attribute this to Marx's extraction → extinction imperative, a Protestant version of ecclesiastical Superpredation ("no conscience, no empathy") emerged when US missionaries in China like Arthur Smith urged white evangelists to take advantage of the "wonderful opening of famine" to increase converts to Christianity in 1879 (in Davis 2002, 77).

Certainly, there was the occasional sincere convert to Catholicism. He or she tended to be well educated and weighed a belief in Catholic doctrine against the inevitable ostracism from family and community that invariably followed conversion. However, bona fide converts were often disappointed with their new faith community. An interesting letter sent by a Chinese Catholic convert to a French priest in the eastern Sichuan vicariate in 1891 ended up in the Zongli Yamen archive of Christian affairs and conflicts. In it, the convert complains that among all the Chinese Catholics, "those who are literate and reasonable (读书明理者) are rare, while there are plenty of vagabonds and scoundrels (游手无赖者多). Furthermore, there are people who . . . are caught up in lawsuits they are afraid they can't win if they don't flee into the Church and take advantage of its power to solve their legal issues. There are even places where the Catholic church is protecting people who are actively involved in crime, and who only use the church as refuge from the magistrate. . . . In other words, none of these people are sincere believers, but find safety in the church for altogether different reasons" (JWJA 5:1465–66).

Altogether Different Reasons

There was a convergence of the motivations for Chinese to convert to Catholicism and for some MEP priests to do missionary work in China. The fact that some Catholic priests were also motivated for "altogether different reasons" than the stated one of spreading the gospel of Christ wouldn't emerge until they penetrated into China's interior after the Beijing Convention was signed in 1860, ending the Second War for Drugs. The 1860 Sino-French treaty both reiterated the two earlier edicts lifting the proscription on Christianity and, in Article 6, greatly expanded the rights available to Catholic missionaries. The most important of these was the right to buy and lease land "in any province . . . to build on as they see fit" (Wei 1991, vol. 2, 590). What I'll call the eighteen-character "privatization clause"[13] in Article 6 was surreptitiously inserted into the Chinese version by three French negotiators, including the Sichuan-based MEP priest L. C. Delamarre (Piolet 1901, 269–70). Although Qing officials were furious when they realized what had been done, they pointed to the absence of this clause in the French version to try to prevent the entirety of China from being put up for sale. However, French officials in Beijing were successful in threatening the Qing with the French soldiers newly stationed there after the Second War for Drugs. The result was the Sino-French agreement known as the 1865 Betheny Convention, which formalized the Chinese version of Article 6 (Young 2013, 31–32). This 1865 agreement also put into law another French demand that the Zongli Yamen reluctantly agreed to in 1862: the exemption of all Chinese converts from their required contribution to local temple upkeep, to festivals, and to Chinese opera performances dedicated to local deities (QMJA 1:195–97).

The privatization clause went a long way in spreading capitalist extraction outside the treaty ports, and until 1876, it allowed Catholics to be the only

Euro-whites to legally play the real estate market—buying land was now allowed, and selling or "flipping" property happened routinely through Chinese Catholic converts (Qin 2006, 77–78). This was a huge advantage as the enclosure of additional treaty ports along the Yangzi in 1860 created mini–real estate booms, and MEP Catholics were perfectly positioned to extract high profits from rent. At the turn of the century, Anglophone capitalists in Sichuan were amazed at all the prime real estate owned by the MEP smack in the center of market towns and cities along the Yangzi and Min Rivers, and insisted that the MEP should not be considered a religious group, but a gang of "land speculators" (BFO 228/1455, April 14, 1902). The writer Han Suyin described the period after 1860 in Sichuan as one where MEP Catholics profited from extreme weather in "buying up entire villages in time of flood and famine" (1965, 64). Moreover, when owners refused to sell property, MEP Catholics ended up "obtaining on threat of military action the best land in the cities for their churches, after evicting the inhabitants and paying no compensation" (64). Introducing even more ambiguity into a rapidly changing situation in central and southwestern China after the Second War for Drugs, the 1860 clause and 1865 Betheny Convention directly contravened the stipulations in the 1858 Treaty of Tianjin against missionaries being involved in commerce. As a result, in addition to buying and selling real estate, white Catholics could now officially import anything they wanted into central and southwestern China tax-free under the category of "products for church use [教堂用品]." As they did in similar cases of juridical ambiguity, the MEP regularly abused this right. For example, an MEP priest was caught smuggling narcotics and weapons from Shanghai into Chongqing in June 1875, but he claimed protection under the "products for church use" stipulation. Understandably, this didn't convince the Chongqing magistrate, who refused to release him and confiscated the goods. When the French delegation heard about the incident, they forced the Qing government to order the release of the priest and to compensate him for the full value of the confiscated contraband (Hu 1986, 21).

The guarantee of private ownership together with missionaries' right to traffic anything at all into the interior under the category of "for church use" operated as a carte blanche for a few white priests to traffic drugs[14] and weapons in the interior. And the basement storage space standard in the brick churches enabled MEP merchants to sit on valuable commodities, waiting until the market price of certain goods rose to the point where they could make handsome profits. Taking advantage of the Society for the Propagation of the Faith's refusal to ban French Catholics from buying and selling opium—the Propagation of the Faith put out instructions to Catholic missionaries in China in 1878 recommending "flexibility" while giving in to pressure to proscribe only poppy cultivation in 1891—the bishop of eastern Sichuan and his underlings were alleged to be selling both opium and weapons stored in the basement vault of the Catholic cathedral in Chongqing (Hu 1986, 20). As many of the MEP priests originally traveled to China in opium clippers from South Asia, we can underline the importance of the clipper-coolie captive-contraband-capital (4C) circuit for the French Catholics (Launay 2008). While most scholarship ignores the extractive practices of the French missionaries in China, we will see that their version of the British 4C circuit replaced the infrastructure of the clipper ship with that of the fired-brick church, allowing some missionaries to traffic contraband from church basements, and even girls out of their brick orphanages (Zhongyang yanjiuyuan 1974, 915).

While new converts were provided with rudimentary education in Chinese and French, Catholic extraction in Sichuan began with the requirement that converts hand over their possessions to the mission priests and subsequently work for free on MEP farms or in their various businesses (for converts who managed to keep their homes, MEP bishops reserved the right to levy taxes on top of those paid to the provincial government [JWJA 3: 1316, 1323]). French Catholic enterprises in Sichuan included climate-interfering copper and gold mining, and pharmacies that featured opiate-based medicines like laudanum and morphine, along with concoctions made from aloes and magnesia (Piolet 1901, 316; 320; JFMA, "Chongqing and Sichuan," 271;).[15] While Catholic converts were generally given medicines for free, the MEP peddled these goods to non-converts at markets throughout the province. A second mode of extraction featured the theft and subsequent obliteration of Daoist temples claimed by MEP Catholics to have been reconfigured from eighteenth-century Catholic buildings; the first of these was the venerable Chongqing temple Chongyin in 1862 (QMJA 1:193–95). Chongyin was situated in the Qixinggang neighborhood, high up on a "prominent sandstone bluff, about two acres in extent, which occupies a commanding position in the center of the city." The long-term resident of Chongqing, Archibald Little, observed that there was nothing more "Feng-shui disturbing" than erecting a large brick monstrosity in that particular location (Little 1898, 165–66).

Later, British consuls in southwestern China F. S. Bourne and W. D. Spence believed that European Catholics were deliberately practicing an anti–feng shui construction policy, as they realized that this would incite church destruction and allow the MEP to inflate the value of the destroyed property in subsequent indemnity claims. If European priests were killed in anti-Christian uprisings, this might also have the effect of increasing donations to missions

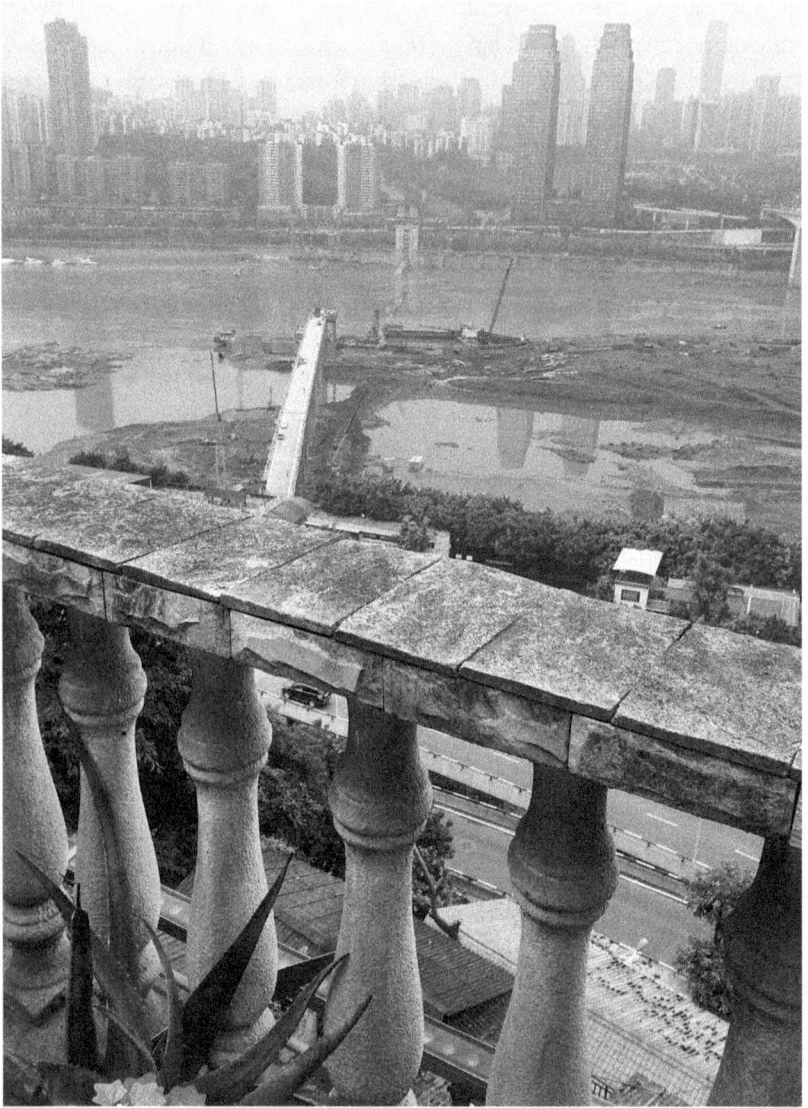

FIGURE 2.2. View from the back of the old MEP Catholic church in Qixinggang, Chongqing. Photograph by the author.

in China that housed Catholic "martyrs" (Coates 1988, 182–97). Nevertheless, Bishop Desflèches, headquartered in Chongqing, claimed to be just following the letter of the new treaties, in particular Article 6 of the 1860 Sino-French agreement, which reconfirmed the repossession of all property any French bishop claimed had previously belonged to Catholics. With both the bishops of western (Delamarre) and eastern Sichuan (Desflèches) pressuring the French legation in Beijing, Qing officials in Sichuan were ordered to transfer the Chongyin temple to the MEP priests, and to pay them a large indemnity of 110,000 *taels*,[16] part of which was compensation for unpaid rent to the Catholic Church on the temple from the city of Chongqing for the previous 135 years (Qin 2006, 23).

This was enough to goad the locals into the first major anti-Christian incident (教案, jiao'an) outside the east coast treaty ports: the Chongqing Uprising of 1863, which saw Desflèches's new church destroyed and Catholic residences in the city sacked (QMJA 1:340). The uprising was preceded by a heated discussion in Chongqing about whether the Chongyin temple and grounds had ever been Catholic property in the first place; most local gentry argued that it had never been. Nevertheless, asymmetric lawfare allowed the MEP to repossess the temple and extract a significant indemnity (for losses on rent) on top of a subsequent second large indemnity after the property was destroyed. The loss of Chongyin cost Chongqing residents not only a popular place of worship, but also a convenient meeting place and storage facility for the local militia (QMJA 1:340). As the preeminent historian of Sichuan Wang Di argues, from this point forward MEP missionaries routinely insisted that Chinese property deeds were unreliable, and this allowed them to repossess land and property that had never belonged to the Church in the first place (2006, 683–84). Similar to the temple-to–Catholic church makeover in downtown Chongqing, MEP repossessions were overwhelmingly of built structures understood by Sichuanese to be integral elements of the local eco-ontology, as the temples dispossessed and then obliterated by Euro-whites had followed feng shui geomancy.

Additional extractive practices of MEP Catholics in Sichuan included a rush of new private purchases of land and property, repeated attempts to dispossess the Qing government of their monopoly salt mines in Sichuan, indemnities for the slightest damage to Catholic property, and the expropriation of all new converts' share of common temple land in their home villages (Wang 1984, 58–59). Indemnities paid out to the MEP in Sichuan also included property damage from weather events and flooding; the assumption inherent in Climate Caucasianism as it was operationalized in China was that even the weather was white (APF 79:117–18).

It was not just the amount of land, but the location of it that increasingly turned the Sichuanese public against MEP Catholics. Catholic enclosures focused on prime real estate in the center of market towns. For example, in the three market towns in Dazu county, Chongqing prefecture, the Catholics enjoyed a formidable presence by constructing imposing churches adjacent to marketplaces, and each of these was the pioneering brick building (BFO 228/829, August 5, 1886). There were 162 brick MEP churches and chapels in Sichuan by the time Chongqing became a treaty port in 1891, a construction boom that began with only around 10 in 1860 (Wyman 1997). Although bricks had appeared in Chinese construction for over a thousand years, local Sichuanese objected to their prominence in the MEP buildings (DX 1:360). In Chongqing, buildings were made primarily of wood, bamboo, mud, manure, and stone. From an object-oriented ontology perspective, fired brick was materially different from wood and mud, which intra-acted with the environment. Wood and earthen structures burned and washed away, while brick was designed in Europe as an extra-active entity impervious to its surroundings (Shammas 2012, 8–11). Bricks became ubiquitous in the enclosed Chinese treaty ports when the first Hoffman kiln was installed in Shanghai in 1868, allowing mass production. In Sichuan, where the MEP owned and operated all the kilns for firing brick until the turn of the twentieth century, the permanence of brick structures announced the fixity of Catholicism on the landscape (Piolet 1901, 321–22).

Non-Catholics were alarmed by both the brick constructions and the MEP's "very extensive property" holdings in Sichuan by the mid-1880s, as the British consul in Chongqing, F. S. Bourne, put it. Much of this property was rented out to Catholic converts and nonconverts alike (BFO 228/829, July 7, 1886). Responding to reports of Catholic rent gouging, Sichuanese wits proffered an ironic critique of these extractions by morphing Catholicism (天主教, *tianzhu-jiao*) into Landlordism (地主教, *dizhujiao*) (Wang 2013a, 132). In other words, as local Sichuanese saw it, the desire structure of the MEP Catholics was not directed to the afterlife (天) as it claimed, but focused solely on earthly (地) dispossessions and repossessions. The Sichuanese writer Han Suyin denounced French priests at this time as using "religious garb to cover [the] most unreligious actions" (1965, 64).

The third major mode of MEP Catholic extraction, and the most lucrative, was indemnification. Indemnification should be seen as part of a logic of capitalism in that it entailed valuing things alienated from their relationality within socio-natural environments. While this was based on the European mechanical philosophy of extra-action pioneered by Descartes,

Sichuanese inhabited very different eco-ontologies and tended to be perplexed by indemnification. This bewilderment was compounded by outrage over the seriously inflated damages often claimed by MEP Catholics. When successful, the indemnity payouts were huge, as we saw in the previous chapter on Japan in the Richardson case. However, to activate the indemnity system in southwestern and central China required the smooth integration of three distinct parts: white supremacist bishops[17] driven to expropriate land, property, and people; French officials in Beijing willing to make good on continuing threats of asymmetric warfare to support the bishops' demands; and at least one Qing official on the ground willing to sign off on dubious indemnity claims.

In the 1860s this willing representative was the most powerful Qing official in western China after the governors general—the high commissioner for border affairs, Chong Shi. He was headquartered in Sichuan's capital city of Chengdu and, as we see in the second epigraph, had a low opinion of white priests' behavior in China. After the Second War for Drugs, Chong's office, normally responsible for relations with Tibetans and Muslims, was saddled with the added duty of managing relations with the newly legitimate Catholic missions in Sichuan. Beginning with the transfer of the Chongyin temple and lasting more than a decade, Chong felt that his responsibility was to, as the 1860 treaty language put it, "protect Catholic rights [保教权]." Moreover, because of the subterfuge carried out by the French legation in cahoots with the MEP in their Chinese rendering of Article 6 of the 1860 Sino-French treaty, he was under the impression that this included corroborating any and all MEP property claims. Chong's willingness to do so frustrated other Chinese officials, and the Qing military commander in Sichuan argued in 1873 that Chong's presence unleashed the "Catholics' predatory desires, that will never stop until they are completely satiated" (JWJA 3: 957–58).

In partnership with Chong, the next requirement for indemnification extraction was the arrogant MEP bishop of eastern Sichuan, Eugène Desflèches, who became notorious among Euro-American officials in China for his outrageous damage claims. But Desflèches also managed to alienate his Chinese converts. For example, in 1865 he succeeded in raking in the Catholics' second inflated indemnity payment of 150,000 taels for the sacking of the newly rebuilt MEP church on the Chongyin grounds and residences of wealthy Chinese Catholics. However, while part of his original 150,000-tael request was earmarked to individual Chinese converts, when Desflèches received the money in 1866 he refused to share any of it. When one of his Catholic converts, Tong Wenhong, personally confronted Desflèches over his promised money,

Desflèches ordered his subordinates to beat up Tong and his brother, seriously injuring them (JWJA 4:1325).

Desflèches thought that in order to keep extracting bloated indemnities he had to establish himself as the supreme authority in Sichuan. Therefore, when he returned to downtown Chongqing in 1864 after having been chased from the city the year before, he did so in Superpredator fashion, surrounded by what Europeans later called an armed "Praetorian Guard" of Chinese Catholics. But the new symbolism of MEP Catholic rule wasn't limited to imperial Rome. As Hu Qiwei points out, from this point on the MEP expropriated the formal structure of Qing rule, and the most important element of this in Sichuan was the prince-like status of the Qing "viceroy" or governor general (1986, 34). Complaining about Desflèches several years later, a senior French diplomat in China elaborated on this in a report to Paris. Claiming that, in addition to his armed security detail, "This prelate had gathered around his apostolic authority about 20,000 Christians, whom he had made into a kind of clientele, as in ancient Rome.... He judges their disputes; assesses as he wishes the taxes each must pay ... if I may use this popular expression, he plays at being viceroy" (in Young 2013, 51).

With his arrival back to Chongqing demonstrating a new commitment to asymmetric warfare, Desflèches launched the first Catholic small war in Youyang county, southeastern Sichuan. Reacting to another questionable Catholic repossession of a Daoist temple there in 1863 and rumors of widespread kidnapping used to expand the pool of Catholic converts, in May and June of 1865 the new church and several Catholic residences were destroyed (QMJA 1:456–57). A Father M. Augustin was killed when he arrived from Chongqing with reinforcements in July. Desflèches began the indemnity battle by once again refusing to accept any MEP responsibility. His October summary of the incident (sent to the French legation, where it was translated into Chinese and sent to the Zongli Yamen) reads like the ravings of a paranoid schizophrenic. First, insisting that the Catholics were persecuted by all non-Christian parties, he then contradicted this martyr narrative by singling out a small band of GLH insurrectionists as the puppet masters behind the attack; it turned out that all the locals secretly liked the Catholic missions. Returning to his focus on absolute victimization—"the rioters plundered countless Catholic valuables; stole incalculable amounts of Catholic money; illegally occupied countless Catholic fields; burned to the ground untold number of Catholic houses; and even after everything was stolen or destroyed, they returned to steal and destroy again"—he broke off unexpectedly to single out the Sichuan governor general's office for continually inciting the locals against the Catholics (QMJA 1:459–61).

FIGURE 2.3. Gelaohui brother decapitated in situ for involvement in Catholic church destruction (Zhao Hong 2006).

Double Indemnity

A second French front was opened when Desflèches's report of the Youyang incident circulated among French officials in Beijing. Minister Betheny immediately demanded a meeting with top Qing officials and threatened them with war if all of Desflèches's indemnity demands weren't met. "China," Betheny blustered, "must realize that a new political situation is at hand after your defeat in the recent war" (QMJA 1:463). With Chong Shi on the ground in Sichuan ready to sign off on even the wildest MEP claims, French warships anchored in Shanghai prepared to navigate up the Yangzi for a drive-by shooting/shelling of Qing offices in Hankou. In the face of asymmetric warfare, the Qing agreed to another punishing 110,000-tael indemnity and to arrest and decapitate the main anti-Catholic perpetrators at Youyang. From this point on, any GLH member caught anywhere near destroyed Catholic property could be immediately decapitated.

Realizing that these indemnity agreements—between 1.5 percent and 2 percent of Sichuan's total annual revenue—were setting a dangerous precedent going forward, Prince Gong's Zongli Yamen wrote a stern note to Chong. No fan of either the Catholic missionaries or secular white narcos, Gong warned him to be sure to double check the cost of damages before tentatively agreeing to any amount proposed by the MEP. This is exactly what happened during the next anti-Christian uprising in Youyang (1868–69), with the important Qing general and diplomat Li Hongzhang (1823–1901) personally going to Sichuan to oversee the process. Consequently, the indemnity agreed to was a fraction of what had been granted previously, with a mere 30,000 taels handed over to the MEP priests in Sichuan (QMJA 1:652–62).

The occasion for this was another uprising against the Catholic mission in Youyang. Responding to alleged abuses of Chinese convert women by priests and another round of accusations of the MEP buying and selling girls out of its orphanages, two churches were seriously damaged by locals between the spring of 1868 and summer of 1869; a Father J. F. Rigaud died when he was unable to escape the flames in the second church burning. According to the Sichuan Governor General Liu Bingzhen's investigation, Desflèches decided at that point to launch asymmetric war. The MEP bishop ordered his Chinese priest Zhi Fangxi to arm as many Chinese converts as possible, and with mercenaries recruited by Zhi from neighboring Guizhou, the MEP forces battled the local population throughout the summer, deploying scorched-earth tactics. With countless houses burned down, Euro-American scholars put the death total at between thirty and two hundred; Chinese sources claim that the combination of dead and wounded reached one thousand (Chen 2010, 168–69; Young 2013, 49).[18]

The French delegation in Beijing was pressured into accepting the low 30,000-tael indemnity because Li Hongzhang's team personally checked that the final requests matched local builders' estimates (JWJA 2: 1110–13, 1142–53). Desflèches was furious at the finalized 1869 agreement, as this was the first time Qing officials hadn't been bullied into accepting his fantastic damage claims. In response, he personally traveled to Beijing and managed to convince the French vice minister to reopen the case. The vice minister was ultimately successful in getting the delegation to support Desflèches's proposal to triple the amount of the 30,000-tael indemnity claim. This time, however, it was the Zongli Yamen's chance to be firm. There would be no triple indemnity.

Desflèches returned to Chongqing itching for vengeance and ordered new mission expansion and church building, both farther out in remote areas in southeastern Sichuan and, more importantly, in areas north of Chongqing such as Dazu county. This expansion led both to new growth in the number of Catholic converts and children taken into its orphanages, and to a new round of anti-Christian incidents. It also began an irreparable rift between the French delegation in Beijing and the two main MEP bishops of Sichuan, Desflèches in Chongqing and M. J. Dunand in Chengdu. Although delighted with the rapid Catholic expansion, more and more French officials in China were worried that the continued reliance on asymmetric warfare and lawfare was hurting the future of French extraction in China. The acting French minister, G. E. Roquette, wrote to Paris in 1873 insisting that there needed to be peace in Sichuan, but that this was "impossible until the bishops put down their firearms" (Qin 2006, 252).

Roquette and French military leaders in Beijing became disconcerted when the Zongli Yamen confronted them in 1871 with detailed findings of Catholic abuses in the two Youyang incidents and in the Tianjin Massacre of 1870, when Catholic priests and nuns were killed and significant damage done to Catholic infrastructure. While French officials thought the Tianjin matter was behind them with the Qing agreeing to a large 400,000-tael indemnity, the Zongli Yamen presented them with eight proposals meant to eliminate further disputes (教民相争). Among them were stipulations that the transfer of abandoned infants and children bought from Chinese traffickers into Catholic orphanages be curtailed and that the widespread practice of Western missionaries intervening in legal cases be stopped (包揽官事). With reference to the problems in Sichuan, another proposal specified that European priests must not feel free to designate any building that caught their eye as formerly confiscated Catholic Church property and demand its immediate return. Rather, French missionaries should make a detailed case for any repossession, including proper documentation. Needless to say, both the MEP leaders and the French and British delegations rejected the proposals out of hand (Taveirne 2004, 181–84).

One final word on the continuing indemnity claims. When Desflèches was successfully recalled to Shanghai in 1877, and then forcefully expelled back to France in 1878, this did little to interrupt French Catholic indemnity gouging. Things quickly returned to the MEP billing Qing officials four and five times what the actual costs to repair damages were. For example, after the Dazu, Chongqing 1898–99 anti-Catholic uprisings, embarrassed Chinese priest whistleblowers leaked the MEP's own estimate of damages in southern Sichuan after they found out how much Bishop Dunand had fleeced the Qing for. The real figure for just the southern Sichuan district was 5,400 taels, while the shakedown put 33,000 taels into the MEP's pocket (SJYD, 618–21). The same Dunand (called "Pig Tiger" by Sichuanese) was said to have seriously inflated the actual costs of damages in Chengdu from the Dazu campaign.[19] Dunand ordered a Chinese priest under him to increase the estimate of destroyed Church property from the actual number of 18,000 to 300,000 taels (*North China Herald*, September 10, 1902).

The evidence suggests that Dunand continued a fourth and final mode of MEP Catholic extraction practiced by Desflèches: human trafficking. The primary means of this was the buying and kidnapping of infants and children for MEP orphanages (Boell 1899, 45). Except for the annual salaries paid to French priests from the Society for the Propagation of the Faith, the only other revenue stream came from the Holy Childhood Association in Paris, and bishops in China were required to report each month the number of infants taken into Catholic orphanages; the more kids, the more money. The MEP "accumulated" children in two ways. The first was the outright buying of them from Chinese human traffickers, something long practiced by wealthy Chinese families. Although illegal, there were many brokers in towns and cities in Sichuan who kidnapped and trafficked young girls and boys; the MEP was a prominent buyer in this traffic (Stapleton 2000, 135). The British consul at Chongqing, F. S. Bourne, reiterated what he called the common knowledge that French Catholics routinely bought young girls "as property" from Chinese human traffickers throughout southwestern China (BFO 228/850, February 7, 1887). The second way MEP priests added to the orphanage total was by paying Chinese converts cash to kidnap children or, alternatively, just baptizing sick children before they died. A 1907 Japanese consul report from Chongqing claims that French Catholic missions in Sichuan paid their catechists between 750 and 1,500 coppers cash for each child brought into an orphanage, and less for a proven baptism (JFMA, "Chongqing and Sichuan," 271).[20] This sum was the equivalent of one or two weeks' manual labor. While the MEP priests welcomed kidnapped Sichuanese into their orphanages, the kids themselves might not have appreciated the change of scenery. While the mortality rate for children under ten was high throughout China at this time, Henrietta Harrison writes that the treatment of the children was so bad in the Catholic orphanages in China that most died on the premises, an ecclesiastical version of the extraction → extinction imperative (Harrison 2013, 101).

The lucky ones who managed to survive MEP orphanages into adolescence often ran out of luck when MEP priests directed some of them to be sold (JFMA, "Chongqing and Sichuan," 272). Most of these trafficked Chinese Catholics were girls sold to desperate families who had unmarried sons. While the MEP offered a small dowry to grooms, it was much less than the standard MEP price for the bride, resulting in a profit for the entrepreneurial Catholics

(Taveirne 2004, 400). As the M E P often required male suitors to be converted Catholics, this was yet another tactic to increase conversions. The French missionary Hugolin Villeret ran a Catholic orphanage in Shanxi province in the 1880s and realized after selling so many young Chinese females that he was nothing more than a sleazy human trafficker, what Villeret himself described as "a merchant in little girls" (in Harrison 2008, 88).

Sexual Superpredators?

After Desflèches was removed, a Father Pons replaced him as bishop of eastern Sichuan. Together with Dunand, they continued to deny that most Sichuanese opposed the Catholic missions and refused to accept that the denunciations of the white Catholic modus operandi in the anti-Western placards reflected popular opinion. Like the gorge-us white guys in Japan discussed in chapter 1, European Catholics only recognized Chinese adulation, and many wanted regular proof of this by requiring converts to kowtow to them (Young 2013, 137). However, for a southwestern Chinese society still without newspapers, the kind of placard cited above served the crucial function of transmitting to illiterate people nonofficial information about political affairs. Locals gathered around the wall a placard was placed on and listened as a literate person read the contents out loud. Against the austere formality of Qing proclamations, the placards were direct and inflammatory. For this reason, they have been either dismissed or marginalized by historians. Mainland Chinese historians of Sichuan like Qin Heping and Hu Qiwei seem almost embarrassed by the placards' combination of a vernacular mythology and a refusal to follow the rules of Euro-American objectivity. Fortunately, a significant number of these were translated into English and French by missionaries. However, the missionary translations were designed in part to highlight the bizarre musings and premodern imaginations of "backward" Chinese. Similar to revising scholarly interpretations of rogue samurai in Japan in the 1850s and '60s in chapter 1, I argue that we need to take a new look at the placards in the light of eco-ontological protection.

One of the most popular placards of the 1880s, "Proclamation against the Criminal Western Religion [讨西洋教匪檄文]," first appeared in 1861, making it one of the earliest of the anti-Western incitements. This is my translation:

> The Western religion is the belief of ignorant predators [夷狄]....
> These predators neither respect the many living things of this world, nor
> worship the deities. They are not filial and disparage the parent–child

relation to the point where sons have incestuous relations with the mother [子淫其母] and the father rapes his own daughter. This is the kind of sleazy and rapacious behavior that epitomizes how they relate with others. . . . Their aggressive temperament drives them to pollute [污] everything they come across. . . . It's easy to see that the Westerners' actions make them indistinguishable from cows and horses. On the contrary, our lives are generated by the five elements [五行] and the cosmic spirits of all things [万物]. So how in the world are we going to coexist with these Westerners who believe they are above everything and everyone? (Wang 1984, 78–81)

The full version of this featured the bullet points of the anti-Christian position in China at this time: Catholic priests kill Chinese children by tearing out their eyeballs; Euro-whites have a deviant, aggressive sexuality including practicing incest; Westerners are actually predatory animals who will persist in their aggressive propagation until each and every Chinese is converted to Christianity; and so on. Clearly, the commitment to myth as the popular form of representation remained strong. But what exactly are the contours of these myths? The notion of tearing out the eyes has an obvious analogue with converts being "blinded" by the totalizing epistemology of Christianity. The code of Euro-white Christians employing a human disguise that camouflages their real identity as pigs or wolves also maps onto the perception of Euro-whites as refusing to recognize limits to what can be expropriated, what I noted in the introduction Robert Hart celebrating as "offensive extraterritoriality."

One of the themes of this book is expressed in the proclamation's reference to a tenet in Chinese philosophy that human and extrahuman life are effects of the intra-action among the five elements or phases of qi (气): wood (木), fire (火), earth (土), metal (金), and water (水). The notion of the five elements posits that human life is a minor derivation from the larger cosmic forces at play in the universe. All entities are produced by what is called "interactive generation [相生]" among the five elements as they unfold as aspects of the primordial element qi.[21] The anti-Western challenge here is to remind Chinese that they exist in an eco-ontological world where the human being is just one of many cosmic forces: deities, emperors, feng shui, and so on. By contrast, the ego-ontology of Christian raciology assumes that transcendentally producing Euro-whites are alone at the center of the cosmos, subordinate only to the one Christian God.

The emphasis on the specificity of the five elements and their intra-acting emergence also brings to the foreground the environmental sensibility of this anti-Western critique. As we saw with the samurai assassin Kiyokawa Hachirô's texts in the previous chapter, the notion of "pollution" [污] here and in other versions of Chinese anti-Western discourse of the late nineteenth century is much more than a wildly xenophobic metaphor. Until now the scholarly tendency has been to dismiss these claims by assuming that readers in both East Asia and Euro-America understand that Euro-white Christians were anything but pathogenic agents corroding everything they come into contact with. But from the perspective of eco-ontology, many kinds of being (ontology) in the house (ecology) are significantly impacted by the polluting forces of Christian Climate Caucasianism. An eco-ontological analysis allows pollution to be understood as, at once, mythic, environmental, and political.

The last thing that calls for elaboration is the frequently ignored accusation of Catholic sexual assault. Even Chinese nationalist scholars back off from commenting on this. I don't agree with this refusal, and recent scholarship by Jessica Delgado (2018) on European Catholic priests' indiscretions and crimes in eighteenth-century Mexico suggests that Sichuanese accusations of persistent attacks on Chinese women and girls by MEP priests were not off the mark. Delgado writes that Spanish Catholic priests routinely told women in private "that sexual acts with them would serve as spiritual remedies" and that nonconsensual sex was more likely to occur between Euro-white priests and Indigenous and Black converts. Whenever a white priest was formally accused of sexual assault, Delgado found a blithe "carelessness and sense of immunity" in the priest's personal defense (57, 59–60). The historian of colonial Mexico John Chuchiak has written eye-openingly of the accusations of Catholic priests sexually assaulting Indigenous Mayan women in seventeenth-century Yucatán. The Spanish colonial authorities routinely dismissed Indigenous accusations as wily fabrications designed to undermine Church authority. Chuchiak argues, to the contrary, that the chorus of Indigenous accusations reveals an endemic pattern of abuse (2007, 83–110).

It's important to understand that the enclosure of Chongqing as a treaty port in 1891 removed the last juridical and commercial restrictions on Euro-whites in Sichuan, putting them above and beyond Chinese law. The paucity of Chinese-language media in Sichuan during most of the 1890s prevented literate Sichuanese from having much information about on-the-ground behavior of Catholic missionaries like George Stenz in eastern Shandong province, who, in all likelihood, serially raped Chinese women (Esherik 1987, 125–26). Nevertheless, Sichuanese knew enough about Euro-Catholics' deportment in their own province to denigrate them as "lawless and Heavenless [无法无天]"—enemies of Heaven because of their despicable behavior on earth. The evidence supporting this charge of "enemies of Heaven" included the claim that Catholics were enemies of all Chinese females. In one of his speeches quoted below, the Gelaohui leader Yu Dongchen (1851–1911) claimed that French Catholics were raping Sichuanese women. In addition to detailing the kind of routine sexual assaults that were perpetrated by white Catholics in Latin America and Africa at this time, Yu's speechwriters may also have been referring to the practice of virginity testing required before a Chinese woman convert could be married into the Church. On occasion, this involved the genital penetration by a priest or Catholic catechist to prove beyond any doubt that the Chinese bride was virgo intacta, with a pure hymen. We only have concrete examples of this in the literary realism of the period. For instance, in Li Jieren's narrative of prerevolutionary Sichuan, a poor female named Zheng was bought by missionaries from human traffickers, converted to Catholicism, and then as a teenager became involved in what appears to have been a nonconsensual sexual relationship with a European named Smith (Li 2012a, 78–79).

I want to draw on yet another anti-Western placard to expand on this. An untitled piece that appeared originally in Sichuan in 1883 is one of the most accusatory of purported sex crimes of MEP priests. This placard begins with the standard denunciation of Catholics who "don't recognize their ancestors or their parents." Because of this violation of proper Confucian respect, all kinds of sexual anarchy ensue: incest, rape, sadism, and so on. The placard then jumps to the claim that when white priests' extractive-eyes/Is settle on a girl they want in a Chinese convert family, they "tell her to come sleep with him." Fantastic white lie? But then the proclamation elaborates that this is done "under the pretext [起名叫] of maintaining her virginity and not allowing her to marry outside the Church." But what really happens is that "the priests are the first to have sex with her, under another pretext of filling her body with the holy liquid [圣水]." Is it completely outside the realm of possibility that a lecherous Father Mirabeau (or Champlain) was laughing to himself that a scared, illiterate Chinese girl would actually believe that his semen counted as "holy liquid"? (Wang 1984, 111–12). This fits perfectly into the virgo intacta scenario. In Sichuan the accusations of Catholic sexual (Super)predation were so public in 1908 and 1909 that an anguished French MEP priest wrote a pamphlet that was translated and distributed in Chinese that tried to shift the imputations to US and UK Protestants. In it, he declared that Luther was a human trafficker and, "according to Protestant doctrine," one Christian man raping 100,000 women a day was pardonable as long as he believed "firmly in Jesus" (BFO 228/1759, January 1, 1910).

Eugenio Menegon's work provides important historical context for late nineteenth-century French Catholic abuses. Menegon uncovered widespread assaults on Chinese women by white priests in Fujian province in the eighteenth century, where "the priest clearly abused his position of authority to obtain sexual favors from unwilling women, using both psychological pressure and physical violence to obtain consent" (2009, 348). In Fujian the private sacrament of confession was an ideal place for white priests—referred to by local Chinese as "ecclesiastical predators [神狼]"—to rape women, after which the priest would then absolve the traumatized woman of her "sin" (346).

My qualified support for the Sichuanese denunciations of some Catholic priests perpetrating sexual assaults during the required annual confessions in Sichuan (Piolet 1901, 326) and in other circumstances can be strengthened by reminding readers of the shift in European understandings of whiteness. While still incipient for European Catholics in China in the eighteenth century, the young Catholic MEP missionaries who worked in Sichuan were educated in a nineteenth century European milieu saturated with the science of raciology. In other words, adding to their previous sense of superiority as Christian men of the cross was a new biological awareness of themselves as inheritors of an advanced Caucasian phenotype. This lawfare further inflated the understanding of their own status, while it deflated as rawfare Chinese women, girls, and boys. When we factor in the sense of captive dependence that characterized the situation of many poor Chinese converts in Sichuan together with the asymmetries in warfare and lawfare, the breeding ground in mid- and late-nineteenth century China for ecclesiastical Superpredators arguably spawned more abuses like those W. E. B. Du Bois enumerates in the epigraph than the eighteenth century.

Moral Ecology and the Second Chongqing Uprising

Before the Chongqing Uprising of 1886, Sichuanese were not prepared to construe political conflicts in racial terms. Rather, they stood against MEP extraction for other reasons: strategic and geomantic. In the terms we are trying to advance in this book, the Christian missionary version of Climate Caucasianism simply ignored (when it didn't deliberately try to obliterate and replace) the ways locals lived intra-actionally among different kinds of entities. And ignoring the geomantic principles of feng shui always angered Sinophone Sichuanese.

With an eye toward the powerful uprisings against Catholicism that took place in the 1890s, the most flagrant rejection of Chinese geomancy wasn't perpetrated by Catholics, but took the form of a US Methodist mission[22] built at Eling on the highest promontory in Chongqing, directly overlooking the main river intersection where the Yangzi divides into the Jialing and flows into Chongqing's central Yuzhong district.[23] About a thousand meters from the matrix of Chongqing's trade traffic at the Chaotianmen wharf, it would have been difficult to choose a more overdetermined locale in southwestern China. Because of its location, its impregnable stone dug out of the surrounding hills, and its blatant violation of feng shui, it was no surprise to any Chinese when, on June 6, 1886, the day of the Dragon Boat Festival, a crowd on their way to the festivities in Yuzhong attacked the Eling mission. Usually supportive of all the Euro-American missions, British Consul Bourne had previously called the new building "obnoxious" and finally agreed to several requests from the magistrate Guo Zhang (who had himself gone twice to speak with the mission superintendent Frank Gamewell) to personally plead with the Americans to halt construction in May, but they refused (BFO 228/829, July 7, 1886).

As Archibald Little revealed later, the Eling mountain location had been the sight of an intense struggle in 1871 and '72 between a rich businessman named Tong and Chongqing gentry.[24] Twenty-four of the gentry filed a lawsuit against a quarrying operation that Tong was undertaking at the spiritual site, complaining that they were extracting too deep into the yin of the mountain, upsetting the earth pulses. The suit was settled by agreeing to give the Tong family some money not to dig deep into Eling, but only scratch away at the light or yang surface. The gentry viewed this compromise as respectful of the geomantic specificity of Eling. Three iterations of the proclamation warning the public not to dig into the dark yin (as this was thought to have catastrophic consequences for the eco-ontology of Eling) or make bricks were carved onto huge slabs of limestone positioned right in the middle of Eling, impossible for any visitors to miss. The proclamation clearly forbade "quarrying of stone, burning of kilns, or digging of ditches, so that the ground pulse may be cherished and handed down (intact) to all ages" (Little 1898, 148–51). But the US missionaries blithely disregarded this and extracted what they wanted from the yin. What the Marxist historian E. P. Thompson (1971) famously called a "moral economy" that allowed for social acceptance of the poor breaking laws during times of duress should be called a "moral ecology" here in Chongqing, as everyone supported the local attacks against the eco-ontological crimes committed by the Gamewells.

Some weeks after the June 6, 1886, attack, a group of gentry and literati from thirty-six neighborhoods in and around Chongqing sent a petition to Sichuan Governor General You Zhikai that was then sent on to Beijing. In it they express complete support for the protectors, reminding the Qing officials in Sichuan about the stone warnings at Eling and the earlier problems with wealthy extractors. Repeating much of the language from the proclamation of 1872, they lectured the officials: "Geomantic vectors from each county in eastern Sichuan merge at the center of Eling. In order to protect the life of these earth pulses it has previously been made public that any building on this site was strictly prohibited. However, Westerners [洋人] have been doing what they always do in cheating and bribing to buy this land; now they are putting up huge buildings on it. Digging way down into the yin has had a devastating impact on the earth pulses. . . . We can see the effect of this everywhere" (JWJA 4:955).[25]

On the fateful day when the locals confronted the missionaries, Mary Porter Gamewell was alone in the mission house and must have been terrified. However, she inflamed the people who had trekked up to Eling by responding to their demands for an explanation by brandishing a hunting rifle and pointing it at the crowd. Her husband, Frank Gamewell, returned home right after this and the couple was subsequently taken hostage and some of the mission property destroyed; the crowd then moved to attack several other houses of white people. The Gamewells were released over a week later, but only after the kidnappers received a promise from magistrate Guo that none of them would be prosecuted.

Within a week of the hostage crisis, a separate group of about thirty Chongqing gentry, students, and merchants submitted a memorial to the governor general providing the first comprehensive explanation of the attacks. The memorial is interesting for its focus on the rapaciousness of the Euro-whites, with one part of this having to do with their evident disdain for the local environment. From this Chongqing perspective, not only did the Euro-whites get what was coming to them, but the arrogant dismissal of Sichuanese political and geomantic sovereignty was certain to produce a mass response: "all the gentry and merchants in Chongqing," wrote the petitioners, "understand the Westerners [西人] to be the source" of the problem" (JWJA 4:951).

Composed by a group including the influential members of the gentry Zhao Zhongxu and Zhou Xinqi, the memorial started off reminding Qing officials about the centrality of Sichuan in Chinese political history: "the entirety of Sichuan is a region blessed by Heaven, and within Sichuan, Chongqing is an especially important place. If you take a historical perspective, whenever Sichuan was at peace, the whole of the Middle Realm [中国] was at peace. Similarly, whenever Chongqing was at peace, all of Sichuan was at peace" (JWJA 4:952–53). It moves on to describe the situation where Euro-whites recently built imposing edifices out of fired brick—"like forts"—overlooking three strategic locations in and around Chongqing: Eling, Tongluoxia, and Liangfengya. Each of these locations is depicted as central and sacred: "Endowed by heaven [天然]

as secure outposts." And owing to the importance of these three locations for Chongqing, it is "especially worrisome that Westerners have built huge stone constructions in each of these places in the name of Catholicism.... This has made the whites the enemy of all the local people" (JWJA 4:953).

The authors then ask the Qing officials to consider the reasons why the Western enemy would be building impregnable structures in these three strategic heights. It can only be because they want to "establish a military bombardment area.... It is well known that there are no markets nearby, and the land is of poor quality and vacant.... But the Westerners are hungry to extend their dominance to our markets, so military means would be a way to do that.... The Westerners are forcing us into a corner [咄咄逼人]" (JWJA 4:953).

The rest of the memorial continues in this vein, elaborating on the obnoxious anxiousness of the Speed Race(r): they "fight and rush to get whatever they want," "lie and cheat in negotiations over indemnities," and "bribe powerful people to get everything they desire." Whenever conflicts arise, "they completely refuse to discuss issues with us," going so far as to "continually violate the terms of the treaties." Whenever Sichuanese try to get the Euro-Americans to take their perspectives into account, "nothing we say has ever been able to stop them [从无片阻], so there's no point in trying to use reason." The authors reach their crescendo by warning Qing officials about impending disaster: "The court in Beijing is known far and wide for humane benevolence. And the gentry and common people try to abide by the conditions in the treaties. However, each and every Westerner demonstrates that rules don't apply to them, as evidenced by their insatiable greed [狼贪] in preying on and devouring [蚕食] our land" (JWJA 4:953–54).

As soon as the Gamewells were taken hostage, locals began hiking up to Eling to offer support, and rumors started to circulate about a mass uprising against Westerners in Chongqing. One additional impetus for the attack was the circulation of articles in the opium rooms and teahouses of Chongqing from the Shanghai newspaper *Shenbao* about the murders of indentured Chinese laborers in Wyoming and elsewhere in the United States by white terrorists, with the US refusing to pay any indemnity to the men's families or the Qing government (BFO 228/829, July 7, 1886).[26] Unlike previous instances, this time leaked information turned out to be more than mere rumors, and on July 1 locals took to attacking Western infrastructure in Chongqing. Within two days, nearly all the Euro-American property in the city was destroyed, including the Catholic church at Qixinggang. The church was also serving the MEP Catholics as a bank, holding 60,000 taels of silver in its vaults—all of which was seized by the insurrectionists (BFO 228/829, July 7, 1886). On July 2, the incident morphed into a pitched battle between anti-Christian locals and the shady Catholic convert and rich merchant Luo Yuanyi. By this time all the white people in Chongqing had fled—rather, they were ushered in carriages pulled by Chinese servants—to magistrate Guo's yamen for protection.

Goddess Worshippers

Although battles in metropolitan Chongqing continued for the next two weeks, the students' plea for a general uprising was answered most fervently in the countryside outside metropolitan Chongqing. The most important of the several rural incidents of July and August 1886 from the perspective of this book was the attack on the new Catholic church in Longshui town, Dazu county, about sixty miles northwest of Chongqing. The incident took place on July 20, on the evening right before the annual celebration of the goddess Lingguan.

The gazetteers wrote later that "in response to rumors of widespread attacks against Christian property, government soldiers led by Liang Fang wouldn't allow anyone to come near" the new Catholic church at Longshui. But as the crowd grew larger and larger, the affective resonance resulted in them being "worked up [憤激] like angry bees. . . . Right then and there it was clear that the crowd intended to trash and burn the church to the ground" (DX 1:360–61). The local militia was able to prevent the church from being completely razed, but it suffered considerable damage. Liang's subsequent report to the governor general on the incident expressed alarm at how spontaneous and bottom-up it was. "Normally a superior hands down orders to those below him in rank, but in the situation at Longshui town there were no leaders [無主] at all. Because of this it was impossible for us to single out any ringleaders for arrest" (DX 1:361). The noticeably acephalic nature of insurrection in Chongqing would soon be linked to a more organized rebel brotherhood, the Gelaohui (GLH).

The GLH Uprisings

Ground zero for the major uprising of 1890 in Chongqing prefecture was in the same county of Dazu. This uprising preceded the long wave of anti-Christian uprisings along the Yangzi River that took place from May to late September 1891. Nevertheless, each of the anti-Christian variants shared a template, and this led Euro-Americans in China and Qing officials to suspect that they weren't at all spontaneous, but rather the handiwork of one large organization with tentacles in many different places—the GLH. What was perplexing to most Westerners was that the GLH was thought to be an anti-Qing group exclusively and relatively unconcerned with Christian missions and the Euro-white presence in China.

In fact, for years Caucasians had been targeted as Enemy #1. The Second Chongqing Uprising of 1886 should have exposed this structure of disavowal as Euro-whites were the first to be attacked. The spark in 1890 was the same as in the 1886 uprising: the annual celebration of the goddess Lingguan. And the target of the protests was similar as well, what Archibald Little called the deliberately "anti–feng shui" Euro-white infrastructure. By the early summer of 1887 the MEP had started the process of rebuilding the church at Longshui—destroyed in the 1886 uprising—thanks to the large indemnity the French wrung from the Qing government. Desflèches's replacement as bishop, Father Pons, forced the local magistrate Qian Baotang to provide militia guards for each annual Lingguan celebration to maintain order. They turned out to be no match for the local insurrectionists, who sacked the church again in 1888. The MEP priests delayed the official opening of the rebuilt church until early 1890, and an official reopening mass took place on May 17. As the next Lingguan celebration grew near, Pons understandably grew concerned. But he made a tactical error by attempting to curtail the Lingguan celebration, mainly by trying to get local officials to not allow workers and peasants the traditional day off (Hu 1986, 69). When this wasn't successful, he again requested militia protection from Qian, but demanded that it consist of the more professional Qing soldiers. Pons got his way, while Qing soldiers, accompanied by European military "advisers," were also sent out into the countryside as a show of force against any potential troublemakers.

One week before the Lingguan celebration, a proclamation (檄文) was put up in the Longshui marketplace, referred to by Chinese historians as the "first Yu Dongchen proclamation." No original has ever been found, only a document that's been cobbled together from eyewitness sources.[27] As far as Yu Dongchen being the author of it, let alone not having the ability to write it, the illiterate Yu was incapable of even reading it. It proclaimed:

These French foreigners are enemies [寇仇] of all that we hold precious.... To get you all to pay attention to their destructive practices, our army of the people put out this proclamation. We found that white people closely resemble dogs and sheep. Although they claim to be like lions and tigers, this invincibility is a sham.... Fortunately, we've started to see the people rise up against them. We realized that there is no other way to change the Westerner, they have always acted like this—just gorging themselves, enjoying their time here at our expense, and stopping at nothing to maintain their life of disgusting luxury. An ox is slaughtered and the criminal is shielded from prosecution [杀牛窝贼]—the many crimes they commit, they do so with impunity. Catholic priests go to Qing offices anytime they want to change wrong into right and right into wrong [颠倒是非]. . . . The foreigners have ruled this whole area for more than ten years, enemies of humanity and Heaven [无法无天] alike. They will suffer the consequences of their actions. (Wang 1984, 90–91)

After the first mass mobilization was subdued by the government forces on August 4, 1890, Longshui remained peaceful, but forebodingly so. One week later a group of over a hundred protectors led by the part-time Sichuan opera singer Jiang Zanchen, but made up primarily of irregularly employed manure collectors, unemployed boat trackers, and destitute peasants, finished what the first wave had started (Davis 1977, 79). Among the hundred were Yu Dongchen and his three brothers, hailing from a poor peasant family who farmed twenty *mu* of inferior land at the foot of the Western Hills in Dazu. Poverty prevented any of the four brothers from receiving an education, and Dongchen and Cuiping had to work long hours as both manure collectors and coal miners, where they most likely came into contact with GLH for the first time (Chen 2010, 172).

Attacking in the middle of the night on August 11, 1890, the insurgents managed to raze the newly rebuilt Longshui Catholic church to the ground (Hu 1986, 68–70). There was no agreement on the accompanying violence; Catholic reports claimed that many Chinese converts were killed, while the local investigation could only confirm one death (JWJA 5:1449–58). On August 14 the uprising spread to the nearby town of Cangzhou, where a new MEP Catholic compound named Mapaochang had just been finished, built cheaply by Chinese converts. That same night Jiang Zanchen and some of his men arrived with several thousand people from Longshui and surrounding areas to try to sack the church and nearby seminary. Although they didn't succeed in doing so, they managed to destroy several smaller church buildings. Mapaochang was attacked twice more by a large group in September, and after the second attempt a group that included GLH members set up headquarters in the two Daoist temples in the market square and declared the town liberated from Euro-whites. From here they would go out into the surrounding countryside to get provisions, forcing Chinese converts to Catholicism to give them rice and other provisions. Wealthy non-Christian landowners were also urged to give food donations to support the uprising.

Attacks on Euro-white infrastructure and converts continued for the next several years, albeit at a slower pace. The Qing government did not try to pacify the protectors until a counterinsurgency offensive was undertaken in 1894 by Qing soldiers against Yu Doncheng's brother Cuiping, who mobilized a separate force of around five hundred to attack Catholics in and around Dazu. The better-equipped government forces eventually captured and decapitated Cuiping, while Dongchen's older brother Haiping surrendered. Dongchen, Jiang Zanchen, and other insurrectionists fled into the highlands area of Dazu's Western Hills. There they remained at large despite huge rewards put on their heads (DX 2:457). Mountains like Sichuan's Western Hills were construed by Climate Caucasianists solely in terms of what could be extracted out of them. In contrast, the eco-ontological protectors viewed these mountains as intra-active sanctuaries. Moreover, the more one ascended, the less likely the mountain land was owned by anyone. Therefore, the commons prevailed at the peak of the Western Hills and, liberated from Qing authority and Euro-American pollution, produced its own unique eco-ontological "high." This intensified the standard GLH opium high, as I will show in chapter 4.

Although the Qing forces thought they had clearly cut off the head of the anti-Catholic movement, skirmishes continued in Dazu until 1893, when Qing soldiers defeated a rebel force of four hundred under the command of Yu's younger brother Cuiping (JWJA 5:1486). Some of the four hundred retreated to the mountains and joined Yu and Jiang Zanchen.

The 1898 Dazu Uprising

The next major rebellion in Chongqing prefecture took place three years after the important insurgency in Chengdu in 1895, where there was significant GLH involvement. The difference with the new uprising was that shared rage against Catholics and Protestants in Sichuan effectively replacing Qing political authority slowly congealed into an ideological understanding that Sichuanese needed to protect themselves against both Euro-white invaders and Qing imperial rule. Just as in the Japanese decolonial experience of the 1860s and 1870s, when the insurgents in the Meiji Restoration synthetically joined white imperialism with corrupt Tokugawa rule, protectors in Sichuan were fated to fight two opponents.

The local spark that kept the long decade of uprisings alive in Chongqing prefecture was the arrest of Yu in April 1898. Local Qing officials took advantage of a GLH attack on the American Episcopal Church mission property in Jiangbei, right across the river from downtown Yuzhong, Chongqing, to frame

Yu as the mastermind and finally imprison him after seven years on the lam on April 17, 1898.[28]

According to the gazetteers, it was Yu's brother Zangchen who called for the jail break: "In less than twelve hours he mobilized many, many followers to help free his brother. When the official in charge of guarding Dongchen, Yang Yinkui, heard about Zangchen's plan he got so terrified that he made up a lame excuse to take a leave from his responsibility" (DX 2:458). With the warden of the Rongchang jail absent, Dongchen was easily freed, and he and his rescuers moved on to a welcoming party on the outskirts of Longshui on April 21. In front of a "crowd of thousands," Yu thanked the people for rescuing him and called for continuing the uprising that had only recently been pacified.

> The trashing of the Christian churches in 1890 had nothing to do with my own grudge [私仇], but everything to do with all of us together being really furious. I've already lost two brothers in this battle and one of my adopted boys has been cut down as well. It's no problem for me dealing with inconveniences like not having a house to come back to at night. . . . But one thing I do know I won't just stand around and watch is that during these last seven years we've seen the Christian wolves [教民狼子] turn greedier and greedier in taking over our land; I know now that their predatory appetites will never be satisfied [野心不足]. . . . The time's gonna come when all of you will make up your own minds not to accept this nonsense; when this moment finally arrives, you should trust the brotherhood to help you.

The gazetteers then described a maudlin pause after this populist oratory. Eliciting tears from the crowd, the locals then shifted affective register into an insurrectionary rage. "The situation quickly escalated to the point where the people were on the verge of rising up yet again. It was becoming obvious that only by risking death [死中] were they going to have another chance at preserving all the things in their land. . . . On the evening of May 15, a group formed to go to Rongchang to kidnap the French priest Hua Fangji and bring him back to Longshui town as a hostage" (DX 2:458).

Longshui was the center of the movement as it had been eco-ontologically protected and placed under "benevolent rule" by the rebels immediately after Yu's release. In what was to be a commonplace for the next six months, the rebels instituted price controls by ordering a 50 percent reduction on rice and other staples at the market. Moreover, all rebels were ordered not to steal or loot from Chinese converts. "Donations" were first requested from wealthy landlords; if the request was rejected, rebels moved to forcefully appropriate the requested sums (Felsing 1979, 122).

After the kidnapping of the MEP priest Fleury (Chinese name, Hua Fangji), the next significant event was Yu Dongchen's call (檄文) for a general uprising, distributed throughout the region. Chinese scholars agree on only one thing about the authorship: it was not written by Yu or any of his men.[29] But there's no doubting the fact that it encodes the protective tendency of the GLH at this time. This is how it read:

> For two hundred years we've lived off the grain grown from nature in the Emperor's land.... We've been brave [敢] enough to follow religions that originate from non-Han areas. But these minority groups are completely different from white people, who do their corrupt trading businesses by sea and spread Christianity along with it. Once here in China, they steal everything that our humble people have, from the food we eat to the clothes on our backs.... Some of us are victimized by their degenerate [淫] practices.... For example, they rape and harass our women and spread chaos among our people. They carelessly insult the Qing court and maintain control over officials. They are an occupying army [占據] in our major cities, which makes it easy for them to steal our money. They are like greedy children carving up a watermelon.... The Qing are attacking us with their soldiers, and at the same time, the predatory wolves and tigers that come from across the oceans are attacking Chinese innocents.
>
> We must convince all our neighbors that we are righteous people and will only assassinate Westerners and Chinese traitors. What is bizarre is that some people in the government regard us as the real enemy and want to aim their weapons at us. Each person who buys into this government lie will be considered no different from a white person.... Christians who are true believers [其奉教] should be able to feel penitent about the sins they have committed and change their immoral ways of the past. Donating money to our cause atones for past sins and allows sinners to be born again [自新] as righteous rebels. (DX 2:459–61)

This astonishing text precedes the slogan of the Boxer Rebellion ("Support the Qing and Wipe Out the Whites") as it moves beyond the narrower, ad hominem gentry attacks against Caucasians like the ones mentioned above. For in its global appeal to the "people of the world" it tries to construct a common sense beyond Western CO2loniality. There is a Fanonian sensibility to the GLH proclamation in that humble, common people have had enough of arrogant Euro-whites. Wretched? Maybe they are, but of the earth and mountains. Importantly, this earthly rootedness derides the white flight tendency of Euro-Americans. Unfortunately, for the Sichuanese wretched of the earth, the only way to cleanse the pollution brought by Climate Caucasianists is by temporarily appropriating their cold-blooded cruelty. But even here, the operationalization of GLH war must maintain the virtues so central to the group's ideology: benevolence and eco-ontological justice. Therefore, only those who have proven their unwillingness to live their lives in terms of a universal morality and humanity—Euro-white and Chinese Catholics—will be targeted for assassination. Demonstrating an awareness of the Christian tenets of introspection and spiritual struggle, they welcome Chinese Christians to rethink their conversion to the religion that has brought such suffering to so many nonconverted Chinese, insults to their gods and goddesses, and so much pollution to their sacred land. They suggest that the best first step toward proper Christian atonement would be in "donating money to our cause."

In these proclamations and in others made by Yu Dongchen, there are the contours of a local eco-ontology distinct from that of the extra-acting arrogance and extracting excesses of Climate Caucasianism (Chen 2010, 175–76). Yu claims above that it didn't bother him to be living without a stable home for seven years in nature, sometimes sleeping outside and at other times in huts in the mountains of the Western Hills. For Yu, the only way to repay the debt to the human and extrahuman life that had supported him for seven years while he was wanted by the Qing and the Euro-white missionaries was to try to eliminate the polluting force—ecclesiastical Superpredators—that was threatening the existence of this ecology. Therefore, in addition to the notions of justice and benevolence foregrounded in the GLH eco-ontology at this time, there is also a salient emphasis on debt—humans are indebted to that which nurtures and gives them life: gods, goddesses, ancestors, and the natural environment. Although illiterate peasants like Yu generally believed, as he says above, that human life is sustained by the "Emperor's land," the attacks on the Qing, in particular, and the lèse-majesté dismissal of the dynastic system that quickly became a focus, established a more horizontal network of debt and intra-action. In the terms established in the introduction, there is an intra-active, other-determination here that couldn't be more different from the extra-active self-determination of the Euro-white Speed Race(r).

In less than two months, approximately ten thousand fighters joined, and appropriations and attacks continued in eastern and southern Sichuan during the summer, fall, and winter of 1898. The rebel campaign caught the local Qing officials off guard with its widespread popularity and its strict discipline.

Their popular support was doubtless enhanced as they reportedly stuck to their promise of only accepting donations from rich gentry, and incidents of looting Chinese Christian residences were rare (*North China Herald*, November 14, 1898). This contrasted with the uprisings in 1886 and 1890 and can only be explained by the mainstreaming of GLH ritual and discipline among the Dazu rebels. Hostile Euro-Americans grudgingly conceded their moral and military discipline (Zhao 2006, 99–100).

Enjoying strong support from Sichuanese of all social classes, the rebel campaign spread quickly in July and August. Another reason for their popularity had to do with Yu's rebels following GLH protocol when moving into a new area: formally announcing their arrival beforehand, inviting all the local GLH leaders for an initial meeting, and then inviting every GLH cadre to a lavish banquet and opium-filled party—all of it paid for by money from rich landlords. In liberated areas, life went on more or less as usual, albeit with the perks of no government taxation and the firm encouragement by GLH leaders to merchants to keep the prices of staple goods as low as possible. Qing officials, soldiers, and militia were the only ones prevented from entering autonomous areas (Felsing 1979, 126). However, the easy liberations of government territory and the ensuing smoking parties became increasingly less frequent as the Qing government—pressured by the French legation in Beijing who wanted the MEP priest Fleury returned alive regardless of the cost—had no choice but to dispatch its armies against the rebels.

In September and October 1898, fierce battles between Qing soldiers and Yu's rebels resulted in military stalemate. At this point, the government authorities thought the time was right to cut a deal with the rebels. In mid-November the commander of the Qing forces in east Sichuan, Reng Xifen, was ordered to begin peace negotiations. He sent his general Zhou Wanshun and the Qing official Ding Ling to begin negotiating with Yu (DX 2:461). This offer succeeded in exacerbating tensions between the different groups, especially between Jiang Zanchen and Yu Dongchen. Jiang was willing to accept almost any terms of surrender, while Yu Dongchen was "unwilling to consider surrender at all and refused to stop fighting" (DX 2:462).

After days of discussion, the opposing sides finally hammered out surrender terms. Nevertheless, there was a weeklong silence from Yu's camp regarding the terms of the final agreement. He had begun to suspect that he'd been betrayed by one of the men from Jiang Zanchen's group, Zhou Wanshun. So, Yu kidnapped Zhou and held him with the MEP priest Fleury in the now-crowded hostage holding area. Beijing was forced to dispatch one of their top military men, General Wang Zichun, to Sichuan, who carried out a new campaign against the protectors (DX 1:462). Yu Dongchen was forced to surrender on January 17, 1899, and Fleury, reunited with his Chinese convert concubine, himself brought Yu's surrender statement to Wang's headquarters (Han 1965, 95). Yu and his men were led away in chains, while Wang's assistant wrote up a memorial to Beijing describing the campaign. The memorial concluded with the recommendation that the "most qualified judge should decide how to adjudicate the situation" (DX 1:463).

———

White Dude's Burden
(The Indifference That Makes a Difference)

Europeans enter into the borders of Asia for the most part with a feeling of indifference or contempt for all that constitutes the life and pride of an Asiatic.—Rutherford Alcock, *The Capital of the Tycoon*, vol. 2, 1863

Arguably the most famous white-guy-in-Japan narrative is *Madame Chrysan-thème*, by the French naval officer Pierre Loti (real name, Louis M. J. Viaud). It tells the autobiographical story of Loti arriving in the Nagasaki treaty port in the summer of 1885 with the intention of hooking up with "a little yellow-skinned female with black hair and cat's eyes. Not much bigger than a doll" (Loti 1985, 7–8; citations to follow). After docking the French warship, Loti hopped into a *jinrikisha* taxi pulled by two "coolies eight or ten years of age . . . with little monkeyish faces" (in other words, neotenized and rawfared) who took him to a brothel to get "married" for two months (25). With the aid of a local pimp Kangerô, he chose a fifteen-year-old for the cheap price "of about eighteen or twenty dollars a month . . . a charming plaything . . . like a china ornament" (46, 49). A few hours later, after Kangerô had leased a house for Loti, the unnamed sex worker appeared with her mother, aunts, and several other young women, arousing Loti's indignation. In a panic he protested to Kangerô that, on second thought, "She is too white . . . I wished for a yellow one" (59).

There are two reasons for Loti's annoyance. First, the skin color of the girl apparently turns out to be too close to his own; the color line of racial capitalism here dictates an optimal situation where the owner is snowy white and the owned sickly and decadently yellow. Second and most important is that, as Loti states clearly, the pimp Kangerô shouldn't have "brought her to me before

friends and neighbors of both sexes, instead of showing her to me discreetly"
(59). Loti understood he was paying for the privatized pleasure of extracting a
girl. Following the presupposition of commodity capitalism, he assumed his
"wife" has been kidnapped and severed from what Marx calls "socio-natural . . .
relations" (1977a, 165). Instead, she shows up accompanied by family and inti-
mates and flaunts these very relations. Loti's freak-out insists capitalism install
what Jacques Lacan called "extimacy," or a walled-off separation eliminating all
connectivity (Miller 2008). Few of us want to know anything about the environmentally destructive practices of extracting African coltan that our com-
puters and cell phones require or the bad labor and environmental conditions
in China where the components are made. We want affordable shiny new machines and turn our backs on the various forms of life and non-life sacrificed
to bring them forth. Like Loti, we participants in commodity capitalism want
to extract a commodity fully "liberated" from what was required to produce it.

To complete Marx's famous formula about commodity fetishism, for Loti
the buyer, the reified, zombie-like exchange of money for commodities "assumes the fantastic form" of a relation between living entities (1977a, 165).
"Fantastic" because it miraculously turns the world upside down, where intimate qualities between living things enmeshed in their sociopolitical and natural environments appear as isolated quantities between nonliving things: commodities and money. What Marx calls "society and nature"—the dense web
of relations required to support life—is what I am calling the eco-ontological
commune that the Japanese sex worker shares with human &bjects, deities, and
entities like built structures, water, trees, and the Nagasaki biome. Established
by Descartes's ego-ontology of separation and Francis Bacon's mechanistic
reduction of all entities to isolated substances, the eco-ontologies this young
woman brings to her "wedding" with Loti in Nagasaki must be denied and
socio-natural beings reduced to quantities of fungible rawfare for white owners
of capital: yellow skin, doll-like, cat-eyed, and so on. These are the fossilized
properties of the seventeen-year-old girl named Kiku Loti extracts to his satis-
faction the next day.[1] While these properties where once small, inconsequential
parts of complicated living entities, capitalist commodification "fantastically"
cleanses the complicated life out of what is to be bought, leaving only the properties to be extracted.

In volume one of *Capital* Marx insists that for commodity fetishism to operate successfully, the owner of capital must actively ignore, or maintain an
indifference to the relational whole that produces the commodity.[2] *Madame
Chrysanthème* shows Loti reveling in this indifference. As he tools around Nagasaki, Loti's encounters function primarily to provoke reminiscences about

his own youth in France. When they don't, his impressions of Nagasaki are judged on whether they correlate to the commodified images of Japan that Loti was familiar with from Europe—on porcelain, on fans, and on Japanese erotic scrolls. These images of Japan were themselves effects of the clipper-coolie captive-contraband-capital circuit. Even Kiku is constantly compared to girls and women Loti has bought previously in the Ottoman Empire and the South Pacific. With few curiosities and fewer contingencies in Loti's experience in Japan, there is very little proof of "human" existence here. When Marx claims that living, breathing humans are killed off in the commodity exchange, this includes the owners of capital as well—neither the erstwhile lively buyer nor the bought escape being extinguished by capitalism; the main subject is $ubject.

Loti demonstrates how he had forfeited his humanity and morphed into a Superpredator ("no conscience, no empathy") in several ways. First, he refuses to recognize human life for what it is when he denies that his Japanese sex servant is a reasoning human being. He writes: "I am almost persuaded that she thinks" (1985, 63). When Kiku threatens to become something other than dehumanized rawfare, he quickly disavows it: "It is a hundred to one that she has no thoughts whatever" (74). Symptomatically, Loti is most drawn to Kiku when she is asleep and hardly breathing, "like a dead fairy" (120). Indeed, in this state she returns to her condition as a supinestupefiedyellow. The only encounter that elicits any emotions for Loti (and the only one that temporarily disrupts his completely alien and alienated existence) is one mediated by nationalism: his French friend Yves. However, it's symptomatic that this is largely defined by jealousy and masculine competition. When Loti starts to sense that Yves is flirting with Kiku, he gets slightly agitated before brushing it off: "I might even feel anxious . . . if it were not a matter of perfect indifference to me" (91). Although Yves comes close to eliciting competition and threat, the Japanese people evoke no emotional response at all in Loti. They are "monkeys" and "dogs," "tiny yellow persons with narrow eyes and no brains" (98, 272). After a month of having sex with the teenager, he depicts their situation thus: "At no time have I ever given myself the trouble to pretend the slightest affection for her, and a certain coldness even has grown up between us" (123). Finally, when Loti hears that his ship has been ordered to deploy to southern China, he wonders if he would feel anything at all about splitting up with Kiku. Ultimately, he is greatly relieved that he doesn't and even more relieved that she doesn't: "no feeling passed through that little brain, that little heart" (320).

Loti's alienated existence in Nagasaki takes place within a lively environment composed of various flora and fauna, spirits, humans, music, built structures, sea and spring water, and the rapidly changing weather during the rainy season in western Japan. This elicits nothing but increasing dispassion from Loti, who had tried to learn a few phrases in Japanese before arriving in Nagasaki, albeit ones that were required to facilitate the cheap purchase of a sex servant—"take to the pimp"; "how much for one month?"; and so on. But once shacked up with Kiku he refuses even this: "Since we've been living together . . . I've neglected studying Japanese—so much so that I feel it completely impossible for me to ever be interested in it again" (122; translation modified).[3] Two pages later, he again declares his "absolute indifference" to her and her eco-ontology.

Marx warned us about how erstwhile "vibrant matter" (Bennett 2010) gets demoted to rawfare and treated with indifference or disdain by capital. As Jonathan Beller points out in *The Message Is Murder*, this "indifference makes a difference" (2017). I would only add that the indifference toward the sociopolitical and natural environment that it leeches off makes *all the difference* for the reproduction of the racial capital in this age of Climate Caucasianism. Capitalism must consign as much of human and extrahuman life as it can to the condition of cheap rawfare, outside the sites (factories, workshops, institutions) where surplus is stolen from labor (Moore 2015). Therefore, capital denies the importance of, and thereby discounts the actual cost of, the rawfare crucial for social reproduction—women, food, energy, people of color, the atmosphere, and so on. If it isn't successful in keeping these human and extrahuman entities down, denigrated, and unpaid, this will raise what Marxists call capitalism's "value composition" and force wages and salaries to go up in factories, workshops, and institutions—seriously diminishing profits. To rephrase Moore and Patel, "to demand that capitalism pay" for the work and energy contributions of rawfare "is to call for an end to capitalism" (2017, 135).

Recalling the analysis of Marx I put forward in the introduction, the reproduction of commodity capitalism requires extra-active indifference both to the relations between people and the intra-active relations all humans have with nature. Loti brags about this indifference throughout *Madame Chrysanthème*. But he was not a "lone wolf" psychopathic extractiv-eye/I. Most white men in Asia shared Loti's modus operandi. Therefore, like "gorge-us" Euro-American men in Japan and ecclesiastical Superpredators in China, Loti's narcissism briefly led him to hope that Kiku would experience sadness about his departure, but ultimately, he is "unconcerned" whether she does or not (1985, 318). His only real feelings are for the eighteen suitcases filled with commodities he has bought in Nagasaki (310). Pleasure has been extracted, and Loti takes white flight to another site of nonreciprocal plunder and purchase, deepening Climate Caucasianism.

Rudyard Kipling's white man of benevolent Euro-American imperialism carries no burden here, leading me to rename him a "white dude," drawing on the utter nonchalance of this popular culture figure of late twentieth-century masculinity. The character traits used to depict white dudes are stoic detachment, principled apathy, and a studied cynical distance. Perhaps their main contribution to Anglophone mass culture in the last forty years is the *cri de coeur* of "Whatever!" Although recently displaced by "It's all good," this vernacular points to the ideological atomism underlining an absence of relationality or intra-action—nothing external to the white dude can impact him in any way. The obverse is even more important: none of the effects his actions have on externalized human and extrahuman life is of any concern to him—his is a *whateveristic* indifference.

The one exception to whateverism is encoded in the white dude's second recognized passionate appeal: "Party on!" Pleasure temporarily displaces whateverism, because with pleasure comes the need for externalized objects to solicit and satisfy it. Therefore, the encounter with objects that pleasure requires contains the potential to disrupt the dude's solipsism; it is only at this point of appropriation that relationality is undeniable. As Mbembe writes about Euro-white predation in the colony: "the colonizer is only conscious of self in the enjoyment of the thing that he . . . possesses" (2001, 189). Therefore, whateverism has to kick in immediately after pleasure is taken to disavow any consciousness of the "self" whose existence contingently depended on some living "other," even if this other is nonwhite rawfare. The function of whateverism is to return the white dude to his extra-active distance from the eco-ontological environment that sustains both his life and the life of the pleasurable object of possession, returning the latter to the condition of a fossilized thing.

Pierre Loti was a proto-dude. And in his extra-action over and against Nagasaki, Japan, he was similar to almost every other Euro-male in—as Rutherford Alcock, the British diplomat in China and Japan, put it—his "indifference . . . for all that constitutes the life" of Asian people. As we have already seen in this book, indifference could often morph suddenly into what Carol Anderson calls "white rage" when white dudes' right to "Party on!" was denied (2017). This normally happened when immediate access to extractable entities was impeded or covered over—what can be called, after Kathryn Yusoff, the White Dude's "overburden" (2018, 28). So, we need to keep alert to the ways in which indifference, nonreciprocal pleasure, and murderous rage are connected reactions to the same dynamic of extra-action. Atomistic white dudes can become first person shooters with minimal provocation. In terms of this book, when indifference turns into rage this becomes the "no conscience, no empathy" of white Superpredation.

Epistemological extra-action and ego-ontological extimacy were crucial for white men in East Asia. Relinquishing them meant racial regress, a terrifying enticement into purportedly "decadent" Asian immorality, and entropic dissipation. In Japan, some earnest Western men accepted positions in the 1870s working for the Meiji government as consultants for capitalist modernization, but were derided as race traitors and ostracized by Euro-American businessmen who maintained a principled self-interest in affairs of trade and an extra-active detachment (except for their sexual and other servants) from Japanese people and the various eco-ontologies that sustained them. In China, treaty port life was even more racially segregated than in Japan. While it is true that many white Protestant missionaries were enthusiastic participants in the white man's burden, on the ground in Asia many Catholic and some Protestant missionaries remained separate from local Chinese and Japanese by their refusal to learn languages, and spatially distant out of racial disdain. I will argue that this surprising indifference to the plight of East Asians on the part of many Euro-white missionaries joined with the self-interested, solipsistic attitude of Euro-white capitalists. The only cumbersome hardship (or burden) lay in convincing everyone else in Asia that whateverism and extra-active separation should be universal. In other words, capitalist white dudes attempted to upload insouciant indifference from an empirical on-the-ground (dis)passion to a general law of individualism through transcendental production. The white dude's burden as self-interested and securely walled off emerged as the personalized expression of Climate Caucasianism in late nineteenth-century East Asia but metastasized into a universalized insistence that consumerist individualism, domination of nature, and the Protestant "personal responsibility" were the ideal subjective condition for all humans. This transformation has been catastrophic for our shared planetary existence.

3

Queer Parenting

Civilization isn't about the splendor of the ruling house, or the lavish possessions of the rich; rather it is based on righteousness. . . . Actually, I can't tell the difference between what white people say is savage and what they say is civilized. If the West is really civilized, then its behavior toward underdeveloped countries should be based on love and mercy. But that's not at all the case. In fact, the more the country is underdeveloped the more violent and cruel the West acts toward it. . . . This should be seen as true savagery.—Saigô Takamori, *Nanshû ôikun*, 1874

It's wild to think that so many Genyôsha heroes who coated the history of the Meiji period with such violence and terror studied Chinese at the school of this queer [変わり] woman Takaba Ran.—Yumeno Kyûsaku, *Yumeno Kyûsaku zenshu*, vol. II, 1936

We saw in chapter 1 how the rogue samurai Kiyokawa Hachirô was trying to mobilize principled protectors (志士) in southwestern Japan in 1861 to join him in bouncing Euro-whites out of Japan to return the emperor to power by overthrowing the Tokugawa clan. While in Fukuoka he met one of the leaders of the Fight the Whites! movement there, Hirano Kuniomi (1828–64). Hirano had previously been radicalized by two years spent in Edo studying Mito School thought and by a trip to Satsuma to meet Saigô Takamori in 1859. After getting energized by his talks with Kiyokawa, he became involved with the failed armed uprising in Kyoto to restore the emperor to political power in April 1862, the Teradaya Incident. Hirano himself plotted an anti-Tokugawa action called the Ikuno Uprising of 1863, for which he was imprisoned. He was unable to survive the harsh conditions and died in jail in 1864 (Harootunian 1970, 310–12).

Hirano was the Fukuoka leader of the main Fight the Whites! group in western Japan from 1860 to 1866, the Revere the Emperor Group (勤王党). This outlaw organization was most active in the western Tosa and Choshu domains, and the Fukuoka branch formed around a group of radical students at the alternative to the Chikuzen (Fukuoka) domain academy, the Kamei school (GYSS, 151). One of these students was Takaba Ran (1831–91), the main teacher of the founding Genyôsha members and close friend of Hirano (Doi 1988, 64–79). Born female in a mid-rank samurai family, Takaba was raised from age ten as a male by her optometrist father and received an education as a doctor, along with the samurai privilege of bearing arms after her father successfully petitioned for permission to the Chikuzen daimyo (Nagahata 1997, 60–65). The domain authorities read the Sino-Japanese character 乱 of her given name as "Osamu," which is a common male Japanese name. Her friends and family all rendered 乱 with the different Japanese voicing of "Ran" which also means "chaos" or "upheaval."

The Genyôsha company history described Takaba in 1919 as someone who was "angry at being born a woman," but who was doing just fine transgendered—they were never seen without a sword and wearing their hair shaved and tied back, "like a man [男子のごとし]" (GYSS, 157).

Warm accounts of Takaba by their students reveal that Fukuoka residents didn't know what to make of the gender-queer sword-wielding scholar, who had a "petite body like a woman, but a booming voice like a man" (GYSS, 156). Genyôsha founding member Narahara Itaru reminisced that this troubling of western Japanese gender norms "scared the shit out of people" in Fukuoka (GY #4, 3). Living up to the name "chaos," Takaba seemed to relish the confusion their appearance elicited in people. Like everyone connected to Genyôsha in its first two decades, Takaba preferred to direct this against the rich and politically powerful. The following is a popular Genyôsha anecdote about Takaba circa 1880 that illustrates this:

> Takaba, crossed-dressed as a man as usual, went out to visit an ex-samurai politician at his mansion. The entrance to the mansion had such a huge gate that it impressed everyone who saw it. . . . Takaba finally arrived and was asked: "Takaba sensei, why don't you come on in?" If Takaba was a normal samurai of low rank she would have to bow and mouth bullshit like, "thank you so much for graciously inviting this loser into your mansion." Instead, Takaba declined in her standard fuck-you [反骨心] way: "Your entrance is too small for me; my balls [肝っ玉] are so big I'll get stuck halfway through." (GY #4, 3)

FIGURE 3.1. Illustration of Takaba Ran from the 1880s (Ishitaki Toyomi 1997).

Presumably, when Takaba matriculated to the Kamei school in 1844, the entrance was wide enough to allow their super-sized testicles to pass through. We can say with more certainty that the educational and political environment in western and southwestern Japan was in crisis, provoked by news of the First War for Drugs in China and rumors of Euro-whites planning to bring a similar scourge to Japan.[1] Unlike most schools in Japan at this time, Kamei refused the official Tokugawa curriculum based on the neo-Confucianism of Zhu Xi. Instead, Kamei offered a mix of Ogyû Sorai (1666–1728) and the Japanese nativism of Motoori Norinaga (1730–1801), which emphasized the student's feeling and passion. By the late 1840s, the Kamei teachers consolidated a new reading protocol that insisted on a passionate engagement with Chinese canonical works, what Doi Atsuko calls an "anti-system pedagogy" (1988, 49–50). Ishitaki Toyomi argues that from the time Takaba first started tutoring students privately in 1856, they brought this subversive pedagogy to Chinese canonical texts like *The Classic of Rites* (礼记) and *The Classic of History* (史记) (1997, 211–12). Considered the expert in politics among all the younger scholars at the Kamei school, Takaba incited an intensely committed sensibility among students, where the teacher demanded that the study of Chinese humanism must lead students to a direct involvement with contemporary politics in Fukuoka and beyond (KTM, 52–53).

Therefore, within the standard structure of mind-numbing repetition of Chinese canonical texts (Takaba was known to recite long sections from *The Classic of History* and *Mencius* with her eyes closed), students were encouraged to come up with their own personal analysis. Not only did this flatten the requisite hierarchy in neo-Confucian pedagogy, where students were expected to deferentially mime the interpretation of the master sensei, Takaba also pushed the students to explain how the Chinese canon was going to guide them in their own practice of transforming an unjust society (Nagahata 1997, 81–82). Relying on classical Chinese humanism as the base, the Daoism of Laozi and Zhuangzi displaced Zhu Xi's neo-Confucian orthodoxy, and Japanese nativist poetics and passion joined Ogyû Sorai's emphasis on action and invention. A short introduction to French republican thought was also used. This global curriculum of Daoism, Japanese nativism, and an explosive hermeneutic approach to the humanist Chinese canon welcomed the young men[2] Takebe Kôshirô, Ôchi Kashirô, Shindô Kiheita, Narahara Itaru, and Hakoda Rokusuke (Itô 1971, 43). The man who would emerge as the de facto leader of Genyôsha after 1888, Tôyama Mitsuru (1855–1944), stayed at the school for over three years, making lifelong friendships there (GYSS, 152).

Takaba worked at Kamei for a decade before starting their own school in 1870, quitting Kamei to devote full time to the new school and the family optometry practice (Itô 1971, 43).[3] As all the pioneering Genyôsha members were educated at this school, Takaba would be referred to around Fukuoka as the "birth parent of Genyôsha" (GY #1, 3). By all accounts they were a loving but disciplining parent and insisted that the young men all follow a few basic rules or risk suspension: (1) no fighting or horsing around during lessons, but after class brawling is allowed in the martial arts area only; (2) no sex between students; (3) drinking is encouraged, but not to the point of intoxication; (4) all housework duties are divided up evenly; (5) all possessions of any kind are to be shared equally (KTM, 59). As far as the last insistence on producing a commons where no private property was allowed, Takaba tried to set an example that whenever something was brought to eat or drink from outside, it was immediately divided up among all the students. In this respect, teachers were no different from students in the confines of the school, officially registered in Fukuoka under the name "Cultivating Humanity [人参畑]."

J-hãd Reset

Genyôsha emerged directly from the defeats of several armed samurai uprisings of 1874–77 against the new Meiji oligarchs and their burgeoning repressive state apparatus. There were multiple motivations behind these uprisings, but I will limit my analysis to explaining Genyôsha's role in them. For the most part, scholars have been dismissive of the anti-systemic energies that drove these uprisings, exhibiting what Linebaugh and Rediker call a "severity of history" that routinely denigrates radical political movements (2000, 158). If Harney and Moten are correct when they write that "Revolution will come in a form we cannot yet imagine," then this can help us understand why the radical impulses of these armed movements have been misrecognized (2013, 11).[4] In my view, there is much to be redeemed in these uprisings, not the least of which is how they folded into and intensified the Autonomy and People's Rights (自由民権) movement (APR). As I will show, many of the surviving combatants rechanneled their antigovernment energies from armed rebellion into the largely peaceful mass APR mobilizations. In fact, for two years, from the summer of 1875 and the first meeting of the APR in Osaka until the fall of 1877, some militants were involved in both, shuttling back and forth between the armed and unarmed APR movement. Several of Takaba's students participated in both forms of political struggle. Finally, a key faction within Genyôsha never fully "matured" from armed resistance into peaceful political work and carried out assassinations well into the 1890s.

After the successful overthrow of the Tokugawa warlord government and the restoration of the emperor (christened with the reign name of Meiji) to the center of political power in April 1868, the new oligarch leaders made several promises, one of which was to decrease the heavy agricultural tax. However, when taxes stayed the same and then went up, farmers rose up against wealthy landlords and the Meiji leaders (Kim 2007, 293–94). One of the largest of these was the Fukuoka Peasant Uprising of June 1873, which involved upward of 300,000 combatants. In addition to the demand for lower taxes, farmers in and around Fukuoka protested the increase in unpaid, forced corvée labor required by the Meiji state, as well as the oligarchs' refusal to provide financial support when they ordered that the new prefectures put in school buildings and universal primary education. In other words, the peasants realized they were being forced to bear the heaviest burden in installing the infrastructure for Euro-American style polities: schools, roads, bridges, and police stations. When a huge group of peasants broke down the gate to Fukuoka castle to force a meeting with local authorities on June 10, 1873, the police opened fire on the protestors and wounded several. Four of the peasant leaders were subsequently decapitated and an astonishing 64,000 imprisoned or fined. Three of Takaba's students joined the peasants in struggle: Hakoda Rokusuke, Miyagawa Taiichirô, and Ôchi Kashirô (Doi 1988, 162–64; GY #11, 2). This was the first concrete effect of the "anti-system pedagogy" that became standard at Takaba's Cultivating Humanity school, but it would not be the last. It's important to underline that all but one of the twenty or so students at Cultivating Humanity at this time were former samurai of low rank, and it was the customary duty of this group to pacify peasant revolts and crack down on protests. For the sons and grandsons of this erstwhile samurai police force to now be fighting shoulder-to-shoulder with peasants in shared political struggle was a remarkable political shift.

In October 1873 a series of high-profile resignations from the oligarch government in Tokyo sent shock waves throughout Japan. While space doesn't allow a full discussion of the causes for the resignations, it will help to go back to some of the events surrounding both the Meiji Restoration and the US invasion of Japan. The first is the indignation that some Japanese experienced when they realized how Euro-whites had racially profiled them as "yellow," meaning "cowardly, deceitful and degenerate" (Mamiya 2010). Although the samurai were given their own distinct profile, many Euro-whites continued to behave as if the contents of Western raciology could be deployed for every interaction with Japanese people. The denigration of yellows in this raciology (sickly, weak, situationally flip-flopping) was especially infuriating for the soldiers, many of whom possessed a self-image that was the polar opposite of this: fiercely loyal, righteously moral, and powerfully resolute. While the expulsionist Fight the Whites! movement had myriad motives for action, into the 1860s the increasing awareness of the rawfared inferior racial status assigned to Japanese people by Euro-whites should be understood as a main one.

Indeed, anti-whiteness figured prominently in the first phase of the Boshin civil war of December 1867–March 1868 against the Tokugawa government. Some in the pro-emperor forces construed the Tokugawa leaders as a surrogate for white Westerners, both of whom were seen as immoral, devious, and obsessed with power for its own sake. I discussed in chapter 1 how Euro-Americans were constantly threatened by rogue samurai, and as the Boshin War drew much of its energy from the ubiquitous "Fight the Whites!" rallying cry, it was unsurprising that Japanese-on-White attacks occurred. Various pro-emperor fighters took advantage of the chaos to attack white enemies of Heaven.[5] Euro-American embassies were routinely targeted, with the most sustained assaults coming in January and February 1868. After a large-scale attack on the British embassy was repelled on March 23, 1868, the emperor's court in Kyoto took the unprecedented step five days later of warning any future attackers that their samurai rank would be stripped from them (Cortazzi 1985, 125–26). What followed in the next five to six years in Japan can't be fully grasped without factoring in this antipathy toward white Westerners and, for some, full-blown opposition to Climate Caucasianism. Finally, the refusal of the Euro-American raciology database had the effect of carving out an antithetical—and in some cases, equally fantastic—schema construing Japanese men as unquestionably righteous and selflessly benevolent.

This fierce critique of Euro-America in the Fight the Whites! movement is usually assumed to have dissipated with the establishment of the new Meiji state, but it is more correct to state that, following Raymond Williams, anti-whiteness became temporarily residual (1978, 121–27). However, we will see its transformed emergence again in the political crisis of fall 1873, and then once again in the 1880s as a weapon to confront the dominance of Euro-American derivations in economic, ecological, juridical, and gendered spheres. To begin to elaborate on this, let's review the famous Charter Oath promulgated at the enthronement of the new Japanese emperor on April 7, 1868. A funeral of sorts for the top-down hierarchy of Tokugawa caste/status society, the first article of the oath seemed to call for immediate democratization by stating that "Public assemblies of debate shall be widely established and all matters decided through open public discussion [公議輿論]." The second article leveled the previous caste/status system by insisting that "high and low shall be made equal [上下を 一心にして] in carrying out affairs of the state." Paralleling the egalitarian impulse of the pro-emperor forces in the battle against the Tokugawa government (and Euro-whites), the oath declared in the third article that "Commoners, no less than civil and military officials, shall all be allowed to pursue their own paths" (JGD, 8; translation modified). What might be surprising is that the egalitarianism salient here derives almost exclusively from East Asian sources, especially the crucial phrase 公議輿論, or "democratic debate."[6] But it was soon obvious to the mushrooming opposition movement that the Tokyo oligarchs were turning their backs on these egalitarian promises.

After assuming power in spring 1868, the oligarch leaders rallied around the emperor and faced the same dilemma as postcolonial states would much later: What should be the appropriate mix of Japanese and Euro-American forms of government and society? In only five short years, and after a delegation of these leaders returned from a fact-finding mission led by the oligarch Iwakura Tomomi to the US and Europe from December 1871 until mid-1873, the decision was made by Ôkubo Toshimichi (1832–78), Itô Hirobumi (1841–1909), Kido Takayoshi (1833–77), and Iwakura to move ahead with a predominantly Euro-American template.[7] Several of the leaders who returned to Japan by mid-1873 had largely reversed their critical stance on Euro-America, which perplexed Saigô Takamori (1828–77) for one. Others in the caretaker government (留守政府) who had run Japan in 1872 and 1873 were disappointed by the returnees' cowardly submission to the white West and frustrated that they were too intimidated to push for a revision of the Unequal Treaties imposed by asymmetric warfare. When the gathering storm around the perceived insult of the new Emperor Meiji by the Korean monarchy left the returnees Kido and Ôkubo refusing to address the issue, several of the new leaders resigned on October 24 and 25, 1873: the leader of the successful military campaign against the Tokugawa, Saigô; Justice Minister Etô Shimpei (1834–74); and two of the loudest voices calling for more democracy, Itagaki Taisuke (1837–1919) and Gotô Shôjiro (1838–97) (Kimura 2010). Although it is difficult to assemble a consensus position among those who resigned (and the factional disputes can also be understood through personality clashes), Itagaki, Gotô, and Etô would soon afterward push for more power sharing and an expanded public sphere for debating the important issues of the day. A critique developed in several places in western and southwestern Japan that held that the sudden pro-Western shift of those returning with Iwakura contradicted the decolonial ideals of the Meiji transformation. Like the Black Jacobins in the Haitian

Revolution seventy years earlier, who C. L. R. James insisted "brought themselves" emancipation through revolutionary sacrifice, some anti-oligarch activists decried how the heavy price paid in the war against the Tokugawa and the Euro-white powers was quickly forgotten in the new pro-Western pragmatism of Kidô and Ôkubo (1980, 85–86). So, several of the departed opted to return to their hometowns to refresh what was understood to be both a social revolution designed to horizontally flatten vertical Tokugawa society—Gotô vowed to "totally destroy the feudal caste system"[8]—and a restoration of the sublime position of the emperor, resulting in formal equality for all Japanese (JTS, vol. 1, 27). It was obvious to many in the anti-oligarch faction that this revostation (combining "revolution" with "restoration") of 1868 needed a reboot.

Party Time

First, Itagaki, Gotô, Etô, and Okamoto Kenzaburo and Komuro Shinobu formed Japan's first major political association of the Meiji era in January 1874—the Patriot Society (愛国社). Next, on January 17 they submitted a memorial to the remaining leaders in Tokyo, the "Proposal to Establish a Popularly Elected Assembly." Published the next day, this proposal jump-started a national debate with its call for the immediate adoption of an elected parliament. Beginning with the egalitarian provocation cited from Emperor Meiji's 1868 Charter Oath, the Patriot Society rejected the argument prevalent among the remaining oligarchs and their elite allies that a democratic assembly would just be an amalgamation of "the people's stupidity and ignorance." Throwing down a revostationary challenge, they asserted, "despotic officials haven't shown themselves to be superior in any way to popular opinion [輿論公議]." Some Patriot Society intellectuals actually inverted the despots' elite disdain and ranked popular opinion above oligarchic policy. But all agreed that there was no alternative going forward: "Democracy is the only way to save our country from ruin" (JTS, vol. 1, 86–89).[9] Next, the Patriot Society put out a platform that promised equal rights to all people: "When heaven gave birth to the people, it granted them inalienable rights, . . . We vow to fight for these rights that are endowed by heaven [天賦] to all people equally" (JTS, vol. 1, 85).[10] This platform would set the terms for a debate that would prove to be just as contentious as the discussion about how to deal with the perceived rebuff of Emperor Meiji by the Korean monarchy in the summer and fall 1873, the "heaven grants equal rights to all debate [天賦人権論]."

While it is true that the most pressing reason for the high-profile resignations was the "Subjugate Korea argument," wherein Saigô, Itagaki, and Etô echoed earlier calls to dispatch a mission to Korea to urge the Korean monarchy to formally recognize Emperor Meiji, by no means did this controversy of 1873 divide cleanly between the supposed itchy trigger fingers of Saigô and his allies—what historians continue to refer to as the reactionary "war party"—and the restrained, pragmatic "peace party" of Ôkubo, Iwakura, and Kido (Arano and Ishii 2010). While all leaders in Japan at this time favored some kind of response to the perceived insult from Korea, a case can be made that the so-called "Last Samurai" Saigô was the least bellicose among them, and that he only committed to tackling the problem well after Kido initiated it in 1869. In the first saber-rattling from the new Meiji government, Kido called Koreans "rude and barbaric" and declared provocatively that "With our military might [兵力をもって] we will invade Korea through their port of Pusan" (Inoue 2010, 203). Knowing that it was the pro-Western "peace party" that called for blood first, it should come as no surprise that this same peace party was the one that followed through on its threat to use military force against Korea in September 1875, eliciting Saigô's denunciation the next month (Ravina 2017, 170):[11] "It's really unfortunate that they went to war against a country we've had peaceful relations with for several hundred years. Without even attempting to negotiate they initiated hostilities. . . . It is a cowardly, shameful act for our country to wage war against a weaker one" (Saigô 1927, vol. 2, 842–43).

The Tokyo oligarchs Kido and Ôkubo chose to use armed force against a weaker opponent with no thought of dialoguing with Korean leaders frankly and honorably. For Saigô and others this was indistinguishable from the barbaric posture the Western powers assumed vis-à-vis Japan and China (Kimura 2010; Yates 1995).[12]

This western Japan critique of the Tokyo oligarchs as having adopted the worldview (extra-active top-down rule by elites, domination of the weak by the strong, etc.) of what we saw in chapter 1, with principled protectors calling Euro-whites "enemies of Heaven" and "ignorant predators," soon became standard in the APR movement. When the focus of scholarship is limited to Saigô and other ex-samurai more or less derisive of Euro-American practices in Asia, it has been easy for scholars to dismiss their anti-Westernism as xenophobic and reactionary. However, the scholarly disregard of the anti-white position of the ex-samurai is revealed as a serious lapse when many of them are shown to be in solidarity with the APR movement, as I will argue. An important correspondence by Saigô established the early parameters for the anti-oligarch position of the 1870s and '80s, and as this language was copied and pasted in many subsequent ripostes, it is worth quoting in full.

Writing to Grand Minister Sanjô Sanetomi on August 3, 1873, Saigô insisted that the military campaign against the Tokugawa in 1868 was victorious only because the Satsuma-Choshu fighters steadfastly followed through on their vow to crush the corrupt Tokugawa and return the emperor to the throne. How, then, Saigô wondered, could the ministers returning from their globe-hopping travels so readily discard those ideals, and in so doing subordinate Japan once again to the white West? This clearly showed how "disgraceful the extent of corruption" was among them, and positive proof of how seriously they were "distorting [転じ] politics and renouncing virtue [仁]," thereby betraying the "principles of the revolution." Finally, this stomped all over the living memory of the thousands of dead men who paid the ultimate price. Saigô here urges his colleagues to practice something close to what theorists of Indigeneity call "keeping faith with death" (van Dooren and Rose 2013). Saigô reiterated his well-known stance that it was his duty to be guided by the "original ideals of the insurrection when all the ministers acted ethically with universal righteousness [天下の義]." Unfortunately, the recent deceitful acts and corrupt policies of the oligarchs are opposed in every way to that earlier righteousness (Saigô 1927, vol. 2, 742–47).

Saigô takes an unconditional stance in his challenge that the Japanese leaders returning from the West must not act like Euro-whites in Asia have. After all, Saigô and Eto's caretaker government successfully prosecuted a case against the Peruvian government for their inhumane treatment of 232 indigent Chinese "coolies" in the *Maria Luz* incident in May and June 1872 (SNKD, vol. 1, 245–52). Many were certain that the Kido-Ôkubo faction wouldn't have done anything at all for these subaltern Chinese. Moreover, together with the resignees' denunciation of the Tokyo oligarchs' lack of righteousness, at issue for Saigô was one's debt to the past, the past being for him that which provides the contours for virtuous action in the present. The nature-worshipping Saigô (some of his most intense relations were with dogs and hot springs) and other decolonial Japanese assumed a debt to the past—configured as the event of the Meiji revostation together with the dense eco-ontological web that endowed the present—that must be honored. The traitors to universal justice Ôkubo, Kido, and Iwakura were turning their backs on this indebtedness by embracing a despicable Euro-American capitalist epistemology serving a myopic self-interest and narrow situational ethics. The Fukuoka writer and son of Genyôsha member Sugiyama Shigemaru, Yumeno Kyûsaku, summed up this decolonial stance circa 1875–80 (with a particular focus on Genyôsha) when he wrote in 1936: "Under the slogan 'Revere the Emperor, Fight the Whites!' the rebel forces from Satsuma and Choshu wiped out the Tokugawa.

But when the new oligarchs took power, what happened to their promise of expelling Westerners from Japan and establishing virtuous government? Instead of doing that, these cowards groveled on the ground in front of barbarian white men wearing his clothes, eating his food, and kissing his ass [媚び る]" (1992, 143).

Bridging Saigô's position to those of his allies Itagaki and Gotô and then to the emerging APR movement insisting that "heaven grants equality to all" can uncover a clear dissensus. In 1874 the anti-oligarch position is calling for the "egalitarian leveling [四民平等]" of the early modern caste/status hierarchy, "expanding democratic discussion [公議興論を張る], and advancing the project of deCO2lonial liberation from Euro-whites. On the side of the Tokyo oligarchs there is a resignation to the cultural and geopolitical subordination to the West and a concomitant embrace of what Jacques Rancière calls a "police logic" (personified here by Ôkubo Toshimichi, who would expand Etô's minimal police force using a Prussian "enlightened despot" template to crush all opposition), featuring a hierarchical ordering of bodies designed to monopolize political power, interfere in the climate, and accumulate capital (1999, 29–30). The years 1873–78 would feature what Japanese leftist historiography calls the "dictatorship of Ôkubo," marked by the marriage of the extractive capitalist conglomerates Mitsui and Mitsubishi with the extra-active oligarchs. Japan's 99 percent were thereby "turned into enemies" of this new CO2lonizing elite by Ôkubo (Gotô 1972, 39, 33).

Horizontalist Horizons

As soon as Saigô and others resigned from the Meiji government, calls for an armed overthrow of the remaining Tokyo oligarchs could be heard throughout western and southwestern Japan, but the volume was turned up the loudest in Fukuoka, Kyushu. Even before the resignations, the fact that not one leader from Fukuoka's domain of Chikuzen was selected to serve in the new government irked locals, who pointed to over two hundred of their men killed or seriously wounded in the Boshin War of 1867–69. Even more infuriating was when a major crisis with the Euro-American powers broke out over the widespread minting of counterfeit coins by many of the Japanese domains. Treasury Minister Okuma Shigenobu concluded the Takanawa negotiations in May 1869 by pledging to England and the US to eliminate the practice (Niwa 1995). While the most powerful western domains of Satsuma, Choshu, and Tosa continued on and off to mint fake coins, Ôkubo argued that the new Meiji government had to show Euro-Americans that is was serious by making an example of the Fukuoka domain leaders (ignoring the loud protests of Saigô and Etô) and ordered five of them jailed and beheaded in November 1869 (Tôyama 1977, 23).

"Tails I win, heads you lose" was the outcome of all the political poker played by Ôkubo, who as home minister went all in on the expensive and environmentally destructive infrastructure projects designed to lubricate the accumulation of capital, and the centralization of power by upgrading the new conscript army with Yamagata Aritomo and the police force with Kawaji Toshiyoshi. In March 1874 Ôkubo and Kawaji divided the expanded police force into two groups: the juridical police, responsible for common crime, and the administrative or national police (国事警察), who were charged with spying on and ultimately crushing all political opposition (Obinata 1987, 30–31). The national police played a central role in fracturing the armed and unarmed opposition movements in the 1870s and was the key counterrevolutionary force against the mass uprisings of the mid-1880s (Chichibu Jiken Kenkyûkai 2004, 173). In October 1876 the role of the national police was significantly expanded when they were asked to crack down on twenty-two new types of crime, unleashing them to harass citizens in the name of defending "homeland security [国安]," administering "modern hygiene," and imposing a more docile and apolitical "popular culture." These new parameters of police action allowed them to search public theaters, inspect restaurants, and spy on married couples in their homes. Police superintendent Kawaji molded his national police into a formidable counterinsurgency apparatus, and his stern force of conservative paternalism was activated to discipline children and educate semiliterate adults—considered "stupid" and "immoral" by Kawaji and Ôkubo, mimicking the same raciological dismissal of Japanese commoners put forward by Eurowhites (Obinata 1987, 41–42).

Even before this arm of Meiji repression was consolidated, Ôkubo crushed Etô Shimpei's samurai-led Saga revolt in 1874, thanks to his own spy network (SNKD, vol. 4, 442–54). During the ensuing armed uprisings in Hagi and Kumamoto in 1876, Ôkubo ordered preemptive sweeps throughout the southwest, resulting in all of the students from Takaba's school being incarcerated and tortured.[13] On Ôkubo's orders, the Fukuoka magistrate Watanabe Kiyoshi sentenced all of these students to death (KTM, 66–67).[14]

From the first arrival of Itagaki and Saigô back to western and southwestern Japan in late 1873, Takaba urged their students to rise up along the lines of the ancient Chinese heroes in the *Classic of History* such as Caomo, the "righteous [正義]" general who "loved force [好力]" (Xi 2011, 454–55). By March 1874, this liberation Sinology lead to the formation of three opposition groups that met regularly at Takaba's school, in blatant rejection of Ôkubo's May 1874 outlawing of unregistered political organizations. The first of the groups was headed by Ôchi and was called the Society of Righteous Protectors (矯志 社). The second group was called the Ninja Assassins League (強忍社), and the third group was the Resolute Protectors League (堅志社) (GYSS 103–6). Hakoda Rokusuke was the only student at the school to be involved in two groups, and he would emerge as the school's leader (and second Genyôsha president in 1883) after Ôchi and Takebe were beheaded on May 3, 1877, for orchestrating Fukuoka's own armed uprising (SNKD, vol. 6, 847–58). Even before this, Hakoda led a group of over four hundred Fukuoka fighters to Saga at the beginning of February 1874 to join Etô Shimpei's uprising, but turned back after hearing that Etô's group had been completely surrounded by the oligarchs' soldiers (GYSS, 101–2).

The lull after Ôkubo's army and police brutally quashed the Saga uprising in April 1874 would be short-lived. By 1876 plans for the whole of southwestern Japan to rise up materialized first in Kumamoto, led by a group calling itself the Divine Wind League (神風連), who despised all things Western, going so far as to spread salt on Euro-American machinery to decontaminate it. Divine Wind League fighters regularly picked fights with government police and soldiers in the streets in preparation for the second major armed uprising in western Japan, beginning on October 24, 1876 (Watanabe 1977). In nearby Hagi, Maebara Issei was having heated discussions with Saigô's people in Kagoshima and insurrectionists in Fukuoka in hopes of establishing a unified armed front to march on Tokyo. Ôkubo was warned of this by his national police spies Yokoyama Shunsuke and Iwamura Takao and ordered all the rebels to be arrested; only Ôchi and Takebe managed to avoid the dragnet (Tôyama 1977, 44). A similar fate awaited the armed group that Ôchi and Takebe were able to organize in Fukuoka in formal alliance with opposition groups linked with Saigô—the January 1877 Academy. With most of the Fukuoka rebels killed or behind bars, Ôchi and Takebe consulted the *I Ching* (through a diviner friend of Takaba's) for the most propitious time, and managed to find fighters who hadn't been arrested for an uprising that started on March 27, 1877, with an attack on the same Fukuoka army garrison Ôkubo had ordered built by unpaid corvée labor in 1875 (GY #23, 2). Pasting up a manifesto in several places around Fukuoka—"we will sacrifice our lives to defend the living and the dead against the thieving oligarchs [官賊] in Tokyo who have been so negligent in their responsibility to protect the health and happiness of all Japanese citizens" (GYSS, 123–24)—this uprising was once again foiled by Meiji government undercover agents. Out of five hundred rebels, more than a hundred were killed, with the five leaders all eventually beheaded (SNKD, vol. 3, 206–9).

Hakoda Rokusuke (1850–88), who at age seventeen fought in the Boshin War on the Tokugawa side but spent most of his time trying to turn his fellow fighters against the government and to join the Fight the Whites! forces, was the first of the students from Takaba's school to be arrested on November 7, 1876, after he was picked up for physically assaulting a government soldier at the Fukuoka garrison (Nagahata 1997, 98). Once he was in jail, two undercover police agents identified him as calling publicly for the assassination of Ôkubo at a large meeting of Fukuoka anti-oligarch activists in mid-September of that year (Hirano and Iida 1974, 248–49). The police subsequently searched his family's house and claimed to have found a pledge signed with his own blood vowing to overthrow the Meiji government and kill all the remaining despots in Tokyo—or die trying. The same blood-signed pledge was uncovered during ensuing house searches of Takaba's remaining students, which led to their immediate arrests on November 8 and 9, 1876.[15]

Takaba's seventeen surviving students were released from prison on September 27, 1877, just three days after the suicidal dénouement of the Satsuma Rebellion (GYSS, 180). After pleading for several months, the Home Ministry official Hayashi Tomoyuki finally convinced Ôkubo and Kawaji to release most of the imprisoned insurrectionists in southwestern Japan after achieving a kind of closure to the antigovernment uprising. Hakoda remained behind bars because he wanted to protect other Fukuoka rebels by claiming he was the sole mastermind behind the Fukuoka Uprising (GYSS, 181).

Specters and Sphincters

Before they were beheaded on May 3, 1877, Takebe Kôshirô and Ôchi Kashirô urged their classmates from Takaba's school to stay strong and focused. Although this final appeal from inside their shared prison to the future core Genyôsha members would resonate intensely, one or two were concerned that their commitment to the struggle was going to cross the line separating moral capacities from basic biological functions. What if they got so caught up in maintaining the purity of the struggle that they neglected to eat? Or worse, given that farting was a central mode of political expression for the Genyôsha militants, what if intense political repression interfered with the smooth working of their bowels? In an offbeat recollection, Narahara Itaru (1851–1919) referred to this dilemma when he described seeing Takebe just before his decapitation.

At that moment four or five people emerged from Takebe sensei's cage.... Sensei stopped in the middle of the courtyard and looked for our cells, yelling out like a courageous roaring lion: "Let's do this!"

All sixteen of us bowed deeply to the ground as several started crying. That was the last time we heard sensei's voice; even now I can feel it deep in my bones. Even now, that voice prevents the shit in my intestines from clogging up [腸の腐り止め] and putrefying everything around them. Even now that voice saves me whenever I get in a tough spot ... and I'm forced to prostrate myself in front of some dog crap official [藩閥の犬畜生]. At times like this I can hear Takebe sensei's brave voice.... I feel that voice swirling round and round in my intestines and I just know that I'll be able to take a shit, which makes me feel strong. It then dawns on me: I don't need anything from dog crap officials and scream out using sensei's words: "Let's do this!" (KKD, 149–50)

This combination of the eschatological with the scatological in Narahara reveals an intense intra-active relationality where the continued existence of one entity is dependent on a physically dead one. In a slightly different version of this, Narahara factors the weather into a situation that is either laxative or costive (GY #26, 2). In other words, Narahara acknowledges his existence to be dependent on at least the following (intra) actors: the hot weather in Fukuoka, his dead comrade Takebe, and his political opposition to powerful government officials—a typical eco-ontology for Genyôsha members at this time.

We will see this intra-active force of the dead on the living again after Saigô Takamori's suicide, effectively ending the Satsuma Rebellion. This 1877 uprising was the major armed action against the oligarch government, one that at its height had twenty thousand fighters singing marching anthems, vowing to take Japan back after it had been stolen by predatory Euro-whites and the craven oligarchs in Tokyo doing their bidding (Nagahata 1997, 31–32).[16] There was no obvious way to achieve this. But at least one thing was clear among the multiple voices in the uprising: the actions of the corrupt oligarchs were dictatorially extra-active and against the expressed idealism of the Meiji revostation. Thus, the Tokyo oligarchs were becoming indistinguishable from Euro-whites who, according to one of the most famous Indian thinkers of this same period, Swami Vivekanada, were "fearsome like wild animals who see no difference between good and evil ... grabbing other people's land and wealth by hook or crook" (in Raychaudhuri 2002, 38).

All of Takaba's students who didn't receive the death penalty were released without being charged on September 27, 1877, with the exception of Hakoda.

As he continually insisted that his friends were innocent of any wrongdoing, Hakoda was reportedly subjected to the most intense torture, making his transition back to normal life quite rough (KTM, 62–63). The fact that he survived the ordeal of a year in prison at all is somewhat surprising given the fact that out of the four hundred or so rebels from Fukuoka imprisoned from October 1876 until November 1877, forty-three died in prison, with "only" five being decapitated; several more died shortly after being released (Ikawa and Kobayashi 2006, 17). Genyôsha researchers attribute the deaths to oligarch-approved torture techniques: floggings (鞭打ち), beatings (打ち叩き), and the withholding of water and food (Tôyama 1977, 42–44, 54).[17]

When Hakoda returned to his small house and settled into a pattern of heavy drinking, it took lots of coaxing by Tôyama and Shindô to convince him to join them in a collective effort to eke out a living. In many ways like Hamas in Gaza and the Black Panthers in 1960s and '70s Oakland, they could only rely on themselves and their surroundings in the face of continued harassment by the police. So, the former Takaba students started what they called the Reclamation Society (開墾社), which included activities like chopping down wood in small forests and selling it, DIY stone masonry, and collecting manure to sell to local farmers (Hirano and Iida 1974, 253–55). After initially making more money than they expected in November and December 1877, by March the members only needed to work from sunrise until the early afternoon and were able to devote the rest of the day to study. Gradually, they drew more and more dispossessed ex-samurai and commoners into their project (GYSS, 181–82).

Firewood and feces weren't the only things being recycled. They were also taking back a project that lay in ruins after the defeat of the Satsuma Rebellion. From the beginning, this reclamation was impelled by both the sense of universal justice they learned from studying the Chinese humanist canon and a rage against the cheap Euro-American copy the Tokyo oligarchs were turning Japan into—what some southwestern rebels called "West infest [西洋かぶれ]" (KTM, 155). More and more people throughout Japan—peasants who were forced to send their sons off for military conscription and their daughters off to the booming brothels, dispossessed low- and mid-rank samurai, all Japanese farmers suffering under the heavy tax burdens[18]—were getting angry about the ways the oligarchs were acting like predatory white people. After all, many of the oligarchs themselves hailed from samurai backgrounds and were therefore inculcated with an ethos to virtuously "serve"—the meaning of *samurai* in Japanese. Just who was being served when the oligarchs used taxpayer money to fund an elaborate system of repression designed to silence most of these same taxpayers?

Although encouraged initially by the successes of the recycling project, things began to get difficult for the Fukuoka rebels as other groups started reclamation projects of their own. In June 1878, while Tôyama was two hundred miles away from Fukuoka in Kôchi learning about the APR movement, some of his younger comrades were growing frustrated at eating only rice with a few vegetables, day in and day out. Then one of them remembered that there was a big cat at the Tôyama house. The anecdote of what they then did demonstrates their ingenuity at "reclaiming":

> One guy suggested, "Since he's not around, why don't we get our hands on that big cat at Tôyama's house?" Thinking this was a great idea, the other guys tried to figure out a way to get the cat so they could eat it, finally coming up with a scheme where they would trick Tôyama's mom into lending them the cat to catch mice. Successfully pulling this off, they then skinned the fat cat, before cooking it up with salt and eating it.... When Tôyama returned he went, "My own guys ate my mom's cat, right?" Subsequently, they were more respectful the next time they came over Tôyama's. But this didn't prevent them from thinking it'd be OK to go after the Tôyama family dogs. (KTM, 639)

When Tôyama first journeyed to Kôchi in March 1878 to find out about the new popular form the anti-oligarch resistance was taking under Itagaki and Gotô (and, more importantly, the younger activist-intellectuals Ueki Emori and Baba Tatsui), Narahara Itaru accompanied him. Penniless, the Fukuoka rebels went directly to Itagaki's house to see if he could put them up and, while he was at it, lend them some money for food and alcohol as well (KTM, 71). It seems that Itagaki did help them out, while one of the stars of the new APR movement—a woman in her mid-forties named Kusunose Kita—offered them her place to stay.

Kusunose (1833–1920) was a widow who had inherited property and written a famous letter to the Meiji government's Chamber of Elders arguing that because she paid taxes, she should be given the vote (Mackie 2003, 19–20). Although ignored by the oligarchs, the letter was published in the Tokyo *Nichi Shimbun* on January 31, 1879, which enhanced her notoriety in Kôchi.[19] The first major female presence in the APR movement, Kusunose was widely referred to as the People's Rights Granny (民権婆さん). Kusunose acted as a kind of political adviser for Ueki Emori, who consulted with her before writing or speaking about many of the political issues of the day. Kusunose also influenced

Ueki's thinking about women's rights as he was the only major APR intellectual to focus on them (Suzuki 1996, 23).[20]

An anecdote related by Tôyama's secretary is the only description I've been able to find about Kusunose's public appearances:

> When APR Granny was traveling around giving lectures with Ueki and Kataoka, at one place she drew loud applause from the audience right before reaching for a glass of water. Suddenly, a police officer who was keeping an eye on the lecture yelled out, "Let's shut this speech down right now [弁士中止]." Although the audience was startled, for some reason People's Rights Granny was nonplussed and quietly drank her water. At that point, she glared right at the cop and said: "This is ridiculous; is drinking a glass of water something that requires the permission of the authorities? I refuse to live in a world where we have to follow the orders of the cops just to drink water or eat food." Then a huge cheer of support rose up. The audience started screaming out: "Let's beat the shit out of the cop [巡査を殴れ]!" At that point the policemen took off real fast. (KTM 95–96)

Although there is some question about whether Kusunose actually did speak in public, her pioneering presence clearly attracted young women to the APR movement.[21] The most important of these was the first major advocate for gender equality in Japan, Kishida Toshiko (1863–1901). Kishida was recruited by the new Liberty Party (the official wing of the APR movement) to be one of its spokespeople after she gave a brilliant speech in Osaka in April 1882 (Sievers 1981, 605–6). Kishida toured throughout Japan on Liberty Party speaking events and was the first woman lecturer most of her audience would have heard, explaining the need for women's liberation and arguing that equality between men and women would strengthen Japan. She was arrested on October 12, 1883, for inciting the audience after one of her famous "Boxed-In Daughters [箱入り娘]" lectures (608).

As soon as Tôyama and Narahara settled in with Kusunose in Kôchi, they started hanging out with a group of young militants involved in a heated discussion about whether or not full representative democracy was feasible in Japan. On most days the group migrated to a cheap restaurant to continue discussions over drinks. Narahara recalled later that he and Tôyama thoroughly enjoyed themselves listening to the discussions and lectures, and became particularly interested in the theory of egalitarianism (KKD, 157).

While Tôyama and Narahara were debating and drinking in Kôchi, an unexpected event in Tokyo delighted all the surviving opposition fighters in western

Japan (Ikawa and Kobayashi 2006, 29–30). On May 14, 1878, Ôkubo Toshimichi was assassinated by Shimada Ichirô and six accomplices while on his way to the imperial palace in Tokyo. Ôkubo was Public Enemy #1 for many ex-samurai, as he was a boyhood friend of Saigô's in Satsuma and went on to work closely with him in the Boshin War. From that point on, Ôkubo consistently opposed the ethics, aesthetics, and politics of the samurai. As finance minister in 1871, he enacted the notorious Hair-Cut Edict (断髪令) outlawing their customary *chonmage* topknot style, and commuted all samurai stipends to cash payments by 1875—resulting in large losses for all classes of samurai. Also, in 1876 Ôkubo forced through the Samurai Disarmament Edict (廃刀令), which prohibited samurai from wearing swords in public. However, the final betrayal was his directing of asymmetric war against Saigô and the Satsuma Rebellion. As Ôkubo had forced both samurai hair and heads to be chopped off, many demanded vengeance (Ochiai 2008, 204–8).

Before the successful hit on Ôkubo, Shimada and his coconspirators composed and signed a document giving the rationale for the killing. They listed six reasons, of which only two are directly concerned with the elimination of the samurai and the death of Saigô. Among them, the first decries Ôkubo's despotic monopolizing of political power. This monopolization betrayed both the will of the emperor and the majority sentiment of the Japanese people. Furthermore, Ôkubo and the other oligarchs had successfully pushed through their Euromimetic policies only by silencing the APR movement and other popular voices in Japan. One of these policies was Ôkubo's borrowing from Climate Caucasianism to require former samurai to wage "war on nature" by draining marshes and rerouting rivers to establish direct navigable routes to Tokyo from all over Japan (GYSS, 183–84).[22]

Although there is no evidence of direct involvement with Ôkubo's assassination on the part of the Reclamation Society, only four days before, on May 10, Hakoda Rokusuke addressed a large meeting of opposition groups in Fukuoka. According to an undercover police report, his "inflammatory address" called on "one hundred samurai willing to die gloriously in assassinating Tokyo despots and provincial representatives of the government" (GY #21, 2). Three years earlier, Hakoda had been arrested and jailed for allegedly calling for the assassination of Ôkubo (Hirano and Iida 1974, 255). The counterintelligence concluded that Hakoda was intending to use the APR movement to overthrow the Meiji government through armed force. After Tôyama and Narahara returned to Fukuoka, Itagaki put out a national call for a second large APR conference in Osaka for September 1878. The Reclamation Society members Hakoda, Shindô, and Katô Tadakichi got their first taste of Japanese national politics at this meeting and returned home eager to spread the APR message (GYSS, 213–14). Yet another conference was called by Itagaki in Osaka in March 1879 to gain support for a popularly elected national assembly, something the oligarchs in Tokyo were fearful of. Hiraoka, Shindô, and Katô represented Fukuoka at this meeting.

The most important event in Fukuoka was Hakoda and Tôyama's decision to start a new political and educational group called Facing the Sun (向陽社), following the model of Rishisha in Kôchi. While Facing the Sun opened a middle school in August 1878, this was only one part of its operation. Arguably, its most influential was the regular Saturday evening teach-ins they sponsored in downtown Fukuoka. The Tokyo weekly *Kinshi Hyôron* of February 13, 1880, reported regular attendances of up to two thousand people at these events. Designed to "nourish the spirit of freedom" and to "incite demands for popular rights," contemporary accounts of this Saturday Night (APR) Fever in Fukuoka never failed to describe the excitement and political intensity (Nishi Nihon 1982, 32). The second most important initiative for Facing the Sun was the hiring of the central APR movement intellectual Ueki Emori (1857–92). After negotiations between Itagaki and Tôyama, Ueki agreed to relocate to Fukuoka as Facing the Sun's main teacher. From August 8, 1878, until March 18, 1879, he taught four days a week at Facing the Sun's middle school, in addition to giving one Saturday evening lecture for the Fukuoka public (Ueki 1990, vol. 7, 129).

Ueki was born and raised in Kôchi as the son of a mid-rank samurai, which provided access to the domain school.[23] At the age of fifteen he left home to study in Tokyo and immersed himself in the new French discourse of representative government and revolutionary justice, studying for a time both at Fukuzawa Yukichi's school and at Nakae Chômin's French academy. In January 1876 he published an article in the *Tokyo Post* newspaper titled "This Government Turns Humans into Apes [猿人政府]," which landed him in prison for two months, one of the first victims of the oligarchs' crackdown on freedom of expression (Ienaga 1974, 215). On June 28, 1875, the Tokyo oligarchs promulgated the Defamation Law, which tightened restrictions on the press declared in the October 1873 Ordinance on Newspapers; this law required that everything published had to be submitted beforehand to the Home Ministry. The Defamation Law was designed to punish news media that criticized ("defamed") the government and authorized harsh punishment for journalists. Article 13 threatened any journalist with one to three years in prison for "advocating subversion of the state," and this was the legal justification for imprisoning the journalist Katô Kuro for three years for merely praising the republican thought of Patrick Henry (JGD, 542).[24]

In Fukuoka, Ueki was lecturing on two main topics: the essential corruption of all governments, and people's rights. In his "There's No Such Thing as a Decent Government Anywhere in the World [世に良政府なる者なきの説]," he was obviously trying to displace the conservative Confucian notion of harmonious, benevolent government that was hegemonic in early modern Japan: "Many people consider the establishment of society to be homologous to that of the family and therefore explain the relation between government and the people in terms of the relation between parent and child. But this is clearly not the case. . . . Between government and the people there are only conflicting interests [利害を異にする]. Governments seek out their own interests and jump at every chance to oppress the people—using everything in their arsenal to do so" (in Ienaga 1974, 9–10),

Ueki also lectured on "The Theory of People's Rights and Autonomy" in Fukuoka, where he introduced Jean-Jacques Rousseau's notion of natural right and the French republican idea of overthrowing corrupt leaders by force.[25] However, while Ueki discussed Rousseau in the second section of the essay and, we can assume, the public lecture that it drew on, his first and third sections commit to using the Chinese canon to argue basically the same point regarding the primacy of the people over secondary, parasitic rulers. Ueki learned from his teacher Nakae Chômin how to transcode Sinological terms like universality (天下) and righteousness (義) to link the French natural rights theory with Chinese ethical discourse, making it easier for his Chinese-trained audience to comprehend the former.[26] As Matsuo Shôichi argues, in the thinking of the APR movement intellectuals at this time, "it was heaven [天] that provided liberty, rights, equality, and prosperity" (1990, 61).

This mediation of European Enlightenment theories of individuality and freedom by Chinese thought is important to highlight because the scholarly consensus on Japan holds that Euro-American "concepts . . . separated both politics and epistemology from the hereditary forms of the Tokugawa regime and placed them in the new categories of Western knowledge" (Howland 2002, 23). With the translations of Rousseau and Mill and the celebrations of atomistic individuality in Samuel Smiles's 1849 *Self-Help*, most scholars assume that Japanese of all classes and backgrounds rushed to mimic Euro-American ideologies of self-determination and the Cartesian binaries of culture versus nature and body versus mind. While large swaths of Japanese society did embrace these foreign concepts, many did not. To arrive at the assumption of a nearly universal downloading of Euro-Enlightenment applications in Japan means one has to ignore (or downplay) the prominent critiques of the white West and Climate Caucasianism. As I will show, these critiques of whiteness were salient in Genyôsha and in other APR groups. Moreover, what will emerge as the revolutionary faction of the APR movement with the Osaka Incident of 1885 (featured in chapter 5) explicitly rejected most of "the new categories of Western knowledge." Even Europhiles like Ueki posited "natural right" not primarily as a ground for the atomized liberal subject of the Euro-Enlightenment but as a collective guarantee to overthrow corrupt rulers by force.[27] While many in the APR movement followed Article 5 of Emperor Meiji's Charter Oath admonishing Japanese that "Knowledge shall be sought throughout the world," many also thought that the East Asian intellectual endowment provided many valuable tools. And for those in the APR who still found East Asian thought valid, the Kantian architecture of universal rationality—which Ferreira da Silva deconstructed in the introduction—insisting that the individual fully separate from and transcend local knowledges and eco-ontologies was considered nonsensical.

The first chapter of *People's Rights and Autonomy* incites the people to "Use your head and heart when dealing with affairs of the state." Ueki continues: "There is a maxim that claims the common people are ignorant of the endowments of heaven, and these days one could add that they are clueless about political affairs as well" (Ienaga 1974, 20; citations to follow). Reminding his readers of some of the ways the Tokyo government should be held accountable, he challenges them to define their current condition in these terms. "Whatever money we have is worthless because of the huge military expenditures of the government, and the price of all goods has increased. Some of us have seen our taxes tripled. How can you remain silent in the face of this tyranny? In fact, silence is the root cause of our misfortune" (22–23).

Ueki then cited Mencius's claim that good citizens are those who understand that government relies on them and not vice versa. Because of the debt that government leaders owe to the people, the very least government can do is guarantee their happiness and comfort. When government fails to do so, and the people don't rise up collectively to challenge it, this passivity is a sign of a lack of virtue in the people. Ueki challenges his audiences in 1878 to understand that the impoverished lives that most of them were enduring at that time could only mean that both the government and the people have lost the path of virtue: "If you people remain satisfied with wretched slave-like conditions, then you aren't being good citizens, but are merely zombie subjects of the state [ほんに国家の死民でござる]" (23).

Chapter 2 discussed Rousseau's thought.[28] Although some in Fukuoka would have heard of Rousseau's name from schools like Takaba's that were introducing French Enlightenment ideas, for most of the audience this would have been truly eye-opening. Ueki started right off in an idiom borrowed from Mencius by saying that "liberty is a universal gift and is something that each one of us possesses inalienably. When people are deprived of their liberty, this is a serious crime against heaven" (24). He points to autonomy as the sine qua non for the human species, claiming that humanity's collective intelligence and each individual's physical strength are compromised when all people aren't free. Moreover, this human potential is further compromised when the people have a "subservient attitude to their government." In what must have been heard by the Fukuoka rebels as a corroboration of their own political praxis, Ueki states that the people have every right to take back their stolen autonomy via violent overthrow of the government. Ueki underlines that the rationale for armed struggle in the Boshin War was "justified by Heaven," owing to the Tokugawa's "obstruction of the people's liberty" and their inability to defend the realm against Western predators (26–27). Influenced by Patrick Henry's emphasis on interdependent (with land and other humans) autonomy, Ueki understood that interdependence would be intensified once the people had achieved liberation from the despotic Meiji government. For him autonomy implied collectivity and interrelationality, albeit one that was freed from co-optation by governments and their industries.

The third chapter is called "The State Must Extend People's Rights and Autonomy," and here Ueki explicitly links the thought of Mencius with that of Rousseau, beginning with his insistence that the government's sole raison d'être is " to serve the people [民為]" (30). However, Ueki also argues that "expanding the people's autonomy will . . . make the state collective more powerful" (31). Although the power of the state will always remain a shadowy effect of people power, a double movement lingers here. He seems to resolve this tension between the people's autonomy and state power through an interpretation of the notion of "universality," or 天下. Universality as universal justice appears three times in this chapter, pointing to a resolution of the tension between popular emancipation and state power. Again, he made this argument easier for his audience to understand by routing it through Chinese thought in insisting that "liberty is an endowment of heaven [天の賜]" (24).

Although we have no record of how Ueki's classes and lectures were received in Fukuoka, the East Asian idea of a heaven-endowed autonomy justifying interdependent collective struggle against the Tokyo oligarchs would have been eye-opening for antigovernment activists—not only in Fukuoka, but in all the other places in Japan Ueki subsequently traveled to as one of the main speakers in the popular Kôchi APR lectures (Ienaga 1974, 308–9). This Chinese canonical justification for rebellion no doubt helped Takaba's students as they were struggling to carve out new political futures after the Meiji counterinsurgency crushed the Satsuma Rebellion. Facing the Sun quickly became the largest APR group in north Kyushu, gaining over a thousand nonstudent members, including three hundred who had fought in the Fukuoka Uprising of March 27 and 28, 1877. These low-ranking samurai and commoners had fled the area after the defeat, but quietly returned to Fukuoka and were convinced by their de facto leader Hakoda that they could continue their struggle against the Tokyo despots in a different political idiom (Nishi Nihon 1982a, 31).

Similar to the discussions that were taking place in many other areas of Japan at this time, the concerns that came to dominate the public and private discussions within Facing the Sun were those of constitutional government and the oppressiveness of the Unequal Treaties. There were over sixty constitutions drawn up in different parts of Japan during this period, several of which were submitted to the quasi-legislative group of oligarchs called the Chamber of Elders as potential templates for the promised Japanese constitution (Emura 1989, 465). One well-known prototype for these was the constitution drafted by Ueki for Kôchi's Rishisha in August 1881, which featured Article 72, allowing the people to overthrow by force (覆滅) a despotic government (Ienaga 1967, 91). Moreover, Ueki's version granted suffrage to all women over twenty.

According to Inada Masatsugu, the very first draft constitution in Japan was written by the umbrella organization for the various APR groups in Fukuoka, the United Patriotic Front (共愛公衆会, UPF), in February 1880, with involvement from several of the Genyôsha pioneers. Inada writes that it was formally adopted by the executive officers of the UPF in November 1880 and signed by the President Miki Ryûsuke and Vice President Hakoda Rokusuke with the affixed date of February 1880 (1960, 352–53). Called "An Outline for a Constitution for the Japanese Nation," UPF's constitution was surprisingly progressive, as it allowed for a female emperor and guaranteed freedom of speech, the press, and assembly. Moreover, reflecting the practice of UPF's intra-active democracy—which included boycotts of Western products, pledges to buy only local products, and opposition to industrial coal mining—their constitution was one of only three throughout Japan that refused to restrict voting rights to property owners. Their Article 77 rejecting wealth qualifications was joined with Article 134, which demanded that all prefectural governors be elected by a vote of all men over twenty. In firmly establishing equality for all (men) before the law (同一の権), Inada sums up his discussion of this pioneering document by saying it reflected the "rebellious spirit" of the APR movement in

Fukuoka (354–62). APR comrades in Kôchi, referencing Fukuoka's location in one of East Asia's typhoon alleys, projected that these characteristics grew from intra-action with local weather systems in calling UPF militants "typhoon-like [台風的]" (Nishi Nihon 1982a, 81).

The first time this Fukuoka typhoon–human hybrid emerged on the national scene after the samurai rebellions of the mid-1870s was at the convention of the Patriot Society in Osaka on November 7, 1879. There were three Fukuoka groups linked to the UPF that were also member-associations of the Patriot Society. But each of the groups, especially the front group for Facing the Sun, the Correct Line Society (正論社), argued both for deepening democracy at the grass roots and for opposing the Unequal Treaties. The perceived obsession with the Unequal Treaties on the part of the Fukuoka groups created a split with Itagaki's Patriot Society, which prioritized the need for a popularly elected national assembly. This was the first public rupture between what I'll call the deCO2lonialists and the liberal constitutionalists (JTS, vol. 1, 249–50). With their focus on the creation of a parliament, Itagaki's liberal constitutionalists thought that the emphasis on petition-memorials would be the most effective way to overthrow the treaty situation. Thinking that a future parliament would be unjustly constrained by Euro-white influences, the deCO2lonialists led by the Fukuoka contingent wanted to keep an open mind about extralegal tactics. They would soon be joined by Ôi Kentarô, Kôno Hironaka, and others embracing armed revolution in the APR.

What was finally agreed on (grudgingly, in the case of the Kôchi APR) is that both groups would draft separate memorials expressing the two central issues of the APR movement in southwestern Japan. Like the Kôchi liberal constitutionalists, the deCO2lonialists planned on submitting these memorials to the Chamber of Elders (GYSS, 216–18). It was the responsibility of the chamber to consider submissions from any representative political group before making legislative recommendations to Emperor Meiji. In fact, the practice of presenting memorials had exploded in Japan in 1879, with 158 submitted to the chamber that year and 198 submitted in 1880 (Kim 2007, 217). The policy paper from the Fukuoka UPF was drawn up by a committee headed by Hakoda and Minagawa Masao and approved at a large meeting of UPF members on December 16, 1879, which at this point featured a majority of commoners (farmers and merchants) as members; sixty-four signed the document (Ishitaki 1997, 108–9). On December 26, the executive council voted to send them to Tokyo to personally deliver the memorials to the Chamber of Elders, which they did on January 15, 1880 (Nishi Nihon 1982a, 37). Narahara Itaru accompanied them.

The UPF memorials encode the political positions of the group that was just about to change its name to Genyôsha, and because of the lack of scholarship in English on Genyôsha, they are worth looking at in depth. The first memorial is the controversial one decrying the asymmetric lawfare imposed by the Unequal Treaties.[29] Called "A Proposal to Reject the Unequal Treaties," the memorial states clearly that "The Unequal Treaties interfere with the inherent sovereignty of an independent country. . . . Therefore, when the West does whatever it wants here, this robs us of our sovereign rights; we must raise our fists against this [之ヲ拳する]. It is enough to see what white people are doing in China and India right now to understand what our future might be" (FKT, Itô box, 34).[30]

Hakoda and Minagawa then delineate the effects of the treaties on Japan: tariff and trade policy effectively stripped, Euro-white capitalists reaping huge profits while Japanese people endure financial chaos (金貨ノ乱出), and the "despotic regime of extraterritoriality" for Westerners making a mockery of Japanese law. Using the trope of the democratic line (公議輿論) throughout to suggest political unanimity among the people in Fukuoka, they argue that East Asia is being "chained down" by the white supremacist logic of "the strong devour the weak" that justified Euro-American profiteering and pillaging. Impelled by the ideology of "selfish individualism [利己主義], obstinate white people are blind to the injustice of their actions. Only by stating the single word 'No!' [否ノ一字] with the collective power of the people are we going to succeed in smashing the arrogance of the Westerners." Hakoda and Minagawa conclude by insisting that it will take an uprising from below to shake off the chains of Euro-white CO₂loniality. "For Japan to be sovereign and independent, please consider the popular voice [輿論] of the Chikuzen people."

The second memorial is the "Proposal for Establishing a Parliament," which went through at least one draft before the final version was submitted to the Chamber of Elders together with the memorial against the Unequal Treaties. It begins with prioritizing the people, which they learned first from Takaba's interpretation of Mencius: "The people are the foundation of the state [人民は国の大本 なり]. It is wrong to claim that there is a government first and then there are people. The opposite is in fact the case: because there are people, a government is possible" (FKT, Itô box, 34).

Next, they go right to one of the fundamental positions of the APR movement at the time: "elect a parliament first, draft a constitution second." Hakoda and Minagawa put it this way: "Though we want a constitution, it is crucial to have a parliament put in place first." Subsequently, almost as if they started off too militantly, they pull back slightly and throw an olive branch to Emperor

Meiji: "But this isn't our own personal opinion. His Majesty has already put out two instructions [叡旨] promising a parliament."[31]

Hakoda and Minagawa then take an interesting tack, one also used by other groups submitting memorials (Emura 1989). They write that the people, "hearing the emperor's edict," proceeded to run around "crazily like a carriage pulled by four wild horses" in their haste to follow Meiji's instructions to set up a democratic parliament. Then what happened? Beginning in 1873, leaders in Tokyo began to subvert this unity of the emperor and the people and tabled any discussion of a democratic parliament. The memorial concludes with a reminder that the government's responsibility is to:

> follow the will of the people [民心]. But to do that there has to be, first, an elected assembly and then a constitution. . . . Remember, the authorities [権理ナル者] don't have a monopoly on political power, therefore the people themselves together with the emperor can take it back by force and move forward. We are seeing something like this already taking place, where all the people are rising up [奮起], trying to retake political power. To guarantee that we the people are successful in this, everyone must be willing to spill fresh blood [鮮血ヲ流す] in the mountains and in the fields. (FKT, Itô box, 34)

Claiming this sense of popular insurrection represented the "people's voice" in Fukuoka, we should understand this memorial as a kind of threat to the Tokyo oligarchs from rebels who just a few years earlier had participated in armed revolts in southwestern Japan, and before that, fought in the Boshin War against the Tokugawa. This time, however, the rebels would be battling with a broad-based coalition made up of farmers, merchants, ex-samurai, and women, intra-actively energized by other entities like "the mountains," "farmers' fields," and typhoons.

All told, the two memorials represent a striking vision for Japan, one that Emura Eichi claims was shared by only two or three other oppositional groups writing petitions (1989, 66–99). Although the general sense of humiliation caused by the Unequal Treaties is foregrounded in the first memorial, it appears in the second one as well, where Hakoda and Minagawa remind Emperor Meiji that Japan is threatened on "four sides" by predatory enemies of Heaven who will stop at nothing to get what they want. This CO2lonial condition exacerbates the political and eco-ontological difficulties the Japanese people face with the oligarch despots. And because of this system of multiple oppression, for substantive liberation to take place, action must be directed at several different levels simultaneously—juridical, economic, and cultural.[32]

Fight Whiteness!

What I find most interesting in these two memorials is the implicit conflation of white imperialists in Asia with the despotic government in Tokyo. Readers will recall that this was the same Fight the Whites! tactic as in the Boshin War against the Tokugawa. Then, Westerners were seen as sharing some of the same characteristics as the Tokugawa rulers: moral corruption, personal selfishness, and an obsession with power for power's sake. This conflation was made explicit by Hakoda Rokusuke at a Fukuoka UPF meeting sometime in the first week of March 1880. As reported by an undercover agent, the executive committee of the UPF was preparing a response to the Patriot Society in Kôchi as to why they felt that overthrowing the Unequal Treaties was so urgent for the Fukuoka militants. Hakoda exclaimed that the oligarchs rejecting the popular will were indistinguishable from Euro-white oppressors. Hakoda continued, "it should be obvious to Kôchi that the battle against white people [西洋人] is the same as the fight against the despots" (FKT, Ôka box, 12).[33]

Before the December 26, 1879, meeting of the Fukuoka UPF, Hakoda, Minagawa, and several others spent two weeks going door to door in northern Kyushu attempting to deepen support for their petitions, and they ended up with approximately twenty thousand signatures (GY #56, 2). On December 28, 1879, they left for Tokyo intending to work the streets and teahouses there to spread the word about the memorials (GYSS, 217–18). Three months later, after the fourth Patriot Society conference in Osaka, society representatives Kataoka Kenkichi and Kôno Hironaka brought a memorial representing twenty-two prefectures and two cities to Tokyo for submission to the chamber. This was the famous Petition for the Establishment of a National Assembly, delivered on April 7, 1880 (JTS, vol. 1, 250).

At this point the political environment in Tokyo was electric, with the oligarchs panicking over the rising tide of petitions. Presciently, in July 1879, army minister and Ôkubo protegé Yamagata Aritomo wrote to the oligarch Itô Hirobumi referring to the viral quality of the APR movement: "every day we wait, the evil poison will spread more and more over the provinces, penetrate into the minds of the young, and inevitably produce unfathomable evils" (Ike 1950, 93). In mid-April 1880, the Chamber of Elders put out the word that they were going to restrict the number of memorials accepted, beginning with the Patriot Society petition. When Kataoka protested that the Patriot Society document reflected the right to free expression of "people from all over Japan," the chamber responded contemptuously that "the people have no rights" (JTS, vol. 2, 321). So Kataoka and Kôno withdrew their memorial and published it as a pamphlet. Earlier, Hakoda, Minagawa, and Narahara also had their memorial rejected, but en route back to Fukuoka they tried to publicize it during several speaking engagements. After other groups copied this tactic, the oligarchs responded by banning distribution of memorials without permission (GY #21, 2). This came on top of the other restrictions dictated in the draconian law of April 5, 1880, which significantly curtailed political meetings.

Two tendencies arose from the crackdown against the freedoms of speech, public assembly, and submission of memorials. The first tendency is well documented and almost mythologized: Ueki Emori and Itagaki Taisuke decided to battle the oligarchs from within and started the Liberty Party (自由党). The second tendency has been decidedly less celebrated, as it concerns the Fukuoka group, the revolutionary wing of the Liberty Party (Ôi Kentarô, Kôno Hironaka) and other insurrectionists who had started carrying out extralegal actions all over the country (Bowen 1980). Never exhibiting much patience or willingness to compromise, after traveling around eastern Japan—stopping to share strategies and tactics in several areas that would see armed uprisings just a few years later—Hakoda, Minagawa, and Narahara returned from Tokyo, chaperoned by both regular police and undercover national police (GY #58, 3). They quickly decided to close the doors of their Facing the Sun middle school and change tactics. Although the Fukuoka rebels kept lines of communication open with the Patriot Society leadership in Kôchi, from this point on their main political alliance was with the militant wing of the APR movement, such as Ôi, Kôno, and the young woman Fukuda Hideko (1865–1927).

Time to Split

Using a boxing metaphor, the Fukuoka writer Yumeno Kyûsaku wrote in 1936 that the combination of incarceration, Western asymmetric warfare, and stifling police harassment delivered a "knockout" punch to Facing the Sun and other southwestern opposition groups just before Genyôsha was formed (KKD 1992, 111). Kyûsaku argued that it was "inevitable" that this would impact the modus operandi of Genyôsha as the core members grew older (112). It should not have been surprising that Hakoda and Tôyama shifted their political tactics at this point to include extralegal actions. They had gone to some lengths to try to work within the shrinking confines of the legal system and had been ridiculed and surveilled by the oligarchs. Genyôsha and other opposition groups in Japan had no choice but to take up arms. Consequently, certain that a broad popular consensus linked Facing the Sun and the Fukuoka people both on the demand for a popularly elected national assembly and on the insistence on a firm rejection of the Unequal Treaties, they shut down Facing the Sun, shifted their focus, and changed their name.

When they renamed their group Genyôsha, it literally marked a turning away from the imperial palace in Tokyo toward the sea and the Asian continent, which in the case of Fukuoka is bridged by the Sea of Genkai. As this political direction is arguably as important for modern East Asian history as anything that would happen in Tokyo, it is imperative that we pause and look at exactly what they are saying when Gen/玄 (from Genkai) yô/洋 (or ocean) is founded. Surely, we will find evidence of their alleged "fascism" and "ultra-nationalism" here.

The founding charter of Genyôsha as it was drawn up in February 1881 was very short and expressed three principal ideals, which the group hoped will be "maintained and handed down forever to generations of our descendants" (GYSS, 225). The three are then given in order:

Respect the imperial house.
Love your home region (本国).
Firmly defend and protect the people's rights (人民の権利).

That's it. Forty years later the company history will add things to the charter, claiming that the founding members really meant this, that, or the other thing. But in 1881 it is simple and succinct.

The first ideal is there to remind people that so many men from southwestern Japan died fighting to overthrow the Tokugawa shogunate, expel Euro-whites, level the hierarchical caste/status order, and return the emperor to the center of political power. This doesn't mean that Genyôsha is necessarily emperorist. In fact, while in the main academic work in English on them by Sabey (1974), he is keen to represent them as ultranationalistic, he admits that Genyôsha clearly did not intend for Emperor Meiji to have any more political power than he had already. In 1881 they simply state that Genyôsha members should respect the emperor, period.

The second ideal should be seen as an extension of the preface to the charter, which expressed hope that the charter would remain to influence people living in the Fukuoka region from time immemorial. In that regard, Genyôsha members should heed the injunction to love the place they come from—its ecology, its past, and its future. Some readers will notice that I've translated the Sino-Japanese characters 本国 as "this region." The Chinese character 国 still maintained the meaning of any clearly demarcated area, as in the sense of "our territory." I would argue that 本国 is best translated as "home region" in the sense of where one hails from, and Genyôsha consistently placed the focus on

Fukuoka and the early modern Chikuzen domain area that included Fukuoka. After all, if they had wanted to, they could have replaced 本国 with 日本 (or 大日本)—"Japan." In his 1935 book on Genyôsha, Yumeno Kyûsaku returns in several places to his emphasis that early Genyôsha wasn't nationalistic at all. Explaining that "people today can't possibly understand this . . . but there existed nothing like the sense of modern nationalism we see today" (KKD 1992, 110). Kyûsaku explains that the early modern notion of *han*, or domain sovereignty, remained strong among Genyôsha during its formative period in the early 1880s. Insisting that it's "impossible to fully grasp the Meiji Restoration without this sense of local sovereignty," he advises readers to refrain from imposing an ahistorical nationalism onto Genyôsha (110). The sense of local Fukuokan identity was paramount for them, although this would weaken somewhat as several main members moved to Tokyo more or less permanently in 1890.

When we read their founding charter together with changing their name from Facing the Sun, where the emphasis was on Emperor Meiji in Tokyo, to one where the emphasis is on moving toward Asia and the sea, this offers further evidence for an absence of Japanese nationalism in Genyôsha. When we realize that one of the foci for Genyôsha for the next three decades would be in Asia, we could reconfigure "home region" as one not moving from western Japan to Tokyo, but from Fukuoka to the Asian mainland.

We can speculate on other reasons for naming a group of humans after a body of water. While some Genyôsha researchers casually depict the members as Shinto-believing "nature worshippers," we shouldn't assume that Shinto as a formally institutionalized religion existed before 1890 (Tôyama 1977, 41). It is more precise to look at their rituals and try to understand how these were parts of an intra-active network. Ueki Emori provided evidence of Genyôsha's devotional practices, whether this took the form of weekly prayer visits to the graves of dead friends and relatives or regular trips to local mountain shrines (Ueki 1990, vol. 7, 134; FKT, Oka box, roll 12, 139). In these sites, at the very least, they would have followed non-Buddhist, nativist protocols of water purification. As I suggested in chapter 1, water purification was understood as one way to cleanse rogue samurai from the various kinds of pollution (mythic, ecological, spiritual, political) brought to Japan by Euro-white enemies of Heaven. But water was also construed in (lowercase) shinto spirituality as a primordial element that generates all other forms of life, including female and male deities.

In other words, the hydrocentrism of shinto spirituality doesn't just insist on humans purifying themselves before encounters with the dead and divine, but is itself a recognition of the other-determining power of water—all forms of life emerge from its matrix. In one of the two main texts of Japanese mytho-history, the *Kojiki* of 711–12, deities themselves emerge from water, and the initial terraforming of the land was caused by the sea. Of course, this hydrocentrism would later be subordinated to the primacy of the Japanese nation. But in 1881 the network of entities that included water, typhoons, the mountains, and Genyôsha members was firmly grounded in a local and regional eco-ontology. In searching for ways to deepen this network and to keep it autonomous from both Tokyo oligarchs and Western CO2loniality, Takaba's students announced a desire to imbricate more tightly with the crucial object of water. Water would cleanse them and flush them out toward a different place, away from the pollution of Euro-America and Tokyo.

Deciding to rename their collective after a body of water was only one of the many assemblages of human and extrahuman nature that the group embraced, what I'll call "humanature hybrids." As we saw above, when the APR leaders in Kôchi referenced the Fukuoka-based rebels as "typhoon-like," several Genyôsha members affirmed this. Locally, Hakoda Rokusuke was conflated as a "mountain [山]" because of his unwavering commitment to Fukuoka (GY #9, 2). While these humanature hybrids have clear Chinese canonical precedents—in *Analects* 2:1 the wise ruler is conflated with a polestar (Lau 1979)—in the 1880s in southwestern Japan they worked to situate humans intra-actively in their eco-ontologies. As we saw in the introduction, Climate Caucasianists from Descartes to Darwin were contrastingly intent on consolidating an ontology and epistemology of separation that positioned Euro-whites spatially above and temporally ahead, where the preferred mode of operation was extra-action.

4

Levelry and Revelry
(Inside the Gelaohui Opium Room)

To organize is not to give a structure to weakness. It is above all to form bonds—bonds that are by no means neutral—terrible bonds. The degree of organization is measured by the intensity of sharing, material and spiritual.—Invisible Committee, *The Coming Insurrection*, 2009

There are many places to party [娱乐] in Sichuan. However, the opium room is the clear favorite among the people.—Popular saying in Chengdu, Sichuan, in the 1930s (in Qin 2001)

In chapter 2 I introduced several Gelaohui (GLH) fighters. The Yu brothers were ideal types of the organization: poor, illiterate, and irregularly employed as manure collectors and seasonal agricultural laborers. Elizabeth Perry calls young men like them the "surplus sons of poor peasant families" (2002, 18). The overwhelming majority of GLH members fit this pattern, particularly in the 1850s, '60s, and '70s (Liu and Mi 2015, 55). As Zhao Hong puts it, "the most important criterion for membership in the Gelaohui was poverty," and with only a few exceptions, GLH Guys in Gowns (袍哥) were paupers (2006, 24). Therefore, during this formative period, the poorer you were, the more likely were your chances to gain membership and thrive in the GLH.

The Qing government's memorial reports of rebellions in the provinces include one started by the GLH member Liu the Second (real name, Liu Tiankui) from Lanzhong county in eastern Sichuan, whose impoverished upbringing is similar to the Yu brothers'. In February and March 1897, several GLH lodges located in the Shaanxi province border area with Sichuan planned a large-scale uprising against Qing rule. When he was finally apprehended, investigators learned that Liu was raised in a struggling peasant family among highland "shack people [棚民]" (Yan 1966). Understanding that, with several older brothers, his father would not be able to leave him enough land from the family plot to survive, he decided to go off to study martial arts. He testified that, as a teenager, he "passed his days wandering from place to place screwing around, before joining the GLH [游荡度日早入哥老会]" (GGZ, vol. 11, 528).[1] In the fall of 1896 he arrived in Heshui county, Shaanxi, right across the Sichuanese border, to form a new lodge with a few friends from his hometown: Wen "Second Skin [二皮]" and Tang "Zit-Face the Third [三麻子]." They quickly assembled a combined force of over a thousand GLH fighters. According to Liu's testimony, one of the inspirations for this mass gathering was that he "got his hands on a righteous book" circulated among the GLH in Sichuan, which convinced him that the "contemporary world was filled with corruption" and it was therefore "best to rise up in rebellion" to rectify it (GGZ, vol. 11, 528).

Several members of the Wen family learned about the planned uprising and, alarmed, managed to get word to the local authorities, despite being placed under GLH guard. The Wen son Zaihong, reportedly earning the nickname "Second Skin" because he was so ugly that his parents attached a second layer of skin to cover up the unsightliness of the first, committed a major error in opposing stricter security measures for his family and letting them move about freely. Just days before the planned uprising, the leaders were captured by local militia forces based on information leaked by the Wens, just as the GLH forces were in the process of "manufacturing guns, explosives, swords, and flags" (GGZ, vol. 11, 527). The mastermind Liu the Second was apprehended hightailing it back to Sichuan.

Shaanxi Governor General Lu Chuanlin's report concluded that because Liu had deliberately plotted "that most heinous of crimes," the most extreme form of Qing vengeance was appropriate: the methodically slow carving off of the fleshy meat of the body, followed by removal of each of the members until the victim bled to death (凌迟处死). This entailed cutting off, first, both the eyebrows, then the meat over both shoulders. This was followed by thick slices off both pectoral muscles, followed by the meat under the upper arms and forearms. Before the hands, arms, and legs were chopped off, the meat from behind the calves and thighs was sliced off.[2] As each slab was carved off, it was caught on a large white plate by an assistant who then showed it to onlookers. Next, the nose was sliced off the rebel's face. Finally, the standard coup de grâce was applied—decapitation, with the bloodless head of Liu hung up for all to observe what happens to those who dare to rebel against the powerful Qing (GGZ, vol. 11, 529).

I want to draw attention to two issues here. The first is that these kinds of mountain areas were attracting rich merchants and landlords by the mid-1700s to set up factories based on wage labor. With the unpredictable highland reclamations most shack people had to undertake just to survive, capitalists knew that there was an abundance of cheap labor in these areas (Wang 2014, 64). Many peasants grew angry at opportunistic factory owners getting rich off their labor, and Liu Tiankui would certainly have been thinking about these capitalists when he critiqued the "contemporary world filled with corruption." The second issue is Liu being a reject from peasant society. Whether because of growing up in a poor, precarious area, bad luck, an arrest,[3] smoking too much opium, homoerotic desires, or a demographic disparity caused by a cultural preference for male children, approximately 20 percent of young peasant men in China were purged from and abandoned by their villages. Adding to the economic crisis in China at this time caused by Euro-American asymmetric lawfare/warfare, the expenses incurred by subduing the Taiping Rebellion (1850–1864), the rise of landlordism, an El Niño weather system, and population pressures all reduced the opportunities for employment previously available in the farming sector and craft and artisan guilds. In the provincial memorials of rebellions in central and southwestern China, we come across the same language depicting young men like Liu as "floating, directionless, and out of work [无业游民]", who ultimately found community and support in the GLH (GGZ, vol. 4, 99–100; vol. 6, 50–53; vol. 11, 255–59). The standard awareness among Qing officials in the years following the Taiping Rebellion was that "the Gelaohui is active in every Chinese province, but nowhere are they as powerful as in Sichuan" (Cai 1987, 197).

Similarly impoverished GLH men rose up in rebellion in the mountainous border region between Sichuan and Shaanxi in the spring of 1892. The GLH leader Zhou "Wild Sword [蛮刀]" was from a poor peasant family and began expanding his lodge membership in Yilong in eastern Sichuan. The memorial reported that Zhou was "ganging up with other like-minded criminals with the intention of stirring up trouble" (GGZ, vol. 7, 255). On May 19, 1892, Zhou's group of over a hundred was challenged by militia in nearby Nanjiang county, but the GLH rebels defeated them, killing several. As was standard for the GLH, whenever one lodge was attacked by government forces, nearby lodges were expected to come to their defense. The Sichuan governor general's office memorial describes this phenomenon as "everywhere Zhou went he was able to convince others to make trouble with him; eventually he was able to expand his group to over one thousand" (GGZ, vol. 7, 256).

Like guerrilla fighters everywhere, the GLH men were able to take advantage of their knowledge of the environment and deepen their intra-actions within the eco-ontology. Moreover, in addition to describing the GLH's ability to blend into the natural landscape, the memorial reports that the GLH benefited from the "floating affect of the people [民情浮动]"—in other words, the people "floated" from their default support for the local representatives of the Qing dynasty to support for the rebels. The writers insist that local officials became "truly terrified" when faced with this excessive intra-activity linking the GLH with the local ecology and linking local people with the GLH; nothing but "more trouble" was bound to result from it (GGZ, vol. 7, 256).

Well-equipped Qing soldiers were finally called in, and the rebels were defeated in two consecutive pitched battles. The GLH spears, waist swords, and hunting rifles proved to be no match for them (GGZ, vol. 7, 257). As the leaders started to get arrested, they only revealed their GLH rank before they were decapitated on the spot. Interestingly, they claimed the same titles as those used in the Qing bannermen army: grand signatory (正印), commander (大帽顶), and so on. The memorial writers wanted to assure Beijing that these titles stolen by the GLH rebels are "fake [伪]," but the GLH provocation is transmitted loud and clear: we are the legitimate army of the people, not you poseurs (GGZ, vol. 7, 257).

When Qing forces routed the rebels again on June 2, the memorial listed the names of several leaders caught and beheaded on the battlefield, including Chen "Pimple-Face," Zhao "Five Dollar," and Tang "Big Ear." Many GLH rebels had some kind of nickname, including Zhou "Wild Sword" and, most famously, Yu "The Savage [蛮子]" Dongchen." Others included Liu "Potty Mouth [歪嘴]."[4] These stigmatizations originated in peasant communities and, in some cases, rationalized their rejection from it. What local girl's family is going to consider marriage to someone known to all as Pimple-Face? Or to someone infamous for slicing up small animals and earning the nickname of Wild Sword? Members seemed to have embraced these nicknames that accentuated their differences from the mainstream. Younger readers may wonder why anyone would embrace something so marked by shame and rejection from straight, conventional society. Michel Foucault called just this paradoxical embrace a "reverse discourse" (1990, 101). Whether taking the form of "mick" or "queer," ethnoracial minorities and sexually subordinated groups often do just what the GLH was doing: turning a stigmatized name into something affirmative, if not absolutely fabulous.

Wild Sword's days came to an end when he was finally apprehended in a skirmish with Qing forces in the middle of June 1892. He testified to his captors that he had been an outlaw for many years, but only recently decided to "help the masses" by organizing a large insurgency. Other detainees' frequent references to greedy landlords and corrupt officials flesh out some of the motivations of the rebels. Right where he was captured and only a few hours later, Zhou was decapitated along with ten other rebel leaders. The heads were subsequently placed in nearby marketplaces as a warning to others contemplating rebellion (GGZ, vol. 7, 258).

Revolutionary Playbook

Let's return to the righteous book that inspired Liu the Second to rise up in rebellion against the Qing. Coming from a poor family in a mountainous area, Liu would have received very little schooling, so it must have been very easy to read, or—more likely—listen to, recite, and memorize. We know of only one book that unquestionably circulated inside the GLH, what the Sichuanese writer Fu Chongju revealed in 1909 as the "*The Ocean Depths* book [海底书]" (1909, 17).[5] *The Ocean Depths* (*Haidi*) also makes an appearance in Li Jieren's trilogy of late-Qing Sichuan; the respected GLH leader in Sichuan and heavy opium smoker Hou Baozhai was said to be able to recite the entire text from memory (2012b, 130). We should clarify how this book transmitted to Liu the Second the ideas and affects inducing him to risk everything in open rebellion against the Qing government and its capitalist allies. Was *The Ocean Depths* really a kind of revolutionary handbook for the GLH?

The Ocean Depths was certainly the manual for starting a new GLH lodge, and because the GLH was an outlawed organization, joining it turned members irrevocably into rebels opposed to Qing rule.[6] As the opening of a new lodge included initiating new members, most of the content of *The Ocean Depths* is dedicated to passing down the rituals, rules, and regulations of the GLH and introducing newcomers to its pantheon and version of history. Unlike elite histories centered on dynasties and imperial courts, the GLH version focused exclusively on idealistic rebels living humbly and intra-actively within a local environment. From that vantage point they opposed corrupt officials and aided and abetted other poor people. One of several extant versions of *The Ocean Depths* begins as a direct address to new members initiated into the GLH:

> We warmly welcome the newcomers and because we don't have very good manners, we hope you will quickly forgive our vulgar and coarse ways. The lodge Elder, the Verification Elder, the Keeper of the Rituals Elder, the #2 Rank Sage, #3 Rank Prince, and the #5 Rank Administrator hereby invite

the newcomers to come into the hall with the young and old members from rows 6, 9, 10. The youngest member will fill the pipe and tea cup for this attendant Elder. We ask all you benevolent ones to forgive our rudeness [恕罪], but our preparations were done quickly like the rushing river.

Even worse, we neglected to travel to your place to personally invite you; we didn't send servants to bring you here; we didn't even properly welcome you when you first arrived. We respectfully beg each member to forgive us by lifting up your sleeve and letting us know you have forgotten our other slights. Once again, we beg you to forgive our coarse manners. (Qunying she 1975, 2–3)

There are three things that should be highlighted here. The first is the salient humility of the group leader welcoming the new members, most likely the lodge's grand supervisor. He repeatedly apologizes for the way the leadership has neglected to treat the newcomers in a manner appropriate to their expansive humanity and righteousness. This would have been a startling inversion of the manner these new members were treated by mainstream society before joining the GLH, either as ex-convicts, petty thieves, or as rejects from peasant society. For a good part of their lives these men would have been subjected to ridicule and shame. When, all of a sudden, those qualities that had determined their wretchedness miraculously caused them to be treated with respect and dignity by a well-known group that promised to provide for their security and welfare would have been a dream come true.

The second aspect to be highlighted here is the repeated reference to the distance that each of the newcomers has traveled to get to the mountain initiation. Distance should be construed here as a metaphor for how far the new members have come in terms of their place in society—from an outcaste one to joining a feared and respected collectivity claiming a continuity with righteous rebels spanning more than a thousand years of Chinese history. In rare cases, distances were less metaphorical, as drifters like Liu the Second would have occasionally traveled from a neighboring province, looking for sanctuary and support.

The last thing that deserves mention is the presence of rows or ranks (牌). The GLH was embedded in the discursive system of traditional China, and although it offered rare opportunities for subalterns to improve their socioeconomic situation, new members usually entered lodges at the lowest of the nine ranks—the fourth and seventh rows were left unoccupied for customary reasons. In both official Qing and opposition rebel groups, each rank carried a different responsibility and status. The GLH was known for rewarding loyalty and dedication to the group by encouraging upward mobility in the ranks (Felsing

1979; Wang 1993). Again, this would have been opposite to most members' socioeconomic status in peasant villages—relentless movement down and out. The Qing government also offered opportunities for advancement, although the primary vehicle for this—the examination system—was often a barrier for less well-off students. Despite the distinct ranking of members, all GLH cadre thought of themselves as equal, and this sense of egalitarianism separated the GLH from mainstream groups in China at this time. The unspoken rule inside the GLH was: "Everyone eats the same food, and everyone bears the same burden" (Wang 1993, 34). As I will show in chapter 6, this egalitarianism would facilitate alliances with the modern revolutionaries in the Tongmenghui that would otherwise have been inconceivable (Zhao 2006, 38–39). Unlike the anthropocentric egalitarianism of the Tongmenghui, however, the GLH's version was multispecies, with human beings just one &bject in an intra-active network of entities including animals, mountains, rivers, deceased predecessors, and deities. There was a version of what object-oriented ontologist Levi R. Bryant calls a multispecies "democracy of objects" inside most GLH lodges (2011).

The top leader in a GLH lodge transcended all the ranks and was known as ship's captain (舵把子) or dragon head.[7] Like the other ranks, the dragon head was expected to mimic the deportment of a rebel hero from Chinese history. The leader's role model was Liu Bei (AD 161–223), the famous warlord of the Eastern Han dynasty during the Three Kingdoms era (AD 220–80), who rose from poverty to become the benevolent ruler of greater Sichuan, or Shu Han.[8]

The first rank or row consisted of first uncles, and there were usually four of these (JFMA, "Chinese Revolutionaries," 660). The four shared power with the top leader inside the lodge, and all GLH cadre had to speak respectfully to them. First uncles were also expected to take Liu Bei as their exemplar. The second row's model was Guan Yu (?–220), the general and sworn brother of Liu Bei, who also came from a poor peasant background. Guan Yu was also the tutelary deity of the GLH, referred to with the divinity name of Guan Di. This row was called the wise second uncle, as there was only one of these. He was chosen on the basis of his moral character and the extent of his learning, which in some lodges in the 1860s and '70s simply meant he could read and write Chinese characters. His most important function was ceremonial, paying proper respect to the deities and ancestors at the beginning of any GLH meeting. According to *The Ocean Depths*, "The second Uncle should follow the ancient sage Guan Yu. He was very loyal to Liu Bei as he risked his life to save Liu's wife after she was taken hostage in Cao Cao's garrison" (Wang 1993, 37).

The third rank's role model was Zhang Fei (?–221), also a sworn brother of Guan Yu and Liu Bei. This rank was called either "manager [当家]" or "keeper of the lodge." He was responsible for dispensing money and provisions. He was situated directly under the top four uncles, and he often passed their opinions on to the rest of the group. The fifth row was called fifth uncle. His main responsibility was taking care of relations with their wharf partners (lodges were normally linked together through an overarching wharf) and with all other nearby GLH wharfs, which called for magnanimity and humility. He was expected to mimic the behavior of Shan Xiongxin, rebel hero of the Sui dynasty (581–618) (Wang 1993, 37).

The sixth rank was called "the carrier of the black flag"; they assisted the supervisor and his helper with maintaining the rules and regulations of the lodge. They were also responsible for gathering information and intelligence from both inside and outside the group; this function was crucial in performing background checks on new members (JFMA, "Chinese Revolutionaries," 985). Moreover, they were also responsible for guarding internal documents and advising on proper ritual procedures. The eighth row was called "the holder of the spirit flag," and this was awarded to "the champion of common people and the destroyer of tyrants [除暴安良]" (Li 1990, 97). The ninth rank was called both the "the ninth river" and "security watch." Their main responsibilities were to put out the new ranks and titles, tutor the new members in proper behavior, and announce promotions at important meetings.

The tenth rank was called "final tenth," or "tail of the phoenix." This rank instructed everyone in the responsibilities of security for all GLH meetings and was supposed to be constantly available in case of emergencies. One or two people from this tenth rank would be chosen for their keen understanding of internal GLH protocols. Those selected needed to excel at interpersonal communication as they often had to pass on sensitive information inside the group. They were also responsible for welcoming other GLH visitors and making arrangements for their own members who were planning visits to other wharfs. This involved dealing with proper invitation cards and making sure security was tight enough for guests to visit safely (Wang 1993, 38).

Membership Has Its Privileges

It's easy to imagine the dramatic transformation for the new GLH initiate, moving from the predicament of being an escaped convict or an impoverished peasant living precariously hand to mouth, to one involving an elaborately coded set of responsibilities and duties. For some this new semiotic world would have been much more than they had asked for in seeking out support and solidarity. But despite the heavy demands placed on new members, the GLH enjoyed explosive growth after the Second War for Drugs ended in 1860 and the Taiping Rebellion was crushed a few years later. Two years before the overthrow of Qing rule in 1911, the official Sichuan provincial publication *Sichuan Guanbao* detailed that GLH lodges "were everywhere and their members included people from all walks of life" (in Liu and Mi 2015, 124). How did this happen when the GLH parent group, Guolu, was in the 1840s a marginalized band of rough-and-tumble levelers and revelers?

There were three main demographic streams that converged in the 1860s to transform the marginal Guolu into the major sociopolitical force Gelaohui. The first was Guolu itself. The second was the decommissioned mercenaries from the Hunan forces fighting the Taiping Rebellion in central China, a significant number of whom came from Sichuan. We know that the GLH recruited intensely inside the Hunan army (Liu 1983, 52–53; Wang 2007, 25). The third and, in my view, the most important stream resulted from the huge peasant uprising from 1859–65 against the Qing and corrupt landlords led by the southwestern Chinese opium dealers and smokers Li Longhe and Lan Dashun (Hu 1983, 118).

Starting in Daguan county in northeastern Yunnan province in 1859, this peasant rebellion spread into southern and western Sichuan, where the main clashes took place. When poor farmers decided they had had enough of the increasing tax burden and Qing corruption, they asked Li and Lan to direct an uprising. Some of them had been selling raw opium paste to Li and Lan and believed they were fair and honest. In the late 1850s in Sichuan, Yunnan, and Guizhou, the GLH controlled opium trafficking, which from the end of the First War for Drugs in 1842 saw the gradual substitution of imported Anglo-Indian opium by local Yunnan and Sichuanese product, called southern (南土) and Sichuanese (川土) mud, respectively (Hu 1983, 20; Liu and Mi 2015, 105). Therefore, owing to the multiple contacts and friendships Li and Lan had established among the GLH in drug routes between Yunnan and Sichuan, and impressed by the organization, in September 1859 along with nine other fellow traffickers they formally became members of the rebel brotherhood. Subsequently, they started organizing fighters, pledging to "kill rich landlords and officials" and "defend the poor peasants" (Hu 1983, 85–87). From February 1860 they took their army to Sichuan, where they eventually mobilized upward of 100,000 GLH fighters to battle for autonomy from landlords and the Qing government. Everywhere the Li/Lan forces went in Sichuan, local GLH lodges would mimic their policy of freeing peasants from rich landlords and setting up fair compensation for opium to be sold directly to GLH dealers. One of their public policies was to liberate peasants to "grow whatever they wanted," and this increasingly became lucrative poppy crops; the pro forma legalization of opium in 1858 at the Shanghai Tariff Conference provided some support for this. The Li/Lan uprising was also one of the first to feature an explicit anti-Western politics, castigating Euro-Americans as "enemies of Heaven" (Hu 1983, 79). The rebellion lasted until 1865 and resulted in Sichuan suddenly becoming the leading poppy-producing province in China (Chen 2010, 120–25). This rapid increase in supply resulted in a lowering of prices, which allowed opium smoking to spread from a practice enjoyed predominantly by the wealthy and Qing officials all the way down to the poorest peasants. The explosion in available opium product in Sichuan (but also in Yunnan and neighboring Guizhou) led to what Hu Hansheng calls a "dramatically transformed situation regarding opium; no one could do without it" (1983, 120). Peasants relied on the extra income from poppy cultivation, the expanding number of GLH members controlled trafficking and the mushrooming opium establishments, and Qing officials and the wealthy required it both for their own smoking and as a status symbol in entertaining friends and extended family at their residences. Finally, with its focus on defending poor peasants and its bragging rights for defeating well-armed Qing forces in several battles, the Li/Lan peasant uprising was, as Liu Yangang and Mi Yungang put it, a "public showcase and a huge promotional exercise crucial for the development of the Gelaohui" (2015, 111). For our purposes here, the Li/Lan movement established an inextricable link between poppy cultivation (and opium use and exchange) and the sociopolitical power of the GLH. No "breaking bad," the production and circulation of opium by the GLH was construed as a beneficent phenomenon throughout southwestern China. As we will see in chapter 6, this emerging conflation of the GLH with opium would prove crucial both for the liberation movement against Euro-American Christian missions, and for the Xinhai Revolution in Sichuan that eventually toppled dynastic Qing rule in China.

Levelry and Revelry

As we saw in chapter 2, despite having converted only 1 percent of Sichuanese by 1900, French Catholic rule enjoyed a powerful presence in the juridical, economic, and environmental realms. And in southwestern and central China, the GLH emerged as the Church's main opponent—confronting legal injustices; subverting Catholic economic power; and, as we saw in chapter 2, defending local eco-ontologies by tearing down deliberately anti–feng shui churches and cathedrals and opposing, Luddite-like, Euro-American mechanization of mining, shipping, and communications (Jabobson 1993; Zhao 2006). The GLH's predecessor Guolu had always been opposed to Qing centralized authority. But as we saw in chapter 2, after the Second War for Drugs of 1856–60, Qing rule was felt to be even more unjust by locals as it became increasingly obligated by the Unequal Treaties to protect Climate Caucasianists and Chinese Christians. Therefore, more and more people looked to the GLH's reputation for defending those victimized by these twin oppressors. When we put the GLH network together, we need to add these conjunctural aspects to the three population streams. In doing so, we can see that the 1860s offered an unprecedented recruiting environment for them (Wang 2018, 40).

And the evidence suggests they didn't screw it up. One of the main reasons for this is that the politics of redistributing wealth and leveling socioeconomic disparities was still foregrounded in the GLH of the 1860s and '70s. This offered both a seductive antigovernment mystique and a clear moral purpose to new members—both of these were revered aspects of Chinese rebel history and myth. In addition to this communistic commitment to what I'll call levelry, or the flattening out of socioeconomic inequality by forceful redistribution, there was an equally salient commitment to festivities and celebrations—revelry. These two were conflated in the organization's tacit promise that, although it would not be easy for recruits to adhere to their strict regulations and codes of honor, for those who did so the GLH would guarantee that members would be well provided for—and that included myriad parties, celebrations, and their own festivals: Ghost Fest (中元会), Reunion Fest (团圆会), Single Sword Fest (单刀会), and the organization's most important annual event, Guan Di (Guan Yu) Fest, occurring on the thirteenth day of the fifth month (JFMA, "Chinese Revolutionaries," 987). All these would normally take place at the GLH wharf's temple to Guan Di and featured fogs of opium smoke and the performance of a classic from the repertoire of Sichuanese opera, often with GLH members in singing roles (Liu and Mi 2015, 101). The same setup would apply for popular Chinese festivals like the Dragon Boat Fest and Chinese New Year, as well as Sichuan-specific holidays like "Liberating All Living Things [放生会]," which took place on the eighth day of the fourth lunar month.

As Wang (1993), Liu (1983), and Liu and Mi (2015) insist, these GLH festivals shared with their most important ritual event—the opening of a mountain (开山) that both formally established new lodges and swore in new members—the ready availability of opium. Opium was deployed both as an offering to their tutelary god Guan Di and as an intoxicant in its own right to alter the consciousness and therefore intensify the ecstatic sense GLH rituals were designed to conjure. Of course, the main element relied on to prepare the ritual space and welcome deities and ancestors was incense (香), and here the

GLH was no different from standard practices in Chinese folk spirituality of the eighteenth and nineteenth centuries. In an authoritative study of the rituals of rebel Chinese brotherhoods, Barend ter Haar underlines the continuity that the centrality of incense in the rituals of the brotherhoods had with mainstream Chinese rituals: "burning incense . . . was used to fumigate and thereby purify places, to get rid of evil influences both on a literal level (especially all kinds of harmful insects) and on a supernatural level (evil demons). Incense was already used as early as the Han dynasty to open up a communication channel with the supernatural world, through which the gods can be invited to attend and messages can be communicated to the supernatural world" (1998, 56).

The description of opening a mountain ritual in *The Ocean Depths* is filled with instructions related to incense. Incense sticks are carried by the initiates into the ritual space, offered as sacrifices to the deities, and lit and placed in specific places and at specific times during the ritual. The deities supposedly love smoke and incense because it both detoxes and helps to create a special, nonmundane environment suitable for intra-action. Opium shared these functions of purifying (through its smoke and sweet smell) and sacralizing, as, like incense, it was a special ingredient that people often spent extra money on. But the added advantage of opium smoking was that it put the participants (especially humans, but it was believed that opium intoxication extended to deities and spirits as well, as I'll show in chapter 6) in an altered cognitive and affective state. Although alcohol was also used for this, the anecdotal evidence shows that opium smoking and drinking "spirits" were frequently combined. In the first Chinese brotherhood initiation ritual ever documented, in 1824 by the Malay Abdullah bin Abdul Kadir, alcohol and opium were consumed off and on during the six- or seven-hour event (ter Haar 1998, 103–4). The increasing availability and low cost of opium in central and southwestern China after the First War for Drugs facilitated its prominence in GLH rituals and celebrations.

Job Placement

In addition to their internal rank and the set of responsibilities that followed from that, poor recruits who were not full-time farmers were generally provided with some kind of job. We should keep in mind that, like the rebel Zhou Wild Sword whose story opened this chapter, the majority of GLH members in Sichuan and throughout China were peasant farmers. Peasants were so central that uprisings in Sichuan and Yunnan were routinely timed to take place in the first, second, and third lunar months so they wouldn't interfere with the rice harvest and spring planting seasons (Liu 1983, 143). Peasants were a new demographic addition to the rebel brotherhoods in Sichuan in the mid-nineteenth century, as all Guolu members in the seventeenth and eighteenth centuries were low-level thieves and hustlers. By the early nineteenth century, the Guolu had stabilized into four distinct occupations for members, which the GLH of the 1860s inherited before adding a new one. The first occupation was robbery, which was divided into experts at breaking into houses, palanquin or car(riage) jacking, and those experienced in river piracy. Nearly all Guolu members were veteran robbers, having practiced it either alone or as part of a larger collective (Wang 1993, 10–12). Like other outlaw groups influenced by traditional Chinese morality, the GLH had a specific set of rules that determined all acts of robbery. The most important drew a clear line between robbery and theft—what was known in Sichuan as "robbery is approved while theft is condemned [认盗不认偷]" (Zhao 2006, 53). Theft was construed as an immoral, selfish act completely bereft of larger sociopolitical and cosmological determinants (Wang 2008, 159–60). Moreover, theft was widely condemned in the other rebel brotherhoods, and the GLH shared with them what David Ownby calls an overarching "brotherhood ideology" (1996, 3).

Contrary to theft, robbery was understood to be an act that repaired unjust social hierarchies and punished the rich and corrupt; in outlaw moral discourse these were inseparable. Wealth brought immorality, spiritual filth, and a blatant disregard for other beings—human, nonhuman, and extrahuman. Readers should recall that while the caste/status hierarchy in China was similar to that in Japan, Chinese society claimed to be more meritocratic because the examination system allowed hardworking young men to rise to the ranks of government officials. However, this happened so infrequently that the unfairness of Qing society became obvious to many. Unlike the false promises of social mobility through success in the examinations, for GLH members the outlaw brotherhoods offered the only existing vehicle to redistribute wealth and correct unfair inequalities in Chinese society, ones exacerbated by the CO2lonial incursion of Euro-whites. As we saw above in the cases of Liu the Second and Zhou Wild Sword, the affective common sense was that "the world was corrupt" and the ethical thing to do was join together with others committed to changing it, ideally by "rising up in rebellion." But J-hād or G(LH)-hād didn't exhaust the available tactics to bring heavenly justice to worldly corruption. Righteous robbery was another, more sustainable one. For the GLH the moral distinction between robbery and theft was a clear reflection of their subaltern position as social outcasts, and it played out as one encouraging hits and jacks on rich landlords, capitalist factory owners, Qing officials, and Euro-white Christians. Similarly, this distinction severely condemned thievery against poorer merchants, peasants, and, naturally, any member of the GLH—the brotherhood code dictated that rebels could only level "up." Although the ideological world of most of the readers of this book will predispose them against organizations like "the mafia," all the Chinese rebel brotherhoods forbade acts that took unfair advantage of the poor; some members were killed for just thinking of doing so. Consistent with this was the moral imperative to rob only those at the top, and acts of redistribution against wealthier Chinese and Euro-Americans were construed as exactly that, especially when the dispossessed goods or money were distributed to those less well off—as it sometimes was (Liu 1983, 139–40). One of the thirty-six oaths of the Triad brotherhood specifically warned rebel brothers to "beware of wealth," while several others elaborated on the danger having too much money brings (ter Haar 1998, 212). Although the streamlined GLH stripped away sixteen of these (leaving only ten laws and ten conditions), this helps explain what GLH researchers like Liu and Mi (2015) and Felsing (1979) mean when they insist that GLH members didn't want to be rich. This was diametrically opposed to the "commandment" handed down to capitalists from the holy men "Moses and the prophets" that Karl Marx sarcastically turned into advocates of private enterprise in ordering believers to "Accumulate! Accumulate!" (1977a, 742). In other words, the majority of GLH rebels were completely different from capitalist $ubjects, wanting only enough to maintain the intra-active lives they shared with other entities and increase their autonomy from rulers—similar to what Indigenous Latin American groups call "*buen vivir*" or living well ("*Sumac Kawsay*" for the Quechua people of the Andes) (Escobar 2018, 148–49). In other words, there was no Christian "prosperity gospel" or "Chinese Dream" urging people to become filthy rich. This was one of the reasons that even after their material situations improved, many GLH Guys in Gowns continued to wear their Guan Yu–inspired tattered and dirty robes (gowns). To look and act poor was living proof of their righteousness and morality.

The most common form that GLH robbery took was forceful entry into the residences of the wealthy (Liu and Mi 2015, 55). A second kind of robbery involved, in the colorful language of the group, cordoning off an area, publicly shaming, and then robbing a rich person—"shut the pig in and cut off its fat [关圈拉肥猪]" (Zhao 2006, 42). As GLH robbery was conceived with an explicit politics of retributive justice and morality, it was also conducted in line with cosmological principles—like some of the samurai uprisings in southwestern Japan discussed in chapter 3. Therefore, GLH robberies could not be carried out on the fifth, fourteenth, or twenty-third of any month. Moreover, consultation with Daoist priests (who were recruited as members) about what object-oriented ontology calls extrahuman "directives" to humans for large leveling operations was strongly recommended (Morton 2013, 141). This normally involved the robbers gathering with the priest and kowtowing to the deities continuously while the priest burned paper amulets and then tossed the ashes into the air, decoding the configuration the ashes made—a ritual called 飘纱 (JFMA, "Chinese Revolutionaries," 661). In other words, GLH robbery was often the result of intra-action among deities, the five elements, lunar movements, ritual figures and shamans, and human &bjects.

It is impossible to ascertain the specific intra-active determinants behind the GLH robbery of British missionaries on October 2, 1884, but there was clearly fat to be shared among those less well off. Two China Inland missionaries decided to leave their mission in northern Guizhou province in late September owing to a lingering illness affecting James Broundon. They hired two single-person carriages with three drivers each and employed an additional six porters to lug all their money and things: some 500 taels in cash and about 500 taels more in possessions carried in three large leather bags and one impregnable iron trunk. This was low-hanging fruit for a GLH team of about fifteen men who surprised them a week into their two week-journey to Chongqing, Sichuan. Although the robbers brandished "clubs, old rusty swords, and one long spear," these were all unnecessary in the end as the leveling action required only threats; no one was harmed. Despite the pleas from Broundon that they weren't French Catholics and therefore presented no direct threat to local Chinese, the action left the China Inland party with nothing except for the clothes on their backs. However, when the twelve Chinese workers told the GLH robbers that the white men had refused to pay them anything in advance and that they would be in serious debt because the robbery made it impossible for the British to make good on their commitment, the GLH proved their righteousness in giving each of the twelve cash money and some of the Englishmen's possessions. Finally, Broundon concluded his own account of the incident by commenting that the GLH appeared to "divide up the money and goods evenly" (BFO 228/746, October 18, 1884). Indeed, what Harney and Moten call the "undercommons" was a prominent feature in this and other GLH actions (2015).

Car(riage) Jackers and River Pirates

When wealthy gentry and merchants began to rebrand themselves as friends of the poor and downtrodden and became members of the GLH in the 1880s and '90s, this left Christians, nonlocal travelers, and boat traffic up and down the Yangzi as the main target of righteous leveling activities for GLH robbers. Most palanquin or carriage carriers performed double duty as security guards and took the brunt of appropriation by force, which the GLH called "intercepting journeys [中途拦截]" (JFMA, "Chinese Criminal Organizations," 625). While the GLH robber carrying out a car(riage) jacking might be referred to as a "*jiaozi* [sedan chair] jacker" or "palanquin poacher," the internal Qing police language was less kind in identifying them simply as "bandits [土匪]."

GLH robbery garnered even more local approval when it targeted perpetrators of sexual assault against women. Violence against women was thought to be carried out primarily by Qing officials (or those with connections to them) and Euro-whites, both largely enjoying immunity from the law (JFMA, "Chinese Criminal Organizations," 624). Although GLH retribution against sexual predators didn't usually involve robbery, two birds were killed with one stoned team of GLH robbers who joined up with women who had been rape victims to rob their attackers. An illustration of this happens in Li Jieren's 1936 realist novel *Sishui weilan* when the landlord Gu Tiancheng is shaken down by a GLH group of heavy opium smokers sometime after 1902 (Li 2012a, 110–16).[9]

Sichuan province has several long rivers, enabling a plethora of opportunities for river piracy in the province—the invocation of which still elicits nostalgia in Chongqing.[10] Organized river piracy (江贼会匪) was less risky than car(riage) jacking or breaking into the houses of the wealthy, as boats traveling up the Yangzi from central China lost some of their protection once they moved into Sichuan. The moral code of GLH river pirates held that the larger the boat, the more righteous the leveling operation. However, Chinese and Euro-white trading companies based in Shanghai adapted quickly to this and began shipping their goods in older, smaller Chinese junks, despite the added transportation costs (JFMA, "Chinese Criminal Organizations," 627). Nevertheless, GLH river pirates used their superior knowledge of the rivers and mountain passes to transmit intelligence about the owners of specific boats. The cat-and-mouse game became even more lopsided in favor of the GLH when they were able to recruit more boat trackers in the 1890s, promising to help block the encroaching substitution of wind- and human-powered river transport by coal-power urged by Climate Caucasianists.

Until Archibald Little's pioneering feat of traveling from Yichang in Hubei some three hundred miles up the Yangzi to Chongqing, Sichuan, by steamship in 1898, every boat, small and large, required multiple pullers to navigate the dangerous passes up the gorges and the river torrents.

GLH boat trackers teamed up with river pirates in complicated actions involving the deliberate grounding of vessels, which could then be easily boarded and leveled by waiting GLH pirates. Of course, the expansion of concession areas in the newly opened ports of Yichang and Chongqing functioned as job

赤身裸体，拉船上游，世上少有的吃苦耐劳群体(民国)

在那个时代，一艘货船逆水上行，只有靠纤夫的"人海战术"了

FIGURE 4.1. Upper Yangzi boat pullers and trackers in 1890s (Wang Chuanping 2013b).

creators for GLH river pirates. And when steamship transport became standard for Euro-white companies in the first decade of the twentieth century, GLH agents figured out which companies combined the transport of goods with paid passenger service. Subsequently, they carried out complicated leveling operations by simultaneously having undercover GLH passengers on the ship subdue sailors and captains from inside, while GLH pirates boarded the ship from the outside (JFMA, "Chinese Criminal Organizations," 666–67). A successful GLH leveling operation against CO_2lonizing Euro-white steamships must have been even more enjoyable payback for the many GLH members who were former boat trackers put out of work by new coal-powered and climate-interfering steamships (663).

The second occupation GLH members inherited from the Guolu was coal mining, which often went together with manure collecting. The GLH dominated the human manure market throughout Sichuan, and in most counties one of their members was the leader of the manure sellers—the so-called "shit head" or 糞頭 (Han 1965, 249). (As in late nineteenth-century Sichuan opium paste was called "mud [土]," we can assert that the GLH primarily sold mud and shit, both recyclable organic products.) Before they became full-time insurrectionists, Yu Dongcheng and his brothers eked out a living by selling manure to farmers during planting season; the rest of the time they worked as hired agriculture workers and in the mines. They probably came into contact with the GLH first at a mining site as the GLH had been recruiting coal miners and porters for over a decade (Felsing 1979, 116). Unlike the kind of extraction practiced by European capitalists like Thomas Glover we saw in chapter 1, however, the GLH insisted on preserving the culture of relating to the spirits and deities of the mountain through daily rituals of thanks and sacrifice (JFMA, "Revolutionary Groups in China," 221). As the mountain was one of the central entities in the GLH eco-ontology,[11] it was impossible to approach it solely as a source of extraction for the $ubject, as it was by Euro-whites like Glover and Archibald Little, who was successful in obtaining mining concessions from Qing officials in and around Chongqing in 1906 (Li 2004). As de la Cadena writes about the relationality with mountains for Indigenous Peruvians, for the GLH a mountain was "not only" a geophysical thing, but something more owing to its "ontological excess" (2015, 15). Acknowledging the exuberant generosity of the mountain, GLH rituals sometimes prioritized mountain entities over human ones. Following from the group's emphasis on rootedness and what theorists of Indigeneity call "ancestrality," mountains occupied a central place in the pantheon of the GLH, second only to the predecessor hero Guan Yu (Di) and Daoist and Buddhist deities (Escobar 2018, 71). Mountains generated minerals for human use, but they also offered crucial protection and security from Qing oppression. Mountains were so life-generating for the GLH that they called the important ritual of starting a new lodge and initiating new members "revealing a mountain [开山]." As these ritual beginnings frequently took place in and around remote mountains difficult for Qing government runners to infiltrate (Chongqing, Sichuan, is surrounded by mountains on two sides), mountains might be said to be insurrectionary entities in their own right (Liu and Mi 2015, 70). Finally, the significant changes in altitude occurring in eastern and western Sichuan's mountains were perfect for creating an atmosphere for rituals as different as possible from day-to-day mundane ones—even better when opium smoking contributed to the "high" of the different ascending zones of a mountain.

The third occupation in the GLH was water hand (水手), which meant anyone connected to boat transport and the complicated hauling procedures that were necessary to get ships up the gorges and rivers to Sichuan from central China. As we saw, water hands worked in tandem with GLH robbers involved in leveling operations by helping them with escapes. To understand the importance of water hands, we should start with the centrality of water for GLH. Many GLH Guys in Gowns in Sichuan referred internally to their organization as simply "rivers and lakes [江湖]" (Wang 2018, 42). This same character compound was understood as something like "poor people's society" in southwestern China of the eighteenth and nineteenth centuries until 社会 (society) borrowed from Japanese became standard in twentieth-century China, displacing the materiality of rivers and lakes.

"Rivers and lakes" signified poverty because without property to live on and land to farm, people were pushed and pulled by the currents of the water. In the upper Yangzi region, water hands/boat pullers were poor, and work was unpredictable. As we'll see in chapter 6, many turned to selling opium to make ends meet. However, as we saw above with the GLH rebels practicing reverse discourse and turning stigmatized names into badges of honor, the same went for rivers and lakes. Although "running [跑] the rivers and lakes" was often the only alternative for surplus sons from peasant villages (often supplemented by gigs like divination, astrology, street performance, manure collecting, etc.), the GLH and other outlaw groups romanticized this. For one thing, leaving peasant villages and immersing oneself in rivers and lakes meant refusing to pay rent to corrupt landlords, and, into the 1890s and 1900s, refusing the capitalist oppression of wage labor. For another, it meant leaving behind the paternal authority of fathers and village elders. Like "going underground" in European rebel discourse, the immersion in rivers and lakes led to a different set of rules and experiences. E. P. Thompson wrote that the time rebels spent underground was "of a richness at which we can only guess" (in Linebaugh 2019, 87). The same applied to dunking in rivers and lakes, where intra-activity was intensified. While eco-ontologies were generally shared by rebels and nonrebels alike—Chinese human &bjects were still one part of a large network of multiple deities, ancestors, and non- and extrahuman beings—the rivers and lakes eco-ontology was more intricate and unpredictable; immersion often meant plunging into the unknown and letting the wild water current take you where it will. Given the centrality of rivers and riparian (river–land) zones to Sichuan, "rivers and lakes" was often more than a metaphor for many, especially the poor sailors and boat pullers. But other GLH members relied on the Yangzi and other rivers to sustain them. We mentioned earlier that riparian zones are known for their intricate biodiversity: plants and birds not found anywhere else call riparian zones home. Evidently, Sichuan's version included diverse kinds of human beings as well. And the GLH, a collection of river and lake entities like no other in Sichuan, was always nearby to throw a life preserver to poor people swept up in the current.

The fourth occupation in the GLH was connected to the first but was so specialized it required an entirely separate system of master and apprentice. The practice of salt smuggling was shrouded in proud memories of antigovernment heroism in Sichuan. As one of the main sources of Qing revenue, the government salt monopoly was an attractive institution for outlaws who wanted to attack the Qing and support their rebel comrades in one gesture. It was considered the most honorable of the expropriative acts in the GLH (JFMA, "Organized Criminals in China," 624).[12]

The final job in the GLH was that of opium entrepreneur (Liu and Mi 2015, 56). As I suggested above, the organization owed much of its early recruitment success to the efforts of the drug dealers and anti-Western activists Li Longhe and Lan Dashun. Moreover, the explosion in poppy cultivation and opium smoking in Sichuan (and Yunnan and Guizhou) between 1859 and 1910 would have been impossible without the efforts of the GLH. Their extensive networks provided channels for peasants to get poppies to makeshift processing sites and then circulate opium from these facilities to town and city opium rooms and parlors, where much of the product was consumed. As we will detail in chapter 6, both Chinese and Euro-American observers were taken aback by the ubiquity of opium establishments in and around Chongqing, claiming that you could see them "everywhere you looked" (Wang 2013a, 40). Most of Sichuan's opium rooms were thought to have direct connections to GLH lodges (Liu 1983, 129).[13]

All this would have been helped by the fact that the GLH was known in Sichuan and throughout central and southwestern China as a group that practiced and preached opium smoking (APF, vol. 80, 14; BFO 228/700, April 20, 1882; JFMA, "Organized Criminals in China," 657–58). Unlike the white British narcos Lin Zexu criticized for not consuming their own product, but similar to any honest drug dealer, GLH smokers were ideally suited as promoters and dealers of homegrown Sichuanese smoke. Ultimately, the ambivalent status of opium in China after the Second War for Drugs—generally condemned, yet also serving as a crucial revenue stream via taxes on its consumption and circulation—also made it perfect as an item of exchange and use for an outlaw group like the GLH. Although I won't fully discuss this until chapter 6, it deserves mention here that Anglo-American Protestants kicked off a major opium suppression campaign in China in the 1880s. Given the fact that the GLH was the unrivaled leader of the anti-Christian insurgency in central and southwestern China, there is no question that this would have stimulated an even richer intra-activity between GLH members, processed opium, and opium poppies (Liu and Mi 2015, 121–22). When the hated Qing caved in to Euro-American missionary pressure and launched its own war on (opium) drugs in 1906, this served as an added impetus for the GLH to expand the production and consumption of Sichuanese smoke.

It's Not Just a Job . . .

After their guaranteed jobs program, a principal reason for GLH membership mushrooming in the 1860s and '70s was its commitment to celebrations and rituals. For all GLH members, weddings, funerals of family members, and new births were celebrated lavishly, with expenses paid by the group's coffers. The modes of celebration were copied as much as possible from narratives in classic outlaw literature like *Water Margin* (水滸傳) (Felsing 1979; Zhao 2006).

The opening of a GLH lodge and initiation of new members was often the place where this was first experienced. The ritual itself featured alcohol, food, and the drinking of each other's blood as a symbol of "blood ties," but these were secondary as both the preparation for the ritual and the celebration afterward centered on opium smoking (Wang 1993, 74). The centrality of opium in the GLH's rituals was the reason that some lodges decided it was more convenient just to conduct them in GLH-owned opium rooms (Qin 2001, 71–72). This was a culmination of sorts to the importance of the opium object in the intra-active network of the GLH. Again, the evidence suggests that regular opium smoking actually aided one's advancement within the rebel brotherhood.

For example, as I will show in chapter 6, the GLH elders who promised the young Tongmenghui activists they would mobilize all of Sichuan's lodges in a mass uprising against the Qing in September 1911 were heavy smokers. The embrace of opium users would also help explain the growth in GLH membership after 1860, as smokers were generally considered disgraceful wastrels in peasant society and the shame of a small village before this changed with the viral spread of opium smoking and poppy cultivation in the 1860s and '70s. For GLH initiates to suddenly have that shame reversed and inverted into something affirmative (all the while guaranteeing access to regular and discounted supplies of opium)—"Well now," a new initiate may have thought, "the Buddha really does have my back."

GLH Conflict Resolution

Any successful outlaw group needs to have proven conflict resolution methods. These are necessary both to maintain group bonding and to disincentivize disgruntled members from going to the local magistrate to rat out brotherhood comrades. Therefore, it's not surprising to find an intricate system of negotiating conflict between GLH members and lodges. GLH conflict management featured two main procedures and took place in two specific establishments: GLH teahouses and opium rooms. The popularity of the GLH opium-induced dispute resolution became such a headache for the Chongqing (Baxian county) magistrate Guo in the mid-1890s that he outlawed any kind of mediation taking place in opium rooms in 1895 (SPA 6:31–01696, October 1895).

The first form of GLH conflict resolution was simply called "dispute mediation." This always involved a GLH elder presiding over the conflict, who was to be deferred to in the last instance. After the establishment was cleared of non-GLH members, each of the parties would tell their side of the story. From there, the main stance of the judging elder was expected to be leniency and flexibility. After asking other GLH members to join in and ask questions or challenge one or both of the parties, the senior GLH member would pass judgment (sometimes taking a day or two to think the situation through) and order the guilty to pay compensation, or "tea money," to the injured party. When the guilty party refused to pay the tea money—a situation referred to as "no other way to discipline the child"—the GLH elder would invoke one of the group's mottos: "We don't care about the reputation of the monk, only the reputation of the Buddha," meaning that the welfare of the group trumped that of the individual, and he would be threatened with death (Zhao 2006, 129–30).

The second form of resolution was called "inculcating the idiot with the wisdom of the ancients [教遇化贤]," and it was deployed when there was still some lingering resentment over a dispute. This involved making young, recalcitrant members mimic ancient rituals of supplication, featuring frequent bowing and kneeling before group elders. These were interrupted by statements from the recalcitrant party that he understood that the violations of filial piety, respect, and obedience were serious crimes. He was, in turn, expected to apologize to the judge and the group's elders three times, before vowing not to be a repeat transgressor. However, the most important criterion in adjudicating any conflict between members was the disparity in material or psychological hardship; all judgments were biased in favor of those who were experiencing some kind of distress. If a member was having problems with a lover or work situation, these were sure to impact his ability to fulfill his rank's responsibilities inside a GLH lodge and would exacerbate interpersonal tensions. Members who were having problems related to excess drug or alcohol use were given extra money to pay for their habits. Finally, distressed members were relieved of most or all of their rank's responsibilities and given time to rest and relax (Zhao 2006, 130).

These mediations were meant to deal with relatively minor interpersonal glitches within a lodge. Obviously, outlaw groups require much more in the way of clear prohibitions to maintain security. And the GLH didn't waste any time in communicating the need for tight discipline. Right at the beginning of their initiation ritual, the master of ceremonies alerted the newcomer to the importance of following rules and regulations:

> Flying in from Shandong and Shaanxi . . . you have crossed many mountains and traveled immeasurable distances to arrive here, spending huge amounts of your own money. Now we have some basic rules to tell you and insist that these are righteous and fair. The first: don't ever say anything about our group around government establishments. The second: don't ever say anything about our group while being tortured by government soldiers [不报武官较场]. As far as what takes place today, you must never utter a word about it. (Qunying she 1975, 3–4)

If warning newcomers that there was something worse than being tortured by Qing executioners wasn't going to put the fear of the goddesses in him, then the clear exposition of the GLH conditions and laws a few days later probably would. These spelled out with brutal frankness the consequences of straying from expected rebel deportment. The conditions and laws form a central part of *The Ocean Depths*, appearing at the end of the formal closure of a ceremony opening a new lodge and initiating new members. The ten GLH laws were:

Terrible vengeance will be meted out to those not pious and sincere;

Punishment will be swift for those not committed to benevolence and righteousness;

Killing another brother will result in you getting your head cut off;

Talking disrespectfully about anyone's mother will get your tongue cut out;

Violating propriety or transgressing any of our laws will result in you hanging yourself;

Sexually harassing or disrespecting any woman will result in you getting tied to a wall with swords thrown at you;

Harming someone weaker than you will result in you getting disemboweled and torn into two pieces;

Traitors of any kind will be shown no mercy;

Members who discuss our internal affairs outside the group will be brutally tortured;

Members who disgrace the old virtues will never be forgiven.

The ten conditions:

Show piety and thankfulness to your mother and father;

Show respect to all male and female elders;

Learn to differentiate between big and small (分大和小);

Be benevolent and righteous in all affairs;

Members should all respect each other;

Don't be carried away with anger (红脸) and kill another brother;

Don't flirt with another brother's wife;

Don't look lustfully at any brother's wife;

Be upright in your dealings with people;

Don't violate propriety or transgress any of our laws. (Qunying she 1975, 27–28)

These are just the basic proscriptions; specific GLH lodges added their own signature punishments. One of the most popular of these accented the ban against unauthorized liaisons with another member's wife. Called with a morbid sarcasm "setting up river lamps [放河灯]" (after the Chinese practice of setting candles inside floating holders and placing them into rivers for holiday celebrations), it featured the condemned adulterer in a kind of crucifixion, with each foot and hand nailed to a door with a long single nail. However, additional contempt for the male GLH transgressor was evident in his being placed in the river already dead by decapitation. The GLH lodge wanted the woman to be alive while she was floated down a river for all to see, but they respected her enough to have her genitals covered—by her lover's severed head roped around her thighs and buttocks. The GLH went so far as to affix a message board describing the couple's transgression and warning people downstream not to try save the woman's life (Zhao 2006, 57). It is safe to say that any version of couples swinging or swapping was never a GLH-approved form of erotic expression.

A GLH member was expected to confront another member immediately if they witnessed violations of group laws. If no other members could be brought in to adjudicate and the crime was particularly egregious (unauthorized murder, leaking information to magistrate runners and spies, stealing from the poor, etc.), then the member was expected to conduct a kind of DIY court hearing (执法堂). If the accused wasn't successful in convincing the accuser of his innocence, the accuser was responsible for overseeing the standard punishment when justice wasn't administered in the presence of the lodge or wharf: the infamous three thrusts and six eyes (三刀六眼). This entailed three sword or knife thrusts going completely through the body in the heart, stomach, and crotch areas. When done properly, the condemned GLH member's body would have a total of six "eyes," or wounds (JFMA, "Organized Criminals in China," 664–65).

Keeping Secrets

Readers should recall how poor nearly all GLH members were in the 1860s and '70s. For the great majority of lodges and even multilodge wharfs, there was no money to have an "office" where group business could be safely carried out. Moreover, an office itself, where members went regularly, would draw the attention of the magistrate and his staff. So many lodges were forced to use public teahouses as meeting places (Liu and Mi 2015; Wang 2008).

But it could be risky to conduct GLH business—conflict resolutions, interviews with prospective members, and so on—in public places like teahouses. Local authorities sent runners and spies there to gather intelligence on anti-Qing activities (Wang 2003, 233). Even if the owner was a GLH member, clearing out non-GLH customers and allowing only certain customers to remain could draw unwanted attention. Therefore, adding to the new responsibilities initiates had to deal with, the GLH required all public speech to be conducted in a special GLH code—really an entirely different language system (Liu and Mi 2015, 82–96). Before an initiate did anything at all, he had to spend weeks studying this new language.

As rebel brotherhoods are often condemned in Anglophone scholarship for being "feudalistic" and bereft of the rational intelligence of modern Euro-American individuals, it's important to underline the wit of the GLH's second language system. The main feature of its structure was that each important

FIGURE 4.2. Sichuanese teahouse in the 1890s (Zhao Hong 2006).

internal code had a different one for public use. For example, when encountering someone at an opium room or teahouse and wanting to ascertain if the person was a GLH Guy in Gown or not, the standard question in Sichuan went: "Do you respect the reasoning of the horse?" If the interlocutor did belong to a GLH lodge, what would be construed as horseshit by a nonmember would be greeted immediately with the name of the group and the person's rank. The GLH tried to make the public code for internal referents as banal as possible. For example, "renting a place to keep dry from the rain" was the public substitute for finding a safe space for GLH robbers to hide out after a successful leveling action. Similarly, "going to the market to pick up a few things for the house" was spoken publicly to refer internally to an upcoming leveling/robbing action. "Going shopping with my buddy" referred to a leveling operation involving two people. More colloquial language was prevalent. For instance, "clean up your shit" referred to a leveling operation that was designed to loot relatively inexpensive items. "Having the shits [拉稀]" referred to forcing someone to confess everything, or shit everything out. "Putting out the decorations" was public language for a heroic GLH robber who lost lots of blood in a leveling action. Interestingly, given the GLH's core membership of rejects and dropouts, "getting rid of your stink [掷臭]" was the public code for "losing one's dignity." The inside joke for poor GLH cadre held that the best way to keep your dignity was to keep it real and stay true to your disheveled, unbathed character (Wang 1993, 71–73).

Three things require elaboration here. The first is the centrality of natural objects in the group's language. "Water" meant "currency," as in the public phrase "How deep is your water? [水有多大深?]" Leaves (叶子) also meant currency. Mountains signified places of celebration and worship. For example, the public phrase "going to the mountain" meant hosting a large party for a visiting GLH lodge, and "opening a mountain" signified the important ritual of starting a new lodge. Second, given the protoracial language emerging in the 1890s and first decade of the 1900s in China, public codes using "white" invariably referred to despised enemies of the GLH. For example, the public phrase "white robe" referred internally to someone who was not allowed to join the GLH under any circumstances. Finally, we get a sense of the importance of opium for the GLH, as its public code was "venerable and awesome [重老]" (JFMA, "Secret Societies in Qing China," 1028, 1031–32, 1027).

The importance of natural entities in the GLH draws attention to the fact that poor &bjects have no choice but to depend on other entities to survive and thrive. Unlike the rich and owners of capital, other-determination is existential for them. We've already seen how GLH fighters relied on mountains and forests as places that nurtured and protected them. Moreover, many GLH members were completely dependent on the larger group—without it, life itself was unthinkable. But in addition to the physiology and sociology of this, there was also a salient ethics of interdependence. As Ferreira da Silva suggests and Marx theorizes in *The Poverty of Philosophy*, humans are different from other entities in that from the beginning they are absolutely dependent on others; extra-action is not an option for them. The GLH was like other subaltern groups in embracing this fundamental intra-activity—life was richer and more righteous because of it.

Human &bjects

There were specific historico-cultural reasons for this. As Zhao Hong writes, the epistemology of the GLH emerged from a long history of nature worship (2006, 43–44). And looking at the rituals in *The Ocean Depths* it's clear how crucial non- and extrahuman entities were in the GLH eco-ontology—mountains, rivers, water, the wind, and so on. Extending from their background as poor peasants and merging with their Daoism—where human

&bjects are not allowed to interfere with Heaven's plans for nature—there is such a respect for earthly processes that nonhuman life is often more powerful to the GLH than humans, living or dead. Without even considering the ways in which humanity owes its existence to dragons, spirits, and the five elements of fire, water, wood, metal, and earth in standard Chinese cosmology, we don't have to go very far to see how crucial environmental forces were for the GLH.

Let's return to the GLH's initiation ceremony. Right at the beginning of the ritual, after the initiates are warned about the life-or-death seriousness of joining a rebel group, the dragon leader of the lodge asks all those present to look up into the sky to welcome the spirit of Guan Yu, the peasant hero from the Three Kingdoms period (AD 220–80). Everyone then recites the "Welcoming the Spirit commandment" in unison:

> Let's welcome the arrival of Guan Yu and his carriage guard; they have come here after a journey long and hard.
>
> Starting in the Peach Orchard many years past, when only one sovereign was going to last.
>
> Praise the upright and outstanding him, whose righteousness is that of Heaven and whose intensity will never dim [于今为烈]. (Wang 1993, 49)

The GLH supervisor, acting as the master of ceremonies, returns to the dais to sing the praises of those past and present in what is called the "Sacrifice commandment [香水令]":

> Use the grass on the ground as incense; drink the plain water as if it were wine.
>
> These ancient rituals endowed by our ancestors and this fragrance released by our comrades, will never fade in thousands of years time.
>
> The hearts of our community unite in the ritual sharing of each other's blood [歃血] like those in the Peach Orchard; and the black cow and white horse are gifts we give to the blue Sky.
>
> Light the third incense stick dutifully following the community of rebels at Liang Mountain, when everyone considered their bonds eternal through death's low and life's high. (Wang 1993, 49–50)

Continuing, the master of ceremonies reminds all those present how important the natural environment of Liang Mountain in Shandong province was for the consolidation of outlaw society, and thus asks everyone to give thanks for the mountains, rivers, lakes, and other natural elements without which they wouldn't be able to exist at all: "Let's give praise to the rivers, lakes, mountains, and sky all around us; if it weren't for these there would be no way to exist thus" (Wang 1993, 50–51).

The wind and the sky usher in ethereal spirits of rebels from the past, while the mountains maintain the actual existence of the rebels of the present. Similarly, human existence is impossible without the gifts generated from the rivers and lakes. Not only do these entities directly nourish rebel life; indirectly they provide crucial security against outside oppressors. External Qing rule, consolidated through built infrastructure like palaces, securitized "great walls," and militarized embankments, treats nature in a completely different, instrumentalized way.

What we see in the GLH eco-ontology, then, is not fetishized nature "out there" waiting in reserve for it to be extra-acted on by humans, but something like the "vibrant matter" highlighted by Jane Bennett (2010). Entities such as water and grass possess the virtual force to become different—alcohol, incense, shelter—yet maintain their original qualities. Relating with human beings doesn't at all drain objects' capacity for change, powers object-oriented ontology insists can never be exhausted through instrumental knowing and extra-active dominance (Harman 2002).

They Came for the Drugs and Stayed for the Politics

The most important entity that made the GLH the sociopolitical force that it became by 1911 was opium. The issue of opium that has lingered around the fringes of GLH and Sichuanese scholarship for decades will be foregrounded here and in chapter 6. Although GLH members were hardly different from 90 percent of Sichuanese males at this time—my approximation of the percentage of regular opium smokers in Sichuan of the late Qing period—opium was the extrahuman force responsible for the GLH combination of revelry, (conflict) resolution, and levelry.

A slogan attributed to the GLH in Sichuan during the 1880s and '90s held that the opium room was crucial because it allowed the organization to conduct three distinct activities: "hold meetings, carry out actions, and relax and get high" (SJYD, 778). As we see in the epigraph from the 1930s, the GLH shared the preference of most Sichuanese to party there, but for them it was much more than a site of recreation. Although the GLH was commercially involved in other consumer sites such as teahouses and gambling parlors, the opium room was understood by Qing officials in Sichuan to be their preferred headquarters. The opium room was so important for the GLH that when a wharf was formally launched, combining several local lodges, often the first major action by the leaders was to open its own opium establishment (Qin 2001, 72). Altars to Heaven and Earth (天地) and Guan Yu were the first accessories installed.

As Wang Di's superb work on the place of the teahouse in urban Sichuan demonstrates, tea establishments were also important spaces for GLH Guys in Gowns (2008). Here the GLH could conduct business using their special language that was impenetrable to nonmembers, or what they called "empties [空子]." They could also communicate with each other using a complicated method of "tea bowl formations" when they sensed Qing spies were trying to crack their group's language code. Moreover, the ubiquity and publicness of the teahouses offered camouflage for the group. Finally, Wang claims that "its crowds and noise provided good cover for surreptitious activities" (2008, 178–79). However, I will argue that the teahouse was not feasible for certain functions and that we can't grasp the full spectrum of GLH intra-action without understanding the centrality of the opium establishment.

The archive of criminal cases in Sichuan during the late Qing period can fill in the gaps about the specific uses of the opium room for the GLH. First, readers should recall the abject poverty that most GLH members were in when they entered the group. Although many quickly found themselves in significantly improved material conditions, some of the poorest members never had a stable living situation. Moving from low-level dive inns in cities and towns to makeshift huts in remote areas, GLH opium rooms were a perfect place to crash after a nightcap smoking session—guests were already stretched out prostrate with pillows or cushions. The problem was the illegality of this, as any establishment that hosted people overnight had to be licensed and pay taxes. In case after case, the Baxian (Chongqing) magistrate's office detailed "criminals [土匪]," "thugs [痞匪]," and "outlaw elements [匪类]" routinely breaking the law by sleeping overnight in opium rooms. One opium room was permanently closed by officials because it "appeared to be in business for no other reason than to harbor criminal elements who stay for two and three days at a time" (SPA 6:50–38521, March 21, 1896[14]). An earlier magistrate's case identified these places as unlawful "smoking inns [吸宿]" where "outlaws flock to as soon as an opium lamp is lit. They don't have a permanent place to live, and stay in these places for months at a time" (SPA 6:50–38507, December 1885). It would take another decade for Sichuanese officials to categorize these stoner sleepovers as "residents of opium rooms [烟馆居民人]." And criminals were said to constitute 100 percent of this population (SPA 6:31–01709, September 10, 1896).

In 1885 the Baxian magistrate issued a rare order to close an opium room "because it invites criminals to make it their permanent home" (SPA 6:50–38522, April 18, 1885). Interestingly, this and other opium room closures still allowed the proprietors to sell processed opium "take-out" (SPA 6:50–38507, December 1883; 6:50–38550, June 16, 1887). These partial closures merely ordered the removal of opium pipes and forbade people from smoking inside the establishment. Partial closures draw attention to the paucity of complete closures in the criminal cases involving opium rooms, especially given the fact that there were upward of a thousand opium establishments in Chongqing and Baxian county by the 1890s. Although several reports from local wardmen urged magistrates to completely shut down establishments, they seem to have been ignored in all but two or three cases (SPA 6:31–01705, April 6, 1896).

In March 1887 Baxian magistrate Yuan sent runners to several opium rooms at night to conduct investigative spot checks, providing a rare glimpse into their goings-on. The usual pattern for low-level opium rooms (with only two to four "lamps") is highlighted in Yuan's subsequent write-up: "homeless people stay overnight [留宿] for days on end"; "denizens are all criminal types"; and "men and women come and go at all hours of the night." The runners reported that the opium room inhabitants refused to cooperate with the magistrate's requests and used rough language. They also exhibited an "openly hostile" attitude to the runners, which matches other depictions of GLH intransigence in the face of Qing law enforcement. Several responded to the threat of arrest for violating license agreements by claiming "we didn't realize we couldn't just come and go freely" (SPA 6:50–38557, December 19, 1889).

Another runner from the Baxian magistrate's office reported with some frustration that government officials had basically lost jurisdiction in and around opium rooms; especially when night fell these drug hangouts were de facto off-limits. Completely different from teahouses, which are "public [公]" and always accessible to the authorities, opium establishments were said to be intimidatingly "obscure" or "shadowy [暗]." The murkiness is compounded by the fact that residents of opium rooms refused to reveal their names to officials and spoke in a language that can hardly be understood (SPA 6:31–01696, November 1895). These are all indications that the GLH was well represented among this population, as their double language was designed to do exactly this: prevent authorities and nonmembers from understanding them.

But the magistrate investigations and reports from neighborhood wardmen surveilling low-level (下层) opium rooms throughout Chongqing managed to reveal at least some of what was taking place inside. The most salient was sex work. Licenses were required when offering women for commercial sex, and few, if any, of these places had them (inter alia, SPA 6:50–38513, August 12, 1884; 6:31–01708, September 6, 1896). However, it's also evident that noncommercial, intra-active sex was taking place at night in Sichuan's opium rooms—hetero- and homoeroticism liberated from the domination of commodification and from the narrowly normative sex allowed within Confucian patriarchy (Li 2012a, 89–91, 176–79; SPA 6:50–38557, December 19,1889). Within the relatively off-limits confines of the rooms people shared their bodies and also "divided up loot [分肥]" (SPA 6:50–38533, February 16, 1886; 6:50–38535, May 8, 1886). In the case of the GLH leveling operation discussed above, the spoils were divided up evenly and publicly. But this occurred in a remote rural area and would have been impossible in a town or city. In more densely populated areas, what was required was a place where people routinely came and went, yet was generally off-limits to the magistrate, his subordinates, and strangers. The opium room was perfect for this. Official reports also suggest that groups kept money and valuables hidden away in these rooms (SPA 6:50–38579, March 22, 1890). Finally, one local headman was certain that rich people kidnapped for ransom were being held captive in a shadowy opium room (SPA 6:50–38621, August 17, 1893).

The opium room also served as a command center for insurgent operations like attacking Christian missions and looting Christian homes. Once again, a semipublic place where people routinely came and went was well suited for a group committed to leveling Christian property. At least this was what a neighborhood wardman named Yang reported to Baxian magistrate Guo when he urged him to immediately close six of these places. Yang wrote that criminal-looking men go out at night in small groups from opium rooms to "break into Christian homes and, whether the victims are killed or left alive [死生], fatten themselves on the stolen goods and reap unfair gains [渔利]." Yang also depicted an upside-down world where opium room denizens "make up and follow their own laws," "spread wild rumors and lies," and completely disregard everything the Qing government says (SPA 6:31–01705, April 6, 1896). In the fall of 1911 opium rooms were singled out as command and control centers in the revolution against Qing rule in Sichuan province (JFMA, "Reports on the Revolutionary Upheaval in Qing China," October 25, 1911).

The material culture of the low-end opium room during this period was yet another reason why it emerged as the party, meeting, and action center for the GLH. Based on the seventy-five or so legal cases where opium establishments appear in the Sichuan Provincial Archives from 1875 to 1910, there were two basic types: upper (上) and lower (下). The lower or popular opium room rarely contained more than three or four opium works or "lamps [灯]," while the upscale parlors tended to have more (SPA 6:50–38560, October 23, 1888). The tax rate on opium establishments was often based on the number of works, and costs were kept low by limiting the number. There is a scene in Li Jieren's 1936 historical trilogy about turn-of-the-century Chengdu that depicts just this. The GLH leader Luo Waizui sets up an opium room during his extended stay at an inn located in the market town of Tianhui, north of Chengdu. This GLH establishment had only two lamps and two beds, with smokers continuously sprawled out on the beds, both GLH members and non (Li 2012a, 43–44).

It was common in opium rooms to find several people smoking together from one lamp—with eight being the limit (Qin 2002, 81). Readers might draw on their own experience with recreational drug smoking to grasp the intimacy of this. Moreover, all the smokers would be lying down on the floor or entwined on large beds. Contrast this intra-active experience with the other "places to party" in Sichuan referred to in the epigraph. The teahouse was also a public site of consumption, but customers didn't drink tea out of the same cup or lie down on a bed with someone else, which is often what happened in opium establishments. The same went for restaurants.

Therefore, the act of entering an opium room to get high was largely self-selecting from the beginning. The overwhelming number of smokers went to places where their acquaintances gathered. Few consumers would want to smoke drugs in such a close-knit, cozy environment with people they didn't know. This only happened in opium parlors, but upscale smokers who frequented these places rarely shared works; they paid more money to have exclusive use of one lamp—often sharing it with a friend or lover.

So while the upscale parlors provided a more private consumer experience, the opium rooms were actually closer to what are known in an Anglophone context as private clubs. Regular clientele at the popular rooms appreciated the opportunity to party with friends, and maybe one or two invited newcomers. Therefore, the practice of getting high in these rooms contributed to the bonding necessary for outlaw insurrectionary groups like the GLH, similar to the Invisible Committee epigraph. Qing magistrates in Chongqing from the 1870s to 1910 understood that antigovernment politics were planned in and carried out from these places, but if they were successful in partially shutting down a handful every year, new ones would pop up immediately (SPA 6:50–38557, December 19, 1889). These new establishments handed over the licensing fees and taxes the Sichuanese government needed; it was not fiscally feasible to permanently close opium rooms in Sichuan. It was also problematic politically to close them. As we will see, while the GLH accrued popular legitimacy, with more and more men joining the organization into the 1890s magistrates grew

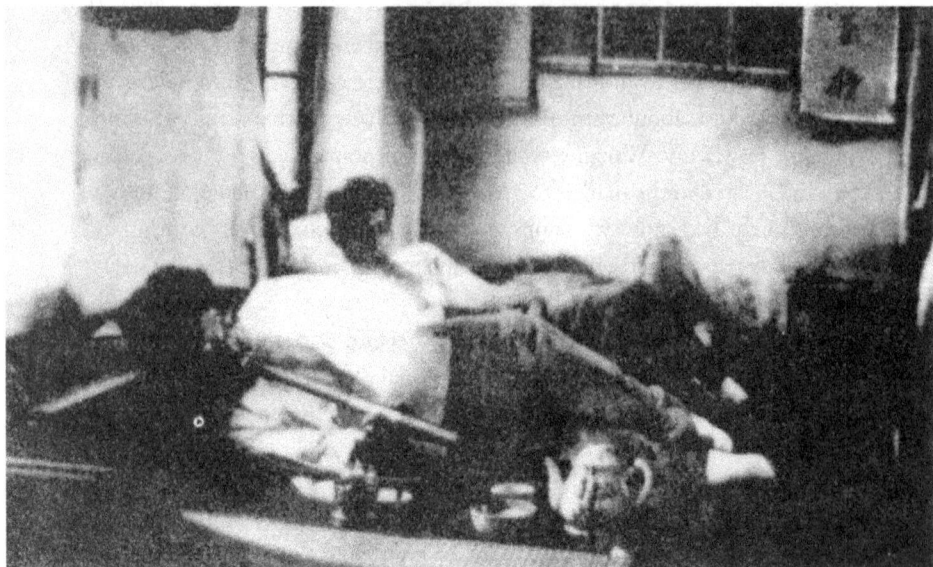

FIGURE 4.3. Opium parlor in Chongqing in the 1920s (Wang Chuanping 2013b).

reluctant to anger locals—anger against Qing officials (反清) being one of the main causes for men to join the rebel brotherhoods in the first place. Finally, almost all government officials in Sichuan were smokers themselves, and they sympathized with the desire to get high among the poorer masses (APF, vol. 68, 20). Many also recognized that workers and peasants had hard lives and getting intoxicated in opium rooms was well-earned recreation (Qin 2001, 71).

But no one understood the popular appeal of opium room smoking like the GLH did. And the evidence suggests that they took advantage of that appeal to expand their membership—the fourth function of the rooms for the GLH. Potential recruits were regularly brought to opium rooms by GLH members, who tried to impress them with lavish smoking and eating sessions. (Teahouses weren't practical for this because potential recruits weren't yet familiar with the GLH public language.) Of course, the euphoria of an opium high was the best sales pitch for the GLH, especially if the smoke was on the house. A phrase that circulated among Chongqing's opium establishments in the 1890s most likely references the GLH practice of taking advantage of the opium room to recruit new members. Using the process of smoking opium as a metaphor for seducing people into joining an organization, it first recommends that recruiters "pick out a good opium pipe [一枪挑下]," or suitable person for the organization. Next, "carefully refine the product [细细烧炼]," or prepare the recruit for the group's sales pitch. Then, "put the opium into the plate, and mold it into a ball with a small stone [小石慢慢的打]," or apply pressure to the recruit when he is lying down and getting ready to smoke, or "in the plate." Next, "jab it with a small needle [小针慢慢的挑]" before placing it under the lamp, lighting it, and "melting it." After the recruit has smoked a pipe or two, "you can easily manipulate the fine powder [揉为膏粉] that is left over into any shape you want" (Qin 2001, 102).

Finally, the GLH opium room highlights the intra-active network found therein. The interwoven mesh of the smoke, the intricate lamps, the other smokers, remembered ancestors, and, at night, the GLH tutelary deities, either in picture or statue form, would have allowed for manipulating more than the human smokers. One could argue that the opium room enabled an intermodulation (what was called "melting or refining [烧炼]") between the various entities and allowed the human &bjects to be affected by the agential force of the other-than-human (intra) actors.

GLH Mainlining and Mainstreaming

A version of the improbable scenario of a wealthy opium smoker finding himself sharing a lamp with a coarse and cursing underclass stranger was in fact taking place inside the GLH in Sichuan and elsewhere. A public announcement put up in the center of all Sichuan's market towns in May 1877 by the governor general of Sichuan, Ding Baozhen, will help generate a fuller picture of this:

> We inform you that thieves and criminals are now running wild [横行] in all parts of our province, mostly in areas that were previously peaceful and orderly.... We have determined that not all of the outlaws are poor and homeless [饥寒]; surprisingly, there are now wealthy merchants and gentry that have joined forces with them. This is obviously because they are terrified by the criminals' brutality and ferocity, and this fear leads them to provide sanctuary and support, as well as giving money in the form of contributions to the criminal leaders. However, the more serious problem is the linking up of the brothers and sons of the wealthy and gentry with the outlaws, who take orders from them and willingly pass along information. It must be said that the wealthy . . . enable criminal activities to extend much further than if carried out solely by people with no social standing. This office is angered and disgusted by this. (Zhengxie Sichuan yanjiu weiyuanhui 1981, 49–50)

This public warning cogently exposes the sociopolitical situation in Sichuan just after the Treaty of Chefoo (Yantai) of 1876, granting Euro-whites in China an expanded array of privileges that Robert Hart called "offensive extraterritoriality." Qing officials in Sichuan are in full panic mode here because its erstwhile supporters, the wealthy gentry, are slowly making new alliances with the outlaw underclass. The rationale given is that in some areas the rebel brotherhoods have garnered enough support from locals to force the wealthy to hand over protection money and other "contributions." Presumably, this extorted shakedown would have guaranteed that the wealthy family would not be attacked by GLH cadre; as long as they paid their protection money, they could continue on with their lives. An investigation by the Sichuan governor general's office of the GLH conducted just a few years before the 1911 Revolution provides final confirmation of this trend: "the organized gang in the beginning consisted solely of outlaw criminal elements, but gradually included a surprising number of wealthy people and local gentry who joined to protect themselves from the thugs" (Wei and Zhao 1981, vol. 1, 134). In 1877 threatening the wealthy into working with the GLH was enabling the outlaws to extend their actions "further than if carried out by people with no social standing." What is evidently part of the Qing government's panic is the realization that the power hierarchy that had sustained their dynastic rule for over two hundred years was being inverted by these losers bereft of any social standing: manure collectors, boat pullers, dropouts, drug dealers, and homoerotic men. Welcome to the world-upside-down reality of politics and society in Sichuan in the late nineteenth century.

The perturbation evident in governor general Ding Baozhen's announcement also allowed a rare admission to slip out of carefully worded Qing government discourse: an acknowledgment that the outlaw underclass has taken up a life of crime not because of weak moral backbones or lapses in character. Rather, most of them were hungry and homeless long before joining the outlaws. A second announcement from Ding Baozhen's office put up all over Sichuan just two months later, in July 1877, inadvertently provides further rationale for the growth of the GLH:

This office has discovered that outlaw societies are also setting up groups that claim the authority of militias [借团练为名] and are providing aid and assistance to people in need. Luring these desperate people into their societies, they then call them "friends" and offer aid and support. This aid consists of these organizations helping them track down enemies and righting injustices inflicted upon them; the new members in turn then provide services for the criminals. . . . Right now, these criminals have the power to do whatever they want in peasant areas, wreaking a particular havoc there. . . . To make matters worse, we are aware that the Emperor's legal system just isn't strong enough to eliminate the criminals. . . . All we can do right now is urge everyone except the criminals to obey the law and respect authority. (Zhengxie Sichuan yanjiu weiyuanhui 1981, 51–52)[15]

In addition to this startling admission that the Qing government has lost political control in peasant areas—80 percent of Sichuan—the most important aspect of this second announcement is the related acknowledgment that because the areas outside Qing law are growing daily, people with legitimate grievances have nowhere to turn to obtain justice but to the outlaw societies, and the largest and most powerful was the GLH. As we saw in chapter 2, the common popular grievance at this time was against Western missionaries and Chinese converts to Christianity. Chinese Christians enjoyed limited protection under the treaties ending the Second War for Drugs, but Euro-white missionaries continued to pressure the Qing government to grant converts the same kind of extraterritorial privileges that white people enjoyed. The Treaty of Yantai was partly successful in expanding immunities for Chinese Christians, resulting in more clashes with government authorities in local areas. As the Sichuan governor general Ding states in no uncertain terms, the outlaw societies emerged as the only force locals could look to in order to correct injustices piling up from this religious war.

The only card Ding could play in this game was to remind the masses in Sichuan of their imperial duty to remain subservient to Qing authorities and obey the law. But what to do about the new sociopolitical phenomenon of the wealthy flooding into the criminal societies? They only had to be subservient occasionally and were exhibiting a blithe disregard for Qing law. For our purposes in this chapter, Ding's announcement exposes a crucial socioeconomic shift that was occurring inside the GLH in the 1870s and '80s: the gradual acceptance of wealthy merchants and gentry as members. It remains unclear exactly why this happened, but there is no doubt that a class division materialized around this time inside the GLH between the original leveler and robber members (now referred to as "muddy water [混水]") and the expanding group of wealthy merchant, literati, and gentry newcomers to the GLH (called "clear water [清水]") (Wang 1993, 26–27). What Ding Baozhen referred to above as the "sons of the wealthy and gentry" became the newest members of the outlaw brotherhood, which had heretofore consisted solely of peasants and poor outcast men surviving through organized leveling attacks against these same wealthy and gentry. What happened?

I'm not aware of any explanation for this emerging class rupture within the GLH, but as we can see from anecdotes in Li Jieren's historical fiction about Sichuan, it is obvious that the upper classes were also being affected by the new power of the Christian missions and Chinese converts (Li 2012a, 32–33). Why not throw one's hat in with the main group committed to battling the Western hegemon? This would have been particularly prudent in an area where the GLH enjoyed mass support. Yet another reason for the wealthy to ally formally with the GLH was the practicality of asking a son or uncle to join the group your family was paying protection money to anyway—in cases where the GLH promised not to threaten your business or property in exchange for regular extortion payments. The subsequent saving of future payments could have resulted in a net gain for the family after the large initiation payments to the GLH lodge were factored in. One final observation about this class transformation within the GLH is that as they extended their reach in the 1880s and '90s, new lodges tended to have as leaders men who were already trusted and respected in their communities. It was inconceivable that these men would suddenly just start breaking into houses, robbing Qing salt mines, peddling drugs, or turning to car(riage) jacking—the modus operandi of the majority of nonpeasant GLH members at the time. Therefore, a de facto separate "clear water" group had to be formed for these respected community leaders and wealthy newcomers (Zhao 2006, 43). Whatever the rationale, this separation between clear and the standard "muddy water" within the GLH certainly did, as Ding observed, "enable criminal activities to extend much further than if carried out solely by people with no status." We will see in chapter 6 some of the ways in which this new class alliance "enabled actions" as encompassing and transformative as anti-dynastic revolution.

Madame Butterfly and "Negro Methods" in China

Now I understand why the civilized European ... kills the Chinaman in America. It is justifiable to kill him. It would be quite right to wipe the city of Canton off the earth and to exterminate all the people.—Rudyard Kipling, *From Sea to Sea*, vol. 1, 1899

Europe has given an exhibition from the coast of Pekin of its newest armaments and its oldest barbarities ... it has used its beautiful weapons of precision for the most part on harmless villagers and unoffending men.—George Lynch, *The War of the Civilisations*, 1901

Puccini's 1905 opera about the Japanese treaty port Nagasaki in the 1890s, *Madame Butterfly*, tells this story: A US naval officer, Pinkerton, extracts the fifteen-year-old sex worker Cio-Cio-san from a Nagasaki brothel and sets up house with her after a sham "Japanese marriage," similar to the experience the writer Pierre Loti documented in intertext I. The Japanese betrothal lasted about a month, after which Pinkerton ships out again, exercising his Speed Race(r) privilege of "white flight." Before leaving, Pinkerton deliberately lies when he promises the smitten Cio-Cio-san that he will soon return. Just before setting up house with Pinkerton, Cio-Cio-san had converted to Christianity. This dramatic transformation was most likely brought about by a combination of hoping to learn some English and being "slut-shamed" by white US missionaries and their Japanese catechists in Nagasaki warning sex workers they were going to rot in hell (Ion 1993, 136–37). Puccini's opera treats Cio-Cio-san's rupturing conversion as equally traumatic as the dissimulating departure of Pinkerton: Cio-Cio-san was disowned by her family, cut off from friendships with her sister sex workers, alienated from her rich spiritual life of Buddhist protective deities and nativist shinto ritual, and abandoned, with no way to make a living. Although Pinkerton left her with some money, this runs out quickly and she and her maid Suzuki descend into serious poverty. This condition was compounded by the birth of an infant son from the sex with Pinkerton.

Puccini's *Madame Butterfly* was based on an 1898 story by US writer John Luther Long. Long's sister, Jeannie Correll, claimed to have heard of such situations while living in Nagasaki from 1892 to 1897 with her missionary husband. In all likelihood, Long was also familiar with the plot of Pierre Loti's 1887 *Madame Chrysanthème* discussed in intertext I (Burke-Gaffney 2004).

Madame Butterfly's popularity derives from the melodramatic force of a fifteen-year-old's innocent naïveté shattered by the extractiv-eye/I practice of Pinkerton—the embodiment of the "no conscience, no empathy" of white Superpredation in Asia. However, the opera also represents the conversion to Christianity as a kind of mountaintop removal of Cio-Cio-san, extracting her from the intra-active web of relations that she grew up in. As in coal mining, where the chief beneficiaries are the fossil fuel capitalists, the Christian missionaries get to add Cio-Cio-san's soul to their conversion account, and Pinkerton gets a month of extracted pleasure from Cio-Cio-san as cheapened rawfare. When Pinkerton does return to Nagasaki with his real (read, white US) wife, it is for the sole purpose of rendering the son back to the United States. Having been ideologically lured into monogamous fidelity and "true love," Cio-Cio-san is devastated when the fiction of what she thought was a Christian marriage is revealed.[1] Her apparent suicide is caused by Pinkerton's insistence that she give up her son, which would leave her ontologically destitute and cut off from friends, family, the deities, and even the ecology of Nagasaki after her house was partly Westernized—what I'll call "eco-ontocide."

Although at face value *Madame Butterfly* seems to be critical of Euro-American asymmetries in warfare and lawfare, it reproduces the fair-skin fantasy that the Asian woman is devastated when "gorge-us" Pinkerton takes his leave. The wrenching separation returns Cio-Cio-san to her rawfared condition as a supinestupefiedyellow—all that she can be without the presence of the white master. This (disavowed) assumption in *Madame Butterfly* that "they love Western guys over there" can help us understand the white rage when the GLH in Sichuan province and the Boxers in Shandong province tried to force these enemies of Heaven to leave, and when Anglo-American officials in Japan in the 1860s advocated bloodbaths to cleanse the country of anti-Western samurai. In these three cases, at the very least, white flight becomes something other than the privilege of an extractiv-eye/I; it emerges as an unconditional decolonial demand issued by nonwhite protectors from within an eco-ontology. For this transgression of raciological hierarchy, the GLH and the Boxers will be denounced and decimated by Euro-American imperialists.

Like the Gelaohui uprisings against ecclesiastical Superpredation I discussed in chapter 2, the subaltern groups that rose up against Christian Co2loniality and capitalist extra-action in Shandong province came to be called the Boxers United in Righteousness (义和团). The Boxer Rebellion of 1898–1900 had multiple causes. A leading one was anger at the German Catholic priest George Stenz, who, in all likelihood, serially raped Chinese women in Juye county, Shandong (which resulted in Boxer attempts to kill him in his mission quarters). Indignation was also strong over the dispossession of local temples and the replacement of them with deliberately anti–feng shui Catholic churches. A temple demolition by Catholics near Juye, similar to the ones in Sichuan discussed in chapter 2, and the subsequent enclosure and construction of a church on the ruins in 1873–74, still infuriated locals in 1898. Finally, the destruction of Chinese burial sites removed as "overburden" for German train tracks and telegraph lines—which helped Euro-Americans to advance meteorological management through forecasting weather—and famine and drought brought both by an El Niño weather system and intensifying Climate Caucasianism added to the Boxer anger (Preston 2000; Xiang 2003). The rebellion was the most serious challenge to what Robert Hart, the powerful inspector general of China's Imperial Maritime Customs, called in 1875 "offensive extraterritoriality" (BPP 1971, 749).

Like Pinkerton from *Madame Butterfly*, the real-life gorge-us white guys in Japan discussed in chapter 1, and a few ecclesiastical Superpredators featured in chapter 2, Hart spent nearly two decades of his life buying rawfared Chinese sex workers and expropriating them as what he called his "absolute possessions." This ended after he fathered three children with a Chinese sex servant and returned to England to start what he configured as a "legitimate" family with the eighteen-year-old, white Hester Bredon. Although Bredon lived in Beijing with Hart for a decade, she took their two children and returned to England alone while Hart returned to buying Chinese women on the cheap in Beijing before ultimately deciding to live celibately in 1883 (Heaver 2013). The Gelaohui uprisings in 1890–91 in the middle and upper Yangzi region against Euro-American power that preceded the Boxer Rebellion upset him so much that he rethought the good cop role (as the "best friend" of the Chinese) he imagined he'd been playing for four decades in China. Thus, Hart applauded in 1895 when Western countries began to replace ministers thought to be too friendly to China with military officers brought directly from the Scramble for

Africa—experts in mass murder like the German Edmund von Heykind and the British Claude MacDonald. Hart wrote approvingly that "MacDonald's appointment will be interesting to watch, and those of us who have succeeded so badly by treating Chinese as educated and civilized ought now be ready to yield the ground to a man versed in Negro methods" (in Wilgus 1987, 79).[2] And like Pinkerton and his missionary fellows' eco-ontocide of Cio-Cio-san in *Madame Butterfly*, these methods would be deployed to do the same to Chinese more generally.

By "Negro methods," he refers to those techniques perfected to strip Africans of all that sustained their lives when they were forcibly extracted and enslaved in the Americas, and subsequently subjected to genocidal and ecocidal scorched-earth campaigns in the full-blown Scramble for Africa (1881–1914). Some commentators on the ground in China saw the butchery of Blacks as a crucial precedent for the campaign of white racial terror carried out against areas imagined to be sympathetic to the Boxers south and southeast of Beijing after their rebellion was finally crushed on August 14, 1900. As Hevia (2003), Li, Liu, and Su (1990), and Sun (1996) have chillingly described, in the organized retribution attacks on suspected Boxer areas from September 1900 to March 1901, the Negro methods carried out by Euro-American forces included: public decapitations of those merely suspected of being Boxers; the looting and burning of all villages with suspected Boxer sympathizers; the "picking clean" through systematic looting of all the valuables in the city of Beijing and many in the Forbidden City, in some cases organized by top Western officials like British minister MacDonald himself; widespread rape of Chinese women and girls; the obliteration of religious and spiritual institutions and burning of sacred texts; demolitions of public buildings; the routine shooting of farm animals and dogs (NARA RG 395, 913, #33); and literal scorched-earth destruction of trees and crops (#21). While the eco-ontocide of Cio-Cio-san in *Madame Butterfly* was brought on by her semi-voluntary conversion to Christianity, the decidedly nonconsensual eco-ontocide in north China followed the template deployed against Blacks.

"Kill Anything That Moves"

Alfred Gaselee (1844–1918) was the head of the British contingent and de facto leader of the eight-nation allied force called together to crush the Boxers. Having served in Britain's Indian army, he was well versed in the different rules of engagement that applied when Euro-American armies waged asymmetric war against nonwhite people and their environments—another manifestation of

Climate Caucasianism. But even he was disconcerted by the general lack of "conscience and empathy" characteristic of some of the Superpredators in his command. Gaselee described the situation in Beijing this way: "Looting of the city, uncontrolled foraging in surrounding country, and seizure by soldiers of everything a Chinaman might have, as vegetables, eggs, chickens, sheep, cattle, etc.... indiscriminate and generally unprovoked shooting of Chinese" (in Gady 2015). (Hence the title of this section, which is a reference to Nick Turse's [2013] history of US atrocities in Vietnam.)

General Adna Chaffee, the head of US forces in China, concluded that "it is safe to say that where one real Boxer has been killed, fifty harmless coolies or laborers, including not a few women and children, have been slain" (in Lynch 1901, 83). White racial terror was intersectionally compounded by sexuality and gender. Sun Qihai writes that after the Boxer siege of the Euro-American embassy area in Beijing ended, "Twenty thousand Western soldiers were unleashed to hunt down the women and girls of Beijing" (1996, 7). But it wasn't just Chinese females who were targeted. Influential US missionary Arthur Brown reported that "for several months after the relief of the legations even respectable American ladies, to say nothing of Chinese women, could not prudently ride out except in closed carts, so great was the probability of indignity at the hands of foreign soldiers." Brown continues his description of the Caucasity of these men by reporting that in consumer establishments and hotels around the Forbidden City, Euro-American officials were compelled to put up signs in English that read "The public is politely requested not to kick the Chinese attendants." Finally, Brown claims that with the exception of a few places in obscure alleys, "every house in Peking was looted.... In the pillaging of property, savages could not have been more lawless than the white men from 'the highly civilized nations of the West'" (1904, 323–24).

Beijing was divided into six districts for the eight-nation allies, and while most of the Euro-American press was silent on the wanton violence carried out by their soldiers, the British *Shanghai Mercury News* did admit that in the German and French districts, white soldiers "burn and shoot right and left" (1901, 115). Concluding their coverage of allied behavior in Beijing in December 1900, the *Mercury* reporter conceded that "loot was king" (121). The staunchly pro-Western missionary Arthur Smith wrote that in addition to burning and looting, Germans "cut off the heads of many Chinese within their jurisdiction, many of them for absolutely trivial offenses" (1901, 727). The US expeditionary forces obviously did the same thing, as we can see from the gruesome trophy pictures of decapitated Chinese men in their jurisdiction in Beijing.

FIGURE INTER.II.I AND INTER.II.2. US sailors and officers posing with the bodies of murdered Chinese men next to their severed heads in Beijing, fall 1900.

Analyzing Euro-American memoirs and testimonies from local Chinese, Sun Qihai claims to have identified "at least" twelve different ways the Allied Forces killed Chinese people in Beijing after the Boxer siege was defeated: decapitation, beating with stones and sticks, stabbing, strangling, shooting, whipping to death, dousing bodies with gasoline and lighting them on fire, gang-raping women to death (奸污致死), and lynching by hanging (吊死) (1996, 287–90).

Despite the ubiquity of racial and sexual assault (all women and any Chinese male "looking like a Boxer") in the Qing capital, most observers considered the actions of the allied forces in the retributive justice missions that took place southeast of Beijing and between Beijing and Tianjin beginning at the end of September even more egregious. The *Shanghai Mercury* depicted the Western soldiers in Beijing and Tianjin at the beginning of October 1900 as "bored and gorged with loot" (1901, 125). Sun sums up the source material depicting the listless allies at this point as "looking to have some fun" (1996, 238). This "fun" should be reconfigured as what Calvin Warren calls the "global sadistic pleasure principle" inherent in white racial terror (2018, 2).

The US Army's 6th Cavalry led one of the first retribution missions out from Beijing on September 13, 1900, directed by the missionary leader W. S. Ament, the so-called "Father of Christian Endeavors in China." The 6th Cavalry's first encounter with what Ament insisted were "Boxer houses" showed no signs of actual Boxers, but the US forces under a Captain Forsyth went ahead and burned down the houses anyway. On September 16, the group did come under pistol fire and responded with a "barrage" of rifle and artillery rounds that struck no one except for their own Chinese guide, killing him. On September 20, Ament directed the looting of several supposed Boxer houses in a small village, which angered Forsyth so much he decided to suspend the mission (NARA RG 395, 913, #19). Some claim that Ament personally executed Chinese men during this outing (LeMaster and Wilson 1993, 24). Later, reports coming back to Beijing of German and French terror in the countryside were so alarming that the US Army sent investigators out to double-check, despite their earlier collaboration. US Captain Grote Hutcheson reported that on their ninety-mile march from Beijing southeast to Baoding (where eleven UK/US missionaries were killed by Boxers), French forces "blazed" every village they came in contact with and "planted the French flag" in the ruins (NARA RG 395, 913, #36). This indiscriminate burning of all Chinese villages that the French (and later German, Italian, and Australian) forces came in contact with elicited the most hand-wringing among concerned Euro-Americans. But the US Army detailed even worse horrors. Lieutenant C. D. Rhodes's "Report on the Investigation into the Burning of Chinese Villages" described German and French troops lighting buildings on fire where peasants had gathered together to protect themselves from Western soldiers. When the innocent Chinese ran out of the burning structures, they were shot and bayoneted (#29). Rhodes noted that word quickly spread among Chinese peasants of white soldiers' intent to rape and summarily execute villagers, so all "able-bodied" people would flee villages ahead of marauding Euro-American men, leaving only children and the elderly. Refusing to be ageist, Italian and German soldiers went ahead and raped old women anyway (#29). In more prosperous villages, the $ubject intervened as soldiers looted all valuables first, then burned what was left. In one instance, a village was looted and the occupants were forced to pay bribes to prevent soldiers from burning everything, and only after the bribes were collected was it burned to the ground anyway by German soldiers (Li, Lin, and Lin 1986, 462).

Australian soldiers in the Victoria and New South Wales contingents reported that German forces were extorting large ransom payments from village leaders in exchange for not torching houses and crops (Nicholls 1986, 109; Smith 1901, 716). The New South Wales soldiers themselves returned to Beijing in early December from their retribution mission having looted, burned, and murdered for four weeks in the countryside. Assistant Paymaster Wynne wrote that they were all growing callous from their "Eastern Education," but it was making them a more effective fighting force: "Until you can bring yourself to regard the Chinamen as something less than human, considerably less, you are at a disadvantage" (in Hevia 2003, 221). Nicholls writes that once the New South Wales contingent was back in Beijing in December, the preferred Australian method of execution "was amended . . . from firing squad to decapitation" (1986, 106). The Australian Victoria contingent was based in Tianjin, and they returned from their twenty-five-day deployment on November 7, 1900. Nicholls summarizes their "educational" outing thus: "During that time they had marched over 200 miles and taken part in innumerable sackings, looting, arson, pillage and executions without coming into contact with the enemy, let alone coming under his fire" (91). In fact, the great majority of the Western retribution missions didn't experience a single enemy shot, but that didn't stop Italian forces from misrecognizing their own troops' gunfire (at farm animals) for Boxer rounds and immediately responding by looting and burning surrounding villages (NARA RG 395, 913, #29). One Italian soldier was killed by this friendly fire.

The British war correspondent George Lynch covered the tail end of the Boxer Rebellion and several months of scorched-earth campaigns, during which he was embedded with different forces. Among his findings was the practice (by German and Italian soldiers) of raping women and girls before burning villages to the ground. Taking advantage of reports of Chinese women and girls committing suicide by jumping down wells in the face of certain rape by Euro-white forces, Germans would try to cover up their atrocities by throwing raped Chinese women down wells and staging the incidents as suicides—"hiding misdeeds and escaping the consequences" (Lynch 1901, 194). After observing the murder of innocent Chinese and the senseless burning of villages, Lynch compared them to incidents of white racial terror against Blacks in the US after the Civil War, calling the atrocities against Chinese the "nigger treatment" (307). Despite being a veteran war correspondent, Lynch admitted that he was psychologically unable to represent some of the worst atrocities he had witnessed: "There are things that I must not write" (142). What could possibly be unspeakable after describing rape, murder, and the bayoneting of Chinese children? Perhaps it was the decapitations via the "Australian method" resorted to when Euro-white soldiers grew bored with just shooting Chinese tied to stakes and found the decapitations more "fun." Amid this atrocity exhibition, Lynch was also disturbed by the enthusiastic participation of some Western Protestant and Catholic missionaries in looting and their overall refusal to criticize Western soldiers' actions. "No voice of protest was raised . . . against the outrages committed by the Allied soldiery" (318). Unbeknownst to him, Christian leaders were in fact "raising voices," but to justify the racial terror against Chinese through transcendental production and asymmetric lawfare.

This justification took two forms. When Euro-white Christian missionaries were caught looting mansions in and around Beijing (a crime Lynch reported on), they rationalized it by claiming "they had a number of converts more or less dependent on them." In other words, there was a "higher cause" motivating ecclesiastical Superpredators to break into Chinese homes and plunder all the valuables (Lynch 1901, 182). The second was a different form of what Hevia calls the "Old Testament" justification for massacres and rapes by Christian soldiers (2003, 289–90). This held that Chinese, by renouncing Christian conversion, demonstrated their proximity to evil and the devil. I show in chapter 6 how a Manichean construal of Euro-American (and Chinese) Christians as good and all other Chinese as evil justified the coercive "hell" of opium withdrawal, which would be facilitated by the "miraculous" cure of injections of Euro-American opioid pharmaceuticals. In the case of the Boxers, the conflation of non-Christian Chinese with the devil was relatively easy, as they were evidently kidnapped by him in their well-known "spirit possession" and other heathen rituals—the "depository," as Fanon critiqued Western colonial discourse, "of maleficent powers" (1968b, 41). Moreover, the justification continues, these anti-Western adults that Rudyard Kipling in "The White Man's Burden" neotenized as "half devil and half child," had carried out cold-blooded killings of Euro-white missionaries.

For Arthur Smith (1845–1932), the main spokesman for the Old Testament justification of European crimes against humanity, these decolonial killings were proof enough of the Chinese "barbaric cruelty" (1901, 734; citations to follow). Smith insisted throughout his best-selling 1901 *China in Convulsion* that the presence of the devil was so strong in the "Chinese race" that some modernized Chinese were ready to admit it and not disavow it by blaming Euro-Americans for the atrocities against suspected Boxer sympathizers: "they recognize with clearness that the worst that has happened in China is but a fraction of what the Chinese would have themselves perpetrated in any foreign country which they might have overrun" (719). This total war logic of good/God versus evil/Devil made the atrocities carried out by Euro-American retribution missions at Baoding and elsewhere "most righteous" and "most salutary" (717).

Smith insists that the superficial changes in China brought by Co2lonial capitalism—commerce, steamships, railways, industrial mining, and so on—have done nothing to transform the inscrutable "Chinese mind," which has shown itself to be so resistant to the truth of Christianity. For Smith, the violent reprisals against the Boxers and the Qing government didn't go far enough in exorcising evil; nothing short of a determined racial cleansing would banish the Devil. But mass murder had accomplished something, as the Qing were forced to sign the Boxer Protocol on September 7, 1901. This allowed the brutal "punishment" to continue, with further decapitations. It also required an indemnity of 450,000,000 taels together with the annual customs revenue of all China's domestic and foreign trade plus that generated from the state salt monopoly for the next forty years (the most punishing indemnity ever paid at that time) (Preston 2000). Moreover, the Qing government was forced to erect monuments at every place a white missionary was killed. Yet according to Smith, even this was "altogether inadequate." What was required was more comprehensive asymmetric warfare that would leave China "pitilessly and irrevocably shattered" (1901, 735, 737). Only at this point, where Chinese are returned to their previous condition as supinestupefiedyellows, could Christianity be introduced to save China once and for all from evil. Capitalism, technology, and objective science were incomplete without a foundation in Christianity, "an integral part of modern civilization" (737).

Smith concludes his call for a Christian crusade by citing the most respected Western secular figure in China, the inspector general of the Imperial Maritime

Customs, Robert Hart. Smith quotes Hart as speculating that if "Christianity were to make a mighty advance, [it might] spread though the land to convert China into the friendliest of friendly Powers.... This would prick the Boxer balloon and disperse the noxious gas which threatens to swell the race-hatred programme, and poison and imperil the world's future" (739). Smith and Hart agree. What Hart invokes as the Chinese "race hatred" of white people has wrought unspeakable chaos, but this is nothing compared to what will come if Euro-Americans don't act preemptively. Only a full-scale Co2lonization of China by the forces of Christianity—married forever to Climate Caucasian-ist science and anti–feng shui extraction indelibly releasing its own "noxious gasses"—can save the world from the Yellow Peril to come. Smith warns Euro-Americans that this is not the time for liberal hand-wringing over what he calls "ten thousand rapists" unleashed on the residents of Beijing or, by extension, condemning the scorched-earth leveling of all villages in a hundred-mile ra-dius south of Beijing; or inquiring into the German, American, French, Ital-ian, and Australian war crimes of decapitating anyone who vaguely resembled a Boxer; or criticizing the white supremacist offensive extraterritoriality that Robert Hart envisioned as enabling the Climate Caucasianist extraction of anything construed as valuable in China. The time is now for the final extrac-tive operation on what Smith calls throughout *China in Convulsion* the hea-then "Chinese mind"—a lobotomy perpetrated on the entire population of Han Chinese.

Climate Caucasianism's Obscene Enjoyment

The most disturbing aspect of the racial terror committed by white men de-tailed in this book is, on the surface, the sheer pointlessness of it. The Western perpetrators in Yokohama, Shanghai, and Beijing and its environs all were sit-ting back, feeling honky dory. Their desires for food, sex, and shelter were met with minimal cost. The typical description of white men in the days and weeks preceding such rampages was that they were "bored and looking to have some fun." As we saw in the introduction, the Euro-Americans in the enclosed treaty ports similarly referred to the nights of assault and rape as "fun." They wanted some "surplus" beyond honky dory.

I find the Lacanian psychoanalytic differentiation of "pleasure" and "enjoy-ment" (*jouissance*) useful to help us understand the dynamics of white racial terror. For Jacques Lacan, pleasure is subject to social restrictions and con-straints, designed by religions and states to guarantee their reproduction. But enjoyment does not follow the same rationality, which is why it often seems illogical. While torture and murder might, perversely, bring a kind of pleasure to the torturer, for Lacanians it is more correct to construe it through the register of jouissance as obscene enjoyment, which is always a "surplus" beyond pleasure. Drawing on Sigmund Freud's notion of the death drive, in the hands of a Marxist like Slavoj Žižek, obscene enjoyment is linked to a homicidal underside lurking within capitalist ideology. Here is Žižek on neo-Nazi skinheads: "The skinhead who gets into a fury and starts to beat 'them' up without any 'deeper' rational or ideological foundation, simply because it 'makes him feel good,' is none other than the narcissistic individual of the so-called 'society of consumption' in a different modality; the line that separates them is extremely thin" (2005, 81).

Of course, the fun the white skinhead has in his encounters with racial others can turn disastrous when the person of color defends him- or herself, as we have seen. Such folks seem to have the most "fun" when backed by overwhelmingly asymmetric force, but the risk that the skinhead himself or the wilding Euro-Americans might themselves get hurt in racial terrorist attacks should be factored into the thrill of obscene enjoyment. Similarly, the risky thrill that the consumer might fall into serious debt must be part of the excitement of "shopping 'til you drop." I would insist, however, on replacing "consumption" with "extraction." When we do so, the obscene enjoyment of "extracting 'til everyone dies" is, unfortunately, much more urgent in 2020 than excess shopping. Environmentalist Bill McKibben's crucial 2012 piece "Global Warming's Terrifying New Math" makes clear that fossil fuel capitalists own oil, gas, and coal reserves equivalent to 2,795 gigatons of carbon. This is more than five times the 565-gigaton carbon budget that the United Nations Intergovernmental Panel on Climate Change's projects has the potential to keep global temperature increases under 2 degrees Celsius. By committing themselves to burning 2,800 gigatons of carbon fossil fuel capitalists are pushing greenhouse gas emissions well beyond the threshold that might allow for sustainable human life beyond the year 2100. White fossil fuel companies and their investors are guaranteeing the extermination of much of planetary life—the concluding Götterdämmerung of Marx's extraction → extinction imperative in capitalism.[3]

The Planet, Dying of Whiteness

Jonathan Metzl's Dying of Whiteness (2019) provides some disturbing examples that—analyzed with McKibben's grim conclusion that fossil fuel companies are cancelling humans' chance at future existence on earth—help flesh out what I call "Climate Caucasianism's obscene enjoyment." Dying of Whiteness features interviews Metzl conducted with a group of working-class white men in Tennessee who are opposed to the Medicare expansion clause in the Affordable Care Act (Obamacare) in particular and to all government assistance in general. What appears contradictory at first glance is that almost all of these white men depend on US government assistance to stay alive. Ending this assistance would mean certain death. But extending government health care to all would mean forfeiting their imagined superiority to racial minorities provided with similar coverage. The fact that some would risk dying rather than give up their most precious possession—white supremacy—can only be understood (if at all) through Lacan's notion of obscene enjoyment/jouissance beyond pleasure. Put differently, for these men the obscene enjoyment provided by white supremacy is more important than life itself.

Metzl's point is clear: white supremacy kills, and its victims include whites. When we extrapolate his provocation about white male supremacy to Climate Caucasianism, we confront the crucial existential dilemma of our time. What if, for white fossil fuel capitalists (who own and are profiting from most of the 2,800 gigatons of carbon they have promised their shareholders they will burn), extra-active domination over non-living minerals, most humans, and the natural environment is worth more than life itself? The jouissance or obscene enjoyment that this provides might be non-negotiable. Many signs point to the fact that for the ego-ontology grounding white capitalists, death is preferable to living intra-actively within shared environmental limits—the equivalent of the white men in Tennessee who would rather give up their own lives than share a government health plan with the Blacks and Latinx people they despise. Like the white racial terrorists looking to have "some fun" at the expense of all the people in Beijing and the surrounding countryside after the defeat of the Boxer Rebellion in August 1900, the Climate-Caucasianists-cum-deranged-fossil-fuel-capitalists might be enjoying themselves too much giving the planet what war correspondent George Lynch called the "nigger treatment" to ever stop digging and drilling.

In the introduction I briefly introduced the founder of the NAACP, W. E. B. Du Bois, and his theory of the psychological wage, arguing that it does some of the same explanatory work as Lacan's theory of obscene enjoyment in helping us understand the extra-economic, psychic dimensions of whiteness. Following new work by Ella Myers, who argues that Du Bois construes whiteness as a psychopathological "dominion" that claims the "title to the universe," it turns out that Lacanian psychoanalysis is even closer to Du Boisian insights (2019, 7–8). Particularly germane to Climate Caucasianism is Du Bois's 1920 essay "The Souls of White Folk," where he links white "race hate" to white people's denigration of nature as "dark lands" and "black earth" (44). For Du Bois, Negrophobia works together with ecophobia. Crucially, dredging up Negrocidal and ecocidal impulses from white people's "awful depths" and activating them in lynching, rape, and crimes against the earth elicits an affect comparable to obscene enjoyment that Du Bois calls a "fierce, vindictive joy" (1920, 33).

Du Bois and Žižek (2005) point to the psychopathology of whiteness subtending extractive capitalists. Their insights deepen an understanding of the ways in which fossil fuel companies like ExonnMobil have tried to hide their own scientific research about climate change, going so far as to financially support climate denialism (Klein 2014, 44–45). While at one level this is obviously a tactic to protect their profits, at a psychic level it points to the irrational drive Du Bois identified as "the rage . . . to own the earth" (1920, 48). When the title deed of white capitalists' ownership of the planet is questioned or usurped, Du Bois warns that a "descent to Hell is easy" (1920, 32). With global emissions doubling since Peabody Coal, ExonnMobil, and other white fossil fuel companies became fully aware in the 1970s and '80s of the destructive effects of their business model on carbon and hydrogen cycles—in the most important climate-intervening event since the Orbis Spike of 1520–1610—it should not be controversial to claim that they have already dragged us across the threshold into that hell. And just as Dante Alighieri depicted it in *The Inferno,* the hell wrought by Climate Caucasianists is indeed unbearably hot.

5

Last Samurai/First Extractive Capitalist

I have merely heard of killing a villain named Zhou, but I have not heard anything about murdering King Zhou.—Mencius; cited in Kurushima Tsuneki's letter to Katsu Kaishû, August 1888 (in Matano 1913)

Meiji Japan's Shock Doctrine

When we concluded chapter 3, Hakoda Rokusuke and Narahara Itaru had just returned to Fukuoka, Kyushu, in early 1880 after their unsuccessful attempt to submit a petition to the Meiji government's Chamber of Elders on behalf of the Fukuoka UPF (United Patriot Front). However, their spirits were lifted when they realized the political atmosphere at home in Fukuoka was still upbeat. Membership in the UPF continued to rise, and in the summer of 1880 there was optimism surrounding the creation of their new group, Genyôsha. More importantly, an inflationary spiral (an effect of the Meiji state borrowing used to defeat the 1876 and 1877 samurai uprisings) was helping to push farmers and merchants into the Autonomy and People's Rights (APR) movement. From the vantage point of borrowers, inflation is most welcome, while it cuts into extractive profits for bankers.

Although the agricultural land tax was set oppressively high by the oligarch government in 1873 (averaging over 40 percent of yields), the fact that it was fixed benefited the majority of Japanese farmers during the inflationary period of 1878–80. Ike Nobutaka tracked an average fifty/fifty split between revenues going to the state and revenue kept by agricultural landowners in 1873 to an average of 17 percent going to the state with 83 percent going to the farmer in 1880 (1950, 145). This resulted in an economic boom in the countryside

(Nakamura 1983, 60–61). The boom made it feasible for farmers to get more involved in politics; their only mode of political expression before this was desperate world renewal (世直し) uprisings against corrupt domain leaders and landlords. Roger Bowen writes that in joining the APR movement, "the farmer changed from the essentially nonpolitical being he was during the Tokugawa period . . . to a political being out to define what was meant by the April 1868 Imperial Oath" (1980, 93). The majority of Fukuoka UPF members were farmers, who also filled the ranks of the many groups across Japan writing up constitutions and memorial petitions.

Inflation following the Satsuma Rebellion also made it easier for full-time activists like the Genyôsha leadership to organize village assemblies, study groups, and schools in addition to running the ubiquitous traveling lecture series (JTS, vol. 1, 236–55). The Meiji oligarchs in Tokyo were horrified at these mass mobilizations. To stop them they revived some of Ôkubô Toshimichi's counterinsurgency techniques and introduced some novel ones: round-the-clock surveillance, agents provocateurs, the planting of fabricated evidence, and expanding restrictions on political speech, with over three hundred fines and jail sentences handed out to writers for violating censorship regulations between 1878 and 1880. Newer tactics included curtailing the popular practice of bringing policy memorials directly to the Chamber of Elders for submission to Emperor Meiji. In mid-1880 orders were sent from Tokyo to all prefectural governors to warn APR groups against submitting indignant "petitions [請願]"; only "constructive proposals [建白]" had a chance for review by the Chamber of Elders. In December 1881 the first of several formal prohibitions against petitioning was announced (Gotô 1972, 145). Obinata Sumio uncovered another innovation in Meiji state repression: a whole new bureau of "national detectives" created in November 1881 and funded through Matsukata Masayoshi's Finance Ministry. In May 1883 funding for this bureau was doubled. The mission of these detectives was "to directly infiltrate APR groups . . . and report word for word to the local police exactly what the groups were saying" (1987, 77).[1]

In an attempt to crack down on the APR after the large Patriot Society conference in Osaka on March 1, 1880, where three thousand activists representing over 100,000 members gathered to push for a democratic Diet, the oligarchs restricted all political meetings. Imperial Decree No. 12, the Public Meetings Law of April 5, 1880, declared that any open association of more than five people required a police permit acquired at least three days before the event, with the names and addresses of all those involved. Article 5 of this decree required "police authorities in uniform" at each event, to "exercise control over the meeting," while Article 7 outlawed students, teachers, and soldiers from being involved with any political organization (JGD, 495–97).

This crackdown targeted the Patriot Society and the UPF, and southwestern Japan activists responded by creating an entirely new group called the League for the Establishment of a National Assembly (国会期成同盟, LNA) that moved to Tokyo in late 1880 to set up a national coordinating center. There the executive committee decided to divide Japan into twelve districts to maintain the level of political agitation they thought was required for the immediate establishment of an elected parliament (JTS, vol. 2, 328–29). The LNA adopted a stripped-down organizational style, both to make it easier to reach a national audience and to avoid problems with police infiltrators and agents provocateurs (Kim 2007, 213). Hakoda Rokusuke was chosen as an executive officer along with two other United Patriotic Front members—one example of how central Fukuoka had become to national opposition politics. It's worth pointing out that Hakoda's existence has been basically expunged from the historical record, and his name doesn't appear in any of the main studies of the APR movement (Bowen 1980; Gotô 1972; Irokawa 1985; Makihara 2012; Matsuo 1990). This should be contrasted with his stature in the early 1880s, when the Genyôsha president was referred to as the second most influential APR activist in all of western Japan after Itagaki Taisuke.[2]

As the Tokyo oligarchs moved to infiltrate and suppress the LNA in mid-1881, the newest tactic of oligarch backlash was already being felt: austerity. As early as mid-1880, APR intellectuals sensed that the Meiji oligarchs would expand their tactics of state repression with the hammer of "retrenchment [紙幣整理]" (Ôishi 1989, 235). The APR leaders feared that a tightening of the money supply would shift resources from small merchants and farmers in peripheral areas to banks and capitalist conglomerates in metropoles like Osaka and Tokyo. In fact, Article 8 of the founding charter of the LNA called for "agreement on matters related to finance" so that the oligarchs wouldn't unilaterally attempt to smother the popular movements via austerity (Ôishi 1989, 248).

While most scholars applaud the Matsukata deflationary retrenchment as the necessary medicine required to get Japan on the global gold standard, some have noted the impact this had on the APR movement.[3] I want to build on their arguments to suggest that the speed and force of shrinking the money supply eviscerated the popular resistance, sucking up monies spent on subscriptions, membership fees for political groups, and action funds for extralegal uprisings and operations.[4] From 1881 to 1884, when the amount of inconvertible paper notes shrank by 19 percent, Tokyo wholesale prices dropped by the same amount. This wasn't the work of Matsukata alone, but a policy proposed by several Meiji oligarchs. As Steve Ericson points out, oligarchs' actions that preceded the Matsukata shock helped trigger the deflation of the early 1880s (2014).

Matsukata himself was surprised at the speed with which, as Sydney Crawcour has argued, his policies "produced a severe recession that reversed the effects of the inflationary boom, transferring resources back to the government and banking system" (in Yamamura 1997, 47). The effects of the shock have been well documented: the price of rice rose dramatically, putting it out of reach for much of the peasantry (with no accompanying *okimai* emergency rations to prevent starvation, which was standard in the seventeenth and eighteenth centuries); state enterprises sold off to cronies of the oligarchs at fire-sale prices; a sharp rise in local taxes[5] when Tokyo cut the money it had promised to the provinces to install the infrastructure for capitalist modernization including roads, bridges, and schools; and dispossession in the countryside where, according to the German economist Paul Mayet, in the three years from 1884 to 1886, "roughly one-eighth" of all Japanese farmland underwent mortgage foreclosure (Mayet 1893, 5). The tenancy rate for the whole of Japan was between 28 and 29 percent in 1873, but increased to 40 percent by 1892 (Nakamura 1983, 56).

This transformation of relatively well-off farmers into beggars and exploited male wage laborers (while what Maria Mies [1986] calls capitalist "housewifization" cheapened everything female spouses did as unpaid "women's work") benefited the capitalist conglomerates Mitsui, Mitsubishi, and Glover and Co., which were Japan's first climate-interferers as principal extractors of coal in western Japan. Deeply aware of ties between the Tokyo oligarchs and Mitsui and Mitsubishi and the way the Matsukata deflation was displacing Kyushu farmers into dangerous and dirty mining jobs, the Fukuoka UPF began to criticize capitalist extraction for export from the region. Fukuoka native Tokushige Masao studied economics in Berlin for two years and was delighted to return home in early 1879 to find widespread resistance to extraction and capitalist centralization. In a new form of eco-ontological protection, with UPF activist Matsuda Toshitari, Tokushige organized several boycotts of Euro-American products in Kyushu and advised merchants on economic strategies that would enhance local and regional autonomy (Ishitaki 2010, 136–38). While not going as far as the rogue samurai ecology protectors who murdered Japanese merchants from 1861 to 1864 for profiting by selling off "the staples of the land" to Euro-white capitalists and then put their severed heads up in public places in Kyoto, Osaka, and Edo affixed with explanations for the killings, Tokushige and Matsuda insisted that Fukuoka must not allow itself to be forced into a CO_2lonial economic situation by exporting primary products like coal and seafood outside the region, either to Tokyo or to Euro/America (Heco and Murdoch 1892, vol. 2, 14). While encouraging locals to use coal for their own families—people normally dug it out themselves or paid day laborers to do so—by the mid-1880s Tokushige and others were denouncing the negative effects industrial coal extraction like that initiated by Thomas Glover at Takashima (discussed in chapter 1) had on local communities: contaminating water supplies and degrading land with uranium and sulfate (GY #19, 2). The Fukuoka UPF was not going to let either Euro-American or Japanese state capitalists extra-act on and exploit their regional environment for the rawfare (in this case, natural resources and cheapened human labor) needed to drive capital accumulation.

The Tokyo oligarchs and the APR movement also disagreed on the causes of the inflationary spiral itself. Meiji leaders blamed antigovernment uprisings in western Japan that "forced" the state to borrow heavily to buy the armaments needed to pacify them. After that, leaders blamed irresponsibly spendthrift farmers and local merchants for exacerbating the problem. Matsukata himself singled out "The farmers, who were the only class to profit from these circumstances, took on luxurious habits, causing a great increase in the consumption of luxury goods" (in Smith 1955, 96–97). Rather than scolding farmers for thinking they could consume like Tokyo oligarchs and gorge-us white guys, the Fukuoka UPF argued that the economic problems in Japan were the result of Japan's CO_2lonized condition in a global market dominated by Euro-Americans. In their view, the fact that the Meiji state couldn't raise tariffs on the foreign machine-produced commodities displacing domestic products was the primary cause of economic instability. In other words, the Unequal Treaties, not uppity farmers, were the main reason behind Japan's persistent trade and current account deficits.

Therefore, the political program of the UPF (which included Genyôsha as a core group) and Kôchi's Patriot Party reiterated the rebel demands from the defeat of the Tokugawa in the civil war of 1867–69: overthrow the Unequal Treaties and level the feudal hierarchies, "horizontally unifying peasants, artisan, merchants and samurai" (Irokawa 1985, 60). As they stated in their founding charter in December 1879, Fukuoka's UPF was formed to "unify all the people in the Chikuzen [Fukuoka] domain" and would work toward eliminating "the hierarchies separating rich and poor of the former four classes" (Ishitaki 2010, 145–46). To put this horizontalist theory into practice, they established a grassroots democratic structure that allowed each town or village to send a representative to the group's congress, which met twice each year. Representatives were chosen by ballot, and each household was allowed one vote, regardless of property or wealth.

Despite these efforts at self-government, the Matsukata deflation put immense pressure on peripheral groups opposing the Tokyo oligarchs, and Genyôsha was no exception. Along with police repression and draconian attacks on political speech, the drying up of money and resources intensified conflicts inside APR groups. These tensions were particularly acute inside Genyôsha as it scrambled to find ways to fund both its above-ground politics and its underground plans for the assassination of Meiji leaders and potential armed overthrow of the Meiji state.

New Alliances

Genyôsha's political ally in nearby Kumamoto was the Mutual Love Society (相愛社), and they shared a link with the APR movement center in Kôchi and hosted their speakers whenever they came to town. However, Tôyama Mitsuru—who, while never holding an official position, always acted as de facto leader of Genyôsha—was growing closer to the leader of the Kumamoto group Shimeikai (紫溟会), political enemies of the Mutual Love Society. Born to a mid-rank samurai family, Shimeikai's leader Sassa Tomofusa (1854–1906) was considered the brightest student at the Kumamoto domain school. But the most important line in Sassa's résumé for Tôyama was that he volunteered to fight with Saigô Takamori in the Satsuma Rebellion. Sassa fought four months before he was seriously injured, after which he was hospitalized and given a two-year prison sentence. Among other things, Sassa was a critic of the APR movement, thinking its emphasis on rights and popular democracy was too Eurocentric for Japan (Motoyama 1997, 280). Instead of this sociopolitical emphasis on autonomy and democracy in the APR movement, Sassa was an ardent proponent of the notion of *kokutai* (国体), or Japanese national essence. His experience as a soldier taught him to value discipline, respect, and loyalty. While the APR intellectuals scanned the Japanese sociopolitical landscape and saw despotic oligarchs and capitalist elites ripping off peasants and small businesses, Sassa and his Shimeikai saw rampant individualism, Westernization, and despotic oligarchs. The main thing linking Shimeikai and the APR movement was a shared enemy: the Meiji oligarchic government in Tokyo.

With the exception of Genyôsha's first president, Hiraoka Kôtaro, all of Genyôsha's original members criticized Tôyama's growing friendship with Sassa and continued to work exclusively with the Mutual Love Society. Unwilling to break off his friendship with Sassa, Tōyama was left with no option but to ally with men from outside Genyōsha's political circle. The first of these was a young accountant from Shimeikai named Yūki Toragorō, who Tōyama brusquely brought into Genyōsha to help with its dwindling finances. But it didn't stop there.

Sometime in the summer of 1884, Sassa told Tōyama that he just had to meet this intense Fukuoka guy named Sugiyama. "Last year he came to see me for cash; says he needs 150 yen for assassination money to whack Itō [Hirobumi]. We throw a few questions back and forth, and then I ask him how in hell's name is he going to pay me back. Sugiyama says the payback will be two freshly severed heads delivered right to my door—one of them Itō's, the other one his own" (Sugiyama 2006b, 69). After hearing this, Tōyama looked forward to meeting the nineteen-year-old Sugiyama Shigemaru (1864–1935), and, hearing that he was living underground in Tokyo, invited him to a Genyōsha get-together there in November 1885.[6]

Sugiyama was living in a rundown room in the Shibaguchi neighborhood of the capital. He had just returned to Tokyo after fleeing to Hokkaidō in northern Japan for six months, just ahead of a sting operation by the national police set up to arrest him for conspiring to assassinate the oligarch and Japan's first prime minister, Itō Hirobumi (Hori 2006, 26). After cooling out in Hokkaidō, he returned to Tokyo in September 1885 to unite with his band of assassins, who called themselves the "Jacobins." He met his two accomplices while studying at Nakae Chōmin's French school in 1883, where he became fascinated with revolutionary politics (GY #12, 4). Despite trying to avoid the police pressure by taking the name of Hayashi Kyōichi, an identity theft Sugiyama pulled off when he overheard a conversation about a young man with that name who had just died, the police dragnet was so tight in Tokyo in October 1885 that the remaining Jacobins were prevented from reuniting. Sugiyama found out in the next few weeks that one of the Jacobins had already been arrested for conspiracy and would be tortured before eventually dying in prison three years later. The other Jacobin committed suicide in Aomori in order to avoid a second round of torture that he was certain would follow from his impending arrest (Muroi 1983, 78). Therefore, when Sugiyama got the invitation from Tōyama, the timing couldn't have been better—he was being hounded by regular and undercover police and was increasingly isolated.

Sugiyama's roommate offered to lend him his battered silk top hat for the occasion of meeting the influential player from Fukuoka. Sugiyama recalled later that he looked truly ridiculous when he donned the top hat in his filthy, tattered kimono and wild greasy hair (2006a, 30). When Sugiyama found the rundown Tanakaya inn that served as the Genyôsha safe house in Tokyo, he was instructed by the owner to go up to the second floor. There he noticed a tough-looking but handsome man about ten years older than himself sitting at a table. When Tôyama called Sugiyama to come over, he noticed four or five other men, all of them appearing slightly older than Sugiyama; they turned out to be the Genyôsha cell in Tokyo: Matono Hansuke, Tsukinari Motoyoshi, Kurushima Tsuneki, and Hisada Tamotsu. Thinking that they were all good guys after exchanging greetings, Sugiyama became nervous when Tôyama told them he wanted to talk to Sugiyama in private.[7]

Sugiyama recalled that he took off his hat and shyly introduced himself. Tôyama refused to reciprocate, only asking brusquely: "Are you some kind of government official? That's the kind of hat only an asshole official would wear." Sugiyama was briefly taken aback, but then replied indignantly, "I've never been a government official! This here is the kind of hat that only a dirt-poor baker would wear at Kimurayas." Tôyama seemed satisfied with that and Sugiyama proceeded to make small talk. After a long silence, Tôyama abruptly lectured him: "Intelligence [才] should always be humble and modest. Bravery [勇] too needs to be a humble and modest bravery; loyalty [忠] should be absolute. Whatever it is you do, do it proudly and with indignant righteousness; don't do anything half-ass . . . I'm feeling right now that you and I must make sure that neither one of us is led off the track by our hot-blooded impulsiveness" (Sugiyama 2006a, 30–31).[8]

Sugiyama was impressed by several things in this first contact with Genyôsha, especially the fierce animosity directed at all Meiji government officials (2006a, 32). Sugiyama would soon find out more about Genyôsha's self-proclaimed rejection of officialdom. When he moved back to Fukuoka for the next eight years, he later heard firsthand of a visit to the governor of Osaka by Tôyama and Shindô Kiheita in 1890. This is how that story was told two decades later by Tôyama's secretary Fujimoto Naonori:

> Because the Osaka governor had a reputation as a real mover and shaker [遣手] Tôyama sensei went to ask him for a favor. After he and Shindô were escorted to a sitting room by a secretary, they waited and waited, but the governor wasn't showing up for their scheduled appointment. All sensei could do was to pretend to wait patiently for the hotshot, but. . . . Just at that moment, Tôyama sensei felt a tapeworm wiggling around inside his stomach, so he swallowed a laxative right there in the waiting room and—wouldn't you know it—sensei soon felt the tapeworm start to crawl out [ムズムズ]. Then, right in public, sensei took his hand and

inserted it right down through his crotch and went digging around in his asshole for it; in no time he pulled out a part of the tapeworm a little over a centimeter. . . . Looking around him, sensei saw a nice hibachi and decided to lay it down right on the edge.

When Tôyama sensei felt the rest of the tapeworm wiggling around, he once again shoved his hand straight through his crotch into his asshole looking for the rest of the little bastard. He pulled out a bigger piece this time and, showing it to all the other people waiting, he laid it down on the edge of the hibachi next to the first piece. . . . At that point, the mayor arrived dressed pretentiously with a holier than thou attitude. He said, "Sorry to keep you guys waiting," and then sat down right next to the hibachi. Accidentally putting his hand on the edge when he went to warm his hands, the tapeworm got stuck on his palm. Suddenly, not knowing what the soft, flat thing was, he put the tapeworm right up to his nose to smell it and was repulsed. Finally, he turned around and said, "Hey, what was that thing on the edge of the hibachi?"

The secretary was already freaked out by sensei pulling small things out of his butt, but she didn't exactly know what they were. Finally feeling compelled to respond, Tôyama sensei opened his mouth: "That's a tapeworm I just now pulled out of my asshole while I was waiting for you." (KKD, 100–102)

The day after their first meeting, Sugiyama was invited to meet again with Tôyama and Yûki Toragorô. Tôyama had done his homework on Sugiyama and discovered that he had basically supported his father and sister from the time he was thirteen—simultaneously working three or four jobs after his mother died of malnutrition in 1870 and his father's samurai stipend was cut in 1871. Tôyama thought that this experience, together with Sugiyama's intelligence and willingness to assassinate oligarchs, made him ideal to assist Yûki in getting Genyôsha's financial house together. Right then and there, Tôyama, Yûki, and Sugiyama agreed to work side by side and commit themselves to five basic principles: overcome the deadlock in Japanese politics, advance universal righteousness, explore new material and intellectual resources that could speed up Japan's full liberation from the West, hasten local economic development in and around Fukuoka, and maintain their focus on the domestic situation in Japan (Noda 1992, 120). Then, by way of a gory samurai ritual that entailed slicing off the top half of one's middle finger (指詰め), they sealed what begs to be called a joint pact (Hasegawa 1974, 43–44).

FIGURE 5.1. Genyôsha in the 1920s. Sugiyama is in the front, second from right, showing off his severed middle finger (Ishitaki Toyomi 1997).

Osaka Incident

One of the reasons Tôyama was in Tokyo was to pressure the Genyôsha cell to halt their involvement with the impending Osaka Incident,[9] which Makihara Norio identifies as "a revolutionary program of the left wing of the APR movement to overthrow by force the despotic Meiji government" (in Matsuo 1982, 84). One part of the plan was to assist Korean independence activists in a coup d'état against the conservatives in the Korean monarchy. While scholars on the left (Inoue Kiyoshi) and right (Marius Jansen) locate the origins of Japanese imperialist expansion in the Osaka Incident of October and November 1885, this is incorrect in my view. The political motivations of the revolutionaries in the Osaka Incident came directly from the left wing of the APR movement: autonomy, egalitarianism, mutual aid, and anti-individualism. The intellectual architects of the action, Ôi Kentarô (1832–1922) and Kobayashi Kuzuo (1856–1920), were staunchly critical of nationalism and state formation. Unsurprisingly, they firmly rejected Japan's imperialist posture toward Korea. In 1876 the Tokyo oligarchs forced the weaker country to sign an Unequal Treaty mimicking the ones the Western powers imposed on Japan and China (Matsuo 1982, 6).

Makihara Norio concludes his essay on the Incident by insisting that "the leaders learned the lessons from the isolation and tragic failure of the previous uprisings [1882–84] and tried to create a situation that would make a totalizing confrontation against the Meiji government a reality" (Matsuo 1982, 85). This kind of clash materialized in the Osaka Incident plan, involving several different parts of Japan rising up in open revolt more or less simultaneously, similar to what happened in the Chichibu uprising of October 1884 but on a national scale. To carry this out Ôi, Kobayashi, and Arai Shôgo (1856–1906) organized small cells with anywhere from five to twenty members based in Kanagawa, Ibaraki, Toyama, Okayama, Tochigi, Nagano, and Fukuoka. They planned on relying on the Liberty Party youth training institutes, called Yûikkans, located in each of these areas, which featured an increasingly militant antigovernment pedagogy by the beginning of 1885 (Machida 2000, 53). Isoyama Seibei was designated to lead the group going to Korea; this collective was the largest, with about twenty-five men and women. With the exception of the Korea-bound group, each cell was charged with mobilizing fighters (挙兵) and gathering money. Groups were supposed to send most of the money raised to Arai and Ôi in Tokyo, keeping only enough to maintain themselves and their training facilities. Ôi himself went out from Tokyo with Kobayashi on several fundraising trips (Nagano, Osaka, Kôchi), but always came back with empty pockets—the Matsukata deflation was having the desired effect. This inability to raise money was arguably the single greatest cause of the failure of the revolutionary program, as several of the groups were forced to turn to robbery, which drew the attention of local and national police.

In addition to trying to mobilize as many rebels as possible, when the simultaneous uprisings were taking place, each group was responsible for assassinating local representatives of the Meiji government. The Kanagawa and Yokohama groups were the most focused on this, plotting to kill high government officials in and around Tokyo. For the Kanagawa leaders Oya Masao and Murano Tsunemon, this was the crux of the "domestic revolution–first plan [国内革命優先]" (Irokawa 1969, 144). As Oya detailed in his court testimony of 1887, the Kanagawa group disagreed with those that insisted on a "Korea revolution–first" plan (June 23, a.m.).[10] Although the judges would not allow him to speak directly about the plan, the details of how they would incite revolution inside Japan—assassinations, bombings, and pasting up revolutionary propaganda in public spaces—leaked out over several months of testimony.

In order to connect the Osaka Incident with Japanese imperialism and nation-centered, raison d'état politics, scholars have to ignore both the left wing of the APR's critique of the Meiji oligarchs' actions in Korea as well as the widespread dismissal within the APR (including Genyôsha) of the Social Darwinist axiom of the "strong devour the weak." Beginning with the public debate between the Tokyo oligarchs' favorite philosopher, Katô Hiroyuki, and the APR movement intellectual Ueki Emori in 1882, the rejection of race and class hierarchies in APR political thought continued right up to the trial of the Osaka Incident revolutionaries in the summer of 1887. Initiated by Arai Shô-go's testimony on June 6, 1887, Ôi's right-hand man claimed that "we are all opposed to the contemporary notion of the 'strong devour the weak [弱肉強食],' as these are the kind of ideas emanating from a truly barbarian world." Linking this critique of Social Darwinism to the savagery of the Euro-American modus operandi in Asia, Arai polemicized that such ideology has been on full display "beginning with England's colonization of Hong Kong and India and now stretching into Central Asia; the Orient has become the wrestling ring within which the Western powers show who has more brute force" (June 6, a.m.). Several of the other defendants at the trial criticized the "barbarity" of the "the strong devour the weak" ideology uncritically adopted by the Tokyo oligarchs from white supremacist Euro-America, especially the revolutionary from Kanagawa, Sakamoto Seijirô (June 11, p.m.). Sakamoto also joined several others in denouncing the ideology of Euro-American atomistic individuality, what I'm calling ego-ontology.

Without having to look closely at their very public denigration of Japanese nationalism, Ôi, Arai, and Kobayashi were explicit that their actions with respect to Korea had nothing whatsoever to do with raison d'état, or that which assumes the primacy of the nation-state and its interests. Ôi insisted that, regardless of how their actions to incite a revolution in Korea were construed by public opinion, "they have no relation whatsoever to Japan" (September 1, a.m.). Kobayashi was the first to declare at the trial that the Korea operation was outside any nationalistic framework: "it should not be seen as Japan interfering in Korea" (July 16, a.m.). Several days later, Ôi hammered this home, claiming that their Korea action wasn't to be undertaken "for the sake of Japan, but out of goodwill . . . in the fashion of a global brotherhood [四海兄弟]" (July 21, a.m.). Iyama Isei from the Toyama group explicitly refused Japanese nationalism, claiming only a local identity and a transnational one: "as Asians we all feel a higher duty to mutually support each other" (June 13, p.m.).

Makihara likens this transnational commitment to the motivations of the fighters in the International Brigades who went to Spain to battle fascism in the 1930s (Matsuo 1982, 60). We could certainly add other global solidarity actions to that list, but first we should pause here to identify the limits to this global sense of solidarity. Ôi, Arai, and Kobayashi did not share Fukuzawa Yukichi and other Japanese liberals' enthusiasm for Euro-American penetration into Asia, because they saw how hypocritical the Western powers were when they mouthed commitments to freedom and liberty while actually using Asia as their CO_2lonial playground. Arai soapboxed at the trial that no Asian "should ever stop opposing the West . . . as the British Empire gets all its means for enjoyment from the blood and tears of Indians [印度人の涙と血] in Asia" (June 8, a.m.). The defendants repeatedly stressed that the struggle for liberation and equality needed to be waged both against repressive and reactionary governments in Asia (the despotic rulers in Japan, the Qing dynasty in China, and the conservative monarchy in Korea) and imperialist Euro-America. As Ôi claimed, "If you want to talk about our position toward Asia, I need to reiterate that we weren't using Korea as 'bait' to be sacrificed, but were trying to bring about a revolution there as a way to improve the situations in Japan and China as well, in other words, throughout all of Asia. Moreover, this should be seen as one part of our larger strategy of Asia [東洋] opposing Europe [欧州]" (July 21, a.m.).

The revolutionaries' view of China was more nuanced than their stance on Korea at the time of the Osaka Incident.[11] Nevertheless, Kobayashi Kuzuo had been in Shanghai's International Settlement in the fall of 1884 trying to convince anti-Qing leaders there to coordinate actions with the Osaka Incident leaders in simultaneously overthrowing corrupt governments in Japan, Korea, and China. At the trial for the revolutionaries involved in the earlier armed uprising known as the Fukushima Incident of 1883—where one of the main issues was opposition to the Meiji oligarchs' environmentally destructive road-building projects—they consistently linked Japan, Korea, and China together, all similarly oppressed by Euro-American imperialism. Kôno Hironaka insisted that "using liberation as the basis of action," their revolutionary plan wanted to bring the benefits of equality "to each country in Asia": "We tried to raise an army of brave volunteers to awaken Japan, Korea, and China from their nightmare; we feel a compassionate solidarity with all Asian people" (in Hirano 1988, 204). Fukushima militant Hanaka Kyôjirô was even more forceful, arguing that, "without the Unequal Treaties being overturned, there's no way for Asians to escape the predations of Westerners" (205). At the 1887 trial for the Osaka Incident militants, the Kanagawa revolutionary Sakamoto Seijirô identified the imperialist right of extraterritoriality in Asia as the central problem: "Japan, Korea, and China are all oppressed by extraterritorial privileges for white foreigners. . . . There won't be liberty in Asia until this is overturned" (June 11, p.m.).

It should not be surprising that Genyôsha was one of Ôi and Arai's central coalition groups, as Hakoda Rokusuke and Shindô Kiheita were close friends and comrades of Kobayashi's. Nevertheless, Genyôsha's involvement in the Osaka Incident hasn't been mentioned in the relevant scholarship (Ishitaki 2010; Sabey 1974; Tôyama 1977). However, primary documents clearly establish their involvement, both financially and politically. Three Genyôsha members were nearly arrested in November 1885 while trying to join up with Isoyama's cell heading off to Korea (Muroi 1984, 111).

The archive of Genyôsha's successor, the Black Dragon Society, provides crucial details pertaining to the Fukuoka group's links to the Osaka Incident. Apparently, Genyôsha donated a significant amount of money (more than 10 percent of the total amount accumulated at the time of the mass arrests) to Inagaki Shime, who was handling some of the finances for Ôi and Arai. They also pledged to have a few hundred fighters prepared for the revolutionary uprising in and around Fukuoka when the time was right (Kuzuu 1936, vol. 1, 119). However, the Black Dragon source material also reveals that tension arose within Genyôsha a few months before the action, as "Tôyama put pressure on the solidarity the young Genyôsha activists" had with Ôi's group (120). In other words, Tôyama ultimately didn't want any Genyôsha members involved in the multisited uprising. Other sources suggest that the emerging split between the leftist APR faction in Genyôsha (Hakoda, Shindô, Kurushima) and the more conservative "states' rights" position represented by Tôyama's alliance with Sassa Tomofusa finally came to a head over the Osaka Incident (GYSS, 250–52; Matsuo 1982, 171). Tôyama visited Tokyo at least three times between spring 1884 and fall 1885, and these visits were probably designed both to deliver pledged money to Ôi and Arai and to begin to move the Genyôsha sleeper cell in Tokyo away from them, and away from Hakoda Rokusuke and Shindô Kiheita (as Genyôsha president and vice president), who promised Genyôsha's support. And this division inside Genyôsha was about to get worse.

Tôyama returned to Fukuoka in early December 1885 (after almost all of the activists in the Osaka Incident had been arrested in two sting operations) and brusquely informed Shindô and Hakoda that a new guy named Sugiyama would be working together with Yûki to boost fundraising for Genyôsha. Shindô immediately derided the two newcomers as the new "business division [実業部]," but Hakoda exhibited an even stronger animosity to Sugiyama. As Hakoda turned up the volume on the public denunciation of Sassa and Shimeikai as anti-egalitarian and reactionary, he focused on forcing Sugiyama out of Genyôsha. In just Sugiyama's second week on the job at the end of February 1886, after a pep talk by Tôyama to all the members at the Genyôsha office,

Hakoda taunted Sugiyama: "When Mitsuru mentioned the glorious Fukuoka heroes, he probably had only you and Yûki in mind, huh?" During the next month, the two came close to blows on several occasions, one that concluded with Sugiyama trash-talking the Genyôsha president: "You can't think outside the box, which is the main reason things are so fucked up around here. You would be nothing without this organization, Hakoda, but I'm completely self-reliant; I can take Genyôsha or leave it whenever I want" (Muroi 1983, 76). Although Sugiyama had been prepped for potential problems with Hakoda and the still-dominant APR faction inside Genyôsha, after several more heated confrontations with Hakoda, Tôyama advised him to take a six-week leave from Genyôsha, and he returned to his old apartment in Tokyo to read and reflect. But unlike the fugitive life Sugiyama was leading in 1884–85, this time Tôyama assigned an armed Genyôsha man to act as his bodyguard—the first time Sugiyama had any protection against the Meiji state terror that had already taken the lives of his two Jacobin comrades. A voracious reader, Sugiyama took the time to revisit some of his favorite texts: Mencius, Rousseau's *Social Contract*, and Miyazaki Muryû's bestseller *A Record of the French Revolution: The Battle Cry of Liberty*. Sugiyama scholar Muroi Hiroichi speculates that this month of reading and thinking in Tokyo marked a shift in Sugiyama's politics from revolutionary terror to a more pragmatic approach (1983, 72).

Depicting Assassinationism

This does not mean that Sugiyama turned into a pragmatist overnight. In Tokyo, Sugiyama not only reread Miyazaki Muryû's loose translation into Japanese of Alexandre Dumas's *Ange Pitou* (*Taking the Bastille*); he devoured the serial publication of Miyazaki's controversial *Demons Softly Crying* (鬼啾々) in the Liberty Party newspaper *Jiyū Shimbun*. Like Miyazaki's *A Record of the French Revolution*, this political novel was not only read in private, but was also proclaimed in groups in the form of communal recitals among APR activists and supporters (Ueda 2007, 59, 67).

Demons Softly Crying depicts the actions of a group of Russian anarchists from 1878 to 1881, beginning with the assassination of a General Mesenchev by Sophia Perovskaya and others and concluding with the execution of Perovskaya after her involvement in the successful assassination of Czar Alexander II.[12] Surrounding these narrative foci are descriptions of rural poverty, police oppression, and the routine torture of political dissidents—in other words, a barely disguised take on western and southwestern Japan in the early 1880s suffering under the oligarchs' surveillance and the Matsukata shock doctrine.

More importantly, the novel details the political program of the revolutionary anarchists: universal franchise, complete freedom of speech and assembly, and workers' ownership of the means of production. With the exception of the last demand, this perfectly reflects the platform of the LPR movement of the early 1880s. More than mere reflection, however, as Miyazaki's text appears just at the end of the period of armed insurrections and just before the preparations for the Osaka Incident, *Demons Softly Crying* should be seen as inflecting its context.

Back to Fukuoka

When Sugiyama returned to Fukuoka and full-time work in April 1886, he continued to face hostility from most of the Genyôsha members. Slowly, he came to understand that this was symptomatic of a general crisis inside the group. Hakoda, Narahara, and Shindô disliked the new nationalistic states' rights (国権) tendency infiltrating Genyôsha; like the Osaka Incident radicals, their political identifications were primarily local (Fukuoka) and transnational (Asia). What must have been perplexing for Hakoda and Shindô is that Tôyama's political commitments to the APR movement in 1885 and 1886 remained consistent with his thinking over the previous seven years, as he continued to support core APR principles including an immediate opening of a democratically elected parliament and the expansion of freedoms of the press, assembly, and speech. Moreover, like Hakoda, Tôyama was considered part of the emerging insurrectionary faction of the APR with Ôi Kentarô and Kôno Hironaka (Hasegawa 1974, 31–32). The difference is that as he got older and more established—and much less anti-oligarch in his politics—Tôyama came to compensate for the mainstreaming of his politics by an overidentification onto subjects with impeccable samurai and oppositional credentials like Saigô Takamori and Sassa. His earlier identifications with leading Fukuoka insurrectionists and his older schoolmates Ôchi and Takebe were consistent with early opposition politics circa 1877. But after Saigô's death and his own sense of melancholic lack at not participating in any of the uprisings in 1876 and 1877,[13] he compensated with an intense transference onto Saigô, whom he started calling 大西郷—"Great Saigô." Configuring identification in the psychoanalytic sense—where an attribute of another person is assimilated by a subject who feels a palpable absence of these desired attributes within him- or herself—suggests that such transference normally trumps one's rational political commitments.

Tôyama's identification with Sassa and Saigô would only intensify as the political and financial pressures added up for Genyôsha into the mid-1880s.

Things almost came to a head in August of 1886 after Sugiyama was sent back to Tokyo to seal two business deals. When Hakoda and several other members threatened to quit Genyôsha if Tôyama didn't terminate his association with Sassa, Tôyama went off on them: "If you want to quit and talk shit [悪口] about me around town, that's OK. If you want to commit suicide after you quit, that would be good too. But the most likely outcome of you quitting is that I'll cut your fucking heads off myself" (Muroi 1987, 142).

At this point, Sugiyama was already having an impact on Genyôsha's finances, getting the group involved in commercial deals with big businessmen all the members had previously been critical of. When Tôyama followed Sugiyama and Yûki to Tokyo in late August 1886 after the confrontation in Fukuoka, Sugiyama told him that he wanted Genyôsha to invest in some extraction businesses in Fukuoka. During his fugitive period in Hokkaido in northern Japan in 1885, Sugiyama met Fukuoka men there who were investigating mining possibilities, looking to build on profitable coal extraction in Kyushu. In April 1886, Sugiyama heard that several ex-samurai from Fukuoka were already making lots of money locally in coal (KTM, 78). After deciding that Genyôsha better get into coal extraction while they still had the chance, he sat Tôyama down for a talk: "If you ultimately want Genyôsha to assume the role of the Japanese state [国家の役], we'll have to operate alongside the Meiji oligarchs for, say, a decade or so. As for how we are going to pay for this, the quickest way to do it would be to just print counterfeit money. Seriously though, the best means to do this aren't counterfeit, but are legal, local, and natural" (Hirai 1987, vol. 1, 320). When Tôyama asked him exactly what he meant, Sugiyama replied, "There are already people making tons of money from coal mining in north Kyushu." Tôyama thought for a minute before growing increasingly agitated. "So you want Genyôsha to be just like those other slimy extractors [鉄山師]?"[14] After a long silence, Yûki told Tôyama about the coal deals that Sassa himself had profited from, which helped assuage Tôyama's anxiety (320).

When they all returned to Fukuoka for the opening of their newspaper, Tôyama brusquely informed the core members that Genyôsha was getting into coal extraction. The outburst was immediate, with all of the members incredulous that Tôyama could be so nonchalant about reversing the group's political opposition to industrial mining in particular and capitalist business in general. Several of the younger members with friends who had worked for Mitsui and Mitsubishi accused Tôyama of betraying their principled refusal of coal extraction. Frustrated, Tôyama responded, "Instead of humiliating ourselves by kowtowing to rich assholes every time we need money, this is going to be easier for all of us to live with" (Muroi 1985, 2).

Hakoda was the founding Genyôsha member most firmly opposed to capitalist business, and he continued to deride Tôyama and Sugiyama's new proposals. The fact that Climate Caucasianists like Thomas Glover and Jardine, Matheson & Co. had been publicly urging all southwestern samurai from 1871 to get involved in coal and copper mining (working for them, of course) may have solidified his opposition (McKay 1993, 106). Since 1882 Mitsubishi had been investing heavily in coal mining in Kyushu, and its operations were so unpopular with the locals that anyone seen as profiting through extractive business was ridiculed with the simple epithet "Mitsubishi" (Muroi 1985, 2). But Mitsubishi was relatively benign compared to the Tokyo oligarchs' own extractive operation at the huge Miike coal mine north of Fukuoka city, opened in 1872. There, the Meiji government solved the problem of labor militancy endemic at extractive sites like Glover's Takashima mine (discussed in chapter 1) by using predominantly convict labor, with the managers and bosses the only paid workers out of approximately two thousand. This Meiji state monopoly at Miike was also freed from having to pay compensation to farmers displaced by the mushrooming pit openings; the oligarchs just ordered people to leave designated areas or jailed them if they refused (Hoshino and Iijima 1992). During the Satsuma Rebellion of 1877, the government forced local men to work for the Meiji army, which caused a labor shortage at Takashima. Since unpaid forced labor had helped Miike become profitable, Thomas Glover's Takashima operation received permission to use convict labor there to keep production steady (Sugiyama 1988, 195). Finally, the new Mitsubishi and Miike mining operations refused to close temporarily during agricultural planting seasons, as had been the case in the seventeenth and eighteenth centuries (Andô 1992).

At this time in 1886, almost all the coal extracted at Takashima, Miike, and other smaller mines north of Fukuoka was shipped out of the two ports of Nagasaki and Kuchinotsu, bound for Hong Kong, Shanghai, or Singapore, where it was sold to Euro-Americans (Andô 1992). Takashima and Miike alone produced around 80 percent of the coal used in East and Southeast Asia in the 1870s, '80s, and '90s, reflecting the CO_2lonial domination of the regional ecology and economy. But the explosion in the number of ships hauling coal out of Nagasaki and Kuchinotsu carried more than just extracted fossil fuel out of Japan. Similar to Saidiya Hartman's reminder that the West African British colony the Gold Coast was called simply "the Mine," because Euro-whites extracted both slaves and gold from it (Hartman 2007, 51), the Nagasaki and Fukuoka mining operations led to an exodus of young Japanese women and girls extracted and trafficked to Shanghai and Singapore for sex work, many stowed away illegally on these same coal freighters (Mihalopoulos 2011, 20–24). The pressure from the Matsukata deflation was compounded in southwestern Japan by forceful land enclosures carried out by Mitsui and Mitsubishi mining operations, leading desperate families to sell their daughters off to human traffickers. By 1920, most of the 100,000 Madam Butterflies sold to Euro-white and Asian men outside Japan came from poor communities in and around Nagasaki and Fukuoka (Driscoll 2010, 57–80).

When Hakoda Rokusuke turned increasingly to public denunciations of Genyôsha's involvement in coal extraction and the larger ecological and economic problems in northern Kyushu resulting from it, people who were already by 1885 financial backers of the group like Yasukawa Keiichirô complained behind the scenes that they were being insulted by Genyôsha's president (Muroi 1985, 4). Hakoda's moral authority was enough to convince most of the other members to remain opposed to Tôyama and Sugiyama's plans to profit from coal. Hiraoka Kôtaro was the only founding member supporting Tôyama; two years earlier, he had quietly tried to break into the local coal business on his own, but failed (Hasegawa 1974, 46–47). Tôyama approached the rift in the same way he had a year earlier, by alternating between a composed persuasiveness and threatening physical violence (Ikawa and Kobayashi 2006, 89).

At this point Sugiyama concocted a way of talking about coal extraction that he hoped would be less off-putting both to the Fukuoka public that was opposed to the large mining businesses and to the anti-extractivists inside Genyôsha. He came up with three talking points to rationalize their involvement with climate-interfering coal mining, a ruse that earned Shigemaru his lifelong nickname of "Bullshitmaru [法螺丸]" (KKD, 123). The first point was "an opportunity from Heaven [天の時]." What he meant to convey by this was that the confluence of factors leading to the boom in coal was a gift from the "natural" world. Since this gift was coming at a time when the both Western shipping firms and the Japanese navy wanted coal resources developed, it would be idiotic for Genyôsha not to take advantage of this chance. It was simply divine fate that their region had a newly valuable resource. Sugiyama's second talking point was "bounty from the land [地の利]." Muroi Hiroichi argues that Sugiyama intended this second talking point to mean that money made from coal located deep down in the land would be "profit coming from our land and not generated from the sweat and blood of working people" (Muroi 1985, 4).

The third talking point was "harmony with people [人の和]." Again, unlike capitalist enterprises where landlords and capitalist bosses exploited workers and poisoned local environments, the coal business contained the potential not to harm people. Coal resources barely had to be developed at all—they just lay there in the earth waiting for people to use them. Moreover, the small amount of labor it took to extract coal took place below the ground and was therefore invisible to most people. For these reasons, it was in harmony with the people of northern Kyushu. Finally, coal was a cheap, domestic source of energy at a time of rapidly developing modern infrastructure. Therefore, Sugiyama emphasized, coal was in harmony with the modernizing imperatives of the Japanese and Kyushu people (Muroi 1985, 4–5).

Sugiyama might have been trying to assuage the ambivalence he and Tōyama were feeling as well. In any case, they were intervening in a Kyushu debate about coal extraction, which was largely understood by locals as something carried out by corrupt Japanese conglomerates like Mitsui for purchase by even more corrupt white Euro-Americans (Hirano and Iida 1974, 135–37). Coal was a big part of the Meiji government's "expanding production [殖産興業]" for export program that Matsukata Masayoshi intensified when he became finance minister in 1881. Under this program, the oligarch government, through the Yokohama Specie Bank, advanced low-interest credit to merchant houses involved in exporting Japanese goods (Ishii 1994, 1–23). Not only did this policy benefit large capitalist corporations, but in 1882 Matsukata discontinued the practice of extending a small portion of this export credit directly to local producers.

As soon as Tōyama warned Genyōsha that he and Sugiyama were going to get into coal extraction regardless of the consequences, he began to work behind the scenes with former political enemies. Critical scholarship on Genyōsha, first published in 1912, details some of the ways that Tōyama started befriending the Fukuoka prefectural governor, Yasuba Tamokazu, who was a protégé of Ōkubo Toshimichi and a close ally of several of the Tokyo oligarchs.[15] Readers will recall that Hakoda Rokusuke had called publicly for Ōkubo's assassination and may very well have been involved when he was eventually killed in May 1878. Less than nine years later, Tōyama is seen several times in Yasuba's office and at his private residence deepening personal connections with the pubic face of Ōkubo in Fukuoka—Yasuba (Yoshida 1912, 41–44). It's safe to assume that Tōyama wasn't leaving tapeworm snacks on Yasuba's hibachi.

This Land Is My Land

The process of privatizing land with coal reserves was a messy, violent one. First, a group or business had to petition the prefectural governor to purchase the land from the owners. This involved a large fee paid by the group to the prefecture, and often the governor's office would OK two or three competing groups to begin the process of purchasing the land. Next, permissions had to be obtained from owners and all nonowner families living on the land. Once most of the permissions were obtained, these were then sent to the Home Ministry in Tokyo, which would usually grant the sale to the group. Yet another fee was required to get final approval for the sale from Tokyo.

Back in Kyushu, although mentions of the "struggles" over which groups would be successful in acquiring the permissions to extract coal survive in the local newspapers, Hirai Banson was the first scholar to reveal the viciousness of the process as it related to Genyôsha's involvement.[16] According to Hirai, Genyôsha's first attempt to gain mining rights was in August 1886 and involved a pitched battle with the Mitsui conglomerate, which had hired local toughs to gather the permissions and "flooded the area" with both bribe money and physical intimidation. At the same time, Tôyama dispatched younger Genyôsha and Shimeikai members with bamboo poles to battle the Mitsui people for the permissions. After the first day of fighting, it became clear that Genyôsha was going to win the battle (Hirai 1987, vol. 1, 322–23). The toughs were coached by Tôyama to tell the residents of the area that Genyôsha wasn't engaged in the extractive process "out of self-interest," and when combined with Genyôsha's reputation, this apparently convinced many locals to sign and sell off their land.

Yûki Toragorô related that in addition to battling corporate giants like Mitsui for mining rights, Genyôsha also took on smaller competitors, and then the gloves really came off. The battle between the Fujita Densaburô group for mining rights in August 1890 included knives and clubs, with Genyôsha resolved to having to kill Fujita's men to eventually win the mining rights; they didn't have to in the end (Muroi 1985, 2). Although it's been difficult to find information about the methods Genyôsha deployed to coax unwilling residents to take the small bribe, sign the permission, and prepare to vacate the area, it's inconceivable that they would have differed significantly from those deployed by conglomerates like Mitsui. Muroi Hiroichi argues that displacing residents from mining areas was probably easier for Genyôsha because of their reputation as unselfish protectors of Fukuoka and leaders of the anti-Tokyo campaign (1986, 152).

But their reputation in Fukuoka only allowed them to begin to negotiate. From that point on, just like the capitalist businesses that many members continued to criticize, when the cash payments didn't do the trick, even Genyôsha insiders like Tôyama's secretary Fujimoto admitted that Genyôsha resorted to "force to obtain permissions from stubborn small landowners" (1967, 76). The histories of resource extraction in and around Fukuoka make it clear that Genyôsha was a major player in coal mining from 1887 on.[17] Not only did Genyôsha buy and sell property with coal reserves on their own, but they partnered with several of their local financial backers like Yasukawa, Kan Meguna, and

Yano Kiheiji to form a major coal extraction conglomerate that operated in northern Kyushu for two decades. This became formalized in 1892 when Kan set up the coal mining business Chikuhô sekitan toriatsukai kaisha, involving Genyôsha centrally in all its operations (Nishi Nihon 1973, 32–39). The profit extracted was in inverse relation to the loss of political credibility, as it was already known in Fukuoka by 1889 that much of the Genyôsha-extracted coal was sold to Euro-American merchants in Nagasaki (Muroi 1986, 153). No matter how loudly Sugiyama and Tôyama proclaimed their three talking points, the dramatic shift from a poor group of idealistic antigovernment rebels to sleazy extractive capitalists came at a price for Genyôsha, and their loss of local credibility must be seen as one factor in expanding their actions in Korea, China, and Tokyo, where Tôyama bought a house in 1890 and relocated there, frequently visiting the Yoshiwara brothels in the manner of the corrupt Meiji oligarchs and white Euro-Americans. The erstwhile critics of extractive venality had become venal extractors themselves, their collectivity of human &bjects reduced to capitalist $ubjects.

What must have been a huge blow to their reputation in Fukuoka was the suicide of Hakoda Rokusuke on January 15, 1888. Remembering that Hakoda had risen to the top echelon of leaders of the national APR movement in the early 1880s, it's interesting that the Genyôsha literature says so little about it. The in-house history published in 1919 lies outright, stating "Hakoda became sick and passed away" (GYSS, 406). Many of the central accounts of Genyôsha or Tôyama neglect to even mention the suicide. It's fitting that the two people most responsible for changing the internal politics of Genyôsha—Sugiyama and Yûki—provide some of the few details. In an interview with the newspaper *Kyûshû Nippô* in 1909, Yûki revealed that Tôyama and Hakoda had a fistfight at one point in mid-1887 (Muroi 1986, 152). Writing in the 1920s, Sugiyama recalled that the suicide happened just two hours after another public yelling and shoving match between Tôyama and Hakoda (2006a, 53). It's easy to imagine Tôyama repeating some of the vitriol he directed at Hakoda and other Genyôsha members during heated discussions in 1885–86: "If you want to commit suicide, that would be OK by me."

In a rare comment on Hakoda's suicide, Hasegawa Yoshiki offers a plausible explanation for the tragic turn of affairs. He writes, "the tension between Hakoda's commitment to the APR movement and its egalitarian values and the intensifying sense of nationalism and traditionalism inside Genyôsha" made some kind of break inevitable (1974, 51–52). Indeed, Tôyama's drift to what we can provisionally call the "right wing" of the antigovernment movement including emperorism, cultural nationalism, and raison d'état must have been a source of constant frustration for Hakoda. Born to a low-rank samurai family and then adopted by a merchant family that became wealthy, Hakoda inherited a significant amount of money in 1876. He reportedly spent every cent of it on building Facing the Sun and Genyôsha (Ishitaki 2010, 166–67). He underwent an astonishing transformation from someone who was arrested and locked away for two years at age fifteen for involvement with the Fukuoka emperorist and anti-Tokugawa group Kin-O to his brutal incarceration in 1876–77 ordered by Ôkubo, before becoming by late 1880 one of the top four or five leaders of the nationwide APR movement. It is important to pause and reflect on what was lost with Hakoda's suicide. He was strongly committed to egalitarian politics and occasionally included extrahuman entities like mountains, water, and local deities in his political alliances. In other words, like the Gelaohui (GLH) protectors in China we discussed in chapters 2 and 4, he was committed to sharing an eco-ontology with multiple forms of being, but NOT with Tokyo oligarchs and extractive capitalists. Tôyama's gradual move from Fukuoka to Tokyo, Hakoda's suicide, and the group's investments in coal mining consolidated a betrayal from being primarily a collective embedded intra-actively within their eco-ontology featuring mountains and the sea into an extra-active organization that worked, not within things, but on and over things from an external location.

Japanese Men Don't Waltz

After a factional power grab among the leading oligarchs, Itô Hirobumi became head of the government, with Inoue Kaoru remaining as foreign minister in December 1885. With the major expansion of the military and the consolidation of the system of peers (mainly top-ranking ex-samurai with some rich merchants), leftist historians see this shift as the beginning of absolutist rule in Japan (Gotô 1972, 190). This period is often emblematized by the Rokumeikan, the large brick complex built near the Imperial Palace in French Renaissance style by the US architect Josiah Conder. Commissioned by Inoue as a five-star hotel for Euro-American diplomats and travelers, it was completed in 1883 and immediately became a target of the APR movement, which derided the expensive, taxpayer-funded deference to whiteness.[18] Some APR activists also criticized the increasing reliance on fired brick as the main material in these Euromimetic buildings. When Kurushima Tsuneki first came to Tokyo in 1881, the prevalence of brick in the new constructions in the "Bricktown" of Ginza and at Rokumeikan angered him (Matano 1913, 71). The only brick construction in Fukuoka circa 1880 was the Meiji government armory ordered built by

FIGURE 5.2. Japanese *ukiyôe* painter Chikanobu's depiction of Meiji oligarchs at Rokumeikan. Courtesy MIT Visualizing Cultures. https://visualizingcultures.mit.edu/.

the hated oligarch Ôkubo Toshimichi, and Kurushima associated brick with Meiji despotism. As William Coaldrake argues, brick was the ideal material in Japan for CO_2lonial capitalism because it could be mass produced cheaply and was extremely durable (1996, 236–38). In the terms of this book, industrially produced brick was not an intra-active substance like the wood, bamboo, mud, and animal feces then featured in most Japanese edifices, but rather an extra-active one that commanded other entities and imposed itself on its environment.

Although Inoue Kaoru strategized that one of the ways to reform the Unequal Treaties was to show the white West that racially inferior Japanese could adequately ape them and their brick buildings, the attempt was derided in the French and English press. Rokumeikan's activities featured Japanese people waltzing under the scrutinizing eyes of European dance instructors, wearing tuxedos and gowns, and promoting French-language-only menus in its restaurant—Euromimetic deportment that became a lightning rod for attacks by the APR and other groups (Tomita 1984).

This was combined with the widespread reports (which turned out to be true) of Itô and other married oligarchs frequenting the brothels at Yoshiwara, and even raping women in the hotel rooms at Rokumeikan (this turned out to be a fabrication). In other words, for Genyôsha the oligarchs were practicing the same modes of extraction as Euro-white men. Even worse, this was happening while people in the countryside were suffering from the effects of the oligarchs' austerity. Things came to a head when Minister of Commerce Tani Kanjô returned to Japan from a trip to Europe and resigned his position in the Itô cabinet, appalled at all the taxpayers' money being wasted by oligarchs on lavish parties at Rokumeikan and in the commercial sex districts (Karlin 2002, 54–55).

What the opening of Rokumeikan did was reignite the controversy that had peaked during the petition-memorial movement when, led by the Fukuoka UPF and other APR groups, activists demanded an end to all the Unequal Treaties. As discussed in chapter 1, the Japanese government was unable to raise revenue from tariffs on Euro-American commodities as white capitalists—living up to the reputation among some Western diplomats as "scum"—regularly avoided paying even the low 5 percent rate. In addition, the new Meiji government couldn't prevent Euro-white soldiers from being garrisoned on Japanese soil. More than even these insults, though, the system of extraterritoriality for civilian whites was the most hated aspect.

A case that highlighted the problems with extraterritoriality shocked the Japanese public in late 1886 and intensified the anti-oligarch and anti-Western movement. On the night of October 24, 1886, the British cargo ship *Norman-ton* left Yokohama for Kobe in western Japan. Caught in a heavy rainstorm, the vessel was shipwrecked off the Cape of Kashinozaki in Wakayama prefecture. Captain John Drake and the Euro-white crew (except for the firemen) escaped the sinking ship in lifeboats, leaving the nonwhite crewmen (twelve South Asians and one Chinese) and the twenty-three Japanese passengers aboard to fend for themselves. While almost the entirety of the white crew was picked up by coastal fishermen and taken to safety, all the Asian passengers and crew perished, together with one British sailor (Clark 2017, 141). On October 28, the governor of Wakayama prefecture telegraphed Foreign Minister Inoue Kaoru an outline of the events, which turned out to be as complete a version as the Japanese side would ever have—Unequal Treaty stipulations robbed the Japanese police of most of their power to investigate incidents involving Euro-Americans. At the hearing at the British consulate in Kobe the following month, Captain Drake was declared innocent of any wrongdoing. Instead, British consul James Troup shifted blame to the Japanese passengers (*Japan Weekly Mail*, November 29, 1886). Despite the fact that Inoue pressed the British for some kind of reparation, resulting in Drake being forced to serve a three-month prison sentence, the opposition movement construed the government's response as weak and insufficient. Illegal speaking tours sprang up all over the country denouncing the Itô cabinet, and the issue was the last one to temporarily reunite Tôyama and Hakoda.

The first mass street protests in Japan erupted in Tokyo in early 1887, with students and activists denouncing the Unequal Treaties and the despicable "Westernization [欧化]" policies of Inoue and Itô. Gotô Shôjiro and Itagaki Taisuke enjoyed a reunion with their old comrades and participated enthusiastically in the snowballing movement. The so-called Grand Coalition of opposition groups succeeded in drafting a memorial called the "Three Cases Petition" to send to the oligarchs' Chamber of Elders in the fall of 1887. The petition called for legal establishment of freedom of speech, a reduction of the oppressive land tax, and the normalization of foreign relations through the revoking of the Unequal Treaties (Gotô 1972, 199).

The opposition to the Unequal Treaties became so focused that the Itô government pushed through a new wave of repression. The Homeland Security Law of December 15, 1887, imposed still tighter restrictions on the press, freedom of speech, and assembly. Article 4 of the law authorized the home minister to banish from Tokyo for three years anyone found to be inciting protests within 7.5 miles of the Imperial Palace. Within three days, 570 prominent antigovernment leaders were swept off the streets and expelled (Makihara 2012, 169). In order to stifle the deafening calls to revoke the treaties, the oligarchs realized state repression alone wouldn't succeed. With the ultimate goal of limiting extraterritoriality, Inoue Kaoru advocated placing Euro-white judges in trials of Japanese citizens and lifting restrictions on foreigners' areas of residence and movements. At this time, Euro-Americans residing in Japan were in theory segregated in the treaty port areas and needed special permission to travel outside of these areas, although many routinely ignored these restrictions. In return for gradually eliminating Western consular jurisdiction over Euro-American conduct in Japan, Inoue proposed removing all of the previous restrictions on white people traveling and buying property.

In 1887 and 1888, deference to white supremacy included proposals in oligarch circles to upgrade the racial stock of Japanese by coercing Japanese women to reproduce with white men, and this uncritical acceptance of Euro-American raciology outraged many APR activists (Oguma 2002, 16–30). In June 1887, Itagaki spoke for the mainstream opposition in decrying the oligarchs' "childish imitation of the West" that started with "banquets at the Rokumeikan" and extended as far as "advocating racial reform of the Japanese by improving Yamato blood with Caucasian blood" (JTS, vol. 2, 162–63). Genyôsha argued that encouraging Japanese women to reproduce with whites basically condoned the frequent rapes of Japanese women and girls by Euro-white men in and around the treaty ports (GYSS, 280–81).

While the oligarchs temporarily solved the problem of mass demonstrations in the streets of Tokyo by banishing 570 opposition activists to western and northern Japan, this also served to incite the movement. Moreover, it confirmed what the assassinationist faction of the APR had long argued: the oligarchs were impervious to nonviolence. Only armed force and political terror could bring about real change.

When Inoue resigned as foreign minister in the face of the protests and Itô stepped down as prime minister in April 1888, they were replaced by Kuroda Kiyotaka as PM and Ôkuma Shigenobu as foreign minister. With opposition to Inoue's proposal extending all the way to cabinet ministers, Ôkuma decided it was best to proceed with negotiations with the Euro-American powers behind closed doors. Despite the precautions, on April 19, 1889, a draft of his proposal for treaty revisions with England was leaked to the *Times* of London by the head of the translation bureau at the Foreign Ministry, Komura Jutarô, and published in Japan. This lit a fuse under the opposition movement, as it was clear that Ôkuma's secret proposal was basically the same as Inoue's, even going further by offering to place a Euro-white judge on Japan's Supreme Court. Moreover, Ôkuma expressed privately that the Japanese government would commit to even more rapid Westernization by promising to increase Euro-American imports into Japan. The internal discussions of the Genyôsha cell in Tokyo at this time show how much the Fukuoka UPF's critique of Euro-American free trade was still influencing their thinking ten years later. Another critique that carried over centered around the ways that industrial extraction was polluting local environments (Matano 1913, 126–28).

From the beginning of the samurai uprisings in southwestern Japan, Genyôsha and other opposition groups insisted on conflating the modus operandi of Euro-white men with that of the hated oligarchs in Tokyo. This tendency intensified in the 1880s as reformers like Itagaki and militants like Hakoda railed on about the shameful ways Japanese leaders were aping a Caucasian modus operandi. In a long letter to the elder statesman Katsu Kaishû in June 1888, Genyôsha militant Kurushima Tsuneki recapitulated this conflation: "The leaders of our government today are the same kind of men who beat their wives to death yet manage to escape punishment because of what white people are calling natural law [自然法], which allows men to do anything they want to women. The oligarchs are the kind of guys who piss away tons of money gambling and who rape women when they go out partying at night" (Matano 1913, 96–97).

As mentioned above, Kurushima despised the Euromimetic galas at the Rokumeikan and complained to Matano for weeks after reading about one ball hosted by Itô Hirobumi there on November 27, 1884 (Matano 1913, 76). This rage affect was enhanced by a strong identification with Hakoda (who also denounced the shameless Rokumeikan events), and this combination drove him toward the suicide bombing of Ôkuma in 1888. His decision to go through with the action was solidified when Kurushima and Matano returned to Fukuoka in the fall of 1887 and met frequently with Hakoda and Tôyama for what Matano called "heated discussions" (1913, 100). According to the Genyôsha in-house history, Kurushima offered to assassinate Inoue Kaoru at this time, but Tôyama was against it (GYSS, 276–85). Apparently, Sugiyama had successfully obtained financing from a Tokyo bank Inoue had a controlling interest in to buy railroad rights in Kyushu and told Tôyama that, for business reasons, any discussion of harming Inoue or his allies had to be tabled (Hori 2006, 49–50). Hakoda was furious that Genyôsha's politics had to be constrained by their business contacts with the hated oligarchs (Nagahata 1997, 190–91). It is evident that Kurushima always supported his role model Hakoda in these debates, as he was quoted at a September 1888 Fukuoka UPF meeting repeating word for word some of Hakoda's lines in denouncing the oligarchs as "obnoxious assholes who were selling off the whole country [売り国] to white people. They shouldn't come anywhere near Fukuoka" (Matano 1913, 100–101).

Tokyo would be Kurushima's base for seven years. He first volunteered to go in the fall of 1881, and he was immediately disgusted by the opulence of the imperial capital, in dramatic contrast to the widespread poverty in Fukuoka and southwestern Japan. It was obvious to him that the heavy taxes imposed by the oligarchs were funding a Euromimetic paradise in the capital. Kurushima wrote to Matano at this time that the oligarchs' obsession with the white West "would tear Japan completely apart" (Matano 1913, 85). Kurushima was bearing witness to what seemed from the perspective of the underdeveloped periphery to be a large-scale social engineering of Japan. The ultranationalist and Asianist Ôkawa Shûmei aptly captured Kurushima's indignation when he described the sensibility of Genyôsha in 1881: "the oligarchs were sacrificing all the Japanese people for their own private gain" (Ôkawa 2007, 99).

The primary responsibility for Kurushima as the Genyôsha representative in Tokyo was day-to-day support for the Korean exiles Kim Oggyun and Pak Yonghyo, who had fled Korea to avoid the crackdown against the insurrectionists after the failed overthrow of the Korean monarchy in December 1882 (GYSS, 241–44). This marked the beginning of a long history of Genyôsha offering sanctuary to Asian revolutionaries, a role that Tôyama Mitsuru would take over after his permanent move to Tokyo in 1890 and whose most famous beneficiary was Sun Zhongsan (Yatsen), the main anti-Qing revolutionary. In addition to staying at the Genyôsha safe house for their first two weeks in Tokyo, Kurushima set up meetings for the Koreans with the most influential Japanese intellectuals, including Fukuzawa Yukichi and Nakae Chômin (Matano 1913, 81–84). The idea for a covert militia to support Kim and Pak's next attempt to overthrow the Yi dynasty in Korea as part of the Osaka Incident arose from some of these meetings in early 1883 (GYSS, 244–45). It took two years for this idea to be fleshed out enough to present to the group in Fukuoka for approval and funding. Hakoda came up with the idea of first setting up a school in Korea to introduce young Koreans to the line of thought hegemonic in the APR at the time: popular democracy, egalitarianism, and a refusal of the Unequal Treaty system imposed by the West throughout East Asia and Japan in Korea (244–47). However, when the Foreign Ministry got wind of it from two police spies, Inoue Kaoru sent word to Genyôsha through Sugiyama threatening reprisals. Nevertheless, a few Genyôsha activists decided they would participate directly in the Osaka Incident, and the group continued to send money to the leaders right up until the time of the mass arrests in November 1885.

In addition to his support for Kim and Pak, Kurushima was also enrolled in Nakae's school for French studies, studying there off and on for two years. Affiliated with Genyôsha's ally the Mutual Love Society in Kumamoto, Nakae personally met Hakoda in Tokyo in 1881, and they became close; afterward many of the Genyôsha members embraced Nakae's teaching and politics. As is well known, Nakae featured an emphasis on French revolutionary and democratic thought at his Tokyo school. What is less well known is that he maintained a lifelong commitment to Mencian humanism, reading Mencius as opposed to Confucius on several important issues (Dardess 1973). Provincializing Europe by underlining the homology between Mencius's focus on a fundamental benevolence in human beings and a similar emphasis in Enlightenment humanism, Kurushima would have been delighted to find Nakae's frequent invocation of Mencius resonating with Takaba Osamu's love for Mencius as one of the centerpieces of Chinese humanist thought. There's no way to know for sure if Kurushima found inspiration for his suicide bombing in Mencius's condoning of assassination in the case of the corrupt ruler Zhou in China's Shandong province (this chapter's epigraph), but at the very least, Nakae's emphasis on virtuous action in the face of sociopolitical corruption would have gone down very well with what Kurushima learned in Takaba's classroom.

The whistleblowing translator Komura Jutarô made the opposition realize that the oligarchs were disregarding the popular will on the Unequal Treaties. Therefore, several opposition leaders concluded that extralegal tactics were the only thing the government would respond to. In dialogue with Nakae and Ôi Kentarô (just released from prison for his leadership role in the Osaka Incident), the Genyôsha cell in Tokyo decided that Foreign Minister Ôkuma had to be killed—the terroristic "propaganda of the deed" would be the next step for the opposition movement (GYSS, 300–301).

The original plan was for three Genyôsha cell members in Tokyo to work together on assassinating Ôkuma. But over the course of September and October, Kurushima remembered how angry Hakoda Rokusuke had been in 1878 when Ôkubo's killer Shimada Ichirô implicated several others, leading to the arrest and imprisonment of nine people. In contrast to this, during the samurai uprisings of 1876–77, Hakoda, Ôchi, and Takebe made sure to shield their teacher Takaba Osamu from any potential criminal charges. Kurushima also understood that his two cell members were married. As a bachelor without a family, he decided the righteous thing would be for him to kill Ôkuma alone, and limit implicating interactions with other Genyôsha members.

Kurushima returned to Fukuoka at the end of July 1889 to arrange some personal things and concretize the assassination plan in a secret consultation with Tôyama and Shindô. After he returned to Tokyo in early September, the atmosphere on the streets was electric, as the indignation over the Foreign Ministry's secret negotiations with Europe peaked when Ôkuma Shigenobu declared publicly that he wasn't going to alter his proposals in the face of the revelations. The opposition to the Unequal Treaties at this time was deep and consistent. In Fukuoka, there was complete unanimity on what was known there as "the argument in favor of suspending the Unequal Treaties [中正論]." Genyôsha had started one of the two major daily papers in northern Kyushu, the *Fukuryô Shinpô*, and beginning in 1888 the paper frequently enumerated the debilitating effects of the Unequal Treaties, especially the inability to set tariff rates (July 13, 1888). Moreover, it routinely referred to the desire to overthrow the Unequal Treaties as the position of "most Japanese citizens" (August 18, 1888). Even the Liberal Party newspaper, the Fukuoka *Nichi Nichi Shimbun*, which was known to critique Genyôsha for its divisive factionalism, supported all their critiques of the Unequal Treaties (July 4, 1889).

On October 16, Kurushima received Ôi Kentarô's bomb from Tôyama, who was in Tokyo, and the next night went out drinking with his sleeper-cell mates in a large public restaurant near Shiba Park in Tokyo to clarify logistics (GYSS, 356–57). On October 18 at 3:55 in the afternoon in front of the Foreign Ministry in Kasumigaseki, Kurushima, dressed in the kind of European clothes he despised, managed to throw Ôi's bomb directly under Ôkuma's carriage, which was completely engulfed in smoke. Satisfied that Ôkuma was dead, Kurushima then bowed once before turning back to Ôkuma's carriage and stabbed himself twice in the neck so deeply that he sliced his head halfway off (Matano 1913, 230).

Miraculously, Ôkuma survived the attack, but had to have his left leg removed at the hip following two operations. Although it would take another decade, the Unequal Treaties would not survive like Ôkuma. While there is some disagreement among scholars about the effect of Kurushima's brave act, the facts are that public opinion was for the most part with Kurushima—this was another instance in Japan of political terror emanating from a broad-based movement. The Kuruda cabinet clearly understood this, as it resigned en masse after the attempted assassination (GYSS, 177–86). Succeeding cabinets, beginning with that of Yamagata Aritomo, withdrew most of the items in the Inoue/ Ôkuma proposals. Finally, Kurushima's attack marked a closure of sorts to the period of mimetic Europeanization of the 1880s.

It also established Genyôsha's nationalist bona fides. As Tôyama and Sugiyama relocated permanently to Tokyo just a few years after this with money from their coal enterprises, Genyôsha became a powerful political lobbying group and an important behind-the-scenes player. Although it continued to have policy disputes with the Meiji state, these became less prominent as the Foreign Ministry took to outsourcing Japan's policy in Asia to Tôyama's operatives. For example, Genyôsha provocateurs planted bombs and carried out assassinations in Korea before these and other actions culminated in the Qing-Japan war over Korea in 1894–95. Genyôsha-linked groups also carried out acts of terror leading up to the Russo-Japanese War of 1904–5. In both wars, independent Genyôsha operatives provided crucial intelligence and logistical support to the Japanese military. In other words, Tôyama and Sugiyama's plan to assume functions of the Japanese state did come to fruition. But it did so at the cost of turning their backs on the communal Fukuoka eco-ontology that had nurtured them.

This is not to say that the extra-active, procapitalist, and Japanese nationalist entity that Genyôsha became after Hakoda Rokusuke's suicide completely rid itself of its earlier intra-active version. As I will show in the conclusion, like the Fukuoka UPF circa 1880, they also became involved from the 1890s in the first major struggle for environmental justice in Japan at the Ashio copper mine.

6

Blow(Opium Smoke)back:
The Third War for Drugs in Sichuan

Looking back at the time Westerners started trafficking drugs to China was when all our money leaked right into their pockets—we wasted so much money buying their opium! But the money made from Sichuanese opium [川土] goes back to the people of Sichuan, meaning it remains in China.—Sichuan Governor General Liu Bingzhen in 1890 (in Qin 2001)

The pernicious results of the soul and body destroying opium vice are all around. Cadaverous looking faces meet one on every side, and the slovenly habits and the filthy appearance of the people generally testify too plainly to the evil it is working.... Humanly speaking, Chinese opium smokers are beyond the reach of conversion.—British Archdeacon Wolfe, in *Correspondence Relative to the Earl of Elgin's Special Missions to China and Japan, 1857–1859*, vol. I, 1896

In June 1907, two officials at the Japanese consulate in Chongqing, Mitsuura Tsûji and Konishi Shin, filed a comprehensive report on Sichuan to the Foreign Ministry in Tokyo. The report began with basic information about Chongqing and Sichuan: population, land mass, geography, and non–Han Chinese populations. The Euro-American presence is highlighted with the detail that in Chongqing at any one time, "one can observe four large Western gunboats, three belonging to England and one to France" (JFMA, "Chongqing and Sichuan," 252; citations to follow).[1] This military threat is said to be more important than the mere human one of 216 French, 262 British, ninety-three from the US, and ninety Japanese. As the gunboats enjoy a monopoly of force over the Sichuanese population, the Euro-whites similarly reside in a walled-off community, preferring their Western food and opulent residences "on the tops of hills and cliffs, far above the local people." The Euro-Americans are biosecurely separate except for male servants who dig their ditches, build their residences, and carry them around in sedan carriages. The gendered division of labor also has Chinese women and girls cooking Euro-Americans their food, cleaning their houses, and catering to the erotic demands of some of the white men (339–40).

The key products that Sichuan generates are opium, salt, and tea, while traditional products like pig bristles and medicinal herbals still bring in some revenue. Mitsuura and Konishi dryly state that the volume of trade for all three primary products has increased since what they call the "opening" of Chongqing, with the top revenue earner, Sichuanese opium, continuing a trend that began in the 1870s of outselling British colonial opium in Chinese drug markets (253). However, five pages of trade tables show the relentless trend toward trade imbalances since the coercive insertion of Sichuan into global capitalism. The value of Sichuanese exports has steadily cheapened, while that of foreign commodities penetrating Sichuan has stabilized, even with the volume of Western and Japanese goods doubling every four years (264). Like most colonial conditions, the balance of trade in Sichuan trends slightly in favor of the imperialist countries. Moreover, the importation of foreign mass-produced goods has threatened the livelihoods of local artisans and weavers, and the increased reliance on steamships has put many Sichuanese boat pullers out of work. Some of these unemployed have been saved by going into the opium business, either as farmers growing poppies on small plots, finding work in the more than three thousand opium rooms in the province, or as drug smugglers working in tandem with others to avoid taxation.

For those recently thrown out of work and unable to find anything connected to the booming opium market, the Japanese investigators hope that desperation will force many to beg for work in the foreign factories. As an added benefit, the growth of foreign-owned factories will provide the proper discipline for Sichuan's "lazy and unmotivated" underclass (64–65, supplement on the city of Chengdu). They remark that two Japanese and several British factories are already profiting from the surplus labor market and exporting goods to other parts of China, including mass-produced opium pipes and other smoking paraphernalia (70).

While the Japanese report performs its CO_2lonial duty of recommending more extraction of copper and coal, it dedicates twenty pages to discussing that most important Sichuanese product, opium, and includes detailed information on its price and popularity in the Chongqing, Yichang (Hubei), and Shanghai drug markets, where it has enjoyed strong sales for more than three decades. A crucial observation reveals that, whereas the salt market is monopolized by the Qing government and the tea market is controlled by merchant guilds or hongs, the much larger opium market is controlled by the "lower classes [下流]" (295). The report doesn't specify just who these poor sellers and producers are, but as I showed in chapter 4, the Gelaohui (GLH) was heavily involved in the opium trade from the beginning of its consolidation in Sichuan and was made up primarily of poor men.

Just four years later, Mitsuura and Konishi will personally witness the ways in which opium provided crucial revenue to the Sichuanese poor, allowing them to overturn two millennia of dynastic rule—and come close to toppling Euro-American imperialism in China as well. The critic of US militarism Chalmers Johnson (2004) concocted the phrase "blowback" to describe the ways militant groups supported and funded by the CIA abroad like al Qaeda often turn against the imperialist agenda of the US. I will demonstrate in this chapter that the narcophilic GLH insurgents will defiantly *blow* opium smoke *back* into the faces of both the Euro-white Protestants and the Qing government trying to eliminate the drug from China. This concluded a remarkable transformation of the opium entity from playing a central role in the Anglo-American clipper-coolie captive-contraband-capital circuit to switching sides and lending what Jane Bennett (2010) calls its "thing power" to the eco-ontological struggle of subaltern Chinese. The GLH conflated the Qing with the hated Euro-American imperialists when Beijing caved in to the combined pressure of a thirty-year campaign of white Protestant missionaries and a more recent push from New Policy factions within the Qing elite to launch a full-scale opium suppression campaign in September 1906.

Stoned Sichuan

I want to expand on two of the points made by the Japanese officials in Chongqing by returning to the 1880s. The first is the improbable turn of events that saw Sichuanese opium come to dominate the smoking market throughout China. The phenomenon that Lin Manhong (1980) calls "import substitution" has been noted by several historians, but the implications of this have yet to be fully developed. Mitsuura and Konishi can coolly point this out, as Japanese companies were just starting to get involved in lucrative narcotic sales to Chinese. In contrast, British officials were markedly less casual about reporting on the declining markets for their Anglo-Indian opium, as opium revenues contributed directly to the consolidation of British CO_2lonialism in Asia and the rise of white racial capitalism globally. Although Robert Hart's Imperial Maritime Customs (IMC) requested reports on the market reach of Chinese domestic opium in 1864 and 1879, the results only pertained to the customs houses at the major ports (Imperial Maritime Customs 1881a, 4–6).

Unlike the rough estimates of the IMC, the British consuls at the new treaty ports of Yichang (W. D. Spence), Chongqing (Alexander Hosie), and Xinjiang (E. L. Oxenham) were given time and resources to carry out investigations of the opium market. After his first stretch of fieldwork in 1881–82, Spence confirmed the fears of British drug capitalists: Sichuanese opium was clearly outselling UK opium at both Yichang and Hankou. Although Spence claims he "wasn't surprised" to find this out, he admitted to being taken aback by how quickly Sichuanese opium had overtaken Anglo-Indian smoke in upper- and middle-Yangzi drug markets (BFO 228/700, April 20, 1882).[2]

Spence concluded that Sichuanese homegrown was selling more than double the volume of Anglo-Indian opium in China. Speculating that the market losses to Euro-whites in central and southwestern China couldn't possibly be as bad in Shanghai and Nanjing (they were, but the losses were masked by the slightly expanding imports of Anglo-Indian opium), he nonetheless warned that the market reach of Sichuan's opium was only going to get wider and deeper. He based this on his personal observation that the pioneering dealers of Sichuanese smoke were lower-class "coolies." There were so many smugglers that one could witness throngs of them arriving in the Hubei river port of Shashi from Chongqing, Fulin, and Fengdu in eastern Sichuan. On any one day the parade of opium peddlers took hours to pass by (BFO 228/700, April 20, 1882).

E. L. Oxenham was technically the British resident at Kashgar in Xinjiang province, the former Silk Road trading hub. His 1883 report focused on the impossibility of cracking down on the booming opium market, as "many of the officials are smokers themselves and have covert sympathies for the offenders." The only good news for British drug capitalists was the near disappearance of Persian opium, formerly their main competition in China. The rest of the 1883 report must have been painful for British officials to read. The most stinging was the observation that Sichuanese opium was overwhelmingly "preferred by the lower classes," although it was also prominent in the mixtures used by everyone else. In other words, except for the wealthiest Chinese "epicures," smoking pure Anglo-Indian had disappeared (BFO 228/724, October 30, 1883). Although Protestant missionaries had been warning their diplomats in China about an explosion in domestic poppy growing and opium smoking, British officials tended to dismiss this as standard Christian anti-opium hysteria. It was only with the opium reports from these consuls that they grasped what was happening: England had fought two Wars for Drugs so that white narcos and their Euro-American investors could profit from the largest opium market in the world. And now? A bunch of revolting peasants and GLH bandits from Sichuan were undercutting them. The Third War for Drugs in China was already underway without a shot being fired.

Despite establishing how and why Sichuanese opium was dominating Chinese markets, Oxenham's subsequent 1884 report tried to reassure British officials in China. From the supply side, the simple reason for the spike in poppy cultivation in Sichuan and the other opium belt provinces of Gansu, Guizhou, and Yunnan was that peasants could earn three to four times the money growing opium as other crops: "an area of land that produces $18 to $20 worth of opium when planted with rice or grain produces a value of $5 or $6." And southwestern Chinese peasants were so protective of these new earnings that any "magisterial interference is provocative of revolt" (BFO 228/747, October 10, 1884).

The Opiate of the People

With the Oxenham and Spence reports filed, there was no longer any doubt about the market reach of Sichuanese opium. In 1882, Sichuan's production alone was estimated to be more than all the imported opium from British India, accounting for roughly 140,000 chests.[3] And these figures didn't take into account black market sales of Sichuanese drugs. When adding the rough annual estimates of opium produced in the opium belt provinces of Yunnan (27,000 chests) and Guizhou (15,000) to Sichuan's official total, this doubled the amount of 98,000 Anglo-Indian chests imported annually (BFO 228/698, October 11, 1882). And Oxenham, Hosie, and Spence all remarked that there remained untapped potential for opium production in southwestern China, to say nothing of consumption—they continually assumed that the Chinese market for opium would increase forever.

Increase it did, but almost all the growth was in Sichuanese opium. In a trend long feared by the pioneering white narcos Jardine, Matheson & Co.—who compared the quality of Sichuan opium to their own smoke in a test at their Guangzhou warehouse on October 15, 1830[4]—Anglo-Indian opium sales would shrink to 54,000 chests by 1906, while Chinese homegrown would explode to over ten times that amount at 584,800 chests (International Opium Commission 1909). Sichuan remained the center of domestic opium production, growing about 40 percent of Chinese product. I am not completely satisfied with the explanations for this in the scholarship, so a new one will be proffered. I have found that the explosive growth in GLH membership and political power correlates almost exactly to the spike in opium production and consumption in Sichuan—beginning with the Li/Lan peasant and GLH-supported war against Qing corruption and landlordism from 1859–64 until the start of the Qing opium suppression campaign in the fall of 1906 (Chen 2010, 120–25). As we saw in chapter 4, without the power and pro-opium narcophilia of the GLH, Sichuan couldn't have transformed into the global center of opium production and consumption in just a few decades.

In the early 1880s, Sichuanese opium was spreading rapidly: north and west to Xinjiang and Central Asia, east to the treaty port markets in Shanghai and Guangzhou, and closer east to the important central Chinese markets of Hankou and Yichang. It was even smuggled across the border of Yunnan into British-occupied Burma, from where some of it made its way to Shanghai, counterfeited and sold for a higher price as Indian (Patna) opium! (BPP 1896, vol. 6, 88). But even more than the wide export reach of Sichuanese opium, what was most important with an eye toward the Xinhai Revolution overthrowing the Qing dynasty in 1911 is that the majority of it stayed home to be smoked by Sichuanese (Ho 2001, 587). A 1904 British embassy investigation detailed that less than 10 percent of Sichuanese smoke was exported out of the province: out of 200,000 *piculs* total, 180,000 remained for local consumption. And others thought that the 200,000 figure was too low (BFO 1908, 39). The British official H. B. Morse, using "the most conservative figures available," put the floor for Sichuanese production at 250,000 chests in 1906 (1907, 345–50).

This far exceeded the amount even heavy urban and town smokers needed. So who were the new smokers in Sichuan in 1906? Indeed, who were the established habitual smokers in 1881 when Alexander Hosie finished his investigations of opium in southwestern China? To answer this, we need to look at one more British investigation, this one carried out by the consul at Yichang, Hubei, W. D. Spence, from September 1881 until January 1882. While he began in Yichang, Spence spent all his time in Sichuan, and he gives us by far the most detailed picture we have of poppy growing and opium smoking there. Spence's observations will ground my main thesis: the Sichuanese peasants and poor represented the new population of smokers in southwestern China. Smoking among them became so widespread that the entrepreneur and Climate Caucasianist Archibald Little observed that in the 1890s in Sichuan, opium was not only tolerated, it was becoming "as they say t'i mien" or de rigueur for everyone in the province (BPP 1896, vol. 4, 342). While ascertaining the staggering amount of smoking that happened in Sichuan starting in the 1870s, I will also displace the contents of the Euro-America raciological database that posited Chinese opium smokers as "wasted" supinestupefiedyellows.

W. D. Spence's "Native Opium" was written in 1882 and circulated internally among British officials. It went viral later when it appeared as an appendix to the second volume of the report of the famous Royal Commission on Opium, conducted in London from 1894 to 1896. Spence begins his report by stating that, "In many parts of eastern Szuchuan [sic] it is the only winter crop; opium has replaced cereals" (BPP 1896, vol. 2, 383; citations to follow). Understanding that readers would find this alarming, Spence reassures them that the opium poppy, "being a winter crop does not interfere with rice the food staple of the people, displacing only subsidiary crops. . . . It can hardly be asserted of Szuchuan that the cultivation of opium seriously interferes with the food supplies of the people. The food, or rice, supplies remain the same" (383).

This optimistic appraisal is immediately supported by a second, wherein Spence provides a crucial hint as to how Sichuan had emerged so quickly as the leading opium province in China. This concerned the system of *metayer*, where the tenant pays the landowner a percentage of the summer crop, leaving the earnings from the winter opium crop entirely to the peasant. "Rent being paid on the summer crop only, the winter crop is the tenants' great source of wealth and it is this fact which makes the question of tenure so important in connection to the cultivation of opium" (384). This is important because the opium crop "brings in twice as much profit as wheat or other winter crops." This figure of double profit is actually on the conservative side, as Alexander Hosie claimed it was "two to four times" higher than the earnings from cereal crops (BFO 228/698, October 11, 1882). Moreover, as the tenant farmer did not have to pay land taxes, Spence underlines that this is a perfect scenario for pulling peasants into growing poppies, "the cultivation of which, so far as officials are concerned, is unfettered, free and open to all. There is no system of excise, no licensing, and no taxation of any kind" (BPP 1896, vol. 2, 384).[5]

Nowhere in China Are the People So Well Off, and Nowhere Do They Smoke So Much Opium

From this point on Spence shifts his analysis to smoking in rural areas. There is potentially a likin tax added if the opium is brought out of the county it is grown in; but if not, "opium pays nothing to the State, and the rural opium smoker smokes the untaxed product of his district" (BPP 1896, vol. 2, 384). Consequently, Spence provides the first explanation for the parallel explosion in opium consumption in southwestern and western China. While the low cost had been cited as a reason for the spread of opium from wealthy consumers in cities and towns to the urban underclass, the reach of smoking to peasants in the countryside was just beginning to be recognized in 1882 (BPP 1896, vol. 1, 39, 47). Although the British consuls didn't know the precise extent of smoking in Sichuan, in neighboring Gansu province Euro-American observers arrived at an 80–90 percent figure for rural smokers. The China Inland Mission secretary Benjamin Broomhall lived and proselytized in Gansu for two years and quipped in the early 1890s that "11 out of 10" adults there were regular smokers (44–45, 40).

After positing that smoking was surprisingly widespread in agricultural areas around his home in Hubei, Spence described rural areas in Sichuan this way: "in Szuchuan [*sic*] country hamlets and villages the state of things is just as extraordinary. Passing along the main street every second house almost is an opium shop" (386). But a peasant smoker didn't even have to go into an establishment. Spence claimed to have observed "farmers everywhere sitting around and smoking," and not necessarily just on work breaks. Peasants smoked both for enjoyment and also as a ritual aspect of community gatherings—religious festivals, holidays, weddings, market days, and, of course, at the occasional "opium fairs" that were unique to Sichuan in the late Qing period (384). It was here that many farmers would deliver their opium paste both to established buyers working for opium rooms or parlors, and to smaller groups of itinerant dealers.

Taken aback by the extent of smoking in rural areas, Spence ventures his first estimate of the percentage of smokers in Sichuan, prefacing this with "It prevails to an extent undreamt of in other parts of China.... Catholic missionaries in Szuchuan say 60% of adult males smoke opium" (385). But Spence disagrees: "Whatever it be the exact percentage of the opium smokers in Szuchuan of the whole population, it is certain that it is many times larger than in the East. The impression one actually gets in a Szuchuan city or village is that everybody smokes opium, and one is surprised to hear on good authority that 40% do not" (385–56).

Spence seems aware of how extreme this assertion of what he calls the "universal practice" of opium smoking in Sichuan is, so he walks it back slightly (387). First, although "many women" smoke as well, the assessment is for adult men only. Second, Spence inadvertently contributes to the de-escalation of the hysteria over Chinese drug use, a phenomenon instigated by the expanding pool of Protestant missionaries in central and southwestern China after the Second War for Drugs. He does this by arguing that very few opium smokers are incapacitated by the drug; the prevailing discourse of the addicted "opium sot" is fallacious. Of course, there are 1 or 2 percent of smokers who let their habits take control of their lives, but doesn't this happen with alcohol as well? (385). The overwhelming majority of smokers partake moderately, or two and three times daily. Spence can find no correlation linking opium smoking with laziness or sloth. Finally, he draws on the work of earlier observers of opium in Sichuan to argue the reverse: opium smoking is a positive force in rural southwestern China, as it contributes to smoother community relations and brings pleasure and contentment to what can be an arduous and precarious life. The first British consul at Chongqing, Colborne Baber, said a few years earlier about Sichuan, "Nowhere in China are the people so well off, or so hardy, and nowhere do they smoke so much opium," and Spence wholeheartedly agrees with this. Consequently, in introducing section 11 of his report, "Effect of Opium-Smoking on People," he inserts the following: "I found the people of Szuchuan stout, able-bodied men, better clad and fed and healthier looking than the Chinese of the lower Yangtze and I did not see among them more emaciated faces and wasted forms. . . . The general health and well-being of the community is remarkable; to their capacity for work and endurance of hardship . . . all travelers bear enthusiastic testimony" (386).

Leaving aside for now the obvious Marxist clue to this puzzle (i.e., the non-alienation of producers from the opium fruits of their labor), Spence indicates that one of the clear positives of the opium issue in Sichuan is that the chain of opium production → circulation → consumption is normally a tight one, with few "cuts" taken out by compradors.[6] The tight farm to (opium room) table circuit is one of the reasons the price is kept low, while allowing the peasant growers the luxury of getting high smoking their own product. And the price was indeed low: in 1881 a standard dose of five-eighths of a mace (about 2.25 grams) cost ten cash[7] in the Sichuan countryside, fifteen to twenty cash in opium rooms in Chongqing, and then went up to thirty in Yichang and Hankou's urban establishments.[8] It's worthwhile highlighting the difference between Sichuanese people smoking homegrown and the multiple links in Anglo-American drug capitalism we analyzed in the introduction. The disparity in carbon footprints between GLH-produced opium in Sichuan and British East India Company opium also couldn't be wider. With the GLH supplying local poppy growers with manure, GLH-connected poppy growers practiced a sustainable form of agriculture using organic fertilizer and crop rotation. In contrast, the East India Company were Climate Caucasianist pioneers in what Marx called the unsustainable form of "robber agriculture" that produced a temporary high volume of poppies, but at the price of destroying soil fertility and degrading the land (1977a, 638). This is one example of the extraction → extinction imperative central to capitalism. Furthermore, when British and American contraband drugs began to be shipped by coal-powered steamships in the 1850s, this added to the climate-interfering character of global narcotrafficking.

Spence estimates that about 100,000 piculs of opium were consumed annually in Sichuan, but lowers this to establish a floor: "certainly no less than 50,000 piculs annually" are smoked "and in all likelihood, much more" (BPP 1896, vol. 2, 386). But how much more? As the processing of opium was different in central and southwestern China from British India, to arrive at 50,000 piculs of smokable opium requires 60,000 piculs of raw Sichuanese opium. Although Spence doesn't mention this, a report circulated in 1879 by the British agent at Hankou for the Imperial Maritime Customs (IMC), T. W. Bredon, put Sichuan's total production of opium for the year 1878 at 150,000 piculs (Inspector General of Customs 1888, 48–49). The British consul Colborne Baber put the total Sichuan production even higher, at 177,000 piculs grown on nearly 1 million acres of land (*Chinese Recorder*, May 1883, 228). Baber, however, claims that only 54,000 piculs remained in Sichuan for consumption there, while 123,000 were exported (BFO 1908, 39). The IMC at Hankou disagreed with Baber's numbers and estimated that only 40,000 piculs of Sichuanese opium were exported each year, leaving 120,000–130,000 piculs to be smoked in the province in the mid-1880s. More precise estimates identify a growing tendency toward exports from a majority of the opium staying in the province in the 1880s, to a 50-50 split in the 1890s, before favoring exports at about a 57-43 percent split in the 1900s (IMC 1902, 153). A conservative way to approach the number of smokers in Sichuan in the early 1880s would be to lower the total estimated output of the IMC to 140 million piculs, and assume that 100 million stayed in Sichuan, which is what W. D. Spence speculates. Using Spence's six-to-five ratio of raw to processed opium gives us 84,000 piculs (11.2 million pounds) smoked annually in Sichuan circa 1880.

Spence's population number for Sichuan in 1880 is 35 million, which is close to the 33 million figure used by Wang Chunwu (1993). With about 25 percent of the population of China at this time consisting of adult men eighteen and over, that calculates to 8 million men. The figure of 11.2 million pounds of smokable opium means 1.375 pounds annually for each male in Sichuan. The median amount of opium smoked daily in China in the late Qing period varied considerably. After four months of investigations in Sichuan, Spence concluded that five-eighths of a mace (1 mace = 3.75 grams) was standard for moderate smokers. The missionary and Sinologist S. W. Williams's research in the late 1870s spoke to the discrepancy in the average amount per smoker by arguing plausibly that a first-time smoker is "content with one or two whiffs," while he or she will often turn into a "temperate" smoker of no more than one mace of opium daily, "which filled twelve pipes" (BPP 1896, vol. 1, 18–50).

Returning to standard opium consumption in Sichuan, Spence claims on "good authority" that moderate Sichuanese smokers sucked up five-eighths of a mace daily (BPP 1896, vol. 2, 386). Taking the 25 percent of men from Sichuan's population, this comes out to 165 maces of opium annually per male, which is a slightly below four-eighths of a mace daily—in Sichuan this is roughly six pipes of opium every day. This tentatively confirms Spence's sense of the universality of male opium smoking in Sichuan circa 1880. Every Sichuanese male in 1880 smoked on average two times a day, every day of the week.[9] And the amount of opium smoked in Sichuan nearly doubled by 1900. But even in 1880 there's more.

We move toward substantiating a "stoned Sichuan" when we go further into Spence's investigation. Building on previous observations of Sichuan by Baber and Baron von Richthofen (1833–1905), the German geologist and geographer who conducted the first European investigations of coal and copper deposits in Sichuan and Yunnan in the late 1870s, he warns readers that the amount of daily smoking doesn't at all stop with one mace of opium smoked every two days. He writes in his detailed section on the specificity of smoking in Sichuan: "For I must explain, three tao or 'drawings' are often smoked from one charge, and from opium unadulterated as many as five. The leavings of the rich smoker are mixed with the opium sold to the poor, the refuse of the poor is smoked by him again, and the unsmokable dregs are drunk in tea" (386).

The British consul's point is that the amount of smoking in Sichuan in 1880 shouldn't be limited to every adult male smoking opium twice daily. The figure of 84,000 piculs of opium needs to be multiplied by the widespread phenomenon of secondhand smoking, or resmoking leftover half-smoked opium, opium ash waste, or other forms of "dregs"—giving Anglophone recreational drug smokers' argot of "wasted" an unexpected literalness.

Yet another way to add to the volume of opium available in Sichuan is smuggling. The IMC estimate of Sichuan's opium production in 1878 at 150,000 piculs does attempt to factor smuggling into its tally, as nonsmuggling totals varied between 50,000 (Spence's absolute floor) and 120,000. Nevertheless, even such a large volume as 150,000 piculs probably didn't reflect the actual amount of Sichuanese opium produced and sold during this period. The explanation for this is linked to Spence uncovering a labor supply issue that perplexed observers at that time. This dealt with the issue of boat trackers and sailors needed for the difficult course up the Yangzi River to Chongqing, Sichuan, from Yichang, Hubei. Let's recall from chapter 4 the complicated method required to navigate boats up the Yangzi. Medium and large cargo ships required anywhere from thirty to two hundred men dragging and lassoing these vessels up through the river's steep passes and gorges (Wang 2013b). These were the famous upper Yangzi boat trackers who travelers like Isabella Bishop admired for their skill, bravery, and ability to work hard while stoned on opium (1972, 138–47). Although some of these trackers worked only one leg of the three hundred miles separating Yichang from Chongqing, many were hired in Yichang to work the entire route and then let go when their loads arrived at ports in Sichuan. What they did then is crucial for understanding both the large amount of opium produced in Sichuan at this time and the growth of the GLH.

Contact High

As many of these men were young and single, they spent at least part of their earnings partying in Chongqing. For six months out of every year in the 1880s and '90s, this added approximately fifty thousand men to the population of Chongqing. The GLH cadre among them would naturally have gone to the opium rooms, gambling joints, and teahouses run by fellow members (Qin 2001, 71–72). After this short period of rest and with much of their earnings up in smoke, the boatmen would have needed to return to work. The problem with the reproduction of labor that arose here was that the cargo boats going down the Yangzi only required one-third the crew necessary to haul them up. So, the boatmen drew on their connections with the GLH and their intimacy with the geography of the eastern Sichuan–Hubei route to transport opium overland. W. D. Spence insists that this form of smuggling was "prevalent, profitable, and, I may add, easy" and sums up the practice this way: "The crews of up-river junks are double and treble the size of down-river ones. . . . There is therefore, no lack of mountain porters. A large number of the trackers on junks bound for Szuchuan have, as the most necessary part of their kit, a yapian pei lou, or back opium carrier. . . . Having completed their voyage to Chungking, they walk to Fuchow, Fengtu or other mart, get a load of opium and trudge back to Hupei with it" (BPP 1896, vol. 2, 385).

Spence conjectures that most of Sichuan's opium exports were moved this way; he summarizes: "The opium is carried on difficult mountain paths from Szechuan to Shashih on the backs of coolies. Each man carries 1000 ounces (60 pounds) receiving 7200 cash or 5 taels from Fuchow to Shashih. At this important river port, 60 miles south of Yichang it is sent all over the East and South" (385).

These men formed the core of the "lower classes" dominating the Sichuanese opium trade noted by the Japanese officials in 1907. But they were willing to be "mules" for more reasons that just the push of labor market reproduction.

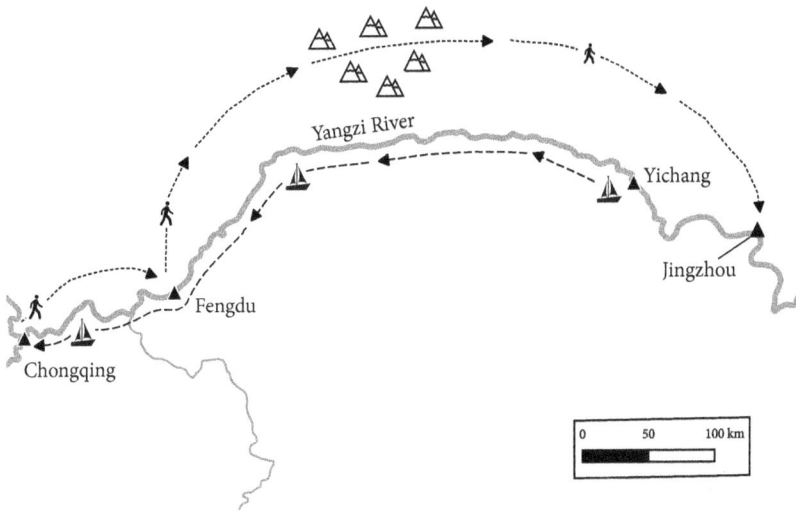

FIGURE 6.1. Map showing movement of Gelaohui boat haulers from Yichang, Hubei, to Chongqing, Sichuan, and these same haulers smuggling opium on foot from east of Chongqing to Jingzhou, Hubei. Map by the author.

The pull of 7,200 cash made from just one successful thirty-day smuggling run on the Chongqing to Shashi (now Jingzhou) route could support the opium habit of moderate smokers for an entire year. The smuggler could then choose between going back to work, doing anti-Western and anti-Qing politics, or just kicking back, playing mah-jongg, and smoking Sichuanese stuff—usually some combination of the three.

Approximately fifty thousand of these boatmen annually worked with vessels traveling up the Yangzi River from Yichang to Chongqing. Upward of 70 percent of them were not needed to work the trip back down the Yangzi from Chongqing, so many bought opium in Fengdu and other opium production centers east of Chongqing and, to avoid the authorities, traveled on foot with it on their backs the three hundred miles over the mountains north of the Yangzi. After a five-week journey they finally sold their opium in Shashi and returned to Yichang to once again find work on a boat going upstream to Chongqing.

So, in addition to the 100,000 piculs that stayed in the province to be smoked, there was even more that went unaccounted for. Therefore, in trying to establish a baseline for per capita opium smoking in Sichuan in 1880, I think it is entirely reasonable to corroborate British consul Spence's intuition of a "universality" of opium smoking. That is to say, on average, every adult male and approximately every other adult female were regular, "temperate" smokers of between six to ten pipes of opium daily.[10] As most Western observers thought that male smoking was much more widespread in Sichuan than in other parts of China, British women residents in China like Alicia Little didn't hesitate to include Sichuanese women in the category of smokers. Speculating that many more Sichuanese women enjoyed opium than women in other parts of China, while living in Chongqing during the late nineteenth century, she recalled hearing several times that well-off men in other parts of China were reluctant to marry otherwise attractive Sichuanese women because "so many of them smoke opium" (Little 1901, 123, 129). Just a few years after Spence's 1881–82 investigation, the American missionary F. D. Gamewell didn't think it was necessary to discriminate against women smokers either, claiming that 80 percent of all people in Sichuan were regular opium smokers (1888, 36).

Although Spence's observations solved the riddle of what happened to the unemployed upper-Yangzi sailors and boat trackers, it's left to us to connect the dots and link this to the explosive growth in GLH membership during this period. Whether the Chongqing-to-Hubei smugglers took the more dangerous Yangzi river route or, more likely, decided to trek overland, the (intra) act of smuggling was more feasible if it was part of a well-connected organization. A successful opium smuggling run involved a team to provide intelligence about provincial officials' runners (who could arrest them) and assistance getting their opium to retailers in the Hubei port of Shashi. The four- to five-week trip also required safe sleeping spaces secure from poaching, and the famous GLH custom of warmly hosting out-of-town members was ideal for this. As I argued in chapter 4, opium use was central to the GLH, and it became more so as prohibition voices among white Protestant missionaries grew louder, becoming deafening by the late 1890s. With the GLH recognized as the main anti-Christian group in southwestern and central China, anecdotal evidence suggests that their pro-opium position became more pronounced. While many of the Catholic missions and nearly all of the Protestant missions refused to accept regular smokers as converts, the GLH, conversely, welcomed them.

The final revelation in Spence's report has to do with the way opium became a central part of the eco-ontology in Sichuan. What I mean by this is that it functioned as an intra-active force, transforming and intensifying relations with the living and dead. In chapter 4 we saw that opium was an integral part of GLH rituals in stimulating connections to different kinds of being: metaphysical, humanly physical, and other-than-humanly physical like water, wind, and animals. Spence observed peasants in Sichuanese rural areas "smearing the lips" of Daoist deities with prepared opium to thank them for all their support, a practice that never failed to horrify white missionaries in Sichuan (Hart 1888, 78). Some of these same rural villages featured opium at funerals. In addition to writing messages of thanks to the deceased, stoned mourners constructed opium pipes out of paper and burned them together with prepared opium "so that the dead may enjoy in the next world the comfort and solace they loved in this" (BPP 1896, vol. 2, 386). While the intra-active connection between humans and goddesses and gods was always strong in peasant societies in China, opium intensified it. And some of the deities who were fed opium paste were in animal form. Whether this spiritual nonanthropocentrism contributed to the widespread practice in Sichuan of giving opium dregs and opium-laced water to farm animals, we can't be certain (Little 1898, 195). But we can state confidently that living human beings weren't the only entities getting high in Sichuan in the late nineteenth century.

Missionary Buzzkill

Euro-American Protestants launched a War on Drugs in central and south-western China beginning around 1880, a largely ignored but potent missionary buzzkill. The attempt was, as Frantz Fanon said about French colonialism in Algeria, to "sack cultural patterns . . . to further the destruction of the social panorama" (1967, 33). The overthrow of cultural patterns included the public shaming of smokers by Chinese-speaking Western missionaries as they left opium rooms and parlors (JFMA, "Chinese Secret Societies," 1091).[11] We don't know exactly when this practice began, but several missionary preaching rooms in urban Chongqing were deliberately placed next to opium establishments to take the war directly to the opium-smoking enemy.

As improbable as it may sound, some missionaries construed the shaming of smokers as a means toward more conversions to Christianity. For example, offering suggestions to her younger China Inland Mission colleagues, a Mrs. Piggot advised that in addition to time dedicated to mild shaming, "We have found that time hangs rather heavily on the hands of these opium smokers while in the opium Refuge . . . as they have nothing to do they are very glad to listen to conversation about the Gospel" (in Wong 2000, 201). Piggot's reference to the "Refuge" indicated a detoxification facility established throughout China by Euro-American missionaries to wean smokers off opium. Although the conditions varied significantly, in all but two of the one hundred or so Protestant refuges in China in the 1890s the treatment centered around morphine, dispensed both in tablet form and by hypodermic injection.[12] The effect of this was to replace opium smoking with the more dangerous pill-popping and shooting up. Chinese widely derided the Protestant opioid pills as "Jesus opium [耶稣鸦片]." As I mentioned in chapter 2, French Catholics were the first missionaries in China to try to substitute opium smoking for ingesting morphine-based medicines.

There is a much larger narrative about this disdain for Jesus opium, and the second epigraph to this chapter from the Protestant Archdeacon Wolfe can help sketch this out. The full version of Wolfe's statement began with the standard narcophobia of "decayed, withered bodies" and "destroyed, lifeless souls" that were the talking points of the Anglo-American zero tolerance message in China. Wolfe then suddenly corroborated the point I made above: "The rapid progress which opium smoking has made among all classes of China's population is a very serious matter" (BPP 1896, vol. 1, 7). What was pressing for missionary leaders like Wolfe was Protestants' frustration over their failure to convert Chinese in central and southwestern China; Sichuan was a particularly bad recruiting ground for Anglophone evangelism. Anglo-American Protestants flooded into Sichuan after the Chefoo Convention of 1876, but a decade later there was almost nothing to show for their efforts. While 1 percent of Chongqing's population of 140,000 were reported to be Catholic converts, the three Protestant missions (China Inland Mission, the US Methodist Episcopal Church, and the Foreign Bible Society) together had twenty converts after nine years of activity (*China's Millions*, 1886, 86).

Protestant missionaries weren't willing to honestly confront the reasons for their frosty reception. Instead, as Wolfe concluded in his statement to the Opium Commission hearings in London in 1893, widespread Chinese resistance to Euro-American missionaries could only have one cause: "opium smokers are beyond the reach of conversion, as the vice unfits them for the perception of any moral or spiritual truths." Other missionary leaders construed habitual smokers as constitutionally foreclosed from Christian proselytizing and, like Wolfe, recommended shutting down missions in areas with high rates of opium smoking (BPP 1896, vol. 1, 43). This advice fell on deaf ears in Sichuan as missionaries took the War on Drugs directly to opium rooms and parlors, which led to even more hostility toward white Christians.

Making Anglo-Saxon Blood Boil

The self-determination, extra-action, and accelerology enabling the white Speed Race(r)s to extract at will faced serious obstacles in southwestern China. Although most Protestant missionaries weren't naïve about China and had internalized the made-in-Europe raciology of Chinese people, all were taken aback by how thoroughly Sichuan tested their patience and faith. Here, with one of the richest natural environments in China—fertile soils, abundant rivers, mountains filled with coal and other minerals—the unwillingness on the part of Sichuanese to focus on accumulating capital was unacceptable. The Canadian Methodist missionary Virgil Hart's first journey to Sichuan in 1887 illustrated this perfectly. After a short stay in Shanghai to visit Protestant missions there, he sailed up the Yangzi and was excited to be finally on his way to Sichuan after a short stop in the Yichang, Hubei, treaty port. But there was one problem: his chartered boat was staffed entirely by a manifestly unmotivated Sichuanese crew. This is Hart's exasperated description:

> After many delays the old sail was hoisted with much ado, and we sailed across the little river, only to anchor again about two hundred yards from the spot we had left! Not half the crew had crawled out from the opium dens. . . . It makes the Anglo-Saxon blood boil to see men sit in indolence to the last possible moment.
>
> Max Müller says that nothing puzzles the mere savage more than our restlessness; our anxiety to acquire and possess, rather than to rest and enjoy. The same remark largely holds good with the more civilized Chinamen. (1888, 29)

Entering Sichuan after two weeks on the Yangzi, Hart grudgingly acknowledged the skill and Herculean effort it took his "opium besotted" crew to haul the boat upstream. Then he returned to his main theme: "The sallow complexion of the people, their emaciated forms, and languid movement attract our attention. . . . The climate seems the acme of perfection—yet there is a want of energy and life among the people" (Hart 1888, 63–64).

The reason for the absence of life is, of course, the opium poppy: "seductive viper, curse of millions!" Smoking opium is what disposes Sichuanese to "rest and enjoy" rather than "restlessly acquire and possess." Although he had been informed that Chongqing was the commercial center of western China, upon entering the city Hart found nothing like the frenetic pace of urban capitalism he admired while living in New York and Toronto. Instead, he found supinestupefiedyellows.

After living in Chongqing for over ten years, Archibald Little provided the best ethnography of what I will call the Sichuanese "ethic of pleasure." Little introduced this with a code he thought was unique to the Sichuanese dialect: 耍 (*shua*) or play. "This word Shwah, which means to play, is constantly in the mouths of the festive Chung-kingites" (1898, 169). He then goes on to describe how eager the gentry of Chongqing were to, as he writes, "tutor" him in the art of having a good time. Although this often meant smoking opium before, during, and after a long and lavish meal, Sichuanese realist fiction about this late Qing period makes clear it also had strong erotic overtones, although the Chinese-speaking Little didn't seem to apprehend this wider sense of shua as "sex play."[13] This wasn't lost on the Euro-American missionaries, though, who linked the "play" of opium smoking to a larger Sichuanese ethic of pleasure that emphasized relaxation, a blurring of gender binaries, and a commitment to multiple forms of sexuality, including widespread male homoeroticism. To counter this, Anglo-American missionary narcophobes and homophobes attacked Sichuan's ethic of pleasure with a stigmatizing discourse of "perversion" and "crimes against nature" (BFO 228/1403, November 2, 1901).

When missionaries witnessed the extent of opium smoking, recreational sex, and "slow life" in Chongqing, they understood that nothing short of a gloves-off War on Drugs was required to induce conversions to Christianity. For them it was clear that opium was what object-oriented ontologists call a "hyperobject" sucking up will, desire, and disposable income (Morton 2013). Winning the War on Drugs, many strategized, would produce the added benefit of implanting the stern discipline of the Protestant work ethic in Sichuan. But this was all just a pipe dream without a battle plan of where to attack first. Although missionaries got their initial glimpse of how widespread and eco-ontological opium was in Sichuan immediately upon leaving Yichang, Virgil Hart knew where Euro-Americans had to take the fight. Scanning the streets of Chongqing on his first arrival, disgusted by "the large class of loafers so degraded by opium," he was the first missionary to insist that ground zero for the War on Drugs would be Chongqing (Hart 1888, 95). There was no other urban area in China where opium so dominated social, commercial, and spiritual realms (Wang 2013a, 40). As Chongqing resident Alicia Little put it, "opium dens are all over the place," resulting in the most consistent "commitment to pleasure" in China (1901, 67, 93). Although Chongqing was known throughout Sichuan as "opium Heaven [烟天]" owing to the omnipresence of places to get high, buzzkilling white missionaries saw only its opposite: the presence of "Satan's mortgage" demanding repayment in an obvious hell on earth (Hart 1888, 78). This time, Euro-whites were determined to make themselves "enemies of opium Heaven."

Protestant missionaries in southwestern China were also forced to confront the epistemological issue of opium-induced animism or, as Methodist missionaries in Chongqing put it in the 1890s, "idolatry" (Young People's Movement 1920, 105). The missionary doctor in Taiwan from 1863 to 1885, E. Maxwell, was one of the first to identify the main obstacle to Christian conversion as one that combined the physical commitment to pleasure with the stoned-on-opium epistemological fog that saw the sacred in all things. Testifying at the Opium Commission hearings in London, Maxwell insisted that while Chinese opium smokers blurred the distinction between truth and falsehood, "the tendency to falsehood" is paramount (BPP 1896, vol. 1, 19). Beginning with their fake gods and extending into their bogus places of worship—where even the Daoist priests are heavy opium smokers—this ultimately scaled up into a completely flawed framing of the world. The only corroboration required, Maxwell continued, was to witness the Chinese commitment to pleasure that followed from opium smoking. It was plainly obvious that while moving up the body to seduce the "mind into falsehood," opium also infects the body's lower regions and "ministers to sensuality" (19). Maxwell concluded his comments by insisting that the heathenish understanding of the human condition as pleasure seeking had to be eradicated if Christianity was to have any chance at all in China. A Hankou-based British missionary summed this sentiment up in 1898: "Opium induces a state of turpitude peculiarly tempting to a people who love to rest and hate to work. . . . The only solution is to take it away from them and give Christianity a chance to lift them to a plane where spiritual joy will take the place of the sensual enjoyment" (Park 1899, 61).

Devil, the Dealer

Not only did missionaries conflate opium smoking with perverse crimes against nature; many abruptly rejected any understanding of the place of relaxation and pleasure in China and simply identified the dealer of opium as Satan himself. Archdeacon Wolfe's fire and brimstone put it in 1888 that "The devil could not have invented a more pernicious vice for the destruction of soul and body than this of opium smoking" (BPP 1896, vol. 1, 7). When Anglo-American Protestants brought this Just Say No! message to central and southwestern China in the 1880s, they were quick to distance themselves and their countries of origin from prior complicity with opium trafficking. This disavowal was pioneered by the Lutheran missionary Karl Gutslaff, who was first sponsored in China by the drug cartel Jardine, Matheson & Co. and then later worked full-time for them as their chief translator in the 1830s, handing Bibles out of the front of Jardines' ships and opium out the back (Platt 2018, 279–81). When missionaries in Sichuan began preaching about the connection between opium and the devil, they were immediately derided as hypocrites. "That country that is compelling China to give up opium" was the same country that "brought it here in the first place" was a common condemnation of British evangelists in the province (BFO 1942, vol. 2, 40–41). In Chongqing the missionary Virgil Hart refused to listen to this common critique and reiterated that "forces of evil" had ushered the opium into China—the devil was the pioneering dealer, not white narcos (Hart 1888, 96).

Free the Sichuanese Slaves!

One way out of the impasse of Chinese decrying the hypocritical Caucasity of Euro-American missionaries waging a War on Drugs in the 1880s, after they had benefited from the earlier Wars for Drugs, emerged in the mid-1880s. Although slavery was on Anglophone missionaries' minds in the 1860s and '70s, it wasn't until the next decade that it began to be articulated to opium smoking. Most of the China-based missionaries testifying at the London Opium Commission stayed on message in using the phrase "opium slaves" to depict Chinese smokers (BPP 1896, vol. 1, 17, 39). Two years after the hearings, the missionary magazine *Chinese Recorder* sponsored an essay contest with prize money for the best entry to expose the "great evils [of opium] that are everywhere rampant in China" in the same way that *Uncle Tom's Cabin* did in "awaking popular opinion against slavery" (July 1895, 330, cited in Lodwick 1996). As some Protestant sects had firmly opposed enslaving Africans, this was an issue that could potentially remove the stain of complicity with narcotics trafficking and remind the global public of their involvement in moral crusades. Moreover, so-called opium slaves restored the rhetoric of moral absolutes that characterized the Christian ideology of "good versus evil" and "Go(o)d versus (D)evil."

We should recall that this invocation of opium slavery was occurring simultaneously with a shift at the highest levels of British policy making in China, from soft to hard techniques of rule. As I discussed in intertext II, Robert Hart and others applauded the necropolitical "Negro methods" the new British minister, Claude MacDonald, promised to bring from Africa to China in 1895. This was a template of racial terror Euro-whites had perpetrated against Blacks in the Americas for nearly three centuries and, more recently, in the Scramble for Africa, where MacDonald had been a military leader. To recognize this contradiction of opposing slavery on the one hand, while praising racial terror against nonwhite populations on the other, would have been to introduce yet more ambiguity into the rhetoric of Protestant moral absolutism. So, missionaries stayed on message; they were henceforth going to liberate a second group of raciological inferiors—Han Chinese—from slavery. This time, the abolition movement in China was directed against the opium version of enslavement, which was seen as even more insidious than the chattel kind practiced on Blacks. As one missionary put it, while African slaves in the Americas had managed to throw off their chains, the opium version of slavery "stealthily... fastens its chain around a man until there is no hope for release" (Park 1899, 74). Writing from Chongqing just before the uprising of 1886, the US missionary Frank Trench described the omnipresent smokers around him as living in a narco-bondage: "once the craving is excited, they are its complete slaves ... any method of setting them free is unknown to the natives. They are doomed for life unless foreigners assist them" (BPP 1896, vol. 1, 39).

The Canadian Methodist mission in Sichuan would be one of the innovators in this "assistance," opening a small opium refuge in 1891. The setting up of opium refuges represented a shift in strategy for the Canadian Methodists, as they along with all the other Euro-white Christians had been forced out of Sichuan after the Second Chongqing Uprising of 1886. Only a single China Inland missionary stayed on to work in Chongqing, while the Catholics fled into their armed brick fortresses in remote areas and Protestant missionaries escaped down the Yangzi to Yichang and Hankou in Hubei. But by 1891 Euro-American Protestants were readying for a second assault on Sichuan, the first one having failed so miserably to convert Chinese. The newest weapon in their arsenal was the opium refuge.

While French Catholics sold morphine-based "opium cure" medicines beginning in the 1850s, the full-blown opium refuge system originated in China in the late 1860s, when Protestant missionary doctors in the east coast treaty ports treated habitual smokers seeking help. Evidently, the great majority of Chinese admitted to the refuges weren't looking to quit smoking entirely. Rather, as opium consumption could adversely affect personal and family finances, many heavy smokers only wanted to cut back. Honest Protestant missionaries in the 1890s estimated that approximately 95 to 97 percent of opium refuge patients continued smoking after their stint in a refuge (BPP 1896, vol. 1, 24). Despite this available information, at the turn of the century, doctors in Methodist refuges in Sichuan refused to deal with why most of their patients abruptly ended the standard monthlong detox cure after only one or two weeks (WCMN, September 1908, 2–3). A phenomenon that occurred with increasing frequency after the Guangxu emperor issued the anti-opium edict in September 1906, it should have been evident that Chinese smokers were merely trying to cut back on money going toward opium consuming, not quit opium smoking entirely. Unfortunately, this didn't fit the new paradigm of (opium) slavery abolitionism. Consequently, with the paternal assistance of white Protestant missionaries, Sichuanese smokers entering refuges were incorrectly construed as enthusiastic participants in their own liberation from idolatrous beliefs, perverse sexuality, and indolence—all of it caused by opium smoking.

The scholar of Protestant missions in China Kathleen Lodwick writes, "the primary aim of missionaries was to cure the addicts so that they might be admitted to church membership" (1996, 130). Similarly, Protestants deployed the issue of opium slavery solely to increase conversions. As the missionary doctor H. T. Whitney, who ran a large opium refuge in the Fuzhou treaty port, reminded his colleagues at the Second Conference of Protestant Missionaries in China in May 1890, the raison d'être for opium refuges was not "philanthropic," which merely considers the "health benefit to the individual." Rather, Protestants involved with opium cures should focus on the "medical missionary point of view, which looks to the salvation of the soul." In arguing against the more popular shock or "sudden withdrawal" method—which by all accounts was not producing any conversions—he urged missionaries to adopt the more time-consuming "gradual diminution method." Regardless of whether or not this resulted in curing patients of their opium habit, with the gradual method "a longer time is afforded for instructing and impressing them with religious truth, the very object for which their care is undertaken" (Protestant Missionaries 1890, 309).

One of the most vocal advocates for opium refuges was the doctor John Dudgeon (1837–1901), who ran the London Missionary Society hospital in Beijing for fifteen years and opened the first refuge there. A notorious narcophobe, Dudgeon put out the pioneering Anglophone call to eliminate opium in China in 1868, published in the missionary magazine *Chinese Recorder*: "If this stumbling block is not gotten rid of, missionaries, charity workers and businessmen will hardly have any bright future in this country" (in Xi 2010, 455). The improbable conflation of missionaries and capitalists represented the dual concern not just of Dudgeon, but of a significant body of Western opium abolitionists in China. Some of these people were sincere proponents of opium suppression, while others were more concerned with opium crowding out the Chinese market for other Euro-American commodities. Dudgeon's voice gained prominence because he was careful to maintain this dual focus. In fact, opium was the only commodity exempted from his lifelong laissez-faire ideology.

While Dudgeon's views on free trade were consistent with British capitalist ideology, his advocacy of refuges was a new approach to ideas of the body and intoxication in China at this time. This was encapsulated in his ambitious "Dudgeon Plan," rolled out in 1886. The seven-point proposal centered on the ultimate eradication of opium smoking, and Dudgeon offered three specific paths leading to this promised land: a widespread campaign of establishing modern hygiene inside opium refuges; substituting opium smoking with morphine tablets and injections (and to facilitate this, Dudgeon sold his own morphine-based "opium cure" tablets and injections both inside his refuge and outside in his private pharmacy); and a campaign to publicly shame opium smokers (*Friend of China*, July 1886, 126). Each of Dudgeon's specific proposals appeared twenty years later in the Qing government's opium suppression initiative of September 1906.

However, the proposal that the Qing neglected to include in 1906 was the most pressing for Euro-white missionaries. For Dudgeon and other missionary doctors emphasized church attendance as essential for a "clean and hygienic" life. Therefore, in the second opium refuge opened in Beijing in February 1878, there was a requirement that patients attend two church services daily, which the different Protestant missions in the city took turns sponsoring (*Chinese Recorder*, May 1880, 200). Regardless of the condition of the patient, he or she was dragged or carried into the Methodist chapel, situated right next to Dudgeon's medical facility. In addition to the compulsory services, Dudgeon urged missionaries to come to patients' rooms and read them the Bible at night. During the day, patients were forced to take a regular dosage of his signature "tablets" made at the apothecary on the premises. Dudgeon designed what he called "white pills" for inpatients and "black pills" that anyone could buy from his pharmacy and take to self-medicate at home (201). White pills cost fifty cash, while black pills went for sixty; both prices were around double the cost for a standard dose of smokable opium in Beijing. Injections of uppers (atropine, ephedrine) and downers (morphine, passiflora) were administered personally by Dudgeon.

By the 1890s, two distinct missionary treatments for kicking the opium habit emerged: the shock or "immediate suppression" method, lasting five to seven days, and "gradual diminution," lasting three weeks to two months. Morphine pills and injections were standard in both treatment protocols. Throughout China there were only two Protestant refuges (out of approximately a hundred) where opioids were refused on principle, although at one of these, the Christian Mission refuge outside Nanjing, Elliott Osgood used cannabis as part of his shock treatment (Osgood 1903). Informed by recent scientific evidence concluding that swallowing and injecting opioids was worse for patients than smoking, Osgood was the rare missionary doctor to avoid morphine-based opium cures. When the leading missionary doctor William Park conducted a survey of Christian opium refuges in 1898, he found that forty-one used the immediate suppression method, while twenty-two used the gradual diminution method; seven combined aspects of both. Only Osgood followed recent scientific recommendations to curtail opioid pharmaceuticals (1899, 48–49). The main problem with the popular morphine injections was that while morphine was chemically similar to opium, it was stronger. And unlike smoking, injections increased the amount of the drug delivered to the body. Compounding this, the total amount of the drug ingested was very different. Recall that the standard daily dose for opium smokers in Sichuan in the 1880s was under two grams. Morphine was measured in grains at this time, and one grain equaled about twenty-eight grams of opium. Chinese patients at opium refuges were often given between five and ten grains of morphine daily, or up to sixty-four times the amount of opiate consumed in daily smoking. Some morphine addicts shot up as much as forty grains a day (Hager 2019, 46). Many wouldn't survive these staggering quantities.

From the beginning of the Protestant refuge system in China, missionary doctors practicing the immediate suppression method deliberately forced their patients to endure what many called the "horrors" of opium withdrawal (Dikötter 2004, 124). As most missionaries believed that opium smoking signaled the presence of the devil, it was considered appropriate that Chinese patients experience the full panoply of withdrawal hell before becoming liberated from Satan's grasp: vomiting, diarrhea, heart palpitations, intense spasms, fierce migraines, and insomnia. Screaming at the top of their lungs and self-inflicted cutting were means to which patients resorted to alleviate some of these symptoms, particularly when relief provided by electric shock and injections didn't help (Osgood 1903, 56). Needless to say, many patients attempted to flee refuges as soon as they underwent any combination of painful discomfort and the corresponding response from the missionaries. But some of the largest refuge facilities were constructed like prisons, with high walls and guards at entrances and exits; escape from these facilities was all but impossible (Lodwick 1996, 132).

Although the physical horrors induced by the shock treatment point to a sadistic mentality among missionary doctors involved in it, we need to recall that Euro-American raciology's profile of Chinese people made torturous medical practices, regarded as inappropriate for Caucasians, routine for Mongoloid patients. As encoded in Arthur Smith's popular 1890 *Chinese Characteristics*, Han Chinese were said to have relatively underdeveloped nervous systems. As Smith put it, the Chinese "absence of nerves" was proven by the their "endurance of physical pain." Similar to Africans for Smith, the "simplicity" of Chinese cognitive functioning extended to their stripped-down nervous system (1890, 115, 55). Whatever the rationale for inducing "horrors," the general disregard of Chinese patients' pain thresholds urges an extension of ecclesiastical Superpredation to white Protestants in China; at least in the opium refuges, they displayed "no conscience, no empathy."

Construing Chinese as less sensitive to pain and remembering that the ultimate goal of opium detox treatment was conversion to Christianity, many missionary doctors saw withdrawal horrors as a means to psychosomatically empty out the patient, leaving them bedridden and confused—resembling the supinestupefiedyellow profile of Euro-American raciology. Bragging about the efficacy of his special sudden withdrawal treatment, Osgood wrote that in just three to five days, "we found a very weak specimen of humanity on our hands whom we at once proceeded to build up.... They are in an impressionable mood and listen willingly to the gospel" (1903, 56). Turning Chinese into emptied-out rawfare was useful for more than conversion to Christianity, though. It also put Chinese patients in a situation to "listen willingly" to sales pitches for the new generation of opioid pharmaceuticals. But that's only if they had a choice in the matter; many of the refuges required patients to purchase the drugs made at their own apothecaries. The refuges that didn't have apothecaries purchased drugs from German and American agents working for early Big Pharma companies like Merck (Hager 2019, 42). The long-distance coal-powered trade bringing Euro-American pharmaceuticals to Asia should be seen as yet another climate-interfering action.

The low cure rate of 5 percent for Chinese who entered into either a shock or gradual diminution treatment shouldn't blind us to the central place the Protestant refuge occupied in the struggle over epistemologies and ontologies. First, the Western innovation of hypodermic injections would leap out of the hospital refuges into the streets and alleys of cities and towns in China— shooting galleries mushroomed as opium smoking establishments were forced to close beginning in September 1906. Euro-American and Japanese morphine-based opium cure drugs competed for market share with smoking, while some Western drug companies diversified their product lines with cocaine, heroin, and more dangerous synthetics (Dikötter 2004, 125). The real "crimes against nature" of Climate Caucasianism were perpetrated by white dealers of synthetic compound drugs trying to force out of the market organic products like opium paste. Here, then, was a new War for Drugs with needles and pills on the Euro-white side and smoking on the Chinese. And with the different forms of delivering drugs to opioid receptors came different forms of interrelating. In opium establishments, smokers shared space, time, and intimacy with other beings—this was one of its attractions. As the GLH recruiting slogan mentioned in chapter 4 put it: in the opium room you could plot political actions, hang out and talk to your friends, or just chill and relax. Contrastingly, pills and injections were generally self-administered in private, and these novel instances of individualism were celebrated by Protestant missionaries eager to dismantle the intertwined, intra-active lives of Chinese.

This transformation in the delivery of opiates to Chinese bodies—away from smoking to pill-popping and shooting up—was so successful that the opium prohibition movement actually increased the quantity of opioids consumed throughout China. This should also be seen as the first global opioid crisis. Obviously, this was not publicized as one of the results of the Protestant War on Drugs. The declared victories were, first, the small but consistent increase in Protestant conversions, and, second, the substitution of so-called feudalistic opium smoking for the modern, hygienic opioids pushed by a new generation of white narcos in China.

The Qing's New Policies and the Spirit of Capitalism

After the disastrous 1895 defeat in the war with Japan and the brutal pacification of the Boxer Rebellion of 1898–1900 discussed in intertext II, the Qing government finally committed in 1901–2 to a process of reform usually referred to as modernization. What were formally called "New Policies [新政]" involved an across-the-board mimicry of Euro-American and Japanese prototypes in education, policing, public health, and governance (Zhao 2014). As Wang Di has shown, the reach of the New Policies in Sichuan extended all the way down to eliminating gambling, public sex workers, and street performers, in addition to arresting people for speaking "bizarrely" in public. The outlawing of incomprehensible speech explicitly targeted the GLH, which was widely known to require its members to use an indecipherable language while out in public (2003, 144–46). In addition to the policing of the GLH and other outlaw groups, the total package of New Policy initiatives was understood by some as an attack on the eco-ontology of many Sichuanese; the province's ethic of pleasure was clearly being served a summons. The Qing government's opium suppression campaign of September 1906 until the fall of the Qing dynasty in December 1911 became a central aspect of this throughout China and was arguably the most disruptive to the everyday life of Sichuanese people. And as the uncontested champions of opium smoking, the GLH was impacted the most.

Because of the ways opium was deeply embedded in the everyday lives of Sichuanese, the New Policies were greeted with both ambivalence and outright opposition in Sichuan (SJYD, 693–808). For sure, some embraced the limited forms of self-rule that were approved by Beijing, although only one out of every thousand men was granted the right to vote. Even this minuscule electorate had to prove that they were not opium smokers before attaining suffrage. The same went for the widely applauded new school system, although by 1909 in Sichuan only one out of 275 school-age kids attended the schools. The new Euro-American–style police that appeared overnight in Chengdu and Chongqing received accolades from some, but the cheerleaders invariably turned out to be government officials and capitalist elites (Wang 2003, 105–44).

As we saw in chapter 3 in the case of Japan's oppressive modernization, farmers bore the heaviest burden. In 1901 Sichuan was ordered by the Qing to hand over a large new tax as its share of the massive Boxer indemnity paid out to the allied countries (Chen 2010, 118). The New Policy taxes (新捐税) were mercilessly added on to this starting in 1903. After the provincial government decided to move ahead with building a railroad from Chongqing to Yichang in 1904, 60 percent of the money came from the land tax. Based on a study focusing on two different counties in Sichuan, Nishikawa Masao estimated that by 1910 the total amount of new taxes was about fifteen times higher than the standard land tax from the 1890s (1968, 131–58). Qing officials in Sichuan at this time didn't let anything go untaxed and, knowing that the poor sold night soil to manure collectors (a trade controlled by the GLH), were finally moved to add human feces to the list of taxable items (Wei and Zhao 1981, vol. 1, 86–91). Once again, as in Japan, these draconian measures caused farm foreclosures throughout China, "liberating" peasants to work for wages set exploitatively by capitalists or send their kids off as indentured workers. The new government's Institute of Agriculture studied the farm situation in Sichuan in the fall of 1912 and determined that the majority of peasants were paying about 60 percent of their annual crop total in taxes. A mere 30 percent owned any land at all (Wei 1981, 33).

The increasing tax burden was only one reason peasants refused to support the New Policies. Many could see that they were never going to have any voice in the limited system of constitutional monarchy, and most couldn't afford to release kids from agricultural chores to attend school. Moreover, those thrown off their land became targets of the new policing designed to cleanse cities and towns of beggars and the informally employed—*bang bang* haulers, itinerant actors and performers, and workers connected to the booming opium trade. Finally, the New Policies banned popular Sichuanese divination practices like "observing the deities [观仙]" and "strolling into hell [走阴]," and intensified the crackdown on astrologers, the latter having been welcomed into the GLH as members since the 1860s (Wang 2003, 153). Needless to say, Euro-American missionaries had long opposed these "heathen" forms of Chinese spirituality and enthusiastically supported these culture war aspects of the New Policies. In Chengdu and Chongqing, new Westernized police forces were authorized to arrest people for almost any reason, including "bizarre speech," "unusual behavior," "weird clothing," and "licentious talk" (132). What Foucault calls the imposition of disciplinary regulations, or "normation," was everywhere on display (2007, 57). But these standards didn't emerge ex nihilo; they had been advocated by Protestant missionaries since the 1880s. Unsurprisingly, the metamorphosis of urban Chongqing via these changes by 1910 was cheered on by the Western missionaries as well as Euro-American visitors, who found the downtown urban space relatively cleansed of filthy "opium sots" and transformed into an "'up-to-date' metropolis for commerce and western civilization" (*North China Herald*, September 2, 1910).

The new policed, Euromimetic makeover of Chongqing intensified the criminalization of idleness and poverty, what Janet Y. Chen in her history of the Chinese urban poor calls "guilty of indigence" (2012). Answering Euro-American missionaries' three-decade call to replace the Sichuanese Stopped Incarce-Raced ethic of pleasure with capitalist discipline and the accelerological Protestant ethic, the police regime element of the New Policies imposed a system of workhouses in Chengdu in 1905, a smaller variant of which spread to Chongqing in 1908. Initially, police were unleashed to arrest anyone who "looked" idle and could not prove employment (WCMN, October 1907, 9). But urban capitalists and gentry realized that a more profitable way to cleanse urban Sichuan of the poor was to turn them into convict labor. After two old temples were appropriated by the Chengdu government, which forced apprehended beggars to do unremunerated labor there, the municipal police built their own workhouse in 1905 explicitly for the poor and irregularly employed, an instance of what Marx called "bloody legislation" against the poor (1977a, 896). The express purpose of this was, as Wang Di insists, to coercively "teach them both working skills and morality" (2003, 145). The Canadian Methodist missionary J. Vale wrote approvingly of the new system, calling it "revolutionary." Vale noted in 1907 that the Chengdu police outlawed the informal hiring of temporary workers, a custom in urban Sichuan going back hundreds of years. With the new workhouse regime, employers could only hire "inmates" in police workhouses, but the carrot for employers was that these convict workers were paid a mere 70 percent of the going wage for private work.[14] For city and provincial public work, the inmates only made 40 percent of the standard wage scale. The working day was ten hours for outside work and fourteen hours for factory-type indoor labor. Most Chinese bosses were no doubt happy that the modernized police regulations allowed them to punch and whip workers like white men at the first sign of laziness, a break from previous custom (WCMN, October 1907, 8).

Just Say No (to Opium Smoking)

Several concatenated events led to the opium suppression proclamation of the Guangxu emperor on September 20, 1906. To try to grasp these, we need to understand that starting with the crisis in the 1830s and the First War for Drugs, there was never a clear consensus within the Qing ruling elite on opium prohibition (Polachek 1992). However, after opium trafficking was legalized in 1858, two prominent Qing officials, Li Hongzhang and Zuo Zongtang, argued successfully that a pragmatic policy of domestic decriminalization and taxing of opium revenues was the only viable way forward (Zhou 1999, 19). Subsequently, opium revenues paid for indemnities arising from anti-Christian uprisings, infrastructure projects, damages after the Taiping Rebellion, military modernization, and the first wave of New Policy reforms. This consensus around legalization lasted until the Japanese defeat of the Qing in 1894–95, which resulted in the loss of Taiwan, a bout of nationalistic soul-searching, and the Hundred Days Reform experiment in the summer of 1898. The fact that Japan had largely managed to keep opium out of the country from 1859 on was put forward as one of the reasons for their surprising military success. By the turn of the century, opium smoking (along with foot binding) was construed by most Chinese reformers as a cringe-inducing feudal remnant that had to be immediately abrogated (21).

An article in the Sichuan government publication *Sichuan Guanbao* in December 1907 insisted that the humiliating denunciation of China as the "Sick Man of Asia" was the result of widespread opium use. "So many of us have been smoking this stuff for so long; whether old or young, rich or poor, 70 to 80 percent smoke opium. Therefore, whenever we negotiate with foreigners we suffer all kinds of losses and humiliations. If you think about the implications of Westerners denouncing us as the Sick Man of Asia [东亚病夫] or if they use a somewhat more honorable designation like 'old venerable empire,' opium is behind this" (in Qin 2001, 127).

A later mention in this same article of the concrete steps the Qing government had already taken was a reference to the September 1906 proclamation promising to eliminate opium smoking in ten years. This happened during ongoing discussions with British officials in China leading to the March 22, 1908, signing of the Anglo-Qing Ten Year Opium Suppression Agreement. Under the accord, Britain promised to reduce Indian opium imports to China by one-tenth annually for ten years, as long as China could prove corresponding levels of reduction.

A November 1906 translation into Chinese of the report of the United States Philippine Commission on Opium circulated widely and spurred Chinese elites into action. Identifying opium as the sole cause of Chinese people to be reduced to the condition of supinestupidyellows, it claimed that "in China there is neither a public opinion which controls nor a national life which welds and consolidates a people. There is no Chinese nation, there is merely a Chinese race" (Lodwick 1996, 113–14).

Diametrically opposed to this representation of supinestupefiedyellows, Sichuan was a late-Qing social and economic success story. Just like the healthy bodies and well-fed mouths that all nonmissionary Western observers saw in rural areas in Sichuan (excepting the famine years of 1894–95 and 1901–2) from the early 1870s to the end of the Qing dynasty, the provincial economy featured a robust glow (Adshead 1984; Chen 2010). The most important manifestation of this was the rapid increase in the number of market towns. Qin Heping identifies the cause as the explosion of opium production and consumption (2001, 16–17). Even more significant than the mere number of them, many of these market towns emerged in poor mountainous areas of eastern Sichuan in Zhongzhou, Kuizhou, and Suiding (Wang 1993, 254). Heretofore cut off from trading centers, the cultivation of opium poppies brought new opportunities for peasant growers in remote areas. Poppies were not only untaxed by landlords, but crude opium paste is light and can be transported to markets fairly easily in regions without roads. Consequently, opium dealers gravitated to Sichuan's frequent opium fairs to buy directly from farmers. Some of these dealers would set up small processing facilities with boilers and strainers right in these mushrooming towns. In turn, some opened opium rooms and restaurants. Before you knew it, a full-blown market town appeared. Here, peasant growers were able to exchange opium for other Sichuanese products and, sometimes, enjoy unimaginable luxuries like eating out at a restaurant or spending time in an opium establishment, where new friendships—including sexual friendships, as we saw in chapter 4—could be made and old ones deepened (Li 2009, 51–52).

At a macro level, Sichuan's opium exports largely paid for the imports of Anglo-Indian cotton textiles and Euro-American machinery that came up the Yangzi. More importantly, the taxes on the opium likin and the transport taxes collected at the Maritime Customs in Chongqing constituted between 11 percent (Qin 2001, 18) and 15 percent (Adshead 1984, 92) of Sichuan's total revenue. This allowed Sichuan to play the feeder role in the Qing welfare system, under which it sent its own revenue through Beijing to poorer provinces. Crucially, reserves that came from Sichuanese opium taxes were used to pay off one-half of the crushing 1 million tael indemnity demanded by the French Catholics for the Chengdu anti-Western uprising of 1895 and slightly more than half of the 1 million indemnity demanded by MEP Catholics after the Yu Dongchen uprising of 1898–99 detailed in chapter 2 (Li 2009, 58). Without the opium money, Qing officials in Sichuan would have had no choice but to impose unpopular taxes on other products. Clearly, revenues from opium delayed the day of reckoning for the Qing dynasty.

Railroad Recovery and Poppy Protection

The scholarship on the Qing opium suppression of 1906–11 is almost unanimous in praising the effort. Recent work by Li Xiaoxing claims it was an unqualified "success" (Li 2009, 71). With the exception of a six-page article published in 1966, no research that I am aware of has suggested that there was even an indirect link between the abrupt suppression campaign and the overthrow of Qing dynastic rule in December 1911. This chapter will conclude with evidence of a direct link. Recall the stock phrase in Sichuan used to depict the sequence of events culminating in the overthrow of the Qing dynasty: "Sichuan was the spark that ignited the fuse of revolution" (which subsequently exploded in Wuchang, Hubei). It is reasonably clear that the same spark was first applied to an opium pipe, and then, with the spark still hot, was used to ignite the fuse of the Xinhai Revolution that toppled the Qing dynasty. While I am aware of how controversial this might sound, I note that historians aren't at all hesitant to argue that when a new opium suppression campaign was launched in Sichuan in the mid-1930s by Governor Liu Xiang, the GLH took up arms to protect poppy growing and defend opium smoking, waging, as Wang Di puts it, "a tenacious resistance" (2018, 130). This was twenty-five years after the GLH had settled into the role of an influential and venerable organization. The stakes were arguably higher and the existential threat to the GLH was even more pressing during the combined Qing and Euro-American Protestant War on Opium of 1906–11. As I will show, the GLH poppy protection and defense of opium smoking was similarly tenacious, resulting in a crucial, but unrecognized, contribution to the beginning of republican rule in China.

One explanation for the neglect of the fierce popular opposition to opium suppression in Sichuan is that the province's railroad recovery movement has attracted most of the attention, and for understandable reasons (Rankin 2002; Zheng 2018). The railroad recovery was, at first glance, a heroic story of mass mobilization against an arbitrary decision by Qing officials in May 1911 to agree to European demands and rescind the province's ownership of the railroad concession linking Chengdu through Chongqing with Yichang, Hubei. The Qing abruptly sold the concession to a European consortium, which infuriated gentry and merchants in Sichuan, many of whom lost considerable investments. One of the first broad-based opposition movements in Sichuan emerged in the wake of this Qing betrayal: the Sichuan Railroad Recovery Movement. And the shift in political consciousness from one of reform to anti-Qing revolution for many Sichuanese happened when the governor general, Zhao Erfeng (1845–1911), arrested the leader of the railroad protection movement and president of Sichuan's constitutional assembly, Pu Diajun; the leader of Sichuan's student assembly, Luo Lun; and seven others on September 7, 1911. During a protest the next day, Zhao ordered his soldiers to fire into the large crowd, killing twenty-six people and injuring many more in what became known as the Bloody Chengdu Incident (成都血案) (Dai 1994, 1132–34; Liu and Mi 2015, 149). The gates in and out of Chengdu were subsequently closed and heavily guarded, but a group of protestors was able to carve messages onto a thousand small oiled boards, which were smuggled out of the city and tossed into nearby rivers, alerting the countryside to Qing atrocities and asking for help. The most popular of these "water telegrams" floated down the Jin and Sha Rivers, suddenly becoming crucial extrahuman actors in the insurgency:

Butcher Zhao arrested Pu and Luo,
Then massacred the Sichuan people.
In all places, friends, arise, save and protect your land! (Han 1965, 249)

Anticipating the arrests of the leaders, railroad protection activists appealed to the GLH for help a few days before the Chengdu Incident in the nearby GLH stronghold of Guanxian (now Dujiangyan). With the Tongmenghui (同盟会) revolutionary leader Wu Yuzhang sent to liaise with the leaders of the GLH, the heavy opium smoker Hou Baozhai and the moderate smokers Zhang Dasan and Zhang Jiexian met in a large Daoist temple in the bedroom of the temple's tutelary sage (Yang 1933–34, 77). They all lay down on the sage's bed and, following GLH custom, smoked opium while debating whether the time was right to commit their muscle to overthrowing Qing rule in Sichuan (Han 1965, 250–51). The decision was ultimately made to rise up, and starting on September 9, a force that quickly expanded to fifty thousand GLH fighters gathered in and around Chengdu, most armed only with swords, knives, and hunting rifles. GLH members constituted the majority of the fighters in Sichuan's "Comrade Army [同志军]," responsible for nearly all the armed confrontations with Qing soldiers and Sichuan government militias (Sun 2007, 117–54). On September 18 and 19, in one of the first major battles of the Xinhai Revolution, Zhao Erfeng's 2,500 modernized New Army soldiers opened fire on the ragtag GLH troops from Chengdu's east and south gates, resulting in over a thousand deaths (Wang 1993, 111–12). With repeating weapons and artillery pieces, the Qing soldiers managed to push back the siege of the city. But for the next two months fighting continued throughout Sichuan, and Qing leaders in Beijing were forced to divert Banner troops, under the command of the Manchu General Duanfang, from Hankou, Hubei, five hundred miles to Sichuan. This transfer significantly reduced Qing military force in central China, one of the reasons the armed uprising in Wuchang, Hubei, beginning on October 10, was successful. Without the lit "spark" of the uprising in Chengdu used to ignite the fuse of anti-Qing rebellion, the better-known explosion in Wuchang wouldn't have happened until much later (103).

The chaotic situation in Sichuan's countryside in October and November made it possible for peasants to resume planting opium poppies free from government interference, and the 1912 crop harvested in March and April was reported to have been larger than that of 1909–10. We will never know the precise number of peasants in Sichuan who thought, in the words of a British IMC investigator, the Xinhai Revolution "meant license to all to do as they pleased, [and] recommenced planting the poppy" (IMC 1913, 253). But there is little doubt that farmers, dealers, and opium establishment proprietors in Sichuan and Yunnan considered the previous two years of strict opium suppression an aberration. Several European observers traveling in postrevolutionary Sichuan in February and March 1912 insisted that the "revolutionary movement had brought a revival of opium cultivation" (BPP 1912, 6). Adshead writes more forcefully that the "freedom to plant opium was one of the things Szechwan [sic] expected from the revolution" (1966, 98–99).

I mentioned above the observation from British consul Oxenham in 1884 that any attempt to curtail poppy growing and opium smoking would lead to open revolt in Sichuan. Several Euro-Americans in Sichuan in the 1890s echoed Oxenham's observation, with Archibald Little in Chongqing stating frankly, "eradicating the vice by edict . . . would amount to a social revolution, such as in the history of the world has never yet been carried out" (1898, 195). And so it went. After the Xinhai Revolution, peasants resumed full opium cultivation, because they could make money from it as an alienated commodity, and, unalienated, they could enjoy smoking their own organic product. We know from the 1920s and '30s that poppy growers often kept one-quarter to one-third of their crop for their own use, and there is every reason to think that this was the case in Sichuan and the other opium belt provinces in the last decades of the nineteenth century (Spence 1992, 237). Peasants with no access to doctors used opium for a variety of medicinal purposes, including malaria, diarrhea, and as what became known as "Chinese aspirin." Most important, however, was that they liked getting high. Opiates channel paths to dopamine receptors in the brain, lifting moods and helping smokers feel motivated. For peasants working long days in the field, the attraction is obvious. When compounded with the fact that opium intensified intra-action with other humans (in the rooms and parlors sprouting up around the new opium fairs in the countryside, and sharing a smoke during work breaks) and deities and spirits (during funerals, weddings, and group rituals), the effect of smoking opiates went beyond mere individual mood enhancement into a communal eco-ontological mode. In other words, most Sichuanese were clearly unwilling to stop cultivating and smoking opium out of some abstract sense of Chinese nationalism, as the scholarly consensus would have us believe. Rather, they wanted to continue to intensify their local intra-activity and commit to what decolonial Latin American theory calls *buen vivir*, or living well. This is to say that the 1911 revolution in Sichuan wasn't undertaken merely to overthrow Qing and Euro-American power; it was fought to protect local intra-actions involving opium poppies, humans, animals, and metaphysical beings.

When the Qing opium suppression hit the ground in early 1907, there was fierce resistance in Sichuan in particular, and the opium belt provinces of Yunnan, Gansu, and Guizhou more generally. The first recorded peasant protests against the suppression campaign took place in Sichuan in June 1907, in Kaixian and Wanxian counties (Adshead 1984). In December 1909, the next wave of organized protest in eastern Sichuan was launched in the opium cultivation center of Fuzhou (Fulin), where Qing soldiers dug up seeds and plowed over fields; two months later, in the middle of skirmishes between soldiers and peasants, two opium wholesalers were decapitated by Qing soldiers (Young People's Movement 1920, 107). Then in 1910, in what proved to be the last year of the Qing suppression, there were at least three additional organized protests in eastern Sichuan against poppy eradication, in Liangshan, Meishan, and Deyang (Zhang and Ding 1982).

The first flush of resistance to opium suppression in Sichuan wasn't limited to protests by peasant cultivators. The Qing government ordered opium taxes to be raised drastically in May 1906, from ten taels per chest wholesaled in the province and twenty-two taels for exported chests to one comprehensive tongshui rate of 115 taels. Sichuan Governor General Xiliang understood better than any other Qing official that this sudden spike was going to be met with fierce resistance, so he delayed its implementation as long as possible. Xiliang finally caved in to pressure from Beijing in January 1907 before opportunistically setting up a transfer for himself to Yunnan province in June (Wyman in Brook and Wakabayashi 2000, 219). This left acting Sichuan Governor Zhao Erfeng to deal with the fallout. Peasant growers, opium dealers, and opium establishment owners launched organized attacks on the new opium tax offices, before widening their targets in Kaixian and Wanxian to the New Policy schools and Euro-American missionary property. Not surprisingly, many GLH members were active participants in these actions (BFO 228/1659, June 7, 1907). Fearing a province-wide uprising against Qing rule in Sichuan, Zhao begged Beijing to lower the tongshui opium tax. Qing officials did relent and lowered the rate for Sichuanese domestic product to thirty-two taels. However, they refused to budge on opium exported from the province, and the rate of 115 taels continued to be enforced.

That was just the beginning of the back and forth within Sichuan over the implementation of opium suppression. Proclamations were put up by local magistrates beginning in the fall of 1907 and extending through the spring of 1909 warning of fines for farmers caught growing poppies and imprisonment for those caught selling—these were completely ignored (Qin 2001, 106–31). In fact, the poppy harvest for spring 1909 was the largest on record in several of the key opium-producing areas. The British consul in Chongqing, J. L. Smith, reported that Kaixian's 1909 harvest was its largest ever, while the outputs in Fuzhou and Nanchuan were six times the amount of the 1908 opium crop. Wanxian's 1909 output was modest by comparison, registering only a 50 percent increase over its 1908 total. But the flagrant violation of opium suppression in Sichuan extended beyond poppy cultivation. While many opium establishments officially closed, their proprietors opened unofficial rooms that did business openly, and the number of semipublic smoking places tended to stay around the same as before 1906 (BFO 1942, vol. 1, part 1, 45–46). Nevertheless, the Euro-American Protestant and Qing War on Drugs had the desired effect of raising the price of opium, from 20–30 cash per mace in 1905 to upward of 150 cash by 1910 in some places far from opium production centers. One consequence of this was to drive some Sichuanese smokers into popping opioid pills and shooting up. This unfortunate trend was made worse by a lack of treatment options for overdoses and addiction. While a large government-run opium refuge opened in Chengdu, everywhere else in Sichuan habitual users who refused to go to white Protestant refuges were on their own. Although the Sichuan government paid a thousand Chinese doctors in December 1909 to undergo training in Chengdu to open up small opium refuges throughout the countryside, no more than three ever opened. What this program was successful at reflected the larger "victory" of the opium suppression campaign. A doctor would end up "selling his [opium cure] medicines" to desperate smokers unable to afford the higher prices for smokable opium in some places (42). Most of these medicines were Euro-American pharmaceuticals sold by Chinese middlemen to doctors. The IMC in Chongqing reported that Western pharmaceuticals returned a 100 percent profit from 1903 until 1912, and Chinese and Euro-American dealers took advantage of the rising price of opium from 1907 to flood southwestern Chinese drug markets with cheap opioids (Hedkte 1968, 31). Protestant missionaries in Sichuan reported that a few areas did experience shifts from smoking to pill-popping and shooting up, and they continued the earlier tendency to cheer this on. However, some Euro-whites who were neither connected to the missionaries nor profiting from the new opioid trade denounced the flood of addictive pharmaceuticals. Robert Hart went so far as to call for a temporary suspension of Western opioid imports to China (RIMC, IG Circular 929, 1899).

Despite the intense pressure, most Sichuanese smokers did resist switching to pills and needles and ignored orders to register with police at local opium bureaus. The British vice consul in Chongqing noticed this defiance in January 1909 and, fearing more anti-Western violence, was relieved to hear from Qing officials that it was too risky to "attempt the entire suppression of public smoking" (BFO 1942, vol. 1, part 1, 23). British missionaries reported to their consulates in Sichuan in 1909 and 1910 about "active hostility" to the opium suppression campaign in the countryside and rebellious "widespread discontent" on the part of smokers (39). Some even noticed hostility being directed at Protestant missionaries, as the alliance between Euro-white evangelists and the Qing in suppressing opium was not only exciting antidynastic opposition, but "has raised strong anti-foreign feelings" (45). Nevertheless, Zhao Erfeng ignored this and pushed ahead. His brother Erxun conceded later that "the knowledge that British eyes were watching . . . served as a great stimulus" (BFO 1942, vol. 1, part 3, 167). Zhao Erfeng himself released the following statement in March 1909: "I'm informing you about our opium prohibition decree, the establishment of which covers all aspects of smoking, growing, and selling the drug. . . . We are going to make sure the opium scourge is removed from Sichuan. If anyone dares to disobey, we will immediately shut your business down. You must not attempt it!" (in Qin 2001, 125).

In addition to the defiance of most cultivators, the British consul in Chongqing, H. E. Sly, confirmed a widespread refusal to quit smoking. Sly sent a questionnaire to some thirty British and American missionaries in eastern Sichuan in September 1909, and they detailed the extensive resistance to the orders to quit smoking. Missionaries reported that in the main opium production centers, "Police have tried to prevent secret boiling and smoking, but the people have obstructed them." While Westerners selectively praised the Sichuan officials' "efforts to suppress it, country people and others are against it." Two missionaries wrote that in the face of ubiquitous protests against the crackdown on opium, Sichuan government officials returning from the countryside to report to their superiors frankly lied about the successes of the suppression campaign. Hearing later about fabricated "successes," the missionaries related that most Chinese understand that these successes are invented, or *yu ming wu shi*—in name only, but not in fact (BPP 1912 42, 46).

Poppy cultivation continued at between 70 and 120 percent of its enormous 1909 total in the 1910 harvest of Fuzhou, at about 50 percent in Fengdu, and around 80 percent in Tianzhang. There was a significant reduction in other areas, but nowhere was there complete eradication despite the presence of magistrates and soldiers in the main opium-producing centers (BFO 1942 vol. 1, part 1, 35; part 2, 19). The harvest at Fuzhou occurred in the face of soldiers uprooting plants, shooting live rounds at peasants, and executing at least one opium buyer by decapitation—a drug war, indeed. According to the veteran British official in China Alexander Hosie, Qing New Army soldiers were also dispatched to Kaixian in January and February 1910 to put down a resurgence of poppy protection attacks against tax offices and New Policy schools. East of Chongqing, the Dachu county market town of Tianzhang witnessed the first appearance of coordinated poppy protection by a group calling itself the Society for Forceful Planting. These defiant poppy protectors provided peasants with rifles and directed pitched battles against New Army forces, killing one and wounding several. A poppy protection leader from the society was decapitated in situ after being caught trying to flee (part 1, 38). There were at least two instances of organized armed peasant resistance in this area in 1911 (vol. 3, part 7, 56).

Almost everything written about the 1911 Xinhai Revolution in Sichuan attributes its primary cause to the railroad recovery movement. As we can see from the sources above, however, many tacitly agreed with Chongqing consul Sly's 1910 assessment that "Opium prohibition involves Szechwan in a . . . revolution" (BPP 1910, 47). Observers on the ground saw the ways in which the two issues of the railroad recovery and poppy protection converged into what the IMC report for Chongqing in 1911 referred to as a "wall hostile to the government: no man, woman or child stood outside" (in Adshead 1966, 98). There were other on-the-ground sources, however, who saw the poppy protection movement as the most important part of that wall separating the people of Sichuan from the Qing government—and against the Euro-American Protestants. The Japanese consular official in Sichuan, Konishi Shin, saw how poppy protection militants identified the Protestant missionaries as the main instigators of the opium suppression campaign, one shamelessly taken up by the Qing government in Beijing, reversing three decades of lukewarm toleration (JFMA, "Reports on the Revolutionary Upheaval in Qing China," November 11, 1911). In the summer of 1908, the MEP bishop of southern Sichuan, Marc Chatagnond, listed the railroad issue and rising taxes as "legitimate" causes of popular discontent. "Less respectable, but just as real and more powerful" was the Qing opium suppression campaign. Chatagnond's vantage point from the major opium-producing area of Yibin elicited a frustrated incredulity: "What do you think would happen in France if there was a complete prohibition on alcohol? . . . What's worse is that the most active groups of Sichuanese outlaws [*les gens de sac et de corde*] and troublemakers are all heavy opium smokers. These groups are well organized and ready to translate their anger into acts of violence and brigandage which, if they are not repressed, will soon take on very serious proportions" (APF, vol. 80, 14).

This Is Not a (Opium) Pipe

In a huge file called "Reports on the Revolutionary Upheaval in Qing China,"[15] Konishi, Mitsuura, and Japanese consular officials in Dali, Yunnan, reported that at the end of November throughout southwestern China, "all Westerners [西洋人] out in public were either attacked or threatened with attack" (JFMA, December 1, 1911). While there were some four hundred Euro-white missionaries in Sichuan at this time, only a handful of Protestants were still living at their missions by mid-October. All the MEP priests had fled to the safety of the French consulates, but ordered their Chinese converts to defend all Catholic church properties with their lives (October 16–17). Even before the arrests of the railroad recovery leaders, there were reports of two kidnap attempts on French priests near Chengdu (September 6). By the first week in October, the British, US, and French consulates in Chongqing had all received repeated warnings to close their facilities and leave China (October 13). In the area between Chongqing and Chengdu, GLH members told the Japanese investigators that the uprising was directed against both the despotic Qing and the Euro-Americans (外国人) (October 14).

Signs of blow(opium smoke)back against Euro-white CO2lonizers were evident in Sichuan's rural areas in the fall of 1911, when the Japanese officials detailed the surprising reach of defiance against the Qing suppression edicts. In one of his reports, Mitsuura highlighted that peasants had vowed to "never stop smoking" and adapted to the opium price increases by adulterating opium paste. Adulteration was so extreme in many cases that the concoctions had to be smoked in tobacco pipes, a tactic that also served to protect them from local magistrates, who were only looking for outlaw smokers using standard opium works.[16] Mitsuura also discovered that organized groups of poppy cultivators were transferring their businesses to more remote, mountainous areas, "where officials never conduct investigations" (JFMA, "Reports on the Revolutionary Upheaval in Qing China," September 21, 1911). The culmination of Sichuanese blowback emerged in Chengdu and Chongqing in mid-October 1911, when most "opium dens reopened publicly." And they evidently continued to be places where smokers could relax, meet with other members, and carry out political actions. Mitsuura and Konishi noted that they were surprised to find that opium rooms were "gathering spaces for revolutionary mob violence" (October 25, 1911).

The New Sichuanese Hegemon

The last three months of 1911 revealed the GLH's surprising degree of mainstream popularity. Although the first few weeks of fighting were carried out primarily by "muddy water" lodges, eventually all GLH members in Sichuan became involved in the revolutionary upheaval. What this meant in practice is that "clear water" members poured money into resources for battle and urged non-GLH militia in local communities not to engage the muddy water insurgents (Zhao 2006, 126). When the fighting subsided by the end of November and Sichuan declared its liberation from the Qing, the GLH emerged as the dominant social organization in the province.

The 1911 GLH was not the same subaltern mutual aid and social bandit organization that had emerged in the 1860s as a formidable enemy of both the Qing and the Euro-American missions. In the fall of 1911, women became prominent for the first time in the GLH, and respected older females like Wang San from Dayi, just north of Chengdu, and Shi Sanmei, from the northern county of Yibing, even assumed the role of military commanders (Wang 1993, 28–29). GLH women like Du Huang—who became known later as one of the "heroines of the revolution"—carried out anti-Qing actions in Beijing with an all-female GLH group called Sichuan Mountain. After the Xinhai Revolution, Du moved back to Sichuan and urged GLH women to form wharves without men; several responded to her challenge, with names like the Women Warrior Society and the Society for Equal Rights for Women (Azumi 2012).

The GLH also saw new groups appear among non-Han groups in southwestern China. As we saw Yu Dongchen in chapter 2 claim in the 1890s, the predecessors of the GLH in Sichuan had always been open to exchanges with Central and South Asian groups. So it wasn't surprising when one of the leaders of the GLH in western Sichuan, Zhang Jie, traveled into remote Tibetan areas of northwest Sichuan and Gansu and developed GLH branches there. For example, the last of twenty-three generations of Wansi Tibetan monks, Suo Daigeng, became a leader of the GLH in Wenchuan and Li counties. Suo commanded a group of more than six hundred Tibetan fighters and directed a famous ambush of Qing soldiers at Sanjiangkou (Zhao 2006, 127).

By far the most important transformation undergone by the GLH was its class composition. In chapter 4 I quoted Qing officials in Sichuan memorializing in the 1870s that many of the sons of wealthy gentry were joining the GLH—some of them because of threats from local GLH strongmen, and some simply because they were bored and looking for thrills in an outlaw group. I will conclude this chapter by suggesting how and why the GLH in Sichuan morphed from being composed primarily of subaltern dropouts from peasant communities in the 1860s, to one whose new members were increasingly merchants and gentry in the 1890s. It's worth repeating that many landlords and merchants had their first contact with the organization by paying shakedown money to the GLH before finding it more practical just to become members outright. A large financial contribution to most GLH wharves could buy a new member a leadership position, a phenomenon that became a regular occurrence in clear water lodges. Also, the biases in all early modern Chinese organizations in favor of education were hardly different inside the GLH. New members who successfully passed examinations at county or provincial levels were usually granted better positions and more power than uneducated GLH members in the 1890s. The discomfort that merchants and landlords reported feeling inside wharves with lower-class members (the tension was usually over the comfort level with "crime" for the bourgeois members) led to a hardening of the distinction between the mainstream clear water and the leveling muddy water factions (Zhao 2006, 43). GLH leaders from Sichuanese peasant families like She Ying and Li Shaoyi wanted to abolish the muddy/clear distinction completely and halt the rush of wealthy men into the group in the early twentieth century (Felsing 1979, 64–65). Because of his opposition to the increasing prominence of clear water capitalists and disreputable landlords, Li decided to splinter off from the GLH with his own group in the mid-1900s, the Xiaoyihui (194). The Xiaoyihui prohibited distinctions based on wealth and privilege and maintained an exclusive muddy water class composition, soon becoming the main coalition partner with the revolutionary Tongmenghui in northeast Sichuan (Wang 1993, 124–26). Major fighting between the GLH and the Xiaoyihui in 1911 and 1912 in northeast Sichuan resulted in serious losses to the latter (Liu and Mi 2015, 136).

This increasing power that bourgeois clear water GLH members accrued from the 1890s greatly reduced the opportunities for a sociopolitical revolution in Sichuan benefiting subaltern groups when the republic was declared on January 1, 1912. In fact, clear water GLH members were already deepening connections with Chinese and Euro-American capitalist enterprises in Sichuan. More important for my argument, when the GLH became increasingly bourgeois and mainstream, it no longer needed to rely on its intricate network of human &bjects and extrahuman entities for survival. Consequently, it shifted from an eco-ontological tendency toward intra-action to one increasingly based on extra-action, similar to the shift taken by the Japanese group Genyôsha discussed in chapter 5. This also meant for clear water (who self-identified as "clean") members a gradual reduction in the amount and frequency of opium smoking and partying. Muddy water GLH wharves remained "smoky" ones, while "clean" signified exactly that in recreational drug users' parlance: no longer getting high. Although I've been arguing that the widely reported victories of the opium suppression campaign in Sichuan were largely fictitious, the combined pressure of Western modernization (and Japanization) with domestic threats and punishment was too much for some educated elites inside the GLH; occasionally, these men "cleaned up." This exacerbated tensions between the muddy/smoky GLH and the clean GLH, one that became so polarized during the fighting in Sichuan in the fall of 1911 that clean members and revolutionaries refused to fight alongside GLH opium smokers (Han 1965, 251).

The Soundtrack for Xinhai: Sichuanese Opera

I don't want to downplay the class and eco-ontological conflicts that finally broke out into pitched battles after December 1911, but there were other reasons that most participants in the Xinhai Revolution in Sichuan ignored the very real differences in class and wealth inside the GLH. The obvious one is a collective sense of being Sichuanese Chinese, what I call "province nationalism." Space doesn't allow for a full discussion of this, but one unrecognized cause of Sichuanese province nationalism was the soundtrack for the Xinhai Revolution in Sichuan—Sichuanese opera. As the writer Li Jieren (1891–1962) described, popular local opera (川剧) played an important role in suturing different classes, ethnicities, and regional differences in the province into one umbrella identification as Sichuanese (Li 2012b, 3–5).

Except for the 2009 collection by the critic Du Jianhua, the 1992 collection by the theater critic Xi Yinzhen, and some fine pages by Wang Di (2008, 144–60), there has been little academic work on Sichuanese opera. According to Du, Sichuan's version differs from Peking and Guangzhou opera mainly in terms of costume style and makeup, and the ways masks and personae are changed rapidly on Sichuan's stages—the so-called face-change, or 变脸. However, she also identifies a main character in Sichuanese opera who isn't nearly as prominent in the other Chinese forms: the fool (小丑角) or uncouth bumpkin (丑) (Du 2009, 7–8). According to the Sichuan opera QQ group 川剧社, Sichuanese opera buffs consistently point to this role of the uncouth fool as the essential element that separates Sichuan opera from the other Chinese variants. One ardent fan estimates that approximately 35 to 40 percent of the canonical works of Sichuanese opera feature this role.[17] From Du Jianhua's synopsis of the canonical operas, the fool appears in multiple guises: as Mangpao (蟒袍) or the emperor's attendant; as the fool in mandarins' clothes (官衣丑); the playboy fool (褶子丑); the dirty and disheveled fool (烟子丑); the old-fashioned fool (老丑); and, arguably the most popular character in Sichuanese opera, the thief fool (襟襟丑). It is not difficult to imagine the strong identification GLH muddy water members would have had with both the dirty and disheveled fool and the thief fool.

How did this contribute both to revolutionary energy in Sichuan and to the inability of the GLH to maintain a focus on poor subaltern members? Wang Di has identified Sichuanese opera as "the most powerful form of popular entertainment" in the province, and an under-recognized force "in influencing the way people thought" (2008, 150). And the way they thought and identified collectively was apparently excited by the fool. To put this very schematically, Sichuanese opera buffs' insistence that the fool is emblematic of Sichuanese opera speaks to the larger sense of marginality in the province—peripheral in relation to Beijing and the major coastal cities. The fool is an uncouth, raucous character without any social graces, and this is how Sichuan was viewed by many in the late Qing period. We should recall how GLH hero Yu Dongchen spoke directly to this denigration of Sichuan in chapter 2. It's inconceivable that the character of the Sichuanese fool didn't elicit a strong identification from the GLH muddy stream, especially given that the fool manages to outsmart and trick elite and better-educated characters. For even more than the uncouth and gruff image that defined Sichuan from the imperial center in Beijing, the trickster fool became the self-image of Sichuan as the GLH rose to prominence. In other words, the progression Sichuan = the fool = GLH helps us understand the sense of injury that Sichuanese of all classes felt toward the increasingly despotic Qing in Beijing. However, this conflation also worked to elide the very real power differences both within the GLH muddy water and clear water factions and between peasants and the new holders of actual political power in Sichuan: the gentry and bourgeois elites.

"Undermining" China and Beyond Climate Caucasianism

Look at the way we have swindled the Chinese in the case of the Pekin Syndicate and still worse in the case of the Chinese Engineering and Mining Company.—G. E. Morrison 1906 (in Phimister 2006, 737)

In agriculture, as in manufacture, the capitalist transformation of the process of production also appears as a martyrology for the producer; the instrument of labor appears as a means of enslaving, exploiting and impoverishing the worker. . . . All progress in capitalist agriculture is a progress in the art, not only of robbing the worker, but of robbing the soil. Capitalist production, therefore, only develops . . . by simultaneously undermining the original sources of all wealth—the soil and the worker.—Marx, *Capital*, 1867

The clipper-coolie captive-contraband-capital (4C) circuit was wildly successful in transforming the Sinocentric trading area (including Japan) from a prosperous and sustainable trading region to a periphery of unsustainable Euro-American CO_2lonial capitalism. The vast Asia-Pacific region, in turn, was becoming what would be called later "the American lake," a process that began with the US invasion of Japan and continued with the brutal subjugation of the Philippines (1898–1901). More importantly, asymmetries in warfare, lawfare, and access to rawfare jump-started by the 4C circuit consolidated an epochal geological shift from the Holocene's twelve thousand years of stability to our present age of the Anthropocene. I have been arguing in this book that the Anthropocene is more correctly called the beginning of Climate Caucasianism, as Anglo-American capitalists transferred massive amounts of wealth from the Sinocentric trading area to a carbon-vomiting capitalism dominated by the US and the UK. As Marx understood and as W. E. B. Du Bois underlined, white racial capitalism was systemically Negrocidal (and Mongolocidal) and ecocidal in that it required the martyrdom of nonwhite workers, soils, water, and air to survive.

Widespread resistance to Euro-American hegemony brought other changes to East Asia. By 1911 Japan had become the first non-Western imperial power, claiming Taiwan, Korea, and South Manchuria on the Chinese mainland as its colonial territory (Driscoll 2010). As we saw in chapter 5, the Genyôsha of Fukuoka, Kyushu, became an important contributor to Japan's own CO_2lonial project. In chapter 6, we saw how opium poppy protectors in the Gelaohui brotherhood, in alliance with the Tongmenghui revolutionaries, successfully overthrew the Qing dynasty in China, leading to republican rule. Multitudes in Asia refused their assigned status as supinestupefiedyellows, leading many to reject the philosophy and raciology subtending Climate Caucasianism. This rejection routinely involved a critique of the unsustainability of Anglo-American global capitalism. For example, Mahatma Gandhi was a paradigmatic deCO_2lonial thinker in that he understood in 1910 that the non-West must not mimic Britain's environmentally destructive capitalism after postcolonial liberation from it. Referring to India's then population of 300 million, Gandhi warned: "If an entire nation of 300 millions took to similar economic exploitation, it would strip the world bare like locusts" (in Bonneuil and Fressoz 2017, 276).

Arguably the most important intellectual in East Asia at the turn of the twentieth century, the revolutionary Chinese philosopher and philologist Zhang Taiyan (1868–1936) was also clear on the unsustainability of Euro-American capitalism. In "The Five Negations" of 1907, he denounced how European economies "exhaust their own enterprises" and "extinguish [化] the fertility [膏腴] of the land." Moreover, Zhang lays bare how white racial capitalist's unwillingness to live reciprocally within nature in their colder environments impelled them to conquer places like India and Vietnam and "plunder resources from these wet and hot countries" (Zhang 1996, 257). While Zhang's Buddhism resisted identity altogether (self, family, nation), he can nonetheless see that in 1907 less powerful countries needed to join together to defend themselves against the white West, each establishing, he hoped, socialist collectives of their own (Murthy 2011, 199). Socialism is for Zhang the only political form capable of defending non-Western societies against what he calls Euro-white "ravenous predators" (Zhang 1996, 275).

In his *Book of Vengeance* (訄書), published first in 1900, Zhang attempted to understand how Euro-whites could rationalize their (Super)predations through the concept of biological race (民族).[1] But as he studied Euro-American raciology and the Japanese interpretations of it, he came across wild claim after wild claim: "Some say that at the beginning of humanity there were two kinds of people, yellow and black, or alternatively, white and black.... We can see that there is absolutely no agreement on the meaning of racial difference" (Zhang 2012, 146). However, Zhang became certain of one thing: there is no such thing as innate differences between racial groups. "Today people of the same race may have belonged to different races in the distant past; similarly, people who today appear to be from different races may actually have belonged to the same race in the distant past. Therefore, we have to consult documented history to delineate what we will call the historical races (历史民族) because decontextualized innate difference is meaningless (Zhang, 144).

With the issue of differences between racialized groups rejected out of hand, Zhang also jettisons the ranking of races from best (White) to worst (Black and Red) axiomatic in Western raciology. For him, the only way to understand human variation is by analyzing how humans reciprocally modulate and mutate within specific ecologies, languages, and histories (Zhang 2012, 145). As such, how could Euro-Americans rank physical environments from best to worst? Are mountains superior to plains? Hot biomes inherently better than cold ones? As he developed in subsequent writings—which Viren Murthy (2011) has so brilliantly analyzed—Zhang urges a decentering of human beings as &bjects into a larger network of relational intra-activity. Therefore, Zhang's distance from Climate Caucasianism based on a white supremacism that understands itself to be temporally ahead of and spatially above and beyond all other forms of life is vast. An East Asian political ecology that understands humans to be only one kind of interdependent being, finds one of its richest philosophical expressions here.

Gentlemanly Capitalism? Yeah, Right

Cain and Hopkins's (1993) influential thesis, arguing that in the late nineteenth century British imperialism in China and elsewhere became "informal" as its locus of power shifted from the Foreign Ministry to the "gentlemanly" investors in the City of London, is basically correct. In terms of the argument presented here, however, it downplays the crucial role investment capital plays in accelerating Climate Caucasianism. That is to say that the London Stock Exchange managed to project extractive capitalism to the whole world; in 1898 more than a thousand mining companies were listed (Bonneuil and Fressoz 2017, 238). As one final example of this, I want to return to Sichuan and the endeavors of the British entrepreneur Archibald Little. As we saw in chapter 2,

Little lived in Chongqing, Sichuan, for over a decade in the late nineteenth century. What brought him fame was his pioneering 1898 climate-interfering effort to get a coal-powered steamship up the Yangzi from Yichang, Hubei, to Chongqing. To do so he ultimately waged war on the riparian zones of the upper Yangzi, with extensive dynamiting and use of naval mines to cut out rock and deepen beds. Little was following the precedent set by the Euro-white engineers working for the Lighthouse Department of the Imperial Maritime Customs in the 1880s, who deployed the instruments of asymmetric war in hydraulic operations.

Little's last extractive operation in Sichuan was the coal concession he purchased in 1906 in Jiangbei, just across the river from metropolitan Chongqing. This was the culmination of a buying spree of Chinese coal deposits by Euro-whites, some of whom were British diplomats recently retired from service in China with insider information that facilitated the corrupt business deals that took place between 1895 and 1907 (Coates 1988, 224). Many were following the widely circulated recommendations of the UK's Blackburn Mission to southwestern and western China in 1896. Headed by British diplomat F. S. Bourne, the mission was tasked with identifying ways to enhance British trade (and to identify new profit opportunities for investors) after the commercial effects of the import substitution of Anglo-Indian opium by Sichuanese smoke began to be felt by British elites in Asia. Silver money had been sucked out of China since the late 1700s through the buying and selling of contraband Anglo-Indian drugs. However, when Euro-American drug profits were visibly drying up, global commodities had to be identified inside China that could pay for both the modern injectable drugs peddled by Euro-American narco missionaries we saw in chapter 6 and expensive Western machines and weapons. Coal would be the solution. Coal, according to the Blackburn Mission, would solve the problem of import-export disequilibrium to the benefit of the new generation of white drug and weapons traffickers. Although copper had been extensively mined by Chinese in Yunnan province since the 1750s, throughout southwestern China coal had not been.

Bourne, who served as British consul at Chongqing, Sichuan, in the 1880s, recommended that while Sichuan should certainly attract more Anglo-American investment for coal extraction, neighboring Yunnan was the place where the British extractiv-eye/I should focus. "No great development of trade is likely to come about until foreign skill and capital are employed in mining. The opening of mines would bring improved communication, immigration from Ssu-chuan, and good wages. A demand for our goods would certainly follow" (Bourne 1898, 98). As the joke circulating among Climate

Caucasianists went, China had for too long been "under-mined" by Westerners (Gibson 1914).

The Euro-white undermining of China reached new heights with the purchase of the Kaiping mines in Zhili province. Kaiping is considered one of the first modern mining operations in China, opening in 1881 with European investment but majority-owned and operated by the Chinese Engineering and Mining Company (CEMC). In 1898, CEMC sought additional European capital to develop the deep-water port of Chingwangtao, finally receiving a large loan from the London mining financiers Bewick, Moreing (Carlson 1971). Pressured by British officials and Robert Hart's Imperial Maritime Customs, mining became one of the first sectors targeted for upgrade by the Qing government and, simultaneous with the Blackburn Mission, Bewick, Moreing set their sights on its huge profit potential. Amid the chaos of the Boxer Uprising, CEMC president Zhang Yi thought the safest way to protect the Kaiping facilities from being swallowed up by Japanese or Russian soldiers was to sell off more of it to Bewick, Moreing, whose main engineer in China was future US President Herbert Hoover. Contracts drawn up by Bewick, Moreing and signed by Zhang replaced the existing company with a new enterprise of the same name and then transferred the entire ownership of the Kaiping mines to Bewick, Moreing and their cronies in the City of London. As Ian Phimister puts it, "the previous Chinese owners were completely defrauded of their property" (2006, 741). Similarly, the European-owned and City of London–financed Pekin Syndicate was very active in buying up mines and fossil fuel reserves after the scramble for concessions following the Qing-Japan war of 1894–95, multiplying sources of climate-intervention. They flipped their purchases for large gains after replacing the older Chinese profit-sharing system with wage labor and then working the Chinese miners into the ground. This prompted G. E. Morrison, the *London Times* correspondent in Beijing, to unmask these erstwhile "gentlemanly capitalists" as tyrants and predatory thieves (see the first epigraph).

Before Chinese mines were transformed by Euro-American capitalists and Zhang Zhidong's pioneering Hanyeping facility in Hubei in the mid-1890s, profit was often distributed among groups of miners called "close friends [亲身]" and the owners of the adits and furnaces. The close friends got 40 percent of the profits and the owners received 60 percent. Workers in other sectors of the operation were paid a monthly wage. Older Chinese scholarship on mining—some wanting to establish a clear Chinese precedent for capitalist wages—presumed that close friends came out with less money than those paid monthly wages (Wang 1965). However, newer work proves the opposite: close friends in profit-sharing situations consistently made more than waged laborers (Kim and Nagase 2013, 108–90). The reasons should be obvious: part ownership increases productivity and enhances collectivity. The shift to European practices in Chinese mining centered on fixed-capital mechanization (especially the increased reliance on coal-powered steam pumps and engines; fossil fuels were now unleashed to intensify further fossil extraction) and outside ownership by financiers, destroying the close friends system. This left the great majority of workers tied to wages. Consequently, the divide between waged laborers and the owners and stockholders turned absolute.

Saitô Kohei argues that Marx's theory of metabolism highlighted that "between humans and nature [there] is an interactive and circular process in which humans not only take from nature but also give back to it" (2017, 286). I have shown how even in extractive operations, mines would close in Japan during planting season so as not to contaminate soils, and in China miners made offerings to the deities while following customary law not to mine on certain days. In terms of the concepts I have put forward in this book, we could call this "intra-active extraction." This means that determinations other than profit and exchange value impacted extraction. But with the shift to wage labor—made possible when the original metabolic rift tore humans from what Marx called our "intimate ties" with the earth—capitalist value irrevocably commands and controls the human (dis)connection to nature in an "extra-active extraction." In the *German Ideology*, Marx pinpointed capital's double domination of wage laborers and nature: "The identity of man and nature also appears in such a way that the restricted attitude of men to nature determines their restricted relation to one another, and their restricted attitude to one another determines men's restricted relation to nature" (Marx and Engels 1975, vol. 5, 44).

Euro-white extraction arrived in Chongqing during the scramble for concessions when a French consortium and several British corporations won mining and railroad rights in Sichuan from the weakened Qing government after the defeat of the Boxer Uprising. In 1903, Archibald Little moved from waging war on the upper Yangzi to extracting coal across the river from Chongqing in Jiangbei. With financing from London, Little became the CEO of a large British-Chinese firm that managed to buy a fifty-year lease to mine coal and build infrastructure in Jiangbei directly from the Qing government in Beijing. The chairman of the Chongqing Chamber of Commerce, Zhao Zhisheng, countered this move by creating a new company with several local partners called the Jianghe Coal and Iron Company. The race for industrial coal extraction in Sichuan had begun (Li 1990, 71–72).

To help him get started, Little hired several British men from a mine prospecting company headed by Pritchard Morgan, then based in Sichuan's capital of Chengdu, including a retired Royal Army engineer with expertise in explosives (Little 1910, 165–66). Little's team moved ahead with major upgrades to the older facilities at the Longwangdong mine in Jiangbei: reinforcing adits, bringing in imported pumps and furnaces from the US, and turning all compensation for workers into wages. In 1907, Little began building a forty-mile road connecting his mine to the Jialing River. As he had done ten years earlier when he launched Climate Caucasianist war on the Yangzi, Little's road construction team deployed dynamite and Harden Star grenades as they blasted their way to the river—destroying private houses, burning down small forests, and outraging local GLH members. According to the British consulate in Chongqing, the GLH retaliated as they had earlier against Euro-American "crimes against nature" by machine-breaking and jamming surveying equipment belonging to Little's company (JFMA, "Chinese Secret Societies," 1068). When Sichuanese gentry joined in the protests, Little asked the Qing attendant for eastern Sichuan to intervene on his behalf. Yet after a year of negotiations, the snowballing local opposition was so powerful that Little was asked to sell his Jiangbei mining operation to the Jianghe Coal and Iron Company. He finally did so in 1909 and made a large profit on his original investment (Jiangbei weiyuanhui 1986, 115). The transfer of the Longwangdong facility and Little's road construction to Sichuanese capitalists was applauded in the popular Shanghai publication *Dongfang Zazhi* as one of the two great events of Chinese mining recovery, together with the buying back of the Kaiping mines (Li 1990, 74). This celebration of the two recoveries happened despite the extensive profiteering by Little; Bewick, Moreing; and other investors in London. Unfortunately, wage labor regimes, dynamiting, and outside investment had CO2lonized the region, becoming permanent features of Chinese mining. Euro-white extra-active lawfare (what Ferreira da Silva [2007] calls transcendental production) appears one last time in this book when the capitalism of Climate Caucasianism refused to allow any mediation other than that of profit to determine the intra-actions of humans in and with extrahuman and nonliving entities in the natural environment. Chinese extractive operations now followed this universalized "rational" template as they added to the number of climate-intervening sites.

Fluidarity Forever!

Japan's first environmental activist, Tanaka Shôzô (1841–1913), was a prominent figure in the Autonomy and People's Rights (APR) campaigns of the late 1870s and 1880s, discussed in chapters 3 and 5. After being elected to the first Japanese Diet in 1890, Tanaka became the most outspoken critic of the industrial pollution unleashed by capitalist extraction throughout Japan. He ultimately focused his attention on the Ashio copper mine in Tochigi prefecture. Opened first in the seventeenth century, Ashio was purchased in 1877 by an industrialist and friend of the Tokyo oligarchs, Furukawa Ichibei, together with several European partners. Anxious to support Jardine, Matheson & Co. in its attempt to monopolize the global market in copper, Furukawa turned Ashio into the most technologically advanced extractive operation in Japan. In Robert Stolz's account, to guarantee profits for its owners, Ashio "externalized" and dumped increasing amounts of pollutants into the nearby Watarase and Tone watersheds—poisoning rivers, contaminating soils, and exterminating wildlife in the area. The nearby town of Yanaka became the first zone sacrificed to industrial extraction in Japan (2014). As this was the most serious consequence of the extraction → extinction imperative to date in Japan, Tanaka and others committed to starting an extinction rebellion.

Tanaka's increasingly vocal indictment of toxic pollution at the Ashio copper mine fell on deaf ears. So, he decided to retire from politics in 1901 to dedicate himself to full-time environmental activism, relocating to Yanaka. We should underline that Tanaka's trajectory is the reverse of the white flight that capitalism takes from an area after it has plundered all that it wants via an extinguishing of workers, soils, and flora and fauna. From Yanaka he produced ethnographies of the effects of pollution (毒, *doku*) and studied the Meiji state's attempt to manage it through levee construction, small dams, and other hydraulic operations. This led Tanaka to the understanding that the unpredictable flow (流れ) of water was so central to the reproduction of life that he called for a "fundamental river law [根本的河川 法]," anticipating recent calls for "water ethics" (Groenfeldt 2013) and Indigenous struggles against fossil fuel extraction, insisting that "Water Is Life!" (Stolz 2014, 108). Rather than capitalism demanding that all forms of life submit to the transcendentally produced law of value (or what is most important for capital, screwing over everything else), Tanaka's incipient hydro-socialism asks humans to consider water as the most powerful determination. Tanaka's sense of urgency in the face of ecological crisis (in 1907!) recommends that, contradictorily, this decentering of human agency through dependence on the natural environment is the only way to maintain freedom (Stolz 2014, 109). Rather than the notion of a grounded "solidarity" that was beginning to influence anticapitalist politics globally at this time, Tanaka urges what I've called a wetter "fluidarity" (Driscoll 2004). This aquatic transformation in the metabolism of humans and nature is the best way to combat what Tanaka calls the life-threatening flowback (逆流) resulting from poisons produced by industrial extraction (110). Although capitalist ideologues insist that capital *flows*, Tanaka disagrees, hinting that it stomps and slays—like a Superpredator. Only water flows.

The course of unimpeded water in oceans and rivers is unpredictable, as we saw earlier in the case of the upper Yangzi in China. Water is actually three-dimensional: vertical, lateral, and horizontal (Nelson, forthcoming). While hydrology couldn't tell Tanaka this in 1907, he clearly grasps that state capitalism intensifies blockages to 3-D hydroflows, trying to CO2lonize them into becoming one-dimensional. As he wrote in his journal in 1910, criticizing government policies like clear-cutting forests and extraction for export that resulted in the "martyring" of entire villages:

> Flowing water must not be blocked, but unleashed. What is called today "water management [治水]" is actually destroying lots of villages. When villages are destroyed this should be called murder [人殺し]. There's absolutely no justice in this. . . . Today people justify anything if it benefits the state: deforestation, mountain obliteration, etc. This happens regardless of the flooding and destruction that ensues. There was never anything like this before where a system created huge oceans of poison [大毒海] that kill and immiserate human beings. If stealing from nature and killing people can be done for the "good of the state," then this state is in fact the enemy. (Tanaka 1989, 84)

Although Tanaka still used the older Chinese humanist language of Heaven and Earth, it is no longer just Euro-whites who are the enemies of Heaven. Rather, the enemy is industrial capitalism everywhere. While Tanaka writes that these forces are unjust in opposing Heavenly morality, his main focus is on their hostility to originary flow. Planetary life is increasingly threatened by the expanding "oceans of poison" unleashed by the extraction of minerals and fossil fuels and the resulting polluted flowback (逆流)—CO_2 is conquering H_2O. Nothing less than the dismantling of entities that produce CO_2 is required to liberate water and generate new life. But the liberation (解放) and autonomy (自由) that Tanaka called for in the last years of his life look nothing like the Euro-white self-determination and solipsism that Ferreira da Silva castigates in the introduction to this book, one that extra-acts on rawfared entities separate from it. Rather, Tanaka's freedom from the oppression of industrial pollution is grounded in a "communally interdependent mutual love [公共協力相愛]" (1989, 77). To me, this resembles what Arturo Escobar calls the Indigenous-inspired "autonomous interdependence" (2018, 166–69) that we saw with the Gelaohui's understanding of eco-ontological immersion in "rivers and lakes" in Sichuan, and in Genyôsha's Hakoda Rokusuke's understanding of the ways water could release human &bjects from the contaminations of both Meiji oligarchs and extractive capitalism.

Although they had become the most powerful behind-the-scenes actors in Japanese foreign policy by the time of the Russo-Japanese war of 1904–5—using the money they made in coal mining in the 1880s and '90s—Genyôsha became a financial backer and public supporter of Tanaka's environmental protests against the Ashio operation (GY #18, 3). Perhaps Genyôsha's leader Tôyama Mitsuru was rethinking his fateful commitment to capitalist extraction. Indeed, in 1880 he and Hakoda had named themselves after a body of water (玄洋) in an attempt to overcome what they called the political "blockage [閉塞]" imposed by the despots in Tokyo and the capitalist conglomerates allied with them. Before Tôyama and Sugiyama Shigemaru turned to coal extraction, Genyôsha had been intra-actively submerged with APR comrades and extrahuman entities in political fluidarity to free and unleash both people and entities like mountains. In publicly identifying Genyôsha with Tanaka Shôzô's attempts in 1908 and 1909 to unblock the flowing water and decontaminate the huge oceans of poisons caused by industrial extraction, Tôyama must have felt some regret for the swerve toward capitalism and nationalism he insisted Genyôsha take in 1885. Did he recall Genyôsha's political impetus of 1880–85 that, as the Antillean writer Édouard Glissant put it in 1958, "the freeing of the waters" is the analogue in the natural world of an uprising of "the people in revolt"? (in Wynter 1989, 638). Was it too late in 1910 and 1911 to reverse Genyôsha's own life-threatening flowback (逆流) and follow Tanaka's path from the Autonomy and People's Rights (APR) movement to the fluidarity of eco-socialism and water rights activism? Indeed, was it too late in 1912 for the Gelaohui in Sichuan to shed its alliances with bourgeois capitalists and return to their humble origins immersed intra-actively in rivers and lakes (江湖)? Unfortunately, from 1912 both groups regressed irrevocably to nationalism and capitalist extraction and turned against their previous commitments to eco-ontological communism and interdependent autonomy. This doesn't mean we can't follow the communist historical tradition established by Walter Benjamin (1969) and Ernst Bloch (1986) and "redeem" those earlier commitments of the Gelaohui and Genyôsha in our present as we search for examples to counter intensifying Climate Caucasianism and ongoing Superpredation. Or, alternatively, we could turn to less Eurocentered inspiration from the Senegalese philosopher Felwine Sarr, who, discussing the work of the Ghanaian architect Kobena Manning, writes: "The concept of *sankofa* is at the epicenter of his thought: 'To drink from the past in order to move forward on a surer foot'" (2016, 143–44). Or we could follow the method of Indigenous Futurism, pioneered by Anishinaabe scholar Grace Dillon to counter the effects of capitalism's myopic and presentist greed. Describing the intra-active connection the past has with the future, Native American scholar and artist Elizabeth LePensée explains that Indigenous Futurism emphasizes both the dynamism provided by the past to futures to come and the ultimate inseparability of the what she calls "past/present/future—the hyperpresent now. . . . We look seven generations before and seven generations ahead" (in Keene 2018).

Notes

INTRODUCTION: THE SPEED RACE(R) AND
THE STOPPED INCARCE-RACES

1. There were two versions of this letter: the one I'm quoting from here and a nearly identical second, cowritten by Lin, the governor of Guangdong Deng Tingzhen, and the vice minister of the Qing Board of War Yi Liang. The second letter was sent to England with the seal of the Daoguang emperor.

2. This isn't a loose comparison. One similarity is that Latin American (crack) cocaine and Anglo-Indian opium were produced at great distances from their centers of consumption in the US and China, respectively. More importantly, the physical effects of both drugs have been exaggerated to (re)consolidate white supremacy. Rather than making people lazy, opium was known as the "work drug" in Japan's Manchukuo colony in the 1930s for its ability to turn even the most degrading labor into something tolerable. Although crack cocaine can be highly addictive in many situations, rather than turning smokers into sociopathic "crackheads" and "crack mothers" as tough-on-crime advocates insist, the half-life of a standard dose of crack is less than one hour, whereas for "white" drugs like methamphetamine or heroin it is up to twenty-four hours.

3. All translations from Japanese, Chinese (modern and classical), French, and Spanish are mine unless indicated.

4. The termination of slavery in the British Empire in 1833 was in part conceivable because white Anglo elites saw the rise of the Asian coolie trade as a substitute source of labor to replace Black slaves (Lowe 2015).

5. See Liu (2004, 118).

6. Marx writes in *Capital*, volume 1, that "a strange God perched himself side by side with the old divinities of Europe on the altar, and one fine day threw them all overboard. . . . It proclaimed the making of profit as the ultimate and the sole purpose of mankind" (1977a, 918).

7. Andreas (2020) also uses War for Drugs.

8. This shares a critical perspective with Françoise Vergès's notion of the "Racial Capitalocene" in Johnson and Lubin (2017).

9. The technical term for this is "indentured labor" (Northrup 1995). However, an estimated 90 percent of Chinese indentured laborers were forced and/or lied to about the conditions of employment, which is the UN definition of forced labor today. While the term "indenture" suggests an above-the-board legality, the majority of Chinese cases belie this, impelling scholars like Yun and Laremont (2001) to use the phrase "forced migration" to depict this human trafficking of Asians. South Asian migration was less coercive, although some of the effects of their forced migration were shared with Chinese "coolies."

10. George Lipsitz (2009) calls this beneficial ownership of pale privilege the "possessive investment in whiteness."

11. Thanks to Diane Nelson for this reference.

12. Miller, Adeney Thomas, and Walker (2013) suggest that Japan and Europe weren't that different in terms of intensifying aspects of the control of nature in the eighteenth and early nineteenth centuries. Federico Marcon's 2015 study makes this point with even more force.

13. Mezzadra and Neilson (2017) and Arboleda (2020) are doing the best work on contemporary extractivism.

14. I'm not arguing that modern raciology was produced ex nihilo in the nineteenth century, but that it built on what Frantz Fanon called the "historical racial schema" (1967). Accumulation by drug and arms possession was both cause and effect of emerging scientific racism. Similarly, the 1980s and 1990s crack epidemic gave birth to an insidious form of postracialism that reversed legal and sociopolitical victories of the civil rights and Black and Brown power movements of the 1960s and '70s; see Alexander's germinal *The New Jim Crow* (2010).

15. An infamous example of this was in Gilbert and Sullivan's 1885 *Mikado*, where an adult Japanese male (referred to as a coolie) was played by a white child.

16. I've benefited from a fine presentation on Down by Mel Chen at Duke University in February 2016.

17. I will not be using "den" in this study, as in English dens are for children and animals. The Chinese for such a place is 鸦片馆 (*yapian guan*), with 馆 (*guan*) denoting an upscale establishment or domicile.

18. On this see Kitahara (2013), where Portuguese are said to have done most of the human trafficking of Japanese and Chinese.

19. See Sufen Sofia Lai in Kowner and Demel (2014).

20. In 1826 the Sino-Japanese characters 神道 didn't have the meaning that they would by 1890 of Japan's state religion, or Shinto. Often translated literally as the "way of the gods," in his fine English translation of *New Proposals* Bob Wakabayashi renders the 神道 compound circa 1826 as "spirit-like processes of nature."

21. What is important here is the ontological monism linking divine reason, primordial matter, and the inscriptions of these in myriad kinds of entities in Japanese neo-Confucianism thought. This should be distinguished from the rupturing dualisms in Cartesian and Kantian philosophy.

22. Thanks to an anonymous reviewer for helping me parse this.

23. I'm collapsing theoretical systems here with significant differences. Philosophically, I agree with object-oriented ontology's insistence that not all objects are &bjects and *every* object possesses the potential (or phase space capacity) to withdraw from relation, as Martin Heidegger insisted (Harman 2018). Actor network theory's flattened ontology disperses questions of power, while decolonial relationality *foregrounds* power, correctly in my view. Decolonial relationality, while appalled by what they see as the apolitical Anglo-white men leading the O O O movement, actually shares some of their insights. For instance, Marisol de la Cadena's (2015) argument that things are "not only" what they are for human phenomenology is an O O O conceit par excellence.

24. Important exceptions include Warren (2018), Bernasconi (2003), Eze (1997) and Osborne (2003).

25. This is worked out in Kant's *Critique of Pure Reason,* part II, book 1, chapters 1 and 2.

26. The most important precedent for a Euro-white subject authorized to extract that which is external to it is John Locke's 1690 "Second Treatise of Government," where he encouraged white settlers in the US to "subdue the earth."

27. I'm critiquing the recent "decolonial" reading of Hegel inspired by Susan Buck-Morss (2009). While Hegel does allow for black slaves to be victorious in a race war with Euro-whites, this can only occur after they have interiorized and subsumed all aspects of Europeans, including self-determination and an extra-active exteriority vis-à-vis nature. Furthermore, Hegel does not preclude white Christian Masters from winning back racial superiority in the rare instances of losing race wars. He recommends as much when he revisits the Master-Slave dialectic in the 1817 *Philosophy of Mind* and suggests that if white Christians recognize the ways in which black slaves have jettisoned their egotism and selfish desires, they can appropriate these for the revanchist project of white Self-Consciousness; see sections 432–35 in Wallace et al. 2007.

28. Cited in Marez (2004, 96).

29. See also Beasley (1955, 158–61) and Inoue (2010, 19–20).

30. Perhaps it bears mentioning that this violence enacted on yellow people by Japanese men dressing up as Blacks occurred on an imperialist ship nostalgically named for a red Native man.

31. "Gemmen" satirizes African American pronunciation of "gentleman," denying, of course, any such status for such a backward caricature. "Olio" refers to the mixture of jokes and songs performed between acts in minstrel shows.

32. 百度百科, accessed April 3, 2018.

33. I learned much about meteorology from Max Conley's 2019 honors thesis, "The World Whole."

34. In reference to US towns where intimidation and threats of violence kept Blacks from living in white towns or even being there after dark.

35. As the discussions over opening Chongqing heated up, Robert Hart refused a Qing government request that Chinese life be compensated when Chinese boats were rammed by Western steamships (BFO 228/886, May 17, 1890). If an incident of White-on-Chinese murder became public—and if the family was of means—consuls in the east coast ports paid damages of ten to twenty dollars; see Coates (1988, 46–47).

36. This changed somewhat with the establishment of the British Supreme Court for China and Japan in Shanghai in September 1865 (Clark 2017, 41). Nevertheless, Chinese victims of Euro-white assaults had to convince Chinese magistrates to open cases against white men, with the consuls representing the Western men who then brought the case to the Supreme Court. It was rare for consuls to initiate investigations against their countrymen, even in capital crimes.

I. J-HĀD AGAINST "GORGE-US" WHITE MEN

1. The Stirling Convention of 1854 was England's first trade treaty with Japan, and its most-favored-nation clause granted British nationals limited trading rights in Nagasaki and Hakodate. When the first British minister, Rutherford Alcock, landed in Nagasaki on June 4, 1859, he found that almost all of the British traders were openly violating the agreements; see Fox (1969, 52–60).

2. There were at least two instances of Euro-white grave robbing, with the first happening outside Nagasaki by Russian mercenaries in 1859. In Hakodate three British employees of the consulate, Henry Frone, George Kernish, and Henry Whitelery, managed to dig up twelve skulls and three whole skeletons in 1865 to sell to dealers in Shanghai before they were found out. These contributed to the phrenological and raciological "proof" of Euro-white supremacy (BFO 46/88, January 31, 1866).

3. Saidiya Hartman makes a similar point about the sexual assault of slave captives in the US South (1997, 43).

4. More honest Euro-whites recognized that most Japanese women were horrified by Caucasian men and did everything they could to avoid them; see Heusken (1964, 93–94) and Cortazzi (1987, 146).

5. After implying as much earlier, Oliphant states clearly that "young ladies" are constantly trying to peek at "the toilet, as performed by an English gentleman" (1860, 376).

6. James Hevia's work (1995, 2003) has been pioneering in this regard.

7. Morikawa Tetsurô claims that the British Legation arranged to buy two sex servants named O'hana and O'kanai to "comfort" Englishmen at Tôzenji, while the 1862 Japanese text *Yokohama Kidan* lists only one woman registered as a *musume*—the common reference to sex servant—to work at the British embassy. See Morikawa (1967, 47–48) and Williams (1963, 109–10).

8. Miyazawa's work is the most detailed description of the incident in any language.

9. Eventually, Anglophone residents of Yokohama in the 1880s acknowledged that Richardson's provocations caused the event. The journalist E. H. Scidmore, who lived in Yokohama for three years in the late 1880s, wrote that Richardson and his friends "deliberately rode into the daimio's train" (1892, 28).

10. This same phrase appeared in Marshall's original testimony given in Yokohama, although this made it seem like Marshall was, nonsensically, yelling at the Japanese.

11. Philip Towle describes the "generalized beating" inflicted on South Asians by British subjects in the nineteenth century (in Kowner and Demel 2014, 287).

12. Grace Fox writes that in Yokohama and Nagasaki, "drunken and disorderly sailors from Western ships repeatedly outraged the peaceful native population" (1969, 77).

13. Cited in McMaster (1992, 186).

14. The incidents that do appear featured Euro-whites assaulting or killing samurai or government officials. On November 27, 1860, the Yokohama merchant Michael Moss shot and fatally wounded a Japanese police officer, Oya Kunitaro. Moss was illegally goose hunting and returning to his home in Yokohama with his prize when he was approached by three policemen. Alcock's description of the incident is in BFO 391/1, January 1, 1861; Moss's explanation of the events is in BFO 46/64, May 31, 1861. The reason that reports of White-on-Japanese abuse are rare in the Japanese archive is that local residents in Nagasaki and Yokohama were ordered by local magistrates not to argue with or harm foreigners, no matter how egregious their behavior (Morikawa 1967, 68). Contrastingly, Japanese locals were urged to report all conflicts with Chinese; see NGB 1:265 and 3:622–24.

15. https://en.wikipedia.org/wiki/Namamugi_Incident, accessed January 21, 2017.

16. Other British officers in China and Japan also thought that what they called "polluting" contact with Asian racial others brought out the worst in white male deportment; see De Fonblanque (1863, 5).

17. This section is based on McMaster (1992, 71–76) and Miyazawa (1997, 156–72).

18. Cited in Proshan (2015, 18).

19. Alcock also used the phrase "goldfield scum" to depict the British merchants (McMaster 1966, 62).

20. Opium was allowed into Japan for "medicinal purposes," but Euro-American traffickers unloaded most of their opium in the Chinatown in Yokohama for use by Chinese.

21. The diplomats had it even better. Ernest Satow had a live-in sex servant, a cook, his own horse, and "drank champagne with every meal" (in Satow 1921, 25–26). Of course, Satow doesn't say anything about his Japanese concubine, but Williams cites an 1863 Japanese book about Euro-whites in Yokohama/Edo in 1862 which claims that one of the registered sex servants (musume) was living at the British legation; see Williams (1963, 110).

22. See Hoare (1994, 35).

23. Japan *Wikipedia* entry for 羅紗緬, accessed April 18, 2018.

24. Japan *Wikipedia* entry for 港崎遊廓 accessed January 3, 2019.

25. The blackface song was credited to George Christy, son of the founder of Christy's Minstrels. See http://www.phrases.org.uk/meanings/hunky-dory.html, accessed January 21, 2017.

26. Even the defender of British capitalists in Japan, John McMaster, admits that many small firms focused primarily on buying gold because it provided "a large profit and quick turnover of funds with little needed in the way of packing, shipping or warehousing" (1966, 45).

27. The Tokugawa negotiators didn't bother contesting this aspect of the US draft treaty, as they apparently trusted Euro-American traders to act in good faith and pay the small tariff. US representative Townsend Harris was "very surprised" by this.

28. Although the standard translation of this is "barbarian," this construal has been largely rejected in Anglophone Chinese studies, and I'm suggesting something similar for Japan studies. In the Chinese usage adopted in Japan, the first character, 夷, signifies,

among other meanings, a person who doesn't read or write Chinese characters. The second character, 狄, signifies lower-than-human life form as the radical means "animal."

29. Japanese native spirituality has a female deity (Amaterasu) as its primogenitor, so it's more precise to call the presence of the divine a "goddess entity."

30. I've chosen not to capitalize Japan's folk spirituality, or 神道, as Shinto, as "Shinto" becomes an ideological tool to justify emperor-centered national rule in the 1890s; in the 1850s and 60s it circulated differently.

31. The new religions that emerged in the 1840s and '50s like Tenrikyô and Kurozumikyô were petitionary, but I can't find any evidence that Kiyokawa was a proponent of them.

32. Readers of Japanese will notice that this first text in Kiyokawa's collected works, *Senchû shimatsu*, has been put into modern Japanese by the editor. The second text I'm citing from, *Senchû kiji*, was published in its original Chinese 漢文 version.

33. I borrow this analysis from Peter Linebaugh (2019).

34. The main employees in Glover's company quit right around this time, apparently over the excessive arms purchases Glover made in his bet that the civil war would be a bloody but profitable one; see McKay (1993, 85).

2. ECCLESIASTICAL SUPERPREDATORS

1. An 1895 Chinese version of this is in SJYD (476–77).

2. Wyman (1997) also analyzes these kinds of stories. The best work done on them is by Li Danke (2004).

3. Paul Cohen was one of the first historians to research these anti-Christian placards; he argued that most of those from the 1880s and '90s were iterations of an 1861 proclamation originating from Hunan he calls "A Record of Facts to Ward Off Orthodoxy"; see Cohen (1963, 45–58, 277–81).

4. I took a two-day boat trip down the Yangzi from Chongqing to Yichang in the summer of 2016, and the guide Wang Zheng helped me figure out these parameters of water flow in consultation with the captain of the ship.

5. This was only one of the several Chinese designations used in Sichuan in the period from the First War for Drugs (1839–42) to the revolution of 1911; others included "Westerner [西洋人]" and "person from across the seas [洋人]." Barend ter Haar parses the various designations of outsiders by Chinese secret societies in his comprehensive 1998 work.

6. The British and Japanese consular officials agreed on the high percentage of Catholic converts in central and western China being petty criminals; see inter alia BFO (228/1064, February 23, 1891) and JFMA ("Chinese Secret Societies," 1064–66).

7. R. Keith Schoppa identifies the Western missionary presence as one of "imperialism's three 'MS': merchants, missionaries, and the military" (2002, 45).

8. The French translation of the edict rendered the explicit Chinese reference to sexual assault as mere "*séduction*," but the second character of the Chinese phrase 诱污 makes clear that Catholic practices of virginity testing and blatant rape—in others words, *defilement* of girls and women—must not be repeated in the nineteenth century. For the French phrasing of the edict, see Young (2013, 25).

9. Although the 1860 Sino-French Convention of Beijing was construed by French Catholics as lifting all restrictions on Catholics' right to buy and repossess as much as possible, some restrictions still applied.

10. In addition to the murders, only thirteen priests (out of about 175 who were living illegally in the Chinese interior) were arrested from 1844 to 1860.

11. Sichuansheng jindai jiaoanshi yanjiu hui (1987, 14); QMJA (vols. 1 and 2).

12. Newer scholarship brings together Chinese and Anglophone work in downplaying the arrival of Christian capitalism, insisting that it merely exacerbated preexisting local tensions; see Tiedemann (2008) and Sun (2011).

13. The eighteen characters read: 并任法国传教士在个省租买田地建造自便. Wei Qingxin was the first scholar to point out the discrepancy in the French and Chinese versions of Article 6 (1991, vol. 2, 590–91).

14. For decades there was an internal debate about whether Catholics could cultivate and traffic opium in China. While growing opium poppies was proscribed by the Society for the Propagation of the Faith in 1891, it doesn't appear that there was ever a ban on buying and selling. Finally, in 1909 the Propagation of the Faith gave the official OK to opium sales, declaring that it was not a violation of Church doctrine; see Young (2013, 273–74).

15. The JFMA file number for this is 1.6.1, 26-1-15 and there are 2 volumes; this report was filed in 1907.

16. One tael was worth roughly one ounce of gold.

17. Claude Prudhomme insists that scientific racism was endemic among European Catholics in China at this time (1994, 264).

18. The entire internal Chinese discussion of this can be found in JWJA (vol. 2, part 2, 1100–1103, 1117–38, 1142–58).

19. See also Qin (2006, 74), who used entirely different source material.

20. JFMA (file 1.6.1, 26–1-15). See also Taveirne 2004, 180.

21. On this see Chen (2010).

22. Zhang Li (1987) argues that 99.9 percent of Sichuanese couldn't distinguish Catholics from Protestants.

23. This US Protestant mission was at this time planning a second church right across the river from Eling, where they had bought a Daoist temple (BFO 228/829, November 6, 1886).

24. Wyman has a concise discussion of this (1993, 168–71).

25. I consulted Wyman's 1993 translation here (167).

26. The Canadian Methodist missionary Spencer Lewis was in Chongqing at this time and wrote that the news of white racial terror against Chinese "coolies" in the US was instrumental in the uprising (Lewis 1933).

27. The one I'm quoting from in Wang (1984) was based on the testimony of a resident of Longshui named Luo Fuchu.

28. The Dazu gazetteers claim that the local rebel Yu Daosheng turned traitor to get the reward money and lured Yu Dongchen to his house. The magistrate then "ambushed him [伏], tied him up with rope and threw him in jail" (DX 2:458).

29. Hu Qiwei (1986) identifies two probable authors: Zhou Ziting, the anti-Western dean of the local Changxiang Academy, and an itinerant Taoist priest, Zhou Zitang.

There was a strong possibility that Zhou Ziting had joined the GLH by this time and therefore would have been the likely author.

1. Kathryn Yusoff's (2018) work on properties has informed my thinking here.

2. My thinking has been influenced by the Marxist-feminist work of Anne McClintock (1995) and Linda Williams (1999).

3. The original French is from Loti (1920, 113).

3. QUEER PARENTING

1. News of Euro-white narcotrafficking in China was disseminated widely in Japan. Books on the First War for Drugs like Shionoya Tôin's 1846 *Ahen Ibun* and Satô Shinobu's 1849 *Suiriku senpôroku* were popular.

2. Genyôsha was an all-male group, although women were affiliates. Related to Genyôsha's early position on women, member Hanbusa Yasuo wrote a well-received book about the issue in 1889 that basically reflects the most enlightened attitudes of the time (GY #14, 3).

3. Takaba's physician father didn't seem to think it would be a problem to get his daughter respectably married off at sixteen. Forced to stop dressing as a man, they played the role of dutiful samurai wife for two years until gender conformity became too unbearable, resulting in a divorce.

4. The authoritative study of the samurai revolts in Japanese remains Gotô Yasushi's 1967 *Shizoku hanran no kenkyû*. In English, the most cited work is Stephen Vlastos, "Opposition Movements in Early Meiji," in Jansen (1989, 367–431).

5. This does not at all mean that most of the Satsuma and Choshu fighters were Fight the Whites! ideologues. What E. H. Norman called the "magical effect of bombardment" accelerated the Euro-Americanization of Satsuma's military and jump-started the pro-Western faction in Choshu (1940, 44). Despite this, many Satsuma and Choshu fighters retained aspects of the Fight the Whites! sensibility that had influenced educational and political environments in Japan since the 1850s.

6. The phrase comes from Japanese neo-Confucianism of the Tokugawa (1603–1868) period, although most often it appears separately as the binomes 公議 or 輿論. Like most elite discourse in the Tokugawa period, these binomes originated in the Song (960–1279) period Confucianism of Zhu Xi; see de Bary and Bloom (1999, vol. 1, 639–41).

7. The authoritative study of this is by Tanaka (2002).

8. Although Gotô spoke in favor of flattening the caste/status system, Itagaki was the most strident in calling for the destruction of the samurai. For his statements on this, see JTS (vol. 1, 27–33).

9. Irokawa (1985) and Gotô (1972) warn readers not to inflate the importance of this proposal, arguing that it was never meant as a call for universal franchise.

10. The European word "right" (and *regt*, *droit*, or *Recht*) was translated into Japanese by Fukuzawa Yukichi as 通義, and by Katô Hiroyuki as 権理. The authors here are

combining both of these renderings. The phrase "endowed by heaven [天賦]" was an early construal for "natural right"; see on this the work of Thomas (2002) and Howland (2002).

11. Gotô Yasushi was the first to invert the "peace" and "war" parties (1972, 18).

12. Môri Toshihiko's groundbreaking 1978 book led to a controversial debate and argument with the historian Tamura Sadao in the 1980s. Môri's first point is the controversial one that claims that although Saigô clearly wanted to lead a mission to Korea, his intention was for this to be peaceful and diplomatic. This position is endorsed wholeheartedly by Charles Yates (1995) and, less enthusiastically, by Mark Ravina (2004). Recent Japanese scholarship by Iechika (2011) and Kimura (2010) continues to oppose Môri's first intervention. Môri's second point has become widely accepted: rather than focusing on the opposed positions among the oligarchs of a focus on domestic (内政) or foreign (外政) problems, what is more important is the brute struggle for power between Ôkubo on one side and Etô (with Saigô and Itagaki) on the other. After reading through Saigô's letters from the fall of 1873, I second Yates and Môri in arguing that a fairly strong case can be made that Saigô did not want a military confrontation with the weaker Korea.

13. For details on the torture see Tôyama (1977).

14. The capital punishment sentence was rescinded for all but two of Takaba's students through the intervention of a Home Ministry assistant, Hayashi Tomoyuki.

15. Genyôsha researchers question the veracity of this pledge, surmising that it was written by one of Ôkubo's agents provocateurs as justification to the Fukuoka mayor who opposed the preemptive incarcerations; see Nagahata (1997, 104).

16. The coalition that fought with Saigô consisted of romantic egalitarians, enraged samurai who wanted mere vengeance against the corrupt oligarchs, progressive samurai groups like the Kyôdôtai who were actively involved in the APR movement, and staunch conservatives who wanted the status of the samurai restored. They were all united under the slogan of "new politics, virtuous government." Several of the marching songs and manifestos of the Satsuma Rebellion are included in volume 6 of SNKD and express disdain for white Euro-Americans.

17. The oligarchs didn't outlaw torture until the fall of 1879 (Tezuka 1986, vol. 3, 3–38). Reports of lacerated backs for all the Fukuoka rebels in SNDK indicate that, at the very least, flogging was routine. Ikawa and Kobayashi write that it was also common for the Fukuoka rebels to be hung upside down for flogging, which continued until they lost consciousness (2006, 41).

18. Mikiso Hane writes that 81 percent of all government revenue came from land taxes in the 1875–79 period, while over 85 percent came from these taxes between 1882 and 1892 (1982, 17).

19. The letter is reprinted in Ichikawa (1980, 102–3).

20. As Ueki was the rare APR intellectual to discuss women's rights, this made the visibility of women like Kusunose and Kishida all the more important. For more on this, see Sievers (1983, 28–29) and Sotazaki (1989, 72), who argue that Ueki's draft constitution of 1881 was the only one in Japan that guaranteed equality between men and women.

21. Ôki Motoko insists that although Kusunose was a popular presence at APR events for several years, she never gave public speeches herself (2003, 38–40).

22. Robert Stolz reveals this oligarch plan (2014, 90).

23. The best essay on Ueki is Julia Adeney Thomas's "Ueki Emori: Singing the Body Electric" (2002). The most recent study of Ueki by Nakamura Katsuaki (2012) reveals how thoroughly antimilitary he was.

24. The information about Katô comes from Kim (2007, 264).

25. This piece was published in Fukuoka in April 1878.

26. I'm disagreeing with Roger Bowen's (1980) fine analysis of Ueki solely on this point.

27. And, as Howland himself argues in his book on the reception of J. S. Mill's *On Liberty* in East Asia, the Japanese translator Nakamura Keiu refused to completely endorse the liberal capitalist individual (2005, 81).

28. I've benefited from the fine translation of this chapter by Katsuya Hirano in *From Japan's Modernity* (2002, 49–52).

29. This resulted in the UPF's voting rights being suspended at the Patriot Society conferences. Hakoda responded to this by creating a "dummy" group that had full voting rights.

30. The Fukuoka Provincial Library (FKT) has the largest collection of Genyôsha-related primary materials in Japan, including the material from the Genyôsha Kinenkan, which closed in 2008. These two memorials have been classified according to the name of the collector, and this collection is called "Itô." These documents can be found on roll 34, 1664. Ishitaki Toyomi includes one of them in an appendix to his 2010 book (373–82).

31. They are referencing the Charter Oath of April 1869 and the 1875 Meiji emperor's edict promising a parliament.

32. Compared to the sampling of memorials from 1879, '80, and '81 included in the book edited by Haraguchi (1956), the Fukuoka proposal doesn't stand out for its emphasis on the CO_2lonial situation facing Japan.

33. This is from the Fukuoka Provincial Library Genyôsha collection, and is roll 12, 139.

4. LEVELRY AND REVELRY (INSIDE THE GELAOHUI OPIUM ROOM)

1. These memorials are from the *Gongzhongdang Guangxu chao zouzhe*, abbreviated as GGZ.

2. The Ming were much more expert at this than the Qing, as the record for slices while keeping the victim alive was 3,335. During the Qing period, the average plummeted to between twenty and thirty slices; 百度百科. accessed June 22, 2018.

3. Jacobson highlights the number of ex-convicts and escapees from prison in GLH lodges (1993, 130).

4. This was a GLH leader and heavy opium smoker from north of Chengdu who is featured in Li Jieren's trilogy (Li 2012a). Also see the 2015 translation of one of these novels, *Ripples on Stagnant Water*, by Bret Sparling and Yin Chi.

5. Other sources at this time identify *The Ocean Depths* as the central GLH text; see Japanese Foreign Ministry Archive's "Investigative Reports on Chinese Revolutionary Groups"" (cited as JFMA, "Chinese Revolutionaries"), 289. The Japanese Foreign Ministry Archive citation for this is 1.6.1, 4–2-1. There are three large volumes here, but

the page numbers consecutively link the volumes. The five named authors, Yamada Yûji, Endô Yasuo, Mitsuura Shin, Nishimoto Shôzô, and Yamaguchi Noberu, all have different styles and investigate the GLH and other underground groups in different parts of China.

6. In 1848 the Sichuanese *juren* Guo Yongtai claimed to have found the original copy of the most important collection of rituals for the rebel brotherhoods, the *True Record of Golden Terrace Mountain*. He edited and reissued the text as 海底 (*Haidi*) because a rumor held that *True Record* was sealed in an iron box and thrown into the bottom of the ocean (海底) to protect it from Qing soldiers when they conquered Taiwan in 1683.

7. I am basing this section on information condensed from Qunying she (1975), Liu (1983), and Wang (2018). Many GLH lodges were also divided into "black" and "red" groups, but space does not allow me to elaborate on that here.

8. The popularity of the historical novel *Romance of the Three Kingdoms* by Luo Guanzhong (published in the fourteenth century) turned out to be excellent posthumous press for Liu Bei, whose fictional double is superhumanly kind and wise.

9. I'm not at all suggesting that the GLH were friends of women. In fact, there's no doubt that they were involved in procuring women for sex work, although this was a minor GLH activity during the late Qing period that unfortunately became more prominent after the 1911 Revolution.

10. At the entrance to one of the main tourist sites in Chongqing, the Hongyadong, there was until summer 2018 a life-size sculpture of Sichuanese river pirates undertaking a leveling operation.

11. For example, the rebel outlaws in *Tales from the Water Margins* lived in the mountains, and mountains were thought to be home to many deities. Also, most rebel brotherhoods thought that one could only arrive at the paradisiacal grotto of the afterlife via mountains (ter Haar 1998, 97).

12. The JFMA archive file number for this is 1.6.1 4–2-1-1, vol. 2.

13. Qin Heping writes that Qing officials in Sichuan understood that the GLH monopolized opium room (but not the upscale parlor) businesses, but were incapable of doing anything to stop it. This was both because the GLH tended to have lots of local support and because the opium rooms served a crucial function as popular sites of rest and relaxation. Local officials also needed the license fees and taxes paid by the opium rooms. In 1894 an opium room was discovered to have been used to ritually open a new GLH lodge (Qin 2001, 70–72).

14. These are all lunar calendar dates.

15. Qing officials in Sichuan often designated the GLH with the characters 党匪 or 会匪 (outlaw society) and nonbrotherhood redistributionist groups as 土匪 (thieves) (Zhengxie Sichuan yanjiu weiyuanhui 1981, 49).

INTERTEXT II: *MADAME BUTTERFLY* AND "NEGRO METHODS" IN CHINA

1. I have consulted Mark Anderson's (2009) work to help me frame *Butterfly*.

2. Ronald T. Takaki (2000) similarly describes how Chinese in the US were subjected to "Negroization" in the 1870s and 1880s.

3. Kim Stanley Robinson used the Wagnerian phrase in his keynote lecture to the World-Ecology annual conference in San Francisco on May 31, 2019.

5. LAST SAMURAI/FIRST EXTRACTIVE CAPITALIST

1. In 1885 there was a push to expand again the resources for these detectives; see Obinata and Yui (1990, 397).

2. Kimura (1967, vol. 14, back cover). This is an October 1880 pamphlet called "Spotlight on the Meiji People's Rights Leaders," in which the main western Japanese personages are ranked in order of importance, with Itagaki in first place and Hakoda in second.

3. Stolz (2014), Kim (2007), Irokawa (1985), and Bowen (1980) don't ignore the impact on the APR movement.

4. On the breakneck speed of Matsukata's shock, see Muroyama (2004, 173–234).

5. The national land tax was fixed in 1873, which worked out to between 30 and 40 percent of a family's yield going to national and local taxes.

6. Genyôsha researchers can't ascertain when this meeting took place. I'm fairly certain it was closer to be the beginning of November, as this visit to Tokyo would have been connected to Tôyama going to plead with the young Genyôsha activists in Tokyo to not participate in the Osaka Incident.

7. This is all taken from Sugiyama's two long memoirs, published in 1926 and 1929.

8. A similar version appears three years later in Sugiyama's 1929 memoir (2006b, 120–21).

9. The main sources for this are Matsuo (1982), Hirano (1988), and Machida Shiritsu Jiyū Minken Shiryôkan (2000).

10. All the citations from the trial are taken from the 1887 coverage in the *Osaka Nippô* newspaper (morning and evening editions), collected in volume 1 of Matsuo and Matsuo (1985).

11. Matsuo Teiko argues that the overall feeling toward Chinese people among the LPR leaders who weren't connected to the Osaka Incident was one of solidarity, which didn't change significantly even after the Gapsin coup of December 1884; see Matsuo (1982, 251–53).

12. I've benefited from the excellent readings of this novel by John Mertz (2003) and Atsuko Ueda (2007).

13. This should be contrasted with Hakoda who fought in the Boshin War to restore the Emperor Meiji to the throne at the age of sixteen and was a combatant in two of the uprisings in southwestern Japan of 1876.

14. Muroi Hiroichi explains that 鉄山師 was used derisively in Kyushu at this time, referencing both the capitalist conglomerates Mitsubishi and Mitsui and the Tokyo oligarchs involved in capitalist extraction (1985, 2).

15. Yoshida Toshio's 1912 book on Tôyama was the first serious study of him. This was followed by the journalist Hirai Banson's *Tôyama Mitsuru to Genyôsha monogatari* in 1914, which pulled very few punches in its depiction of Genyôsha's de facto leader. Responding to these critiques of Tôyama, Genyôsha published its own history in 1919.

16. *Fukuryô Shimpô* of August 1, 1890 mentions the "struggle [闘争]" between Tôyama and Fujita Densaburô from Osaka for extraction licenses in a mountain area north of Fukuoka.

17. The most comprehensive treatment of the coal business in northern Kyushu is that of Nishi Nihon (1982b).

18. Jacques Rancière describes similar ways in which French workers denounced the Paris Exposition of 1867 as just another way to dispossess them (2011, 64–88).

6. BLOW(OPIUM SMOKE)BACK: THE THIRD WAR FOR DRUGS IN SICHUAN

1. The JFMA file number for this is 1.6.1, 26–1-15, and there are two volumes.

2. Spence would have been more surprised that by the late 1890s the only appearance of British opium in the hundred or so "opium crime" cases written up by the Chongqing (Baxian) magistrates from 1890 to 1900 was limited to its stronger potency, making it perfect for the three suicides and one poisoning; see inter alia SPA (34–07882, 34–07878, 34–07839, 34–07810).

3. Opium chests were actually measured in piculs in China, with one picul = 133.3 pounds. British chests weighed 140 pounds, but opium tended to dry and become lighter as it aged.

4. Zheng (2005, 101–2).

5. The scholar with the best grasp of the Chinese sources, Li Xiaoxiong, insists that in Sichuan there were "no direct taxes on poppy growers" until the New Policy campaign began in 1903 (Li 2009, 46).

6. Of course, peasant producers are in the most important sense alienated from the land, as the great majority of it was owned by wealthy landlords.

7. "Cash" were copper coins.

8. The US missionary Frank Gamewell wrote in 1887 that Chongqing opium rooms normally charged 16 cash for the standard 2.25 grams of processed opium (Gamewell 1888, 36).

9. I've been inspired here by Richard Newman's (1995) groundbreaking attempt to quantify opium consumption in the late Qing period.

10. A missionary study of doctors' views of opium in China in the 1890s detailed the surprising reach of smoking to women (Park 1899). Zheng Yangwen has focused attention on the phenomenon of women smokers (2005, 116–30).

11. The file number is 1.6.1 4–2-1-1.

12. Although I haven't been able to locate much data, this situation appears to have been similar for Chinese converts to Catholicism in Sichuan who took advantage of the morphine-based medicines dispensed liberally and freely (Piolet 1901, 316–17).

13. Right at the beginning of Li Jieren's 1936 novel *Dabo* about prerevolutionary Chengdu, Sichuan, there is a scene where the male friends Huang Lanshen and Wang Wenbing are reminiscing about the homoerotic sex they had when they were younger. At least in this context, 耍 (shua) meant "queer sex play" (Li 2012b, 5). In Li's 1938 novel *Sishui weilan*, 耍 signifies both hetero- and homoeroticism. *Sishui weilan* also features a primarily homoerotic GLH man.

14. I have benefited from Stapleton's discussion of workhouses in Chengdu (2000, 126–29).

15. The Japanese for this is 清国革命動乱に関する情報, and the JFMA file number is 1.6.1, 46–1.

16. In her monograph on opium politics in Fujian province, Joyce Madancy found that opium smokers there also used tobacco pipes to avoid detection (2003, 158–59).

17. This QQ member posing as Mistress Celebrate (小三庆) exaggerates the centrality of the fool role somewhat. Anecdotally, among the thirty or so Sichuan operas I have seen performed in Chongqing and Chengdu over the last eight years, roughly one-third have featured a version of the fool.

CONCLUSION

1. I am using the final edition of *Book of Vengeance*, published in 1918.

Works Cited

ARCHIVES AND REFERENCE SOURCES WITH ABBREVIATIONS

Annales de la propagation de la foi [Annual Report of the Propagation of the Faith]. 1828–1912. Vols. 3–84. Lyon and Paris. Cited as APF.

Fujimoto Naonori. 1931 [1922]. *Kyojin Tōyama Mitsuru Ō* [The Great Tōyama Mitsuru]. Tokyo: Yamazuisha Shobō. Cited as KTM.

Fukuokaken Toshōkan [Fukuoka Provincial Library]. Cited as FKT.

Genyōsha [Newsletter published by the Genyōsha kinenkan]. 1979–2001. Fukuoka. Cited as GY.

Genyōsha shashi [Genyōsha company history]. 1992. [1919]. Edited by Genyōsha shashi hensankai. Tokyo: Ashi Shobō. Cited as GYSS.

Gongzhongdang Guangxu chao zouzhe [Guanxu period memorials in the Palace museum archive]. 1973. 11 vols. Taibei: Guoli Gugong Bowuyuan. Cited as GGZ.

Japanese Government Documents. 1979. 2 vols. Edited by W. W. McLaren. Washington, DC: University Publications of America. Cited as JGD.

Jiaowu jiaoan dang [Archive of Christian affairs and anti-Christian conflicts]. 1974–80. 7 vols. Taibei: Zhongyang Yonjiuyuan. Cited as JWJA.

Jiyūtō shi [A History of the Liberal Party]. 1955. 3 vols. Tokyo: Aoki Shoten. Cited as JTS.

Jindaishi Yanjiusue. National Archives and Records Administration, Washington, DC. Cited as NARA.

Nihon Gaikō Bunsho [Diplomatic Archives of the Ministry of Foreign Affairs of Japan]. Cited as NGB.

Nihon Gaikō Shiryōkan [Japanese Foreign Ministry Archive]. Cited as JFMA.

Qingmo jiaoan [Anti-Christian incidents during the late Qing period]. 1996–2000. 5 vols. Edited by Fujian shifan daxue lishi xi. Beijing: Zhonghua Shuju. Cited as QMJA.

Records of the Imperial Maritime Customs Service of China (1854–1949). 1971. Farmington Hills, MI: Gale. Cited as RIMC.

Seinan Kiden [Remarkable Stories of Southwest Japan]. 1908–11. 6 vols. Edited by Kuzuu Yoshihisa. Tokyo: Kokuryūkai Honbu. Cited as SNKD.

Sichuan Dangan Guan, Baxian ziliao [Sichuan Provincial Archive in Chengdu, Baxian materials]. Cited as SPA.

Sichuan jiaoan yu Yihequan dangan [Archive of anti-Christian incidents and the Boxers in Sichuan]. 1985. Edited by Sichuansheng Dangan Guan. Chengdu: Sichuan Renmin Chubanshe. Cited as SJYD.

West China Missionary News (Published in Chengdu, Sichuan). Cited as WCMN.

Yumeno Kyûsaku. 1992 [1936]. *Kinsei kaijin den* [Stories of Eccentric Early Modern Heroes]. Vol. 11 of *Yumeno Kyûsaku zenshu*. Tokyo: Chikuma. Cited as KKD.

BOOKS AND ARTICLES

Adamson, Rebecca. 2017. "Vulnerabilities of Women in Extractive Industries." *ANTYA-JAA: Indian Journal of Women and Social Change* 2, no. 1: 24–31.

Adshead, S. A. M. 1966. "The Opium Trade in Szechwan 1881 to 1911." *Journal of Southeast Asian Studies* 6, no. 2 (September), 93–99.

Adshead, S. A. M. 1984. *Province and Politics in Late Imperial China: Viceregal Government in Szechuan, 1898–1911*. London: Curzon.

Ahuja, Ravi. 2009. "Networks of Subordination—Networks of the Subordinated: The Ordered Spaces of South Asian Maritime Labour in an Age of Imperialism." In *The Limits of British Colonial Control in South Asia*, edited by Harald Fischer-Tiné, 13–48. London: Abingdon.

Aizawa Seishisai. 1931 [1858]. "Shinron." In *Nihon shisô tôsô shiryô*, edited by Washio Junkei, 445–522. Tokyo: Tôhô Shoin.

Alcock, Rutherford B. 1863. *The Capital of the Tycoon*. 2 vols. London: Longman & Green.

Alexander, Michelle. 2010. *The New Jim Crow: Mass Incarceration in the Age of Colorblindness*. New York: New Press.

Anderson, Carol. 2017. *White Rage: The Unspoken Truth of Our Racial Divide*. New York: Bloomsbury.

Anderson, Mark. 2009. *Japan and the Specter of Imperialism*. New York: Palgrave McMillan.

Andô Seiichi. 1992. *Kinsei kôgaishi no kenkyû*. Tokyo: Yoshikawa Kôbunkan.

Andreas, Peter. 2020 *Killer High: A History of War in Six Drugs*. Oxford: Oxford University Press.

Antrobus, H. A. 1957. *A History of the Assam Company, 1839–1953*. Edinburgh: T. and A. Constable.

Arano Yasunari and Ishii Masatoshi, eds. 2010. *Kindaika suru nihon*. Tokyo: Yoshikawa Bunkan.

Arboleda, Martin. 2020. *Planetary Mine: Territories of Extraction Under Late Capitalism*. New York: Verso.

Arnold, David. 2000. *Science, Technology and Medicine in Colonial India*. Cambridge: Cambridge University Press.

Ashizu Uzuhiko. 1984. *Daiajiashugi to Tôyama Mitsuru* (DTTM). Tokyo: Nihon Kyōbunsha.

Azumi, Kyôko. 2012. *"Sôchin" no nabi to Xinhai kakumei*. Tokyo: Hakusuisha.

Baptist, Edward. 2014. *The Half Has Never Been Told: Slavery and the Making of American Capitalism*. New York: Basic Books.

Barad, Karen. 2007. *Meeting the Universe Halfway*. Durham, NC: Duke University Press.

Barr, Pat. 1968. *The Deer Cry Pavilion: A Story of Westerners in Japan, 1868–1905*. New York: Harcourt, Brace and World.

Bauer, Rolph. 2019. *The Peasant Production of Opium in Nineteenth-Century India*. Leiden: Brill.

Beasley, W. G. 1955. *The Perry Mission to Japan*. Oxford: Oxford University Press.

Beasley, W. G. 1972. *The Meiji Restoration*. Stanford, CA: Stanford University Press.

Beijing shifan daxue lishi xi. 1985. *Xinhai Geming qian shi nianjian minbian dang'an shiliao*, vol. 2. Beijing: Zhonghua Shuju.

Beller, Jonathan. 2017. *The Message Is Murder: Substrates of Computational Capital*. London: Pluto.

Bello, David A. 2016. *Across Forest, Steppe, and Mountain: Environment, Identity, and Empire in Qing China's Borderlands*. Cambridge: Cambridge University Press.

Benjamin, Walter. 1969. *Illuminations: Essays and Reflections*. Translated by Harry Zohn. New York: Schocken.

Bennett, Jane. 2010. *Vibrant Matter: A Political Ecology of Things*. Durham, NC: Duke University Press.

Bernasconi, Robert, ed. 2003. *Race and Racism in Continental Philosophy*. Bloomington: Indiana University Press.

Bernstein, Richard. 2009. *The East, the West, and Sex*. New York: Alfred Knopf.

Bickers, Robert. 1999. *Britain in China: Community Culture and Colonialism, 1900–1949*. New York: St. Martins.

Bickers, Robert. 2011. *The Scramble for China: Foreign Devils in the Qing Empire, 1832–1914*. London: Allen Lane.

Bickers, Robert. 2012. "The Foreign Inspectorate of the Chinese Maritime Customs." In *Twentieth-Century Colonialism and China*, edited by Bryna Goodman and David S. G. Goodman. New York: Routledge.

Birkett, Paul. 2014. *Marx and Nature: A Red and Green Perspective*. London: Verso.

Bishop, Isabella. 1972. *The Yangtze Valley and Beyond*. Taibei: Cheng Wen.

Black, John R. 1880. *Young Japan*. 2 vols. London: Trubner.

Blaser, Mario. 2010. *Storytelling Globalization from the Chaco and Beyond*. Durham, NC: Duke University Press.

Blaser, Mario, and Marisol de la Cadena, eds. 2018. *A World of Many Worlds*. Durham, NC: Duke University Press.

Bloch, Ernst. 1986. *The Principle of Hope*. Translated by Neville Plaice, Stephen Plaice, and Paul Knight. Boston: MIT Press.

Blue, Gregory. 2000. "Opium for China." In *Opium Regimes: China, Britain, and Japan, 1839–1952*, edited by Timothy Brook and Bob Wakabayashi, 31–54. Berkeley: University of California Press.

Blumenbach, Johann Friedrich. 1795. *De generis humani varietate nativa* [On the Natural Variety of Mankind]. 3rd edition. Gottingen: Vandenhoeck & Ruprecht.

Blussé, Leonard, and Harriet T. Zurndorfer, eds. 1993. *Conflict and Accommodation in Early Modern East Asia*. Leiden: E. J. Brill.

Boell, Paul. 1899. *Le protectorat des missions catholiques en Chine et la politique de la France en extrême-orient*. Paris: Institut Scientifique de la Libre-Pensée.

Bonneuil, Christophe, and J. B. Fressoz. 2017. *The Shock of the Anthropocene*. London: Verso.

Botsman, Dani. 2005. *Power and Punishment in the Making of Modern Japan*. Princeton, NJ: Princeton University Press.

Bourne, F. S. A. 1898. *Report of the Mission to China of the Blackburn Chamber of Commerce, 1896–7*. Blackburn: North-East Lancashire Press.

Bowen, Roger R. 1980. *Rebellion and Democracy in Meiji Japan: A Study of Commoners in the Popular Rights Movement*. Berkeley: University of California Press.

Bowler, Peter J. 1983. *The Eclipse of Darwinism: Anti-Darwinian Evolution Theories in the Decades around 1900*. Baltimore: Johns Hopkins University Press.

Bressan, David. 2012. "Namazu the Earthshaker." *Scientific American*, March 10.

British Foreign Office (BFO). 1908. *Correspondence Respecting the Opium Question in China*. London: Harrison and Sons.

British Foreign Office. 1974. *The Opium Trade, 1910–1941*. 5 vols. Wilmington, DE: Scholarly Resources.

British Foreign Office. 2012a. *Correspondence Respecting Anti-Foreign Riots in China, 1891*. London: Ulan.

British Foreign Office. 2012b. *Further Correspondence Respecting Anti-Foreign Riots in China, 1891*. London: Nabu.

British Parliamentary Papers (BPP). 1859. *Correspondence Relative to the Earl of Elgin's Special Missions to China and Japan, 1857–1859*. London.

British Parliamentary Papers. 1894. *First Report of Royal Commission on Opium with Minutes of Evidence and Appendices*. London.

British Parliamentary Papers. 1896. *Report of Royal Commission on Opium*. 7 vols. London.

British Parliamentary Papers. 1912. *Report of the British Delegates to the International Opium Conference Held at The Hague*. London.

British Parliamentary Papers. 1971. *Correspondence, Dispatches and Other Papers Respecting Western China, 1864–98*. Shannon: Irish University Press.

Brook, Timothy, and Bob Wakabayashi, eds. 2000. *Opium Regimes: China, Britain, and Japan, 1839–1952*. Berkeley: University of California Press.

Brown, Arthur J. 1904. *New Forces in Old China: An Unwelcome but Inevitable Awakening*. New York: F. H. Revell.

Bruner, Katherine F., and John K. Fairbank, eds. 1986. *Entering China's Service: Robert Hart's Journals, 1854–1863*. Cambridge, MA: Harvard University Press.

Bryant, Levi R. 2011. *The Democracy of Objects*. New York: Open Humanities.

Buck-Morss, Susan. 2009. *Hegel, Haiti, and Universal History*. Pittsburgh: University of Pittsburgh Press.

Bulfoni, Clara and Pozzi, Anna. 2003. *Lost China: The Photographs of Leone Nani*. Milan: Skira.

Burke-Gaffney, Brian. 2004. *Starcrossed: A Biography of Madame Butterfly*. London: EastBridge.

Burkett, Paul. 1999. *Marx and Nature: A Red and Green Perspective*. New York: St. Martins.

Cain, P. J., and A. G. Hopkins. 1993. *British Imperialism*. 2 vols. New York: Longman.

Cai Shaoqing. 1987. *Zhongguo jindai huidangshi yanjiu*. Beijing: Zhonghua Shuju.

Carlson, Ellsworth. 1971. *The Kaiping Mines, 1877–1912*. Cambridge, MA: Harvard University Press.

Carter, Marina. 1995. *Servants, Sirdars and Settlers: Indians in Mauritius, 1834–1874*. New York: Oxford University Press.

Casey, Bart. 2015. *The Double Life of Laurence Oliphant: Victorian Pilgrim and Prophet*. New York: Post Hill.

Cassel, Par Kristoffer. 2012. *Grounds of Judgment: Extraterritoriality and Imperial Power in Nineteenth Century China and Japan*. Oxford: Oxford University Press.

Césaire, Aimé. 2000. *Discourse on Colonialism*. New York: Monthly Review.

Chakraborty, Gorky. 2012. "Roots and Ramifications of a Colonial 'Construct': The Wastelands in Assam." Occasional Papers #39, 1–32. Kolkata: Institute of Development Studies.

Changjiang Liuyu Guihua Bangongshi, ed. 1979. *Changjiang shuili shilue*. Beijing: Shuili Dianli Chubanshe.

Checkland, Olive. 1989. *Britain's Encounter with Meiji Japan, 1868–1912*. London: Macmillan.

Checkland, Olive, and Sydney Checkland. 1984. "British and Japanese Economic Interaction under the Early Meiji: The Takashima Coal Mine 1868–88." *Business History* 26, no. 2: 139–55.

Checkland, Sydney. 1988. *The Elgins 1766–1917: A Tale of Aristocrats, Proconsuls and Their Wives*. Aberdeen, UK: Aberdeen University Press.

Chen, Janet Y. 2012. *Guilty of Indigence: The Urban Poor in China, 1900–1953*. Princeton, NJ: Princeton University Press.

Chen, Mel Y. 2012. *Animacies: Biopolitics, Racial Mattering, and Queer Affect*. Durham, NC: Duke University Press.

Chen Shiqi. 2002. *Zhongguo jindai haiguanshi*. Beijing: Renmin Chubanshe.

Chen Shisong, ed. 2010. *Sichuan tongshi*, vol. 6. Chengdu: Sichuan Renmin Chubanshe.

Chen Yinkun. 1991. *Qingji minjiao chongtu de lianghua fenxi (1860–1899)*. Taibei: Taiwan Shangwu Yinshuguan.

Chesneaux, Jean, ed. 1972. *Popular Movements and Secret Societies in China, 1840–1950*. Stanford, CA: Stanford University Press.

Chichibu Jiken Kenkyūkai. 2004. *Chichibu Jiken: assei o henjite jiyū no sekai o*. Tokyo: Shin Nihon Shuppansha.

Christopher, Emma, Cassandra Pybus, and Marcus Rediker. 2007. *Many Middle Passages: Forced Migration and the Making of the Modern World*. Berkeley: University of California Press.

Chuchiak, John. 2007. "Secrets behind the Screen: Solicitantes in the Colonial Diocese of Yucatan and the Yucatec Maya, 1570–1785." In *Religion in New Spain*, edited by Susan Schroeder and Stafford Poole, 83–110. Albuquerque: University of New Mexico Press.

Chung-ying Cheng. 2010. "On Internal Onto-Genesis of Virtuous Actions in the Wu xing pian." *Journal of Chinese Philosophy* 37, no. S1: 142–58.

Clammer, John, and Sylvie Poirier. 2004. *Figured Worlds*. Toronto: University of Toronto Press.

Clark, Douglas. 2017. *Justice by Gunboat*. Hong Kong: Earnshaw.

Clinton, Maggie. 2017. *Revolutionary Nativism: Fascism and Culture in China, 1925–1937*. Durham, NC: Duke University Press.

Coaldrake, William H. 1996. *Architecture and Authority in Japan*. New York: Routledge.

Coates, P. D. 1988. *The China Consuls*. Oxford: Oxford University Press.

Coble, Parks M. 1991. *Robert Hart and China's Early Modernization: His Journals, 1863–1866*. Cambridge, MA: Harvard University Asia Center.

Cohen, Paul. 1963. *China and Christianity: The Missionary Movement and the Growth of Chinese Antiforeignism, 1860–1870*. Cambridge, MA: Harvard University Press.

Comaroff, Jean, and John Comaroff. 1986. "Christianity and Colonialism in South Africa." *American Ethnologist* 13, no. 1: 1–22.

Cortazzi, Hugh. 1985. "Britain and Japan: Did the Diplomats Make Any Difference?" *Asian Affairs* 36, no. 1: 54–66.

Cortazzi, Hugh. 1987. *Victorians in Japan: In and around the Treaty Ports*. London: Athlone.

Cortazzi, Hugh, ed. 2003. *Mitford's Japan: Memories and Recollections, 1866–1906*. New York: Routledge.

Cortazzi, Hugh. 2008. *Britain and the "Re-Opening" of Japan*. London: Japan Society.

Coulthard, Glen Sean. 2013. "For Our Nations to Live, Capitalism Must Die." *Unsettling America*, November 5.

Coulthard, Glen Sean. 2014. *Red Skin, White Masks: Rejecting the Colonial Politics of Recognition*. Minneapolis: University of Minnesota Press.

Cunningham, Alfred. 1895. *A History of the Szechuen Riots*. Shanghai: Shanghai Mercury News.

da Cunha, Dilip. 2019. *The Invention of Rivers: Alexander's Eye and Ganga's Descent*. Philadelphia: University of Pennsylvania Press.

Daggett, Cara. 2019. *The Birth of Energy: Fossil Fuels, Thermodynamics, and the Politics of Work*. Durham, NC: Duke University Press.

Dai Zhili, ed. 1994. *Sichuan baolu yundong shiliao*. Taibei: Zhongyang Yanjiu Jindaishi Yanjiusuo.

Daniels, Gordon. 1996. *Sir Harry Parkes: British Representative in Japan 1865–83*. Abingdon, UK: Routledge.

Dardess, Margaret Beckerman. 1973. "The Thought and Politics of Nakae Chomin (1847–1901)." PhD dissertation, Columbia University.

Davis, Fei-ling. 1977. *Primitive Revolutionaries of China*. Honolulu: University of Hawai'i Press.

Davis, Mike. 2002. *Late Victorian Holocausts: El Niño and the Making of the Third World*. London: Verso.

de Bary, Theodore, and Irene Bloom. 1999. *Sources of Chinese Tradition*, 2nd ed. New York: Columbia University Press.

De Fonblanque, E. B. 1863. *Niphon and Pe-chi-li*. London: Sanders, Otley.

de la Cadena, Marisol. 2015. *Earth Beings: Ecologies of Practice across Andean Worlds*. Durham, NC: Duke University Press.

Delgado, Jessica. 2018. *Laywomen and the Making of Colonial Catholicism in New Spain, 1630–1790*. Cambridge: Cambridge University Press.

Desmarais, Annette Aurélie. 2007. *La Vía Campesina: Globalization and the Power of Peasants*. New York: Fernwood.

DiAngelo, Robin. 2018. *White Fragility: Why It's So Hard for White People to Talk about Racism*. Boston: Beacon.

Di Giminiani, Piergiorgio. 2018. *Sentient Lands: Indigeneity, Property, and Political Imagination in Neoliberal Chile*. Tucson: University of Arizona Press.

Dikötter, Frank. 1992. *The Discourse of Race in Modern China*. London: Hurst.

Dikötter, Frank, with Lars Laaman and Zhou Xun. 2004. *Narcotic Culture*. Chicago: University of Chicago Press.

Doi Atsuko. 1988. *Amagakeru: Takaba Osamu*. Tokyo: Shinchôsha.

Down, John Langdon. 1866. "Observations on an Ethnic Classification of Idiots." *Clinical Lectures and Reports of the London Hospital* 3: 259–62.

Driscoll, Mark. 2004. "Idiorogi vs. Naizaisei" [Ideology vs. Immanence]. *Gendai Shisô* 1 (January): 33–51.

Driscoll, Mark. 2010. *Absolute Erotic, Absolute Grotesque*. Durham, NC: Duke University Press.

Du Bois, W. E. B. 1920. *Darkwater: Voices from Within the Veil*. New York: Harcourt, Brace and Co.

Du Bois, W. E. B. 1935. *Black Reconstruction in America, 1860–1880*. New York: Harcourt Brace.

Du Jianhua. 2009. *Chuanju jinghua*. Chengdu: Sichuan Chuban Jituan.

Dussel, Enrique. 1992. *1492: El encubrimiento del Otro*. Bogotá: Antropos.

Dussel, Enrique. 2008. *Twenty Theses on Politics*. Translated by George Ciccariello-Maher. Durham, NC: Duke University Press.

Dussel, Enrique. 2012. *Ethics of Liberation: In the Age of Globalization and Exclusion*. Edited by Alejandro A. Vallega. Durham, NC: Duke University Press.

Elgin, James. 1872. *Letters and Journals*. London: John Murray.

Elmore, H. M. 1802. *The British Mariner's Directory and Guide to the Trade and Navigation of the Indian and China Seas*. London: T. Bensley.

Elvin, Mark. 1998. "Who Was Responsible for the Weather? Moral Meteorology in Late-Imperial China." *Osiris* 13: 213–37.

Emura Eichi, ed. 1989. *Kenpô kôsô*. Tokyo: Iwanami Shoten.

Ericson, Steven. 2014. "The 'Matsukata Deflation' Reconsidered: Currency Contraction in a Global Depression, 1881–85." *Journal of Japanese Studies* 40, no. 1: 1–28.

Escobar, Arturo. 2018. *Designs for the Pluriverse*. Durham, NC: Duke University Press.

Escobar, Arturo. 2020. *Pluriversal Politics: The Real and the Possible*. Durham, NC: Duke University Press.

Esherick, Joseph W. 1987. *The Origins of the Boxer Uprising*. Berkeley: University of California Press.

Esherick, Joseph W. 2013. *China: How the Empire Fell*. New York: Routledge.

Etô Shinkichi. 2004. *Etô Shinkichi chosakushû*. 9 vols. Tokyo: Tôhô Shoten.

Eze, Emmanual Chukwudi. 1997. *Race and the Enlightenment: A Reader*. Boston: Wiley-Blackwell.

Fairbank, J. K., and K. F. Bruner, eds. 1975. *The I. G. in Peking: Letters of Robert Hart, Chinese Maritime Customs, 1868–1907*. Cambridge, MA: Belknap Press.

Fanon, Frantz. 1965. *A Dying Colonialism*. Translated by Haakon Chevalier. New York: Grove.

Fanon, Frantz. 1967. *Black Skin, White Masks*. Translated by Charles Lam Markmann. New York: Grove.

Fanon, Frantz. 1968a. *Toward the African Revolution*. Translated by Haakon Chevalier. New York: Grove.

Fanon, Frantz. 1968b. *The Wretched of the Earth*. Translated by Constance Farrington. New York: Grove.

Farooqui, Amar. 1998. *Smuggling as Subversion: Colonialism, Indian Merchants, and the Politics of Opium*. New Delhi: New Age International.

Farooqui, Amar. 2005. *Smuggling as Subversion: Colonialism, Indian Merchants, and the Politics of Opium, 1790–1843*. Lanham, MD: Lexington.

Fay, Peter Ward. 1975. *The Opium War, 1840–1842*. Chapel Hill: University of North Carolina Press.

Federici, Silvia. 2004. *Caliban and the Witch: Women, the Body, and Primitive Accumulation*. New York: Autonomedia.

Federici, Silvia. 2012. *Revolution at Point Zero: Housework, Reproduction, and Feminist Struggle*. Oakland: Common Notions/PM.

Feifer, George. 2006. *Breaking Open Japan*. New York: HarperCollins.

Felsing, Robert H. 1979. "The Heritage of the Han: The Gelaohui and the 1911 Revolution in Sichuan." PhD dissertation, University of Iowa.

Ferguson, Niall. 2011. *Civilization: The West and the Rest*. New York: Penguin.

Ferreira da Silva, Denise. 2007. *Toward a Global Idea of Race*. Minneapolis: University of Minnesota Press.

Finck, H. T. 1895. *Lost Time in Japan*. London: Laurence and Bullen.

Foster, J. B. 2000. *Marx's Ecology: Materialism and Nature*. New York: Monthly Review.

Foucault, Michel. 1990. *The History of Sexuality*, vol. 1: *An Introduction*. Translated by Robert Hurley. New York: Vintage.

Foucault, Michel. 2007. *Security, Territory, Population*. Translated by Graham Burchell. New York: Palgrave McMillan.

Foucault, Michel. 2008. *The Birth of Biopolitics: Lectures at the Collège de France, 1978–1979*. Translated by Graham Burchell. New York: Palgrave McMillan.

Four Arrows. 2016. "Is Standing Rock the Oil Industry's Last Stand? It's Up to Us to Make It So." *Truthout*, October 17. http://www.truth-out.org/opinion/item/38008. Accessed October 24, 2017.

Fox, Grace. 1969. *Britain and Japan 1858–1883*. Oxford: Clarendon.

Fu Chongju. 1909. *Chengdu tonglan*. Chengdu: Chengdu Tongsu Baoshe.

Fujimoto Naonori. 1967 [1920]. *Kyojin Tôyama Mitsuru*. Tokyo: Sekkasha.

Fukuoka-ken jimukyoku. 1952–60. *Shōsetsu Fukuoka-ken gikai shi.* 9 vols. Tokyo: Fukuoka-ken.

Fukushima Shingo and Hirano Yoshitaro. 1968. *Ôi Kentarô no kenkyû.* Nagoya: Fûbaisha.

Fuse Kenji. 2006. *Kakyû bushi to bakumatsu Meiji.* Tokyo: Iwata Shoin.

Gady, Franz-Stephan. 2015. "When Americans Ruled Beijing." *The Diplomat,* June 4. https://thediplomat.com/2015/06/when-americans-ruled-beijing/. Accessed July 12, 2018.

Gaimushô. 1969. *Gaimushô no hyakunen.* Tokyo: Hara Shobô. Cited as GSNH.

Gamewell, F. D. 1888. "From Shanghai into Western China." *Gospel in All Lands* 14 (January): 33–37.

Gardiner, Michael. 2007. *At the Edge of Empire: The Life of Thomas Glover.* Edinburgh: Birlinn.

Gerson, Jack. 1972. *Horatio Nelson Lay and Sino-British Relations.* Cambridge, MA: Harvard University Press.

Gibson, Rowland R. 1914. *Forces Mining and Undermining China.* New York: Century.

Gilroy, Paul. 2000. *Against Race: Imagining Political Culture beyond the Color Line.* Cambridge, MA: Belknap Press.

Goldsby, Jacqueline. 2006. *A Spectacular Secret: Lynching in American Life and Literature.* Chicago: University of Chicago Press.

Goldstein, Jonathan. 2011. *Stephen Girard's Trade with China, 1787–1824: The Norms versus the Profits of Trade.* Honolulu: University of Hawai'i Press.

Gong Pengcheng, ed. 2010. *Gaibian zhongguo lishi de wenxian.* Beijing: Zhongguo Gongren Chubanshe.

Gotô Yasushi. 1967. *Shizoku hanran no kenkyû.* Tokyo: Aoki Shoten.

Gotô Yasushi. 1969. "Meiji jûshichinen no gekka shojiken ni tsuite." In *Jiyû minken-ki no kenkyû,* vol. 2, edited by Horie Hideichi and Tôyama Shigeki, 205–69. Tokyo: Yûhikaku.

Gotô Yasushi. 1972. *Jiyû minken: Meiji no kakumei to hankakumei.* Tokyo: Chûkô Shinsho.

Graves, R. H. 1895. *Forty Years in China; Or, China in Transition.* Baltimore: R. H. Woodward.

Griffis, W. E. 1877. *The Mikado's Empire.* New York: Harper & Brothers.

Groenfeldt, David. 2013. *Water Ethics.* New York: Routledge.

Guha, Ranajit. 1983. *Elementary Aspects of Peasant Insurgency in Colonial India.* Delhi: Oxford University Press.

Guo Honghou, Chen Xishan, et al., eds. 1977. *Dazu xianzhi.* 2 vols. Taibei: Chengwen chubanshe. Cited as DX.

Guth, Christine M. E. 2004. *Longfellow's Tattoos: Tourism, Collecting, and Japan.* Seattle: University of Washington Press.

Hager, Thomas. 2019. *Ten Drugs: How Plants, Powders, and Pills Have Shaped the History of Medicine.* New York: Abrams.

Hamaya Masaki. 1984. *Kurofune to bakufu.* Tokyo: Kôbundo Shuppansha.

Hane Mikiso. 1982. *Peasants, Rebels and Outcastes: The Underside of Modern Japan.* New York: Pantheon.

Hanes, Travis W., and Frank Sanello. 2002. *The Opium Wars: The Addiction of One Empire and the Corruption of Another*. Naperville, IL: Sourcebooks.

Hani Goro. 1978. *Meiji Ishinshi kenkyū*. Tokyo: Iwanami Shoten.

Han Suyin. 1965. *The Crippled Tree*. New York: G. P. Putnam's Sons.

Hao Yenping. 1986. *The Commercial Revolution in Nineteenth Century China: The Rise of Sino-Western Mercantile Capitalism*. Berkeley: University of California Press.

Haraguchi Takaaki, ed. 1956. *Meiji jūsannen zenkoku kokkai kaisetsu genrōin kenpakusho shūsei*. Tokyo: Meiji Shiryô Kenkyû Renrakukai.

Haraway, Donna. 1988. "Situated Knowledges." *Feminist Studies* 14, no. 3: 575–99.

Haraway, Donna. 1991. *Simians, Cyborgs, and Women: The Reinvention of Nature*. New York: Routledge.

Haraway, Donna. 1997. *Modest_Witness@Second_Millennium. FemaleMan_Meets_Onco-Mouse: Feminism and Technoscience*. New York: Routledge.

Haraway, Donna. 2007. *When Species Meet*. Minneapolis: University of Minnesota Press.

Haraway, Donna, Noboru Ishikawa, Gilbert Scott, Kenneth Olwig, Anna L. Tsing, and Nils Bubandt. 2016. "Anthropologists Are Talking—About the Anthropocene." *Ethnos*, 81:3, 535–64.

Harman, Graham. 2002. *Tool-Being: Heidegger and the Metaphysics of Objects*. New York: Open Court.

Harman, Graham. 2005. *Guerrilla Metaphysics: Phenomenology and the Carpentry of Things*. New York: Open Court.

Harman, Graham. 2018. *Object-Oriented Ontology: A New Theory of Everything*. London: Penguin.

Harney, Stefano, and Fred Moten. 2013. *The Undercommons: Future Planning and Black Study*. New York: Semiotext.

Harootunian, Harry. 1970. *Toward Restoration*. Berkeley: University of California Press.

Harootunian, Harry. 2015. *Marx after Marx: History and Time in the Expansion of Capitalism*. New York: Columbia University Press.

Harrison, Henrietta. 2008. "'A Penny for the Little Chinese': The French Holy Childhood Association in China, 1843–1951." *American Historical Review* 113, no. 1: 72–92.

Harrison, Henrietta. 2013. *The Missionary's Curse and Other Tales from a Chinese Catholic Village*. Berkeley: University of California Press.

Hart, Evanston Ives. 1917. *Virgil C. Hart: Missionary Statesman*. New York: Hodder and Stoughton.

Hart, Virgil C. 1888. *Western China: A Journey to the Great Buddhist Center of Mount Omei*. Boston: Ticknor.

Hartman, Saidiya V. 1997. *Scenes of Subjection: Terror, Slavery, and Self-Making in Nineteenth-Century America*. Oxford: Oxford University Press.

Hartman, Saidiya V. 2007. *Lose Your Mother: A Journey along the Atlantic Slave Route*. New York: Farrar, Strauss, and Giroux.

Harvey, David. 2005. *The New Imperialism*. Oxford: Oxford University Press.

Hasegawa Yoshiki. 1974. *Tōyama Mitsuru hyōden: ningenko to shôgai*. Tokyo: Hara Shobô.

Hawkes, Francis. 1856. *Narrative of the Expedition of an American Squadron to the China Seas and Japan: Performed in the Years 1852, 1853, and 1854, under the Command of Commodore M. C. Perry*. Washington, DC: Beverly Tucker.

Hayes, Jack Patrick. 2019. "The Opium Wars in China." https://asiapacificcurriculum.ca/learning-module/opium-wars-china. Accessed March 3, 2019.

Heaver, Stuart. 2013. "Affairs of Our Hart." *Post Magazine*, November 9. https://www.scmp.com. Accessed August 6, 2016.

Heco, Joseph, and James Murdoch. 1892. *The Narrative of a Japanese*. 2 vols. Yokohama: Yokohama Printing.

Hedkte, C. H. 1968. "Reluctant Revolutionaries: Szechwan and the Qing Collapse, 1898–1911." PhD dissertation, University of California–Berkeley.

Hegel, G. W. F. 1956. *The Philosophy of History*. London: Dover.

Hegel, G. W. F. 1977. *The Phenomenology of Spirit*. Translated by A. V. Miller. Oxford: Oxford University Press.

Heidegger, Martin. 1977. *The Question Concerning Technology and Other Essays*. New York: Harper.

Hershatter, Gail. 1997. *Dangerous Pleasures: Prostitution and Modernity in Twentieth-Century Shanghai*. Berkeley: University of California Press.

Hesselink, Reiner. 1994. "The Assassination of Henry Heusken." *Monumenta Nipponica* 49, no. 3: 331–51.

Heusken, Henry. 1964. *Japan Journal*. Translated by Jeannette Van der Corput and Robert Wilson. New Brunswick, NJ: Rutgers University Press.

Hevia, James. 1995. *Cherishing Men from Afar: Qing Guest Ritual and the Macartney Embassy of 1793*. Durham, NC: Duke University Press.

Hevia, James. 2003. *English Lessons: The Pedagogy of Imperialism in Nineteenth-Century China*. Durham, NC: Duke University Press.

Hidemura Senzo. 1977. *Meiji zenki Hizen sekitan kogyo shiryô shu*. Tokyo: Bungei Shuppan.

Hirai Banson. 1987 [1914]. *Tôyama Mitsuru to Genyôsha monogatari*. 2 vols. Fukuoka: Ashi Shobô.

Hirano Kunio and Iida Hisao. 1974. *Fukuokaken no rekishi*. Tokyo: Yamakawa Shuppansha.

Hirano Yoshitaro. 1938. *Bajô Ôi Kentarô den*. Tokyo: Ōi Bajō Den Hensanbu.

Hirano Yoshitaro. 1988. *Ôi Kentarô*. Tokyo: Yoshikawa Kôbunkan.

Hoare, James. 1994. *Japan's Treaty Ports and Foreign Settlements: The Uninvited Guests, 1858–1899*. Folkestone, UK: Japan Library.

Hobsbawn, Eric. 1979. *The Age of Capital 1848–1875*. New York: New American Library.

Hobsbawn, Eric. 2000. *Bandits*. New York: New Press.

Ho Honwai. 2001. "Qingji guochan yapian de tongjuan yu tongshui." In *Xinhuoji: Chuantong yu jindai bianqian zhong de Zhongguo jingji*. Taibei xian Banqiao shi: Daoxiang Chubanshe.

Hori Masaaki. 2006. *Sugiyama Shigemaru: Ajia renpô no yume*. Tokyo: Genshoin.

Hornsby, Edmund. 1867. *Instructions to Her Majesty's Consular Officers in China and Japan on the Mode of Conducting Judicial Business*. Shanghai: A. H. De Carvalho.

Horowitz, Richard S. 2006. "Politics, Power and the Chinese Maritime Customs: The Qing Restoration and the Ascent of Robert Hart." *Modern Asian Studies* 40, no. 3: 549–81.

Hoshino Yoshiro and Iijima Nobuko. 1992. "The Miike Coal-Mine Explosion." In *Industrial Pollution in Japan*, edited by Jun Ui. Tokyo: United Nations University Press.

Hosie, Alexander. 1897. *Three Years in Western China*. London: George Philip & Son.

Howland, Douglas R. 2002. *Translating the West: Language and Political Reason in Nineteenth-Century Japan*. Honolulu: University of Hawai'i Press.

Howland, Douglas R. 2005. *Personal Liberty and Public Good*. Toronto: University of Toronto Press.

Hu Hansheng. 1983. *Li Lan qiyi shigao*. Chongqing: Chongqing Chubanshe.

Hu Qiwei. 1986. *Dazu renmin fanyangjiao douzheng*. Dazu Xian: Dazu Xian Zhengxie Wenshi Ziliao Yanjiu Weiyuanhui.

Ichikawa Fusae, ed. 1980. *Nihon fujin mondai shiryô shûsei*, vol 8. Tokyo: Domesu Shuppan.

Iechika Yoshiki. 2011. *Saigô Takamori to bakumatsu ishin no seikyoku*. Tokyo: Minerva Shobo.

Ienaga Saburô. 1967. *Kakumei shisô no senkusha: Ueki Emori no hito to shisô*. Tokyo: Iwanami Shoten.

Ienaga Saburô. 1974. *Ueki Emori senshû*. Tokyo: Iwanami Shoten.

Ikai Takaaki. 1992. *Saigô Takamori: Seinan sensô e no michi*. Tokyo: Iwanami Shoten.

Ikawa Satoshi and Kobayashi Hiroshi. 2006. *Hito arite: Tôyama Mitsuru to Genyôsha*. Tokyo: Kaichosha.

Ike Nobutaka. 1950. *The Beginnings of Political Democracy in Japan*. Baltimore: Johns Hopkins University Press.

Imada Shûsaku. 2000. *Pakusu buritanika to shokuminchi indo: igirisu indo keizaishi no sôkan haaku*. Kyôto: Kyôtodaigaku Shuppankai.

Imperial Maritime Customs (IMC). 1881a. *Opium*. Special Series no. 4. Shanghai: IMC.

Imperial Maritime Customs. 1881b. *Reports on Trade at the Treaty Port for the Year 1880*. Statistical Series no. 4. Shanghai: IMC.

Imperial Maritime Customs. 1902. *Decennial Reports, 1892–1901*. Shanghai: IMC.

Imperial Maritime Customs. 1913. *Reports and Returns of Trade, 1912*. Shanghai: IMC.

Inada Masatsugu. 1960. *Meiji kenpô seiritsushi*, vol. 1. Tokyo: Yûhikaku.

Inoue Katsuo. 2010. *Bakamatsu, Ishin*. Tokyo: Iwanami Shinsho.

Inoue Kiyoshi. 1965. *Nihon no rekishi*. 3 vols. Tokyo: Iwanami Shoten.

Inoue Kiyoshi. 1970. *Saigô Takamori*. 2 vols. Tokyo: Chûô Kôronsha.

Inoue Masaji. 1910. *Kyojin Arao Sei*. Tokyo: Sakuma Shobô.

Inoue Tentarô. 1995. *Higashi Ajia ni okeru Fubyôdô Jôyaku Taisei to Kindai Nihon*. Tokyo: Iwata Shôin.

Inspector General of Customs. 1888. *China Imperial Maritime Customs*, vol 2: *Native Opium*. Special Series no. 9. Shanghai: Inspectorate General.

International Opium Commission (IOC). 1909. *Report of the International Opium Commission, Shanghai, China, February 1–February 26, 1909*, vol. 2. Shanghai: IOC.

Invisible Committee. 2009. *The Coming Insurrection*. Translated by Robert Hurley. New York: Semiotext.

Ion, Hamish. 1993. *The Cross and the Rising Sun*, vol. 2. Toronto: Wilfrid Laurier University Press.

Irokawa Daikichi. 1969. *Murano Tsuneemon den*. Tokyo: Chûô Kôron Jigyô Shuppan.

Irokawa Daikichi, ed. 1970. *Minshû kenpô no sôzô: Umoreta tama no jinmyaku*. Tokyo: Hyôronsha.

Irokawa Daikichi. 1984. *Konmintô to Jiyûtô*. Tokyo: Yôransha.

Irokawa Daikichi. 1985. *The Culture of the Meiji Period*. Edited by Marius Jansen. Princeton, NJ: Princeton University Press.

Irokawa Daikichi. 1990. *Jiyû minken no chikasui*. Tokyo: Iwanami Shoten.

Ishii, Kanji. 1994. "Japanese Foreign Trade and the Yokohama Specie Bank, 1880–1913." In *Pacific Banking, 1859–1959: East Meets West*, edited by Olive Checkland, Shizuya Nishimura, and Norio Tamaki. New York: St. Martin's.

Ishii Takashi. 1976. *Kotô Yokohama no tanjô*. Yokohama: Yurindô.

Ishitaki Toyomi. 1997. *Genyôsha hakkutsu: Mô hitotsu no jiyû minken*. Fukuoka: Nishi Nihon Shinbunsha.

Itô Ishirô. 1971. "Joju Takaba Osamu." *Chikushushidan* 46 (March): 41–49.

Jacobson, Carl Whitney. 1993. "Brotherhood and Society: The Shaanxi Gelaohui, 1867–1912." PhD dissertation, University of Michigan.

Jaffer, Aaron. 2015. *Lascars and Indian Ocean Seafaring, 1780–1860: Shipboard Life, Unrest and Mutiny*. London: Boydell.

James, C. L. R. 1980 [1938]. *The Black Jacobins: Toussaint L'Ouverture and the San Domingo Revolution*. London: Secker & Warburg.

Jansen, Marius. 1952. "Ôi Kentarô: Radicalism and Chauvinism." *Far Eastern Quarterly* 2, no. 3: 305–16.

Jansen, Marius. 1989. *The Cambridge History of Japan*, vol. 5: *The Nineteenth Century*. Cambridge: Cambridge University Press.

Jiangbei weiyuanhui, ed. 1986. *Jiangbeixian wenshi ziliao*. Chongqing: Chongqing Chubanshe.

Jin Xiangming and Zhong Youling, eds. 1992. *Ba Yu minjian wenxue huicui*. Chengdu: Sichuan wenyi Chubanshe.

Jocelyn, Robert. 1841. *Six Months with the Chinese Expedition; Or, Leaves from a Soldier's Note-Book*. London: John Murray.

Johnson, Chalmers. 2004. *Blowback: The Costs and Consequences of American Empire*. New York: Holt.

Johnson, Gaye Theresa, and Alex Lubin, eds. 2017. *Futures of Black Radicalism*. London: Verso.

Joos, Joël. 2011. "The Genyôsha (1881) and the Premodern Roots of Japanese Expansionism." In *Pan-Asianism: A Documentary History*, vol. 1: *1850–1920*, edited by Sven Saaler and Christopher W. A. Szpilman, 61–68. Lanham, MD: Rowman & Littlefield.

Karl, Rebecca. 2002. *Staging the World: Chinese Nationalism at the Turn of the Twentieth Century*. Durham, NC: Duke University Press.

Karlin, Jason. 2002. "The Gender of Nationalism: Competing Masculinities in Meiji Japan." *Journal of Japanese Studies* 28, no. 1: 41–77.

Katsuya, Hirano, trans. 2002. "Discourse on Popular Rights and Liberty." In *From Japan's Modernity*. Select Papers no. 11. Chicago: University of Chicago, Center for East Asian Studies.

Keene, Adrienne. 2018. "Wakanda Forever: Using Indigenous Futurisms to Survive the Present." *Native Appropriations*, February 24. https://nativeappropriations.com/2018/02/wakanda-forever-using-indigenous-futurisms-to-survive-the-present.html. Accessed August 3, 2019.

Keevak, Michael. 2011. *Becoming Yellow: A Short History of Racial Thinking*. Princeton, NJ: Princeton University Press.

Kikuchi Akira. 2005. *Bakumatsu tenchû zankanroku*. Tokyo: Shinjinbutsu Oraisha.

Kim, Djun Kil. 2005. *The History of Korea*. Westport, CT: Greenwood.

Kim, Kyu Hyun. 2007. *The Age of Visions and Arguments: Parliamentarianism and the National Public Sphere in Early Meiji Japan*. Cambridge, MA: Harvard University Press.

Kim Nanny. 2009. "River Control, Merchant Philanthropy, and Environmental Change in Nineteenth-Century China." *Journal of the Economic and Social History of the Orient* 52, nos. 4–5: 660–94.

Kim Nanny and Nagase Keiko, eds. 2013. *Mining, Monies and Culture in Early Modern Societies*. Leiden: Brill.

Kimura Ki, ed. 1967. *Meiji bunka no zenshû*. 32 vols. Tokyo: Nihon Hyôronsha.

Kimura Naoya. 2010. "Higashi ajia no naka no Seikanron." In *Kindaka suru nihon*, edited by Arano Yasunari and Ishii Masatoshi. Tokyo: Yoshikawa Bunkan.

Kipling, Rudyard. 1899. *From Sea to Sea and Other Sketches: Letters of Travel*. 2 vols. New York: Doubleday & McClure.

Kirihara Mitsuaki. 1984. *Kabasan Jiken to Tomimatsu Masayasu*. Chiba-ken Nagareyama-shi: Ron Shobô.

Kitahara Michio. 2013. *Porutogaru no shokuminchi keisei to Nihonjin dorei*. Tokyo: Kodansha.

Kiyokawa Hachirô. 1913. *Kiyokawa Hachirô icho*. Compiled by Yamaji Alzan. Tokyo: Minyusha.

Klein, Naomi. 2007. *The Shock Doctrine: The Rise of Disaster Capitalism*. New York: Knopf.

Klein, Naomi. 2014. *This Changes Everything: Capitalism vs. The Climate*. New York: Simon & Schuster.

Koch, Alexander, and Chris Brierley. 2019. "Earth System Impacts of the European Arrival and Great Dying in the Americas after 1492." *Quarternary Science Reviews* 207 (March): 13–36.

Konishi Shiro. 1966. *Kaikoku to Jôi*. Tokyo: Chûô Kôronsha.

Kornicki, P. F., Mara Patessio, and G. G. Rowley, eds. 2010. *The Female as Subject: Reading and Writing in Early Modern Japan*. Ann Arbor: University of Michigan Press.

Kowner, Rotema, and Walter Demel, eds. 2014. *Race and Racism in Modern East Asia*, vol. 1. Leiden: Brill.

Kowner, Rotema, and Walter Demel, eds. 2015. *Race and Racism in Modern East Asia*, vol. 2. Leiden: Brill.

Kuzuu Yoshihisa, ed. 1936. *Toa senkaku shishi kiden*. 3 vols. Tokyo: Kokuryûkai Shuppanbu.

Lane-Poole, Stanley. 1901. *Sir Harry Parkes in China*. London: Methuen.

The Last Year in China to the Peace of Nanking. 1843. London: Longman, Brown, Green & Longmans.

Latour, Bruno. 1993. *We Have Never Been Modern*. Translated by Catherine Porter. Cambridge, MA: Harvard University Press.

Lau, D. C. 1979. *The Analects*. London: Penguin Classics.

Lau, D. C. 2005. *Mencius*. London: Penguin Classics.

Launay, Adrien. 1894. *Histoire Générale de la Société des Missions Étrangères*, vol. 3. Paris: Société des Missions Étrangères.

Launay, Marcel, ed. 2008. *Les Missions Étrangères*. Paris: Editions Perrin.

Lees, Willam Nassau. 1867. *The Land and Labour of India, A Review*. London: Williams and Norgate.

LeFevour, Edward. 1974. *Western Enterprise in Late Ch'ing China: A Selective Survey of Jardine, Matheson & Company's Operations, 1842–1895*. Cambridge, MA: Harvard University Press.

LeMaster, J. R., and J. D. Wilson, eds. 1993. *The Mark Twain Encyclopedia*. New York: Taylor & Francis.

Lensen, George Alexander. 1959. *The Russian Push Toward Japan: Russo-Japanese Relations, 1697–1875*. Princeton, NJ: Princeton University Press.

Leopold, Aldo. 1949. *A Sand County Almanac*. New York: Oxford University Press.

Lesourd, Paul. 1947. *Histoire générale de l'Oeuvre Pontificale de la Sainte Enfance depuis un siècle*. Paris: Imprimerie Les Presses Continentales.

Leupp, Gary. 2003. *Interracial Intimacy in Japan: Western Men and Japanese Women, 1543–1900*. New York: Continuum.

Lewis, Simon, and Mark Maslin. 2018. *The Human Planet: How We Created the Anthropocene*. New Haven, CT: Yale University Press.

Lewis, Spencer. 1933. "Pioneering in West China." *China Christian Advocate*, September–December.

Li Danke. 1990. "Culture, Political Movement, and Revolution: The Formation of the Chinese Communist Movement in Chongqing, 1890–1930." PhD dissertation, University of Michigan.

Li Danke. 2004. "Popular Culture in the Making of Anti-Imperialist and Nationalist Sentiments in Sichuan." *Modern China* 30, no. 4: 470–505.

Li Dezheng, Liu Tianlu, and Su Weizhi, eds. 1990. *Baguo lianjun qinhua shi*. Jinan: Shandong Daxue Chubanshe.

Li Jieren. 2012a [1936]. *Sishui weilan*. Chengdu: Sichuan Wenshu Chubanshe.

Li Jieren. 2012b [1936]. *Dabo*. Chengdu: Sichuan Wenshu Chubanshe.

Li Wenhai, Lin Dunkui, and Lin Keguang, eds. 1986. *Yihetuan yun dongshi shiyao lu*. Jinan: Qilu Shushe.

Li Xiaoxiong. 2009. *Poppies and Politics in China*. Newark: University of Delaware Press.

Li Zifeng, ed. 1990. *Haidi*. Shijiaya: Hebei Renmin Chubanshe.

Lin Manhong. 1980. "Qingmo benguo yapian zhi tidai jinkou yapian." In *Zhongyang yanjiuyuan jindiashisuo yanjiu jikan*, vol. 9. Taibei: Zhongshu Chuban.

Linebaugh, Peter. 2019. *Red Round Globe Hot Burning*. Berkeley: University of California Press.

Linebaugh, Peter, and Marcus Rediker. 2000. *The Many-Headed Hydra: Sailors, Slaves, Commoners, and the Hidden History of the Revolutionary Atlantic*. Boston: Beacon.

Lipsitz, George. 2009. *The Possessive Investment in Whiteness: How White People Profit from Identity Politics*. Philadelphia: Temple University Press.

Little, Alicia E. 1901. *Intimate China: The Chinese as I Have Seen Them*. London: Hutchinson.

Little, Alicia E. 1902. *The Land of the Blue Gown*. London: T. F. Unwin.

Little, Archibald J. 1898. *Through the Yang-tse Gorges*. London: Sampson Low.

Little, Archibald J. 1910. *Gleanings from Fifty Years in China*. London: Marston.

Liu, Andrew. 2010. "The Birth of a Noble Tea Country: On the Geography of Colonial Capital and the Origins of Indian Tea." *Journal of Historical Sociology* 23, no. 1: 73–100.

Liu Cenghe. 2005. *Yapian shuishou yu Qingmo xinzheng*. Beijing: Xinhua Shudian.

Liu Cheng-yun. 1983. "The Ko-lao Hui in Late Imperial China." PhD dissertation, University of Pittsburgh.

Liu Guangdi. 1986. *Liu Guangdi ji, nanxuanji*. Beijing: Zhonghua Shuju.

Liu, Lydia He. 2004. *The Clash of Empires: The Invention of China in Modern World Making*. Cambridge, MA: Harvard University Press.

Liu Yangang and Mi Yungang. 2015. *Sichuan Paoge shigao*. Chengdu: Sichuan Jiaoyu Chubanshe.

Locke, John. 1988. *Two Treatises of Government*. Edited by Peter Laslett. Cambridge: Cambridge University Press.

Lodwick, Kathleen L. 1996. *Crusaders against Opium: Protestant Missionaries in China, 1874–1917*. Louisville: University of Kentucky Press.

Loti, Pierre. 1920 [1887]. *Madame Chrysanthème*. Paris: Calmann-Lévy.

Loti, Pierre. 1985. *Japan: Madame Chrysanthemum*. London: Kegan Paul.

Lott, Eric. 1991. "'The Seeming Counterfeit': Racial Politics and Early Blackface Minstrelsy." *American Quarterly* 43, no. 2: 223–54.

Lott, Eric. 1993. *Love and Theft: Blackface Minstrelsy and the American Working Class*. New York: Oxford University Press.

Lowe, Lisa. 2015. *The Intimacies of Four Continents*. Durham, NC: Duke University Press.

Lu Zijian. 1984. *Qingdai Sichuan caizheng shiliao*. Chengdu: Sichuansheng Shehui Kexueyuan Chubanshe.

Lubbock, Basil. 1935. *Coolie Ships and Oil Sailers*. Glasgow: Brown, Son & Ferguson.

Lucid, Robert F. 1968. *The Journal of Richard Henry Dana, Jr.*, vol. 3. Cambridge, MA: Harvard University Press.

Lutz, Jessie. 1984. "Karl F. A. Gützlaff: Missionary Entrepreneur." In *Christianity in China*, edited by Suzanne Wilson Barnett and John Fairbank. Cambridge, MA: Harvard University Press.

Luxemburg, Rosa. 2003. *The Accumulation of Capital*. New York: Routledge Classics.

Lynch, George. 1901. *The War of the Civilisations, Being the Record of a "Foreign Devil's" Experiences with the Allies in China.* London: Longmans, Green.

Machida Shiritsu Jiyū Minken Shiryōkan, ed. 2000. *Osaka Jiken: Minken to kokken no hazama de.* Tokyo: Minshu Bukkusu.

Mackie, Vera. 2003. *Feminism in Modern Japan: Citizenship, Embodiment, and Sexuality.* New York: Cambridge University Press.

Madancy, Joyce. 2003. *The Troublesome Legacy of Commissioner Lin: The Opium Trade and Suppression in Fujian Province, 1820s to 1920s.* Cambridge, MA: Harvard University Press.

Maddison, Angus. 2007. *Contours of the World Economy 1–2030 AD.* Oxford: Oxford

Makihara Norio. 2012. *Minken to Kenpô.* Tokyo: Iwanami Shinsho.

Malm, Andreas. 2015. *Fossil Capitalism: The Rise of Steam Power and the Roots of Global Warming.* London: Verso.

Marcon, Federico. 2015. *The Knowledge of Nature and the Nature of Knowledge in Early Modern Japan.* Chicago: University of Chicago Press.

Marez, Curtis. 2004. *Drug Wars: The Political Economy of Narcotics.* Minneapolis: University of Minnesota Press.

Martinez, Maria Elena. 2008. *Genealogical Fictions: Limpieza de Sangre, Religion, and Gender in Colonial Mexico.* Stanford, CA: Stanford University Press.

Marx, Karl. 1968. *Marx on China.* London: Lawrence & Wishart.

Marx, Karl. 1977a. *Capital,* vol. 1. Translated by Ben Fowkes. New York: Vintage.

Marx, Karl. 1977b. *Grundrisse: Foundations of the Critique of Political Economy.* Translated by M. Nicolaus. New York: Vintage.

Marx, Karl. 1981. *Capital,* vol. 3. Translated by David Fernbach. New York: Vintage.

Marx, Karl, and Friedrich Engels. 1972. *On Colonialism: Articles from the* New York Tribune *and Other Writings.* New York: International Publishers.

Marx, Karl, and Friedrich Engels. 1975. *Collected Works.* New York: International Publishers.

Marx, Karl, and Friedrich Engels. 2004. *Collected Works.* 50 vols. London: Lawrence & Wishart.

Matano Hansuke. 1913. *Kurushima Tsuneki.* Tokyo: Jûensha.

Matsuo Shôichi, ed. 1982. *Ôsaka Jiken no Kenkyû.* Tokyo: Kashiwa Shôbo.

Matsuo Shôichi. 1990. *Jiyû minken shisô no kenkyû.* Tokyo: Nihon Keizai Hyôronsha.

Matsuo Shôichi and Matsuo Teiko, eds. 1985. *Ôsaka Jiken kankei shiryôshû.* 2 vols. Tokyo: Nihon Keizai Hyôronsha.

Matthews, James. 1999. "The Union Jack on the Upper Yangzi." PhD dissertation, York University.

Mayet, Paul. 1893. *Agricultural Insurance in Organic Connection with Savings-Banks, Land-Credit, and the Commutation of Debts: Proposals for the Amelioration of the Condition of the Japanese Agriculturalist.* Translated by Arthur Lloyd. London: Swan Sonnenschein.

Mbembe, Achille. 2001. *On the Postcolony.* Berkeley: University of California Press.

Mbembe, Achille. 2017. *Critique of Black Reason.* Translated by Laurent Dubois. Durham, NC: Duke University Press.

McCauley, Edward York. 1942. *With Perry in Japan*. Princeton, NJ: Princeton University Press.

McClintock, Anne. 1995. *Imperial Leather: Race, Gender, and Sexuality in the Colonial Contest*. New York: Routledge.

McKay, Alexander. 1993. *Scottish Samurai: The Life of Thomas Blake Glover*. London: Canongate Books.

McKibben, Bill. 2012. "Global Warming's Terrifying New Math." *Rolling Stone*, July 19.

McMahon, Keith. 2002. *The Fall of the God of Money: Opium Smoking in Nineteenth-Century China*. Lanham, MD: Rowman & Littlefield.

McMaster, John. 1963. "The Takashima Mine: British Capital and Japanese Industrialization." *Business History Review* 37, no. 3: 217–39.

McMaster, John. 1966. *Jardines in Japan, 1859–1867*. Groningen: Druk.

McMaster, John. 1992. *Sabotaging the Shogun*. New York: Vantage.

McNeill, William H. 1982. *The Pursuit of Power: Technology, Armed Force, and Society Since A.D. 1000*. Chicago: University of Chicago Press.

Meillassoux, Quentin. 2010. *After Finitude: An Essay on the Necessity of Contingency*. Translated by Ray Brassier. London: Bloomsbury.

Menegon, Eugenio. 2009. *Ancestors, Virgins, and Friars: Christianity as a Local Religion in Late Imperial China*. Cambridge, MA: Harvard University Press.

Merchant, Carolyn. 1980. *The Death of Nature*. Berkeley: University of California Press.

Merchant, Carolyn. 2002. *The Columbia Guide to American Environmental History*. New York: Columbia University Press.

Mertz, John Pierre. 2003. *Novel Japan: Spaces of Nationhood in Early Meiji Narrative, 1870–88*. Ann Arbor: University of Michigan, Center for Japanese Studies.

Metzl, Jonathan M. 2019. *Dying of Whiteness: How the Politics of Racial Resentment Is Killing America's Heartland*. New York: Basic Books.

Mezzadra, Sandro, and Brett Neilson. "On the Multiple Frontiers of Extraction: Excavating Contemporary Capitalism." *Cultural Studies* 31, nos. 2–3 (2017). doi.org/10.1080/09502386.2017.1303425

M'Ghee, R. J. L. 1862. *How We Got to Peking*. London: Richard Bentley.

Michie, Alexander. 1900. *The Englishman in China during the Victorian Era, as Illustrated in the Career of Sir Rutherford Alcock*. 2 vols. London: W. Blackwood and Sons.

Midnight Notes Collective. 1990. *The New Enclosures*, issue 10.

Mies, Maria. 1986. *Patriarchy and Accumulation on a World Scale: Women in the International Division of Labour*. London: Zed.

Mihalopoulos, Bill. 2011. *Sex in Japan's Globalization, 1870–1930: Prostitutes, Emigration, and Nation-Building*. London: Pickering and Chatto.

Miller, Ian, with Julia Adeney Thomas and Brett Walker, eds. 2013. *Japan at Nature's Edge: The Environmental Context of a Global Power*. Honolulu: University of Hawai'i Press.

Miller, Jacques Alain. 2008. "Extimity." *Symptom 9*, Fall. https://www.lacan.com/symptom/extimity.html. Accessed December 13, 2018.

Miller, Joseph. 1988. *Way of Death: Merchant Capitalism and the Angolan Slave Trade, 1730–1830*. Madison: University of Wisconsin Press.

Mills, Charles W. 1997. *The Racial Contract*. Ithaca, NY: Cornell University Press.

Minear, Richard. 1999. *Dr. Seuss Goes to War*. New York: New Press.

Mishra, Amaresh. 2008. *War of Civilisations India AD 1857: The Road to Delhi and the Long Revolution*. 2 vols. Delhi: Rupa.

Mita Munesuke, ed. 1968. *Meiji no gunzo*, vol. 5: *Jiyû to Minken*. Tokyo: Sanichi Shobô.

Miyazaki Muryû. 1974. "Kishûshû." In *Meiji seiji shôsetsu shû*. Tokyo: Kadokawa Shuppan.

Miyazawa Shin'ichi. 1997. *"Bakumatsu" ni korosareta otoko: Namamugi Jiken no Richadoson*. Tokyo: Shinchôsha.

Moore, Jason. 2015. *Capitalism in the Web of Life*. London: Verso.

Moore, Jason, ed. 2016. *Anthropocene or Capitalocene? Nature, History, and the Crisis of Capitalism*. Oakland: PM Press.

Moore, Jason. 2020. "Spaceship or Slaveship?" Keynote presentation to annual World-Ecology workshop, Binghamton University, February 7.

Moore, Jason, and Raj Patel. 2017. *A History of the World in Seven Cheap Things: A Guide to Capitalism, Nature, and the Future of the Planet*. Berkeley: University of California Press.

Morck, Randall. 2007. "Business Groups and the Big Push: Meiji Japan's Mass Privatization and Subsequent Growth." Working Paper no. 13171. Cambridge, MA: National Bureau of Economic Research.

Môri Toshihiko. 1978. *Meiji rokunen seihen no kenkyû*. Tokyo: Yûhijun.

Morikawa Tetsurô. 1967. *Bakumatsu Ansatsushi*. Tokyo: Sanichi Shobo.

Morse, H. B. 1907. *The Trade and Administration of the Chinese Empire*. Shanghai: Kelly & Walsh.

Morse, H. B. 1910. *The International Relations of the Chinese Empire*. 3 vols. London: Longmans, Green.

Morton, Timothy. 2013. *Hyperobjects: Philosophy and Ecology after the End of the World*. Minneapolis: University of Minnesota Press.

Motoyama Yukihio. 1997. *Proliferating Talent: Essays on Politics, Thought, and Education in the Meiji Era*. Edited by J. S. A. Elisonas and Richard Rubinger. Honolulu: University of Hawai'i Press.

Murata Shizuko and Ôki Motoko. 1998. *Fukuda Hideko shû*. Tokyo: Fuji Shuppan.

Muroi Hiroichi. 1981–99. *Sugiyama Shigemaruron no-to*. Tokyo: Higashichikushi Tanki Daigaku Kenkyû Kiyô.

Muroyama Yoshimasa. 2004. *Matsukata zaisei kenkyû*. Tokyo: Minerva Shobo.

Murray, Dian. 1987. *Pirates of the South China Coast, 1790–1810*. Palo Alto, CA: Stanford University Press, 1987.

Murthy, Viren. 2011. *The Political Philosophy of Zhang Taiyan: The Resistance of Consciousness*. Leiden: Brill.

Myers, Ella. 2019. "Beyond the Psychological Wage: Du Bois on White Dominion." *Political Theory* 47, no. 1: 6–31.

Myers, Norma. 1994. "The Black Poor of London." *Immigrants and Minorities* 13, nos. 2–3: 7–21.

Nagahata Michiko. 1997. *Rin: Kindai Nihon no jokai, Takaba Ran*. Tokyo: Fujiwara Shoten.

Nakae Chômin. 1965. *Nakae Chômin bunshû*. Tokyo: Bunka Shiryôchôsakai.

Nakafuji Hitori. 2008. *Sorekara no Kaishû*. Tokyo: Chikuma Bunkô.

Nakamura Katsuaki. 2012. *Ueki Emori: Kenkyû to shiryô*. Tokyo: Kantô Gakuin Daigaku Shuppankai.

Nakamura Takafusa. 1983. *Economic Growth in Prewar Japan*. New Haven, CT: Yale University Press.

Nakano Takeshi. 2012. *Nihon shisôshi shinron: Puragumateizumu kara nashionarizumu e*. Tokyo: Chikuma Shinsho.

Nelson, Diane. Forthcoming. *Riparian Worlds*. Durham, NC: Duke University Press.

Newman, Richard K. 1995. "Opium Smoking in Late Imperial China: A Reconsideration." *Modern Asian Studies* 29: 765–94.

Nicholls, Bob. 1986. *Bluejackets and Boxers*. Sydney: Allen and Unwin.

Nishi Nihon Bunka Kyôkai, ed. 1973. *Chikuhō sekitan kōgyōshi nenpyō*. Tokyo: Nishi Nihon Bunka Kyôkai Shuppan.

Nishi Nihon Bunka Kyôkai, ed. 1982a. *Fukuokahenshi*, vol. 16: *Jiyû minken undô*. Tokyo: Nishi Nihon Bunka Kyôkai Shuppan.

Nishi Nihon Bunka Kyôkai, ed. 1982b. *Fukuokahenshi*, vol. 20: *Chikuhô Sekitan*. Tokyo: Nishi Nihon Bunka Kyôkai Shuppan.

Nishikawa Masao. 1968. "Shisen horo undo: Sono zenya no shakai jôkyô." *Tôyô Bunka Kenkyûjo Kiyô* 45: 109–77.

Nishio Yôtaro. 1981. *Tôyama Mitsuru-ō seiden*. Fukuoka: Ashi Shobô.

Niwa, Kunio. 1995. *Chiso Kaisei Hô No Kigen: Kaimei Kanryô No Keisei*. Tokyo: Minerva Shobô.

Noda Yoshihiro. 1992. *Sugiyama Shigemaruden: Mogura no kiroku*. Tokyo: Shimazu Shobô.

Norman, Edward Herbert. 1940. *Japan's Emergence as a Modern State*. New York: Institute of Pacific Relations.

Norman, Edward Herbert. 1944. "The Genyôsha: A Study in the Origins of Japanese Imperialism." *Pacific Affairs* 17, no. 3: 261–84.

Noro Eitaro. 1983. *Nihon shihonshugi hattatsushi*. Tokyo: Iwanami Shoten.

Northrup, David. 1995. *Indentured Labor in the Age of Imperialism, 1834–1922*. New York: Cambridge University Press.

Nozawa Keiichi, Kawasaki Masaru, and Hirose Yoshihiro, eds. 1984. *Hoshi Tôru to sono jidai*. 2 vols. Tokyo: Heibonsha.

Obinata Sumio. 1987. *Tennôsei seikatsu to minshû*. Tokyo: Nihon Hyoronsha.

Obinata Sumio and Yui Masaomi, eds. 1990. *Kanryôsei keisatsu*. Tokyo: Iwanami Shoten.

Ochiai Hiroki. 1999. *Chitsuroku shobun: Meiji Ishin to bushi risutora*. Tokyo: Chûô Kôron Shincho.

Ochiai Kô. 2008. *Ôkubo Toshimichi*. Tokyo: Nihon Keizai Hyôronsha.

O'Connor, James. 1998: *Natural Causes: Essays in Ecological Marxism*. New York: Guilford,

Oda Hiroshi. 1993. *Japanese Law*. Oxford: Oxford University Press.

Office of Strategic Services (oss). 1944. "Japanese Infiltration among Muslims in China." Document no. 890.1. Unpublished report, Research and Analysis Branch.

Oguma Eiji. 2002. *A Genealogy of "Japanese" Self-Images*. Translated by David Askew. Melbourne: Trans Pacific Press.

Oishi Kaichirô. 1989. *Jiyû Minken undo to Ôkuma, Matsukata zaisei*. Tokyo: Daigaku Shuppankai.

Ôkawa Shûmei. 2007. *Tôyama Mitsuru to kindai Nihon*. Tokyo: Shunfûsha.

Ôki Motoko. 2003. *Jiyû minken undo to josei*. Tokyo: Domesu Shuppan.

Oliphant, Laurence. 1860. *Narrative of the Earl of Elgin's Mission to China and Japan in the Years 1857, '58, '59*. New York: Harper & Brothers.

Oliphant, Laurence. 1887. *Episodes in a Life of Adventure, or Moss from a Rolling Stone*. London: Westwood.

Osborne, Peter. 2003. *Philosophies of Race and Ethnicity*. London: Bloomsbury.

Osgood, Elliott. 1903. "Some Experiences with Patients Breaking Opium." *China Medical Missionary Journal* 17 (April): 54–56.

Otte, J. A. 1910. "Treatment of the Opium Habit." *China Medical Journal* 4 (July).

Owen, David Edward. 1934. *British Opium Policy in China and India*. New Haven, CT: Yale University Press.

Ownby, David. 1996. *Brotherhoods and Secret Societies in Early and Mid-Qing China*. Stanford, CA: Stanford University Press.

Parenti, Christian. 2015. "The Environment Making State: Territory, Nature, and Value." *Antipode* 47, no. 4: 829–48.

Park, W. H., ed. 1899. *Opinion of over 100 Physicians on the Use of Opium in China*. Shanghai: American Presbyterian Press.

Parker, E. H. 1909. *John Chinaman*. New York: E. F. Dutton.

Parkinson, C. N. 1966. *Trade in the Eastern Seas, 1793–1813*. New York: A. M. Kelley.

Parsons, Willian Barclay. 1900. *An American Engineer in China*. New York: McClure, Phillips.

Partner, Simon. 2018. *The Merchant's Tale: Yokohama and the Transformation of Japan*. New York: Columbia University Press.

Paske-Smith, M. 1930. *Western Barbarians in Japan and Formosa*. Kobe: J. L. Thompson.

Pedlar, Neil. 1990. *The Imported Pioneers: Westerners Who Helped Build Modern Japan*. New York: St. Martin's Press.

Perry, Elizabeth. 2002. *Challenging the Mandate of Heaven: Social Protests and State Power in China*. London: M. E. Sharpe.

Perry, Matthew Calbraith. 1854. *On Board the Powhatan*. Shimoda: Japan Expedition Press.

Phimister, Ian. 2006. "Foreign Devils, Finance and Informal Empire: Britain and China c. 1900–1912." *Modern Asian Studies* 40, no. 3: 737–59.

Piolet, J. B. 1901. *Les Missions Catholiques Françaises au XIXe siècle*. Tome 3. Paris: A. Colin.

Platt, Stephen. 2018. *Imperial Twilight: The Opium War and the End of China's Last Golden Age*. New York: Knopf.

Polachek, James M. 1992. *The Inner Opium War*. Cambridge, MA: Harvard University Asia Center.

Pomerantz, Kenneth. 2000. *The Great Divergence: China, Europe, and the Making of the Modern World Economy*. Princeton, NJ: Princeton University Press.

Pong, David. 1994. *Shen Pao-Chen and China's Modernization in the Nineteenth Century.* Cambridge: Cambridge University Press.

Porter, Bernard. 2004. *The Absent-Minded Imperialists: What the British Really Thought about Empire.* London: Oxford University Press.

Powdermaker, Hortense. 1966. *Stranger and Friend: The Way of an Anthropologist.* New York: W. W. Norton.

Pratt, Mary Louise. 1992. *Imperial Eyes: Travel Writing and Transculturation.* London: Routledge.

Preston, Diana. 2000. *The Boxer Rebellion: The Dramatic Story of China's War on Foreigners That Shook the World.* New York: Bloomsbury.

Proshan, Chester. 2015. "'. . . Behind a Screen': Early Intercultural Exchange in the Yokohama Treaty Port and the Michael Moss Court Case." *East Asian Journal of Popular Culture* 1, no. 1: 11–32.

Protestant Missionaries. 1890. *Records of the General Conference of the Protestant Missionaries of China Held at Shanghai, May 7–20, 1890.* Shanghai: Missionary Press.

Prudhomme, Claude. 1994. *Stratégie Missionaire du Sainte-Siege sous Léon XIII (1878–1903).* Rome: Palazzo Farnese.

Qin Heping. 2001. *Sichuan yapian wenti yu jinyan yundong.* Chengdu: Sichuan Minzu Chubanshe.

Qin Heping. 2002. "Er sanshi niandai yapian yu Sichuan chengzhen shuijuan guanxi zhi renshi." *Chengshi shi Yanjiu* 2: 76–96.

Qin Heping. 2006. *Jidu zongjiao zai Sichuan chuanbo shigao.* Chengdu: Sichuan Chuban Jituan.

Quijano, Anibal. 2000. "Coloniality of Power, Eurocentrism, and Latin America." *Nepantla: Views from the South* 1, no. 3: 533–80.

Qunying she, ed. 1975. *Jianghu haidi.* Taibei: Kuding Shuwu.

Rancière, Jacques. 1999. *Disagreement: Politics and Philosophy.* Translated by Julie Rose. Minneapolis: University of Minnesota Press.

Rancière, Jacques. 2011. *Staging the People: The Proletarian and His Double.* Translated by David Fernbach. London: Verso.

Rankin, Mary Backus. 2002. "Nationalistic Contestation and Mobilization Politics." *Modern China* 28, no. 3: 315–61.

Ravina, Mark. 2004. *The Last Samurai: The Last Battles of Saigô Takamori.* Hoboken, NJ: John Wiley & Sons.

Ravina, Mark. 2017. *To Stand with the Nations of the World: Japan's Meiji Restoration in World History.* Oxford: Oxford University Press.

Raychaudhuri, Tapan. 2002. *Europe Reconsidered: Perceptions of the West in Nineteenth-Century Bengal.* Delhi: Oxford University Press.

Reichert, Folker. 2013. "Mord in Namamugi." *Damals* 45, no. 3: 66–69.

Richards, John F. 1981. "The Indian Empire and Peasant Production of Opium in the Nineteenth Century." *Modern Asian Studies* 15, no. 1: 59–82.

Robinson, Cedric J. 2000. *Black Marxism: The Making of the Black Radical Tradition.* Berkeley: University of California Press.

Roger, Nicholas. 2004. *The Command of the Ocean: A Naval History of Britain 1649–1815*. New York: Penguin.

Rose, Deborah Bird. 2004. *Reports from a Wild Country: Ethics for Decolonisation*. Sydney: University of New South Wales Press.

Rose, Sarah. 2011. *For All the Tea in China: How England Stole the World's Favorite Drink and Changed History*. New York: Penguin.

Ruskola, Teemu. 2013. *Legal Orientalism: China, the United States, and Modern Law*. Cambridge, MA: Harvard University Press.

Ruxton, Ian C. 1998. *The Diaries and Letters of Sir Ernest Mason Satow (1843–1929), a Scholar-Diplomat in East Asia*. Lewiston, NY: Edwin Mellen.

Saaler, Sven, and Christopher W. A. Szpilman. 2011. *Pan-Asianism: A Documentary History*, vol. 1: *1850–1920*. Lanham, MD: Rowman & Littlefield.

Sabey, John Wayne. 1974. "The Genyôsha, the Kokuryûkai and Japanese Expansion." PhD dissertation, University of Michigan.

Said, Edward. 1978. *Orientalism*. New York: Vintage.

Said, Edward. 1993. *Culture and Imperialism*. New York: Vintage.

Saigô Takamori. 1927. *DaiSaigô zenshu*. 3 vols. Tokyo: DaiSaigô Zenshu Kankokai.

Saigô Takamori. 2017 [1874]. *Nanshû ôikun*. Edited by Takaaki Ikai. Tokyo: Kadokawa.

Saitô Kohei. 2017. *Karl Marx's Ecosocialism*. New York: Monthly Review.

Sarr, Felwine. 2016. *Afrotopia*. Paris: Éditions Philippe Rey.

Satô Kiyohiko. 1991. *Kidan tsuiseki Bakumatsu*. Tokyo: Daiwa Shobô.

Satow, Ernest. 1921. *A Diplomat in Japan*. London: Seeley, Service.

Scarth, John. 1860. *Twelve Years in China*. Edinburgh: Thomas Constable.

Schoppa, R. Keith. 2002. *Revolution and Its Past: Identities and Change in Modern Chinese History*. Saddle River, NJ: Prentice Hall.

Scidmore, Eliza Ruhamah. 1892. *Jinrikisha Days in Japan*. New York: Harper & Brothers.

Seddon, Toby. 2010. *A History of Drugs: Drugs and Freedom in the Liberal Age*. New York: Routledge.

Shammas, Carole, ed. 2012. *Investing in the Early Modern Built Environment: Europeans, Asians, Settlers and Indigenous Societies*. Leiden: Brill.

Shanghai Mercury News. 1901. *The Boxer Uprising*. Shanghai: Shanghai Mercury.

Sharpe, Christina. 2010. *Monstrous Intimacies: Making Post-Slavery Subjects*. Durham, NC: Duke University Press.

Shen Congwen. 1983. *Chen Congwen xuanji, sanwen*. Chengdu: Sichuan Renmin Chubanshe.

Shiva, Vandana, and Maria Mies. 2014. *Ecofeminism*. London: Zed.

Sichuan Daxue lishixi diaocha. 1956. "Yibabaliu zhi yibajiuba de Dazu jiaoan shimo." *Sichuan Daxue Xuebao, Shehui Kexue* 1: 110–26.

Sichuansheng jindai jiaoanshi yanjiu hui. 1987. *Jindai Zhongguo jiaoan yanjiu*. Chengdu: Sichuansheng Xinhua Shudian.

Sichuan wenshi ziliao weiyuanhui, ed. 1993. *Sichuan wenshi ziliao xuanji, 1961–1992*. Chengdu: Sichuan Wenshi Chubanshe.

Sievers, Sharon. 1981. "Feminist Criticism in Japanese Politics in the 1880s: The Experience of Kishida Toshiko." *Signs: Journal of Women in Culture and Society* 6, no. 4: 602–16.

Sievers, Sharon. 1983. *Flowers in Salt: The Beginnings of Feminist Consciousness in Modern Japan*. Palo Alto, CA: Stanford University Press.

Simpson, Audra. 2017. "The Ruse of Consent and the Anatomy of 'Refusal': Cases from Indigenous North America and Australia." *Postcolonial Studies* 20, no. 1: 18–33.

Singh, Narayan Prasad. 1980. *The East India Company's Monopoly Industries in Bihar with Particular Reference to Opium and Saltpeter, 1773–1833*. Muzaffarpur, India: Sarvodaya Vangmaya.

Singh, Vipul. 2018. "Flood, Avulsion and Governance: The Ganges River in the Nineteenth Century." Presentation at Duke University, February 16.

Smith, Arthur. 1890. *Chinese Characteristics*. Shanghai: North China Herald News.

Smith, Arthur. 1901. *China in Convulsion*. 2 vols. New York: Fleming H. Revell.

Smith, Thomas C. 1955. *Political Change and Industrial Development in Japan: Government Enterprise, 1868–1880*. Stanford, CA: Stanford University Press.

Société des Missions Étrangères, 1912. *Annales de la Société des Missions Étrangères et de l'Oeuvre des Partants, 1900–1901*. Paris: Société des Missions Étrangères.

Sotozaki Mitsuhiro. 1989. *Nihon fujinron shi*. Tokyo: Domes Shuppan.

Spence, Jonathan D. 1992. *Chinese Roundabout*. New York: W. W. Norton.

Spivak, Gayatri Chakravorty. 1999. *A Critique of Postcolonial Reason: Toward a History of the Vanishing Present*. Cambridge, MA: Harvard University Press.

Stanley, Amy. 2012. *Selling Women: Prostitution, Markets, and the Household in Early Modern Japan*. Berkeley: University of California Press.

Stanziani, Allesandro. 2018. *Labor on the Fringes of Empire: Voice, Exit and the Law*. New York: Springer.

Stapleton, Kristin. 2000. *Civilizing Chengdu: Chinese Urban Reform, 1895–1937*. Cambridge, MA: Harvard University Press.

Statler, Oliver. 1969. *Shimoda Story*. New York: Random House.

Stewart-Harawira, Makere. 2005. *Indigenous Responses to the New Imperial Order*. London: Zed.

Stolz, Robert. 2014. *Bad Water: Nature, Pollution, and Politics in Japan, 1870–1950*. Durham, NC: Duke University Press.

Stone, Allison. 2005. *Petrified Intelligence: Nature in Hegel's Philosophy*. New York: State University of New York Press.

Sugiyama Shigemaru. 2006a [1926]. *Hyakuma*. Tokyo: Shoshi Shinsui.

Sugiyama Shigemaru. 2006b [1929]. *Zokusengokusaku*. Tokyo: Shoshi Shinsui.

Sugiyama Shinya. 1988. *Japan's Industrialization in the World Economy, 1859–1899*. London: Athlone.

Sun Jiang. 2007. *Kindai Chugoku no kakumei to himitsu kessha, 1895–1955*. Tokyo: Kyuko Shoin.

Sun Jiang. 2011. "Yangjiao or the 'Other'? Christianity and Chinese Society in the Second Half of the Nineteenth Century." *Frontiers of History in China* 6, no. 1: 53–73.

Sun Qihai. 1996. *Baguo lianjun qinhua jishi*. Beijing: Huawen Chubanshe.

Suzuki Yûko. 1996. *Nihon josei undô shiryô shûsei*, vol. 1. Tokyo: Fuji Shuppan.

Swinton, Captain, and Mrs. Swinton. 1859. *Journal of a Voyage with Coolie Emigrants, from Calcutta to Trinidad*. Edited by James Carlile. London: Alfred W. Bennett.

Tadano Masahiro. 2014. *Mitogaku shôyô*. Tokyo: Kinseisha.

Takahashi Tetsuo. 1970. *Fukushima Jiken*. Tokyo: Sanichi Shobo.

Takaki, Ronald T. 2000. *Iron Cages: Race and Culture in Nineteenth Century America*. Oxford: Oxford University Press.

Takasugi Shinsaku. 1916. *Tôkô sensei ibun*. Edited by Tôkô gojûnensai kinenkai. Tokyo: Min'yūsha.

TallBear, Kim. 2019. "Decolonizing Settler Sexuality." Keynote presentation to Duke Feminist Theory Workshop, March 23.

Tan Chung. 1978. *China and the Brave New World*. Durham, NC: Carolina Academic Press.

Tanaka Akira. 2002. *Iwakura shisetsu no rekishiteki kenkyû*. Tokyo: Iwanami Shoten.

Tanaka Manichi. 1990. *Seinan sensô shiryôshû*. Tokyo: Aochôsha.

Tanaka Shozo. 1989. *Tanaka Shozo senshu*, vol. 7. Edited by Anzai Kunio. Tokyo: Iwanami Shôten.

Taveirne, Patrick. 2004. *Han-Mongol Encounters and Missionary Endeavors: A History of Scheut in Ordos (Hetao) 1874–1911*. Leuven: Leuven University Press.

Taylor, Carl. 1989. *Dangerous Society*. East Lansing: Michigan State University Press.

ter Haar, Barend. 1998. *Ritual and Mythology of the Chinese Triads: Creating an Identity*. Leiden: Brill.

Tezuka Yutaka. 1986. *Meiji keihô shi no kenkyû*. 3 vols. Tokyo: Keiô Tsûshin Kaisha.

Thomas, Julia Adeney. 2002. *Reconfiguring Modernity: Concepts of Nature in Japanese Political Ideology*. Berkeley: University of California Press.

Thompson, E. P. 1917. "The Moral Economy of the English Crowd in the Eighteenth Century." *Past & Present*, no. 50: 76–136

Tianzhujiao Chengdu Jiaoqubian. 1986. *Tianzhujiao lishi ziliao huibian*, vol. 2. Chengdu: Tianzhujiao Chengdu Jiaoqubian.

Tiedemann, R. G. 2008. "Indigenous Agency, Religious Protectorates, and Chinese Interests: The Expansion of Christianity in Nineteenth-Century China." In *Converting Colonialism: Vision and Realities in Mission History, 1706–1914*, edited by Dana L. Robert, 206–41. Grand Rapids, MI: William B. Eerdmans.

Tomita Hitoshi. 1984. *Rokumeikan: Giseiyoka no sekai*. Tokyo: Hakusuisha.

Totman, Conrad. 1980. *The Collapse of the Tokugawa Bakufu, 1862–1868*. Honolulu: University of Hawai'i Press.

Tôyama Mitsuru. 1974. *DaiSaigô ikun*. Tokyo: Shigensha.

Tôyama Motokazu. 1977. *Chikuzen Genyôsha*. Tokyo: Ashi Shobô.

Trocki, Carl A. 1999. *Opium, Empire and the Global Political Economy: A Study of the Asian Opium Trade 1750–1950*. London: Routledge.

Tsai, Henry. 2003. "The History of Eunuchs, Explorers, and Chinese Immigration to America." *University of Arkansas News*, March 25. https://news.uark.edu/articles /11667/the-history-of-eunuchs-explorers-and-chinese-immigration-to-america. Accessed April 21, 2019.

Turse, Nick. 2013. *Kill Anything That Moves: The Real American War in Vietnam*. New York: Picador.

Ueda, Atsuko. 2007. *Concealment of Politics, Politics of Concealment: The Production of "Literature" in Meiji Japan*. Stanford, CA: Stanford University Press.

Ueki Emori. 1955. *Ueki Emori nikki*. Kōchi: Kōchi Shimbunsha.

Ueki Emori. 1990. *Ueki Emori shū*. 10 vols. Edited by Ienaga Saburo. Tokyo: Iwanami Shoten.

Ujifusa, Steven. 2018. *Barons of the Sea: And Their Race to Build the World's Fastest Clipper Ship*. New York: Simon & Schuster.

Urabe Noboru. 2009. *Daizaifutenmangû no teienkan*. Tokyo: Genshobô.

Ushioda, Sharlie C. 1984. "Fukuda Hideko and the Woman's World of Meiji Japan." In *Japan in Transition*, edited by H. Conroy, S. T. W. Davis, and W. Patterson. London: Associated University Presses.

van de Ven, Hans. 2012. *Breaking with the Past: The Maritime Customs Service and the Global Origins of Modernity in China*. New York: Columbia University Press.

van Dooren, Thom, and Debora Bird Rose. 2013. "Keeping Faith with Death: Mourning and De-Extinction." http://extinctionstudies.org/2013/11/10/keeping-faith-with-death. Accessed November 12, 2016.

Varma, Nitin. *Coolies of Capitalism: Assam Tea and the Making of Coolie Labour*. Berlin: De Gruyter Oldenbourg, 2017.

von Siebold, Phillip Franz. 1981 [1841]. *Manners and Customs of the Japanese in the Nineteenth Century*. Rutland, VT: Tuttle.

Wakabayashi, Bob Tadashi. 1986. *Anti-Foreignism and Western Learning in Early Modern Japan: The New Theses of 1825*. Cambridge, MA: Harvard University Press.

Wallace, William, A. V. Miller, and Michael Inwood, eds. 2007. *Hegel's Philosophy of Mind*. Oxford: Clarendon.

Wang Chuanping, ed. 2013a. *Lao hangdang*. Chongqing: Chongqing Chubanshe.

Wang Chuanping, ed. 2013b. *Lao matou*. Chongqing: Chongqing Chubanshe.

Wang Chunwu. 1993. *Paoge tanmi*. Chengdu: Bashu Shusha.

Wang Di. 2003. *Street Culture in Chengdu: Public Space, Urban Commoners and Local Politics, 1870–1930*. Palo Alto, CA: Stanford University Press.

Wang Di. 2006. *Kuachu fengbi de shijie: Changjiang shangyou quyu shehui yanjiu, 1644–1911*. Beijing: Zhonghua Shuju.

Wang Di. 2008. *The Teahouse: Small Business, Everyday Culture, and Public Politics in Chengdu, 1900–1950*. Palo Alto, CA: Stanford University Press.

Wang Di. 2018. *Violence and Order on the Chengdu Plain: The Story of a Secret Brotherhood in Rural China, 1939–1949*. Palo Alto, CA: Stanford University Press.

Wang Kaiyun. 2007. *Xiangjun shi*. Changsha: Hunan Renmin Chubanshe.

Wang Meiying. 2008. *Minguo Jianghu*. Beijing: Tuanjie Chubanshe.

Wang Minglun. 1965. "Yapian zhanzhen qian Yunnan tongkuangye zhong de zibenzhuyi mengya." In *Yunnan kuangye shi lunwenji*, edited by Yunnan lishi yanjiusuo. Kunming: Yunnan Lishi Yanhuiyuan.

Wang Minglun. 1984. *Fanyangjiao shuwen tiezhan xuan*. Jinan: Qilu Sushe.

Wang Wenjie. 1947. *Zhongguo jinshi shishang de jiaoan*. Fuzhou: Zhongguo Wenhua Yanjiu Hui.

Wang Wensheng. 2014. *White Lotus Rebels and South China Pirates: Crisis and Reform in the Qing Empire*. Cambridge, MA: Harvard University Press.

Wang Xiuyu. 2011. *China's Last Imperial Frontier: Late Qing Expansion into Sichuan's Tibetan Borderlands*. Lanham, MD: Lexington.

Warren, Calvin L. 2018. *Ontological Terror: Blackness, Nihilism, and Emancipation*. Durham, NC: Duke University Press.

Watanabe Kyôji. 1977. *Kamikazeren to sono jidai*. Tokyo: Hara Shobô.

Weber, Max. 2002. *The Protestant Ethic and the "Spirit" of Capitalism and Other Writings*. London: Penguin.

Wehrle, Edmund S. 1966. *Britain, China, and the Anti-Missionary Riots, 1891–1900*. Minneapolis: University of Minnesota Press.

Wei Qingxin. 1991. *Faguo duiHua chuanjiao zhengce*. 2 vols. Beijing: Zhongguo Shehui Kexue Chubanshe.

Wei Yingtao. 1981. *Sichuan baolu undong shi*. Chengdu: Sichuan Renmin Chubanshe.

Wei Yingtao. 1990. *Sichuan jindaishigao*. Chengdu: Sichuan Renmin Chubanshe.

Wei Yingtao and Zhao Qing, eds. 1981. *Sichuan Xinhai geming shiliao*. 2 vols. Chengdu: Sichuan Renmin Chubanshe.

Wilgus, Mary. 1987. *Sir Claude MacDonald, the Open Door, and British Informal Empire in China, 1895–1900*. New York: Garland.

Williams, Harold S. 1958. *Tales of the Foreign Settlement in Japan*. Tokyo: Charles E. Tuttle.

Williams, Harold S. 1959. *Shades of the Past*. Tokyo: Charles E. Tuttle.

Williams, Harold S. 1963. *Foreigners in Mikadoland*. Tokyo: Charles E. Tuttle.

Williams, Linda. 1999. *Hard Core: Power, Pleasure, and the "Frenzy of the Visible."* Berkeley: University of California Press.

Williams, Raymond. 1978. *Marxism and Literature*. Oxford: Oxford University Press.

Williams, S. Wells. 1895. *The Middle Kingdom*. 2 vols. New York: Scribner & Sons.

Wong, Bin R. 2000. "Opium and Modern Chinese State-Making." In *Opium Regimes: China, Britain, and Japan, 1839–1952*, edited by Timothy Brook and Bob Wakabayashi. Berkeley: University of California Press.

Wong, J. Y. 1998. *Deadly Dreams: Opium, Imperialism, and the Arrow War in China*. Cambridge: Cambridge University Press.

Wood, Frances. 1998. *No Dogs and Not Many Chinese*. London: John Murray.

Wyman, Judith. 1993. "Social Change, Anti-Foreigners and Revolution in Sichuan." PhD dissertation, University of Michigan.

Wyman, Judith. 1997. "The Ambiguities of Chinese Antiforeignism: Chongqing, 1870–1900." *Late Imperial China* 18, no. 2: 86–122.

Wynter, Sylvia. 1971. "Novel and History, Plot and Plantation." *Savacou* 5: 95–102.

Wynter, Sylvia. 1989. "Beyond the Word of Man: Glissant and the New Discourse of the Antilles." *World Literature Today* 63, no. 4: 637–48.

Xi Gao. 2010. "The Truth and Evils of Opium: The Anti-Opium Activities of British Missionary to China John Dudgeon." *Frontiers of History in China* 5, no. 3: 453–70.

Xi Han. 2011. *Shiji*. Kunming: Yunnan Renmin Chubanshe.

Xi Yinzhen. 1992. *Chuanju zhi*. Beijing: Wenhua Yishu Chubanshe.

Xiang Lanxin. 2002. *The Origins of the Boxer War: A Multinational Study*. New York: Routledge.

Xiang Lanxin. 2003. *Yihetuan zhanzheng de qiyuan*. Beijing: Huadong Shifan Daxue Chubanshe.

Yamamura Kozo, ed. 1997. *The Economic Emergence of Modern Japan*. Cambridge: Cambridge University Press.

Yan Ruyi. 1966 [1827]. "Pingding jiaofei zonglun." In *Huangchao jingshi wenbian*, vol. 89, edited by He Changling. Taibei: Wenhai Chubanshe.

Yang, Shaozhuan. 1933–34. "The Revolution in Szechwan, 1911–1912." *Journal of the West China Border Research Society* 4: 63–90.

Yates, Charles L. 1995. *Saigo Takamori: The Man behind the Myth*. New York: Routledge.

Yellin, Victor F. 1996. "Mrs. Belmont, Matthew Perry, and the 'Japanese Minstrels.'" *American Music* 14, no. 3: 257–75.

Yokohama Yakusho, ed. 1973. *Fûzoku hen*. Yokohama: Yokohama Shuppankai.

Yoshida Hiroji. 1976. *Katô Hiroyuki no kenkyû*. Tokyo: Ôhara Shinseisha.

Yoshida Toshio. 1912. *Tenka no kaiketsu, Tôyama Mitsuru*. Tokyo: Seikō Zasshisha.

Young, Ernest. 2013. *Ecclesiastical Colony*. Oxford: Oxford University Press.

Young People's Movement. 1920. *Our West China Mission*. Toronto: Missionary Society of the Methodist Church.

Yun, Lisa, and Ricardo Rene Laremont. 2001. "Chinese Coolies and African Slaves in Cuba, 1847–74." *Journal of Asian American Studies* 4, no. 2: 99–122.

Yusoff, Kathryn. 2018. *A Billion Black Anthropocenes or None*. Minneapolis: University of Minnesota Press.

Zhang Li. 1987. *Zhongguo jiaoan shi*. Chengdu: Sichuan Sheng Xinhua Shudian.

Zhang Taiyan. 1996. *Gegudingxin de zheli: Zhang Taiyan wenxuan*. Shanghai: Shanghai Yuandong Chubanshe.

Zhang Taiyan. 2012 [1900]. *Qiu Shu*. Shanghai: Zhongxi Shuju.

Zhang Zhenhe and Ding Yuanying. 1982. "Qingmo minbian nianbao." *Jindaishi ziliao* 49: 108–81.

Zhao Hong. 2006. *Paoge, Limen, Yiguandao*. Beijing: Tuanjie Chubanshe.

Zhao Yuntian. 2014. *Qingmo xinzheng yanjiu*. Haerbin: Heilongjiang Jiaoyu Chubanshe.

Zheng Xiaowei. 2018. *The Politics of Rights and the 1911 Revolution in China*. Palo Alto, CA: Stanford University Press.

Zheng Yangwen. 2005. *The Social Life of Opium in China*. Cambridge: Cambridge University Press.

Zhengxie Sichuan yanjiu weiyuanhui, ed. 1981. *Sichuan Baolufeng yulu*. Chengdu: Sichuan Renmin Chubanshe.

Zhongguo renmin xieshang huiyi weiyuanhui. 1981. *Xinhai Geming huiyi lu*. 3 vols. Beijing: Wenshi Ziliao Chubanshe.

Zhongyang yanjiuyuan, ed. 1974. *Jiaowu jiaoan dang*. Vol. 1. Taibei: Zhongyang Yanjiuyuan Jindaishi Yanjiusuo.

Zhou Sanpei. 1959. *Xinhai Sichuan zhenglu qin liji*. Chongqing: Renmin Chubanshe.

Zhou Yongming. 1999. *Anti-Drug Crusades in Twentieth-Century China: Nationalism, History, and State Building*. Lanham, MD: Rowman & Littlefield.

Žižek, Slavoj, 1989. *The Sublime Object of Ideology*. London: Verso.

Žižek, Slavoj. 1993. *Tarrying with the Negative: Kant, Hegel, and the Critique of Ideology*. Durham, NC: Duke University Press.

Žižek, Slavoj. 2005. *The Metastases of Enjoyment: On Women and Causality*. London: Verso.

Index

face-change, in Sichuan opera, 296–97
Facing the Sun movement, 157, 161–62, 166–67, 245
Fanon, Frantz, 31, 50, 217–18, 269, 312n14
farmers' uprisings, Meiji economic shocks and, 223–28
Federici, Silvia, 9
feng shui geomancy: Christian missionaries and, 103–8, 117–21, 211–12; Gelaohui and, 122–24
Ferreira da Silva, Denise, 26–29, 31, 34, 81, 91, 159
First Opium War, Climate Caucasianism and, 3–6
First War for Drugs: Chinese and Japanese elites and, 16; Climate Caucasianism and, 3–6, 30; "coolie" captives in, 17; defensive extraterritoriality and, 37; shipping technology and, 12
"Five Negations, The" (Zhang Taiyan), 300–301
Fortune, Robert, 17
Foucault, Michel, 51, 174, 282
Fraser, E. H., 89
freedom of speech, Japanese crackdown on, 159–66
French nationals: as Catholic missionaries in China, 96–101; indemnification demands in China by, 109–13; land expropriation by, 101–8; violence in Boxer Rebellion retribution by, 215; violence in Japan by, 79–80
French Religious Protectorate (China), 96–101
Freud, Sigmund, 220
Frone, Henry, 314n.2
Fu Chongju, 175
Fujimoto Naonori, 155, 230–31, 243
Fujita Densaburô, 243
Fukuda Hideko, 166
Fukuoka Peasant Uprising, 142–45, 161, 319n17
Fukushima Incident, 235–37
Fukuzawa Yukichi, 157, 235, 251
Furukawa Ichibei, 306

Gamewell, Frank D., 119–20, 268
Gamewell, Mary Porter, 119–20
Gandhi, Mahatma, 300
Gankirô commercial sex brothel, 68–71
Gaselee, Alfred, 212–13

Gaspin coup (1884), 322n11
Gelaohui organization (GLH): anti-Christian uprisings and, 121–24, 211–12; capitalism adopted by, 295–97; Catholic persecution of, 98, 109–13, 180–82; conflict resolution in, 192–95; Dazu uprising and, 126–29; eco-ontological environmentalism of, 307–8; festivals of, 181–82, 191–92; human-nonhuman entities and, 197–99; initiation ceremony, 191–93, 198; jobs program of, 185–91; literary inspirations for, 175–78; mainstreaming of, 205–8; membership privileges in, 178–80; occupations within, 182–85; opium suppression campaign and, 280–83, 293–97; opium trafficking and, 43–44, 181–82, 199–205, 266–69, 321n13; origins of, 171–75; peasant uprisings and, 179–80, 182–83, 260–61; piracy by, 185–91; Qing dynasty overthrow and, 171–75, 293–97, 300; railroad recovery movement and, 285–92; ranking system for, 176–78; rituals of, 181–82, 191–93; rules and laws of, 193–95; secrecy of, 195–97; Sichuan opium production and, 259–61; as sociopolitical force, 199–205; white resistance to, 210–12; women in, 293–97; Yangzi River development and, 90
gender equality, Japanese movement for, 154–64
Genyôsha group (Japan), 44–45; anti-oligarchs uprisings and, 140–45, 151–53, 159–64, 246–48, 252; assassination plots and, 237–38, 249–53; environmentalism in, 308–9; formation of, 166–69, 223; inner crises in, 236–42; land privatization and, 242–45; Meiji economic shocks and, 224–28; Osaka Incident and, 232–37; political alliances of, 228–31; village assemblies organized by, 224–28; women in, 318n2
German Ideology (Marx), 14, 94
German nations, violence in Boxer Rebellion retribution by, 215
Gilroy, Paul, 20
Glissant, Édouard, 308
"Global Warming's Terrifying New Math" (McKibben), 220
Glover, Thomas, 57, 62–63, 71, 80–83, 188, 227, 240, 316n34

Mitsui company, 44–45, 148, 226, 242
Mitsuura Tsûji, 255–58, 293
Miyagawa Taiichirô, 142
Miyanoshita family, 69–70
Miyazaki Muryû, 237–38
Miyazaki Shin'ichi, 63
Miyozaki commercial sex district, 68–71
Mi Yungang, 180–81
modernization, Qing dynasty and, 280–83
"Mongoloid" profiling, Anglo-American raciology and, 20–23, 47–51, 213–14, 278–79
monocrop cultivation, Anglo-Indian opium trade and, 7–9
Moore, Jason, 3, 10, 134, 343
moosme/musume (sex servant), 67, 314n7
moral ecology, Christian missionaries and, 117–21
Morgan, Prichard, 304–5
Morikawa Tetsurô, 79–80, 314n7
Môri Toshihiko, 319n12
morphine-based opium drugs, Euro-American and Japanese development of, 279–80
Morrison, G. E., 299, 303
Morse, H. B., 260
Moss, Michael, 315n14
Moten, Fred, 141, 185
Motoori Norinaga, 140
mountains, Gelaohui reverence for, 188–91
multi-species democracy, 7
Murano Tsunemon, 233
Muroi Hiroichi, 237
Mutual Love Society, 228–31, 251
Myers, Ella, 221–22

Nakae Chômin, 157, 230, 251–52
Namamugi Incident, 59–60
Namazu (demon catfish), 78
Narahara Itaru, 138, 140, 151–52, 154–57, 162, 166, 223, 238
Narrative of the Earl of Elgin's Mission to China and Japan in the Years 1857, '58, '59 (Oliphant), 48, 54
"Native Opium" (Spence), 261–66
Natural Varieties of Mankind (Blumenbach), 20
nayboen, Japanese code of, 49–53
Neal, Edward, 63–66
"Negro methods": African extractive colonialism and, 212; slavery of opium consumption and, 274

neo-Confucian cosmology, opium trafficking and, 2–3
neoteny, 20–21; in Japan, 47–53
New Policy initiatives, Qing embrace of capitalism and, 280–83
New Proposals (Aizawa Seishisai), 22–23, 50, 75
Nice, Desus, 42
Nichi Shimbun newspaper, 154, 252
Ninja Assassins League, 150
Nishikawa Masao, 281–83
Normanton incident, 247–48

Obinata Sumio, 224
Ocean Depths (Haidi), The 175–77, 193–94
Ôchi Kashirô, 140, 142, 150–51, 238, 252
O'Connor, James, 14–18
offensive extraterritoriality, 99–101; Boxer Rebellion and, 211–12; Catholic missionaries and, 114; Gelaohui and, 206–8
Ogyû Sorai, 140
Ôi Kentarô, 232–39, 252–53
Okamoto, Kenzaburo, 145
Ôkawa Shûmei, 250
Ôkubo Toshimichi, 144–51, 156–57, 224, 242, 245–46
Ôkuma Shigenobu, 148–49, 249–53
Oliphant, Laurence, 48–59, 68–70, 73, 77
opera in China, provincial nationalism and, 295–97
Opium Agency, 7
opium trafficking and consumption: capitalism and climate regime and, 6–14; Catholic missionaries' involvement in, 102–8, 317n14; Chinese expansion of opium production and, 259–61; Chinese lifting of restrictions on, 85–90; Climate Caucasianism and, 3–6; decriminalization and taxation policies and, 283–85; detox cures for, 275–80, 289–92; dominance of Sichuan production in, 259–61; Gelaohui and, 43–44, 179–82, 190–91, 199–205, 321n13; in Japan, 21–23; legalization in China of, 34–37; market town development and, 284; missionaries' criticism of, 271–73; missionaries' involvement in, 44, 102–8, 262–66, 269–70, 317n14; opposition to suppression campaign, 285–92; Qing dynasty suppression of, 44, 280–85; raciology perspective on, 19–21, 278–80;

refuges from, missionaries' establishment of, 276–80; in rural China, 261–66; Sichuan drug war and, 255–97; smuggling activities and, 265–69

Orbis Spike, 3, 222

Ordinance on Newspapers (Japan), 157

orphanages, Catholic human trafficking for, 112–13

Osaka Incident of 1885, 44–45, 159, 232–37, 251

Osgood, Elliott, 277–79

"Outline for a Constitution for the Japanese Nation, An" (United Patriotic Front), 161–62

Ownby, David, 183–85

Oxenham, E. L., 258, 287–88

Oya Kunitarô, 315n14

Oya Masao, 233

Pak Yonghyo, 250

Parenti, Christian, 12

Park, William, 277–78

Parker, E. H., 91

Parkes, Harry, 41, 57, 80–82

Parkinson, C. N., 11

Patel, Raj, 10

Patriot Party, 227–28

Patriot Society (Japan), 145–48, 162, 165–66, 224–25

peasant uprisings: in China, 142–45, 161, 171–76, 319n17; GLH and, 179–80, 182–83, 260–61; Qing opium suppression and, 285–97

Pekin Syndicate, 303

People's Rights and Autonomy (Ueki), 159–64

People's Rights Granny. *See* Kusunose Kita

Perry, Elizabeth, 171

Perry, Matthew, 30–34, 56

Petition for the Establishment of a National Assembly, 165–66

Phenomenology of Spirit (Hegel), 28

Philosophy of Nature (Hegel), 28

Phimister, Ian, 303

Physics and Politics (Bagehot), 29

piracy, by Gelaohui organization, 185–91

pollution, eco-ontology of, 78–79

Pons (Father), 122–24

poppy cultivation: East India Company monoculture practices and, 7–14; economic

growth linked to, 43–44; Qing opium suppression campaign and, 285–92

post-Enlightenment philosophy, European supremacy in, 26

Pratt, Mary, 51

primitive accumulation, drug wars and, 14–18

"Proclamation against the Criminal Western Religion," 113–17

"Proposal to Reject the Unequal Treaties, A" (United Patriotic Front), 163

"Proposal for Establishing a Parliament" (United Patriotic Front), 163–64

"Proposal to Establish a Popularly Elected Assembly," 145

province nationalism, Xinhai Revolution and, 295–97

Public Meetings Law (1880) (Japan), 224–25

Puccini, Giacomo, 209

Pu Diajun, 286

Pybus, Cassandra, 5

Qian Baotang, 122

Qing dynasty: British victory over, 13–14, 30, 34–37; capitalism embrace of, 280–83; career advancement in, 176–78; Caucasian hypermobility and, 24–25; Chongqing anti-Christian uprisings and, 117–24; economy under, 6–14; France and, 97; Gelaohui and, 171–75, 195–97, 300; indemnity demands of Catholics and, 109–13; missionary expansion during, 87–90; New Policies of, 280–83; opium suppression campaign of, 44, 280–92; opium trafficking and, 1–3, 5–6; outlaw underclass during, 205–8; overthrow of, 285–92; Sino-French treaty and, 101–8; uprisings against, 179–80, 182–83, 260–61

Qing-Japan war (1894–1895), 303

Qin Heping, 113, 284, 321n13

Qiying (Chinese negotiator), 97

racial capitalism: color line of, 131–36; gorge-us ideology and, 47–53; in Japan, 21–23; White-on-Chinese violence and, 39–43; white racial domination and, 19–21

racial terrorism: Boxer Rebellion retribution as, 213–19; obscenity of, 219–20 raciology, 20–21; Anglo-American sexual obsession in Japan and, 55–59; East Asian rejection of, 300–301; European supremacy and, 26–27, 314n2; in Japan, 24–25; opium trafficking and consumption and, 19–21, 100, 213–14, 278–80; sex trafficking in Japan and, 55–59, 69–71

railroad recovery movement, opium trafficking and, 285–92

Rainier, Peter, 11

Rancière, Jacques, 148

rape, Euro-White predation including, 41–45

real estate: Genyôsha involvement, 242–45; privatization of, 101–8. *See also* land rights

Reclamation Society, 153, 156

Record of the French Revolution: The Battle Cry of Liberty, A (Miyazaki), 237

Rediker, Marcus, 5, 141

"Report on the Investigation into the Burning of Chinese Villages" (Rhodes), 215–16

Resolute Protectors League, 150

Retreat of the Elephants (Elvin), 15–16

Revere the Emperor, Fight the Whites! movement, 74–76, 81, 137–38, 143–45, 165–66, 318n5

Rhodes, C. D., 215–16

Rice, Thomas, 32

Richardson, Samuel, 59–66, 314n9

Richter, Danial, 18

Richthofen, Manfred von (Baron), 265

Rigaud, J. F., 110

Rishisha movement, 157, 161

river traffic: Climate Caucasianism and, 7; Gelaohui and, 185–91; opium smuggling and, 265–69

robbery: by Gelaohui network, 185–91; as restorative justice, 183–85

Robertson, D. B., 39

Robinson, Cedric, 19

Rokumeikan complex, 245–48, 250

Romance of the Three Kingdoms (Luo Guanzhong), 321n8

Roquette, G. E., 111

Rose, Sarah, 18

Rousseau, Jean-Jacques, 158–60, 237

Royal Commission on Opium, 261, 270, 274

Ruskola, Teemu, 26, 30, 37

Russell & Co., 12–13

Russia, Japan Expedition of, 21–22

Russo-Japanese War (1904–1905), 253

Sabey, John Wayne, 167

Saga revolt (1874), 149–51

Said, Edward, 26

Saigô Takamori: anti-oligarch campaigns and, 150–52, 156, 319n12, 319n16; Fight the Whites! movement and, 137–38; Genyôsha and, 238–39; Meiji austerity measures and, 228; Patriot Society and, 145–48, 150–52

Saitô Kohei, 304

Sakamoto Seijirô, 234

salt smuggling, 256–57; GLH and, 190–91

samurai: Anglo-American view of, 54–55, 80–83; gold profiteering and, 66–68; J-hâd of, 74–76, 141–45; peasant uprisings against, 153; raciologist perspective of, 57–59; violence in brothels and vengeance by, 79–80

Samurai Disarmament Edict, 156

Sanjô Sanetomi, 147

Sarr, Felwine, 308

Sassa Tomofusa, 228–31, 236–42

Satow, Ernest, 21–22, 47, 315n21; on Anglo-American foreign policy, 81; Anglo-Japanese relations and, 53, 57; assaults commited by, 59, 61; Japan posting for, 59

Satsuma Rebellion, 151–53, 156, 161; economic impact of, 224; forced labor used in, 240; Genyôsha and, 228

Satsuma samurai: Anglo-American violence against, 59–66; J-hâd by, 72–76

Scarth, John, 39

Scidmore, E. H., 314n9

Scottish Carron Company, 11

Scramble for Africa, 211–12

Second Chongqing Uprising, 275

Second War for Drugs: Climate Caucasianism and, 5–6; end of drug trafficking restrictions in, 85–90; Gelaohui brotherhood and, 179; legalization of opium trade and, 34–37

self-determination, extraction as vehicle for, 28

Self-Help (Smiles), 158–59

Senchû Kiji (Kiyokawa), 78–79, 316n32

Senchû shimatsu (Kiyokawa), 316n32

Serres, E. R. A., 20

sexual dimorphism, in Euro-American raciology, 47–53

weapons trafficking, 81–82; Climate Caucasianism and rise of, 4–6; in Japan, 57–59
Wei Yuan, 22
Whitelery, Henry, 314n.2
whiteness: East Asian profile of, 24–25; eco-ontology and, 220–22; minstrel shows as affirmation of, 32–34; superpredation of, 37–38, 314n2
White-on-Chinese violence, 37–43, 313n35, 314n36; in Boxer Rebellion retribution, 213–19; by missionaries, 87–90; myths concerning, 87–90; reports of, 61–62
White-on-Japanese violence: Anglo-American incidents of, 59–66, 315n14; in brothels, 79–80; gold profiteering and, 67–68; samurai J-hād against, 73–76
white supremacy: of Euro-Americans in Japan, 70–71, 314n2; extra-action and eco-ontology and, 136; fatality of, 220–22; racial terror and, 213–20
"White Man's Burden, The" (Kipling), 218
Whitney, H. T., 276
Williams, Raymond, 143
Williams, S. W., 264
Willis, Dr. William, 50
The Wire (HBO series), 13
Wolfe, J. R., 255, 270
women: Euro-American rape and violence against, 213–19, 247–48; in Gelaohui network, 293–97; Gelaohui retribution for violence against, 186–91, 321n9; Japanese movement for rights of, 154–56, 161–64; opium consumption by, 268; sex work and violence against women, 79–80
Women Warrior Society, 293
Wu Yuzhang, 286
Wynter, Sylvia, 7

xenophobia, in Japan, 79
Xiaoyhui group, 294–97
Xiliang, 288–89
Xinhai Revolution, 285–92, 295–97
Xi Yinzhen, 296

Yamagata Aritomo, 149, 165–66, 253
Yamaguchi Nobu, 95
Yangzi River: Climate Caucasianism and development of, 90–96; Gelaohui piracy on, 185–91; opium smuggling on, 265–69
Yano Kiheiji, 244
Yasuba Tamokazu, 242
Yasukawa Keiichirô, 241–44
Yates, Charles, 319n12
"yellow" Oriental racial classification, narco-capitalism and, 19–21
Yokohama Kidan, 314n7
Yokoyama Suhunsuke, 150
Young, Ernest, 85
Youyang Catholic war, 108–13
You Zhikai, 118–19
Yu Dongchen, 116, 122–29, 171, 188, 294, 296
Yûikkans (Japanese youth training institutes), 233
Yûki Toragorô, 230–31, 239, 243–44
Yumeno Kyûsaku, 137, 147–48, 166–69
Yusoff, Kathryn, 135
Yu Zangchen, 125, 171

Zhang Dasan, 286
Zhang Fei, 177–78
Zhang Jie, 294
Zhang Jiexan, 286
Zhang Taiyan, 45, 300–301
Zhang Yi, 303
Zhao Erfeng, 286–87, 289
Zhao Hong, 171
Zhao Zhisheng, 304–5
Zhao Zhongxu, 119–20
Zhi Fangxi, 110
Zhou ("Wild Sword"), 173–75, 182–83
Zhou Wanshun, 128–29
Zhou Xinqi, 119–20
Zhurong (Daoist fire deity), 89–90
Zhu Xi, 140
Žižek, Slavoj, 2, 220, 222
Zongli Yamen, 101, 110–11
Zuo Zongtang, 283